# Law of Compulsory Purchase and Compensation

# Law of Compulsory Purchase and Compensation

Fourth edition

Keith Davies, MA, LLM, JP
of Gray's Inn, Barrister
Reader in Law at Reading University

London
Butterworths
1984

| England | Butterworth & Co (Publishers) Ltd, 88 Kingsway, LONDON WC2B 6AB |
|---|---|
| Australia | Butterworths Pty Ltd, SYDNEY, MELBOURNE, BRISBANE, ADELAIDE and PERTH |
| Canada | Butterworth & Co (Canada) Ltd, TORONTO<br>Butterworth & Co (Western Canada) Ltd, VANCOUVER |
| New Zealand | Butterworths of New Zealand Ltd, WELLINGTON |
| Singapore | Butterworth & Co (Asia) Pte Ltd, SINGAPORE |
| South Africa | Butterworth Publishers (Pty) Ltd, DURBAN |
| USA | Mason Publishing Co, ST PAUL, Minnesota<br>Butterworth Legal Publishers, SEATTLE, Washington; BOSTON, Massachusetts; and AUSTIN, Texas<br>D & S Publishers, CLEARWATER, Florida |

First edition     1972
Second Edition  1975
Third edition    1978

© Butterworth & Co (Publishers) Ltd 1972, 1975, 1978, 1984

Davies, Keith
  Law of compulsory purchase and compensation.—
  4th ed.
  1.  Eminent domain—England
  I.  Title
  344.203'252     KD1185

  ISBN hardcover 0 406 57187 2
       softcover  0 406 57188 0

Printed in Great Britain by
Thomson Litho Ltd, East Kilbride, Scotland.

# Preface

The fourth edition of this work comes after a longer interval than those between earlier editions. On this occasion the work of revision has required extensive updating and amendment, rather than wholesale recasting in the light of any sweeping alterations in the structure of the law. Despite the absence of major legislative changes, we have in the intervening years seen the abandonment of the concept of 'community land' and the ripples (fast subsiding) that this has caused on the surface of politics. A number of Acts have been revised and consolidated; and developments in case law have continued apace, providing some interesting, though as a rule not very controversial, decisions in the courts.

I should like to express my appreciation once again of help and enlightenment obtained in discussions with colleagues, students and others. It may be that may people studying and practising in the field of public land law, viewing the subject from the standpoint of the private as well as the public sector, will continue to find the book useful—perhaps not least because of the diagrams, which I hope will illuminate points that may not be so easy to accept by verbal presentation alone.

Department of Law                                      Keith Davies
University of Reading                              February 1984

And Ahab spake unto Naboth, saying, 'Give me thy vineyard . . . and I will give thee . . . the worth of it in money'.
(1 Kings 21, v 2)


'The best way would be . . . to send 'em away with a flea in their ear, when they come spying and measuring,' said Solomon. . . . 'It's all a pretence . . . about their being forced to take one way. . . . And I don't believe in any pay to make amends for bringing a lot of ruffians to trample your crops. . . .'

'Brother Peter, God forgive him, got money out of a company', said Mrs Waule. 'But that was for the manganese. That wasn't for railways to blow you to pieces right and left.'

'Well, there's this to be said, Jane,' Mr Solomon concluded, lowering his voice in a cautious manner— 'the more spokes we put in their wheel, the more they'll pay us to let 'em go on. . . .'
(George Eliot *Middlemarch* ch 56)

# Contents

# Table of Statutes

References in this Table to *Statutes* are to Halsbury's Statutes of England (Third Edition) showing the volume and page at which the annotated text of the Act will be found.

# Table of Cases

PAGE

PAGE

# Introduction

In the six years between the last and the present edition of this book, comparatively little of fundamental significance has changed in the law of compulsory purchase and compensation relating to land in England and Wales. Even so, more than enough has happened to necessitate a new edition. There has been a constant stream of cases in the Lands Tribunal, the High Court, the Court of Appeal, the House of Lords, even the Privy Council, to illustrate and develop a great many strands of the law in this area. There have been some notable statutory changes as well.

Two Acts in 1981, the Acquisition of Land Act and the Compulsory Purchase (Vesting Declarations) Act, have re-cast earlier provisions governing the procedure for making compulsory purchase orders and general vesting declarations respectively. Almost every year since 1978 a Finance Act has made some alteration to development land tax. The Local Government, Planning and Land Act 1980 repealed the Community Land Act 1975 and put paid to its scheme for transferring development value to the public sector.

Despite the attention drawn by these changes to the question of development land generally, the famed 'compensation-betterment problem' which received so much attention in the post-war years has dropped out of sight. But it is merely submerged and will reappear one day. In the meantime there is the *Pointe Gourde* doctrine to think about which now (in Hilaire Belloc's phrase) 'is accepted everywhere'. Yet it is a house built on sand. Its lack of any foundation in the principles of law or valuations[1] has led to the utterance of judicial strictures (see chapter 7, p 133, below). When it supports the 'willing seller' rule of market value it is redundant; when it does not it produces confusion. It entails much earnest discussion over 'schemes' and the marvellous 'no-scheme world'. Yet in many compulsory purchases 'schemes' are irrelevant; and what really needs to be discounted in every case is the fact or prospect of *compulsion*.

Compulsory purchase, for all its peculiarities, will long continue to be of practical importance, just as it has been since governments began. It is

---

1 On the relationship between law and valuations, see the article in *The Chartered Surveyor* for May 1971, based on the First Royal Institution of *Chartered Surveyors' Invitation Address*, which was delivered by Lord Denning MR and entitled 'The Law and the Professional Man'.

public-sector conveyancing, whose standard forms can be studied along with the legislation in the *Encyclopaedia of Compulsory Purchase* which forms part of the Local Government Library. Compensation, on the other hand, is a specialised part of arbitration and so, ultimately, of the law of contract (and, to a lesser extent, tort). This is true even of planning compensation, the most arcane part of which—the Town and Country Planning Act 1971, Sch 8—has at last come under the searchlight of the Court of Appeal in *Peaktop Properties (Hampstead) Ltd v Camden London Borough Council* (see chapter 16, p 324, below).

Everyone remembers how Sir Edward Coke described an Englishman's house as his castle. But few people remember just how ruthless our rulers have been towards castles, none more so than the founder of the common law himself, King Henry II. On his accession 'he quickly ordered new castles . . . to be flattened except for a few in suitable locations which he decided to keep under his own control or that of reliable custodians for the purposes of national defence'.[2] He did not even pay compensation.

Thus the power of the central government over landownership was always great, and remains so. Today's constitutional forms and administrative ramifications, extensive though they are, cannot disguise this fact. Every landowner's tenure depends on the system by which the state sustains the legal framework of property. It follows that at no point can the state be expected to relinquish its right or its power of acquiring private land to meet its needs.

2  'Mox castella nova . . . complanari praecepit, praeter pauca in locis opportunis sita quae vel ipse retinere vel a pacificis ad regni munimen retineri voluit' (AD 1154 –William of Newburgh, ii c.1: see H.W.C. Davis *Stubb's Select Charters from the beginning to 1307* (9th ed, O.U.P.).

# Part one

# Compulsory purchase procedure

# Chapter 1

# The background and the statutes

## A. Eighteenth-century origins

### 1 COMPULSION AND THE 'PUBLIC GOOD'

The law of compulsory purchase of land in England, as a subject of coherent study, begins with Blackstone.

So great, moreover, is the regard of the law for private property, that it will not authorise the least violation of it; no, not even for the general good of the whole community. If a new road, for instance, were to be made through the grounds of a private person, it might perhaps be extensively beneficial to the public; but the law permits no man, or set of men, to do this without consent of the owner of the land. In vain may it be urged, that the good of the individual ought to yield to that of the community; for it would be dangerous to allow any private man, or even any public tribunal, to be the judge of this common good, and to decide whether it be expedient or no. Besides, the public good is in nothing more essentially interested, than in the protection of every individual's private rights, as modelled by the municipal law. In this and similar cases the legislature above can, and indeed frequently does, interpose, and compel the individual to acquiesce. But how does it interpose and compel? Not by absolutely stripping the subject of his property in an arbitrary manner; but by giving him a full indemnification and equivalent for the injury thereby sustained. The public is now considered as an individual, treating with an individual for an exchange. All that the legislature does is to oblige the owner to alienate his possessions for a reasonable price; and even this is an exertion of power, which the legislature indulges with caution, and which nothing but the legislature can perform.[1]

Embedded in these resounding phrases, so expressive of the flavour of the eighteenth century, is the statement that Parliament not only can

---

1 1 Bl Com (14th edn) 264. See also Dicey *Law of the Constitution* (10th edn) p 48: 'Coke (it should be noted) particularly chooses interference with private rights as specimens of Parliamentary authority.... Parliament ... habitually interferes, for the public advantage, with private rights. Indeed such interference has now (greatly to the benefit of the community) become so much a matter of course as hardly to excite remark, and few persons reflect what a sign this interference is of the supremacy of Parliament. The statute-book teems with Acts under which Parliament gives privileges or rights to particular persons or imposes particular duties or liabilities upon other persons. This is of course the case with every railway Act, but no one will realise the full action, generally the very beneficial action of Parliamentary sovereignty, who does not look through a volume or two of what are called *Local and Private Acts*.'

compulsorily purchase land (though non-one else can) but 'indeed frequently does'. The deprecating statements that follow—'a full indemnification and equivalent', 'a reasonable price', 'indulges with caution'—do not alter the fact that compulsory purchase in all its essentials has existed for two centuries and more.

The best known kind of compulsory acquisition in Blackstone's day, leaving aside the prerogative right (and duty) of the Crown to take land for the defence of the realm in an emergency,[2] was the inclosure movement. Inclosures meant the compulsory extinction of rights in land to make possible the re-allocation of that land so as to apply more efficient methods of farming. The rights to be extinguished included separate holdings and rights of common, ie not only the possession of land but lesser rights superimposed on such possession. Rights to pasture cattle were of chief importance, but there were also rights to take turf, wood, gravel, and so forth, and to catch fish and to pasture pigs. These profits à prendre were enjoyed by the copyholders and others in the village or the manor, in common over uncultivated land of which the title was vested in the lord of the manor ('common lands') or over land cultivated separately as arable by copyholders and freeholders for part of the year ('commonable lands').[3]

An allotment of land or money was made to all 'commoners' whose rights were expropriated, even to the lord of the manor himself to the extent to which he shared in those rights. But since the benefit of the change was most obviously to be reaped by the more prominent owners and cultivators, the lesser ones tended to object to expropriation. Blackstone's concept of 'a full indemnification and equivalent', which is the same as the modern 'full market value', was just and adequate between the expropriated asset and its new equivalent. But it did not meet the point that in such a case the owners of assets may not wish to be compelled to make the change at all. There is such a thing as a quid pro quo for consenting to an exchange as well as a quid pro quo within the terms of that exchange. A compulsory purchase can be justly equated with a free transaction only in respect of the compensation, not of the compulsion.

What justifies compulsion is in Blackstone's phrase, 'the general good of the whole community', 'the public good'. The protection of every individual's private rights' is as he says, essential to the public good, but not in isolation, even allowing that it includes freedom of contract.

---

2   *Case of the King's Prerogative in Saltpetre* (1606) 12 Co Rep 12. 'And therefore by the common law, every man may come upon my land for the defence of the realm ... for this is for the public, and everyone hath benefit by it; but after the danger is over, the trenches and bulwarks ought to be removed, so that the owner shall not have prejudice in his inheritance. ... *Princeps et respublica ex justa causa possunt rem meam auferre.*' Nowadays, of course, the danger is never over.

3   See Cooke's *Inclosure Acts* (4th edn).

Otherwise the uniqueness of the legislature's power to impose compulsion, which he emphasises, is beside the point. That power, even though unique, is not justified purely by its own existence. Might is not right per se, but only on some independent justification. Adequate compensation balances the acquisition, but only 'the public good' can balance the compulsion.

Whether 'the public good' calls for any particular expropriation is outside the scope of this book. It depends neither on fact nor on law, except incidentally, but on policy. All that the law can do is to show the boundaries within which policy, or 'discretion', is to be allowed to operate.

## 2 INCLOSURES

Opinions differ as to whether inclosures, like other expropriations, were for 'the public good'. Advocates of inclosures promoted them on the grounds of better farming. In the eighteenth century objections turned largely on the harshness with which small cultivators were said to be treated; in the later nineteenth century they turned more on the threat to amenity and recreation. The latter objections prevailed while the former did not, which sheds light on public attitudes and other practical realities. Nowadays 'commons', instead of being areas of land with special agricultural uses and a complex pattern of property rights, are almost entirely used and thought of as places of public recreation. To reduce to order the remaining problems caused by their survival Parliament thought it necessary in 1965 to introduce the modern system of registration of commons and village greens,[4] and it may be hoped that this will settle the matter once and for all.

The most uncharacteristic thing about inclosures, by comparison with later forms of compulsory purchase, is the fact that to a great extent the expropriators and the expropriated were the same people. From the legal standpoint, inconvenient property rights were being bought out, but from the practical standpoint the land was simply being redistributed on a more efficient basis. On the former view it was a question of justice; on the latter a question of profit. Nevertheless the basic continuity of the legal approach to expropriation can easily be traced from that day to this. The entire process is statutory; the common law is confined to its irreducible minimum in relation to any branch of statutory law: reasonable interpretation.

Inclosures were first permitted, in relation to uncultivated land, by general statutory provisions in the thirteenth century, which, so far as they went, were still being applied six centuries later.[5] In the seventeenth

4 Commons Registration Act 1965.
5 Statute of Merton 1236, c 4; Statute of Westminster II 1285, c 46; *Robertson v Hartopp* (1889) 43 Ch D 484 (encroachments by lord of the manor resisted). See Pollock and

and eighteenth centuries the modern inclosure movement got under way, whereby cultivated land was included in the process; and medieval 'open fields' were by this procedure rearranged in consolidated separate holdings more suitable for the new methods of farming introduced in the 'agricultural revolution'. At first this was often done by inclosure agreements made between the various proprietors involved and registered in the Court of Chancery. But recalcitrants might spoil such schemes by holding out, and there might be disagreement about the extent of rights of common as distinct from full possession. To make such schemes more certain in their legal effect, to ensure that recalcitrants could not spoil the new pattern of ownership, to deal comprehensively with all rights and alleged rights, and to meet the concern voiced by Blackstone about reconciling private property with the general good, it became increasingly common to apply for Parliamentary confirmation.

Unlike the earlier inclosure statutes, however, the Acts procured in the eighteenth and nineteenth centuries were private local Acts, petitioned for externally and not introduced internally as public general Acts. This reflected their very different purpose, which was to make particular provision in great detail for complex transactions of which the essential character was that of private land transfers but which needed an element of compulsion to ensure their success; whereas the medieval statutes had merely delineated in general terms the boundary which marked off the extent of a manorial lord's rights from those of manorial tenants.

Parliament must be taken to legislate, in this field as in any other, for the 'public good'; though a distinction might have to be drawn between ends and means. In regard to inclosures a Parliament of landowners obviously saw no difficulty in placing a general reliance on the judgment of other landowners—an eighteenth-century attitude roughly equivalent to 'what's good for General Motors is good for the nation'. There was a great consistency about it, and hundreds of inclosure Acts between 1750 and 1850 transformed the economic and social pattern of rural England from its medieval to its modern form in a manner which would have continued to satisfy Blackstone.

## B.   Emergence of modern compulsory purchase

### 1   ORIGINAL RELIANCE ON PRIVATE ACTS

Compulsory purchase of land in England and Wales today comprises a legal process containing four main elements. Each of these elements has a

Maitland *History of English Law* Vol 1, p 623; Plucknett *Legislation of Edward I* pp 84–86; Law of Commons Amendment Act 1893.

separate statutory code, though the codes are closely connected and even overlap. They are:

(1) Authorisation of compulsory purchase.
(2) Selection of land.
(3) Acquisition of land.
(4) Compensation.

The four modern statutory codes are in general terms, though of course they are applied by specific procedures in each particular case. The purpose has been to economise in the expense of statutory procedures and Parliamentary time. On the other hand the body of statutory provisions has been made more confusing by this elaborate treatment, which must therefore be examined with care.

Each private inclosure Act contained all four elements within itself, largely undifferentiated. The interested landowners, including the lord of the manor and the 'commoners' anxious as a group to exchange their various rights of common for separate blocks or 'parcels' of land in full and unincumbered ownership 'in severalty', obtained authorisation to do this. The requisite concerted action, with coercion of recalcitrants, by this means became clearly lawful, and the boundaries of freedom of contract could be transcended. The other three elements then presented no difficulty. The exact land was specified in the Act, at least by reference to a map or plan or other means of identification; so were the actual expropriation and creation of rights and the payment of such money compensation as might be necessary if the new interests in land were not equivalent to all the rights expropriated.

The outcome of a successful inclosure was, in modern jargon, a 'package deal' in which compulsion made good any shortage of consent. The detailed work of redistribution was carried out by 'commissioners', appointed by the 'promoters', that is the most prominent of the landowners anxious for the inclosures, with professional assistance as necessary. Meetings were held to hear and determine all claims and objections, and to draw up the necessary plans. The completed work of the 'commissioners' was termed the 'award', from which by Parliamentary sanction the title to all the new interests would be derived. The award often included the setting aside of land for the sites of public and private roads, schools, work-houses, 'fuel and field garden allotments' and other special purposes, if any. It may not be too fanciful to draw a comparison between this comprehensive rearrangement of the land pattern and the twentieth century 'comprehensive development' or 'urban renewal', even though the inclosure award was rural and the other is normally urban. Neither would be fully practicable without compulsory purchase.[6]

6 See Clapham *Concise Economic History of Britain to 1750* ch 7.

This kind of procedure was a success. The expense and trouble were outweighed by the benefits. So it became increasingly common by the early nineteenth century for groups of 'promoters', whether incorporated or unincorporated, to obtain powers by private Act to acquire land for purposes the scope of which called for compulsion to be made available. Building canals and railways obviously needed this kind of authorisation, for the long route involved could not be allowed to be imperilled by any particular landowners, large or small, who wished to remain undisturbed, or for that matter to apply blackmail in bargaining.[7]

There was also the question of ultra vires. The great capital outlay required for such projects could seldom be found by individuals; the need was for incorporation and limited liability, granted by Parliament in return for a clear demarcation of the limits of the purposes to which other people's money and land could be applied—in a word, control. An even more elaborate body of law grew up to safeguard the 'public good', which freedom of contract cannot secure unaided in such circumstances.

While entrepreneurs were building canals and railways, and also docks and markets, hoping to reap large commercial profits thereby for themselves and their shareholders, others were constructing water works, gas works and (later) electricity works. Here the hope of commercial profit was probably shorter-lived; and although public utility companies survived until they were nationalised, or until this day (in the case of water companies), they tended to become in effect a public service. In many cases local authorities took over or promoted these activities themselves. The point to note is that the boundary-line between private enterprise and public service is very indistinct in this area, and that the ultra vires rule and the need for compulsory purchase powers dominate the scene on either side of that boundary line. The ultra vires rule is especially relevant to the first of the four elements in compulsory purchase set out above—its authorisation. If an Act authorises body A to carry out purpose X, such statutory authorisation does not extend to purpose Y,[8] nor does it give body B power to carry out any purpose.

It is highly unlikely that any such purpose can be carried out at all except by using some land or other. Each authorising statute, therefore, will need to provide for acquiring necessary land; but if it does not such acquisition will be ultra vires. Powers of compulsory acquisition may be necessary or desirable and the statute may authorise them also; but if it

7  'Women both old and young regarded travelling by steam as presumptuous and dangerous, and argued against it by saying that nothing should induce them to get into a railway carriage; while proprietors . . . were yet unanimous in the opinion that in selling land, whether to the Enemy of mankind or to a company obliged to purchase, these pernicious agencies must be made to pay a very high price to the landowners for permission to injure mankind.' (George Eliot *Middlemarch* ch 56)

8  *Ashbury Railway Carriage and Iron Co v Riche* (1875) LR 7 HL 653.

does not any *compulsory* acquisition will be ultra vires. The mode of procedure for compulsory acquisition will also have to be prescribed in the statute, because if it is not any procedure at all will be ultra vires.

## 2 BEGINNINGS OF STANDARDISATION

In 1801 Parliament decided to simplify the involved and expensive private bill procedure in so far as it applied to inclosures. The need for private legislation was not dispensed with; but the disadvantage of it, namely the fact of the repetitive similarity of its bulk of detailed terms, was turned to good account by enacting it in a standard form in a public general statute, the Inclosure (Consolidation) Act 1801, and providing therein that the standard provisions should apply henceforth to each individual private Act unless otherwise indicated. Thus the earlier procedure, by which inclosure agreements were given subsequent approval by private Act of Parliament in each specific case, had now given way to a procedure which Parliament prescribed in advance in general terms and which was adopted for each specific case, as a rule, by a separate shorter private Act afterwards. There was little basic change in the procedure itself. The private Act in each case specified the land and the inclosure commissioners. The latter held meetings, determined claims, and produced the award. Thus the Act of 1801 was the forerunner of the mid-nineteenth-century spate of 'clauses' Acts.

In 1845 the inclosure system pioneered another advance in compulsory purchase. The Inclosure Act of that year did away with the need for private Acts altogether and set up a single statutory body of Inclosure Commissioners for England and Wales. Petitions by 'commoners' were now dealt with administratively by the Commissioners, who gave or withheld approval in a manner essentially similar to that in which government departments today confirm or reject compulsory purchase orders. The Commissioners were in effect a central government department, whose work was later taken over by the Minister of Agriculture and Fisheries. Thus the 1845 Act was the authorising Act; groups of commoners acting by petition were the acquiring bodies, empowered by the Act to expropriate by use of a prescribed method; the method in question resembled that under a modern compulsory purchase order in that the petition indicated the land to be inclosed and also required the Commissioners' approval; and there was even a system whereby valuers were separately chosen to adjudicate on claims. In this primitive forerunner of the modern system, however, the third and fourth elements in compulsory purchase set out above, namely expropriation and compensation, were not kept separate from each other. Perhaps they could not be. But since a valuer and not a lawyer conducted this single undivided procedure, any legal problems arising in relation to doubtful or disputed claims were not to be adjudicated by a legal tribunal. However, before that stage was reached, the Commissioners despatched an assistant to hold a meeting to hear objections to the petition itself, essentially like an inspector today holding a public inquiry in relation to a modern compulsory purchase order.

### 3 THE LANDS CLAUSES CONSOLIDATION ACT

In that same year, 1845, Parliament brought other varieties of expropriation to the point that inclosures had reached in 1801. That is, the need for private Acts was not done away with, but their procedure was simplified by enacting a standardised set of provisions which would be incorporated into each Act unless otherwise stated. The statute that did this was the Lands Clauses Consolidation Act:

> This Act shall apply to every undertaking authorised by any Act which shall hereafter be passed, and which shall authorise the purchase or taking of lands for such undertaking, and this Act shall be incorporated with such Act; and all the clauses and provisions of this Act, save so far as they shall be expressly varied or excepted by any such Act, shall apply to the undertaking authorised thereby. . . .[9]

Any Act authorising any such 'undertaking', and incorporating the 1845 Act as stated in the above provision, was known as 'the special Act'.[10] Also, 'undertaking' meant any undertaking 'of whatever nature'; and no distinction was drawn between public and private bodies or persons; but the long title of the Act does clearly specify 'undertakings of a public nature'.

The 1845 Act deals with purchases by agreement as well as with compulsory purchase. All such purchases are governed by the ultra vires rule: they are all for public purposes, all dependent upon their 'special Act' for their validity. There are two strict limitations on purchase by agreement when the purchaser is a public body: the purchase itself must be covered by statutory authority, and if it is so covered the price agreed must be a proper one and not excessive. Where the public body is a local authority the auditor is nowadays entitled to challenge any expenditure on a purchase which infringed either of these rules, and indeed would be in duty bound to do so;[11] and the authority would also be liable at the suit of any ratepayer on the footing of breach of trust, as implied by law, in respect of misapplication of the authority's funds.[12] In particular it is ultra vires for a public body's decisions (contracts, for example) to

---

9 Section 1.
10 Section 2.
11 Local Government Act 1972, s 161.
12 *A-G v Wilson* (1840) Cr & Ph 1; *A-G v Newcastle-upon-Tyne Corpn* (1889) 23 QBD 492; *A-G v De Winton* [1906] 2 Ch 106.

'fetter' the exercise of discretion in a way which is incompatible with Parliament's intentions.[13]

The main body of law relating to compulsory purchase, contained in the statutory provisions of the Lands Clauses Consolidation Act 1845, and later enactments, did not apply to inclosures, though it applied (and applies) to most other expropriations, for three reasons. The first is that the statutory procedure for inclosures had already been developed to a stage not reached until later for other forms of acquisitions: this has been referred to already. Second, the nature of the expropriation in an inclosure award is very different from expropriation in other cases, in that most or all of the parties whose rights are expropriated reappear as the parties acquiring rights from the expropriation, so that in practical or economic terms as distinct from strictly legal ones the operation is a compulsory redistribution rather than a compulsory purchase of land. This too has been touched on. Third, the inclosure movement was virtually at an end after 1850; though the new procedure laid down in the Inclosure Act 1845 was enacted in an attempt to galvanise the movement back to life, and some notable inclosure disputes occurred, especially in relation to open spaces near London, in the 1860s and 70s.[14]

### 4 THE LATER NINETEENTH CENTURY

The Inclosure Act 1845 also enacted that certain kinds of petition should be laid before Parliament as well as before the Commissioners.[15] This rule was applied to the inclosure of areas of specified sizes within specified distances from towns of specified population. Like the general procedure, it has a parallel within the modern system, in that certain kinds of compulsory purchase order even now have to be laid before Parliament in addition to being approved by a Minister: and commons and open spaces are included within the scope of this requirement. But the need to lay inclosure petitions before Parliament as well as before the Commissioners was made general in 1852.[16] As a result, as soon as public opinion began to move in opposition to inclosures—partly out of sympathy for local inhabitants with customary rights which would be lost when land was inclosed, but more strongly from the new standpoint of the need to preserve public open spaces to keep pace with increasing urban development—Parliament began to reflect this opposition. Within 30 years, the Indian summer of inclosures came to an end. The Commons Act 1876 gave effect to the new policy of ensuring that 'inclosures will be of benefit to the neighbourhood as well as to private

13 See footnote 17 p 32.
14 *Willingale v Maitland* (1866) LR 3 Eq 103; *Chilton v London Corpn* (1878) 7 Ch D 735. See also *Robertson v Hartopp* (1889) 43 Ch D 484, above, p 7.
15 See Cooke's *Inclosure Acts* (4th edn).
16 Inclosure Act 1852, s 1.

interests',[17] which in practice meant that 'benefit to the neighbourhood' would normally prevail and commons be transformed into public open spaces.[18] Local authorities of various kinds obtained power under this and other statutes to acquire common land and either expropriate the owners of common rights, as well as the owners of the freehold, or make special provision to control and protect such rights.[19] Inclosures can still be made.[20] The Secretary of State for the Environment[1] may submit a provisional order to Parliament if satisfied, after receiving the report of a public local inquiry into the matter, that an inclosure of land should take place. But it must be shown that inclosure of the land is preferable to its being used as a public open space; and this in modern conditions is likely to be acceptable only in special circumstances.

In spite of the definite and comprehensive wording of the Lands Clauses Consolidation Act 1845—'This Act shall apply to every undertaking'—it seemed to be assumed in this century that it did not do so automatically; therefore it would be wise to say expressly that the Act applied to any particular authorising Act. The reason may be that s 1 envisaged express exclusion of parts of the Act—'all the clauses and provisions of this Act, save so far as they shall be expressly varied or excepted'—which might be acted on by negative wording such as, 'the following sections are excluded'. Yet it tended instead to be brought into effect by positive wording such as: 'the Lands Clauses Consolidation Act 1845 shall apply, *except for* the following sections'. This implies contrary to section 1, that it does not apply without express wording in some other Act. As a result it has been found possible to replace the 1845 Act by a more modern statute[2] without repealing it.

In the later nineteenth century several minor Acts[3] were passed amending some of the provisions of the Act of 1845. The Interpretation Act 1889, provides[4] that these Acts, from the principal statute of 1845 onwards, may be collectively referred to as 'the Lands Clauses Acts'. As a matter of fact this phrase, rather than 'compulsory purchase', was for a long time favoured as a title for the subject as a whole, as early textbooks bear witness. But in the twentieth century, it became the fashion to word

17 Preamble to the Act.
18 Hence the modern assumption that a 'common' is land which all people may use in common for recreation. But see Law of Property Act 1925, s 193.
19 Metropolitan Commons Acts 1866 to 1898; Commons Act 1899.
20 Commons Act 1876; Ministry of Agriculture and Fisheries Act 1919.
 1 To follow how functions have devolved upon the Secretary of State, see SI 1965/319; SI 1967/156; SI 1970/1681.
 2 The Compulsory Purchase Act 1965.
 3 Lands Clauses Consolidation Acts Amendment Act 1860; Lands Clauses Consolidation Act 1869; Lands Clauses (Umpire) Act 1883; Lands Clauses (Taxation of Costs) Act 1895.
 4 Section 23. See now Interpretation Act 1978, Sch 1.

differently the titles of compulsory purchase statutes; and now to speak of 'the Lands Clauses Acts' wears a very old-fashioned look.

## C. Replacement of private by public legislation

### 1 STANDARDISED PROCEDURE FOR ACQUISITION

In relation to the four main elements in compulsory purchase of land, referred to earlier—namely: authorisation, choice of land, acquisition procedure and compensation—the Lands Clauses Acts transferred the third and fourth from the individual private Acts to a general, standardised code contained in public general legislation to be incorporated by reference into each 'special Act'. In fact the Lands Clauses Acts concentrated upon acquisition procedure, and treated compensation as a minor question of fact of which acquisition procedure has to take account as one item among many.

In the twentieth century, Parliament had to concede that compensation is not merely one aspect of procedure and evidence, but a major element in compulsory purchase in its own right, depending on important rules of assessment quite apart from the mode of procedure. Victorian legislators had assumed that the only problem was whether the procedure for assessment should require the compensation to be fixed by an arbitrator, an umpire, a jury, a surveyor, or two lay magistrates.[5] But the courts soon found it necessary to settle disputes by evolving principles to govern the basis of assessment, regardless of the procedure. Parliament eventually took a hand; and it in part endorsed principles evolved by the courts in various leading cases, in part altered them. Statutory compensation provisions now govern the law in detail over the purchase price of land actually acquired under compulsory powers; but the principles evolved by the courts for incidental heads of compensation are still largely untouched by statute. A modern provision openly concedes the reliance of statute on precedent in these cases:

This section shall be construed as affording in all cases a right to compensation for injurious affection to land which is the same as the right which section 68 of the Lands Clauses Consolidation Act 1845, has been construed as affording. . . .[6]

Broadly speaking, the third and fourth elements in compulsory purchase are now dealt with by separate codes contained in public general Acts. The third element, acquisition procedure, until recently the preserve of the Lands Clauses Acts, is now contained in the Compulsory Purchase Act 1965, with an important variation to be found in the Compulsory Purchase (Vesting Declarations) Act 1981. The fourth

5 Sections 22, 23, 25, 27, 38 and 58 of the 1845 Act.
6 Compulsory Purchase Act 1965, s 10 ('construed' in cases discussed in ch 9).

element, compensation, is now dealt with by the Land Compensation Act 1961, supplemented by the Land Compensation Act 1973; certain incidental matters, however, are governed in principle by the Compulsory Purchase Act 1965 and in detail by judicial decisions.

## 2 INCLOSURE PETITIONS AND PROVISIONAL ORDERS

In 1845 the first and second elements were still commonly dealt with by 'special Act' in the sense of private, local legislation dealing with specified land; but they soon underwent a change. It became increasingly common for the authorisation of compulsory purchase to be conferred by public general Act. Thus the Public Health Act 1875, authorised local authorities of various kinds, in general terms, to acquire land compulsorily for various purposes under that Act.[7] Most public general Acts are not intended to specify particular land and not an appropriate method of specifying it. In the rare cases where they do specify particular land, they are scarcely distinguishable from private local legislation. Typical public general Acts which authorise compulsory purchase are the Public Health Acts and the Housing Acts which authorise various authorities to acquire land compulsorily in connection with their public health and housing functions, the Education Act 1944, which does so for education functions, the Post Office Act 1969, which authorises the Post Office to acquire land for its various functions, and many other statutes.

Such legislation is clearly very different from the type envisaged by the framers of the Lands Clauses Consolidation Act 1845. The private local Act which itself specifies land to be taken is not unknown today,[8] but it is less often met with. The fashion for compulsory purchase by public general Act made it necessary to provide by statutory authority for a separate stage in the procedure for selecting particular land in each case. For inclosures this had been provided for by the Inclosure Act 1845 in the manner described above by which the promoters presented to the central authority, the Inclosure Commissioners, for confirmation a petition specifying the land concerned; and in many cases at first, and in all cases after 1851, Parliamentary approval was needed. The comparable procedure devised for compulsory purchase under the Lands Clauses Acts when authorised by public general Acts was the 'provisional order'—a procedure which was itself applied to inclosures by the Commons Act 1876,[9] referred to above.

It became customary, therefore, for authorising Acts to prescribe

---

7 The provisions of this Act have largely been re-enacted in later statutes, such as the Public Health Act 1936.

8 Many local authorities obtain additional powers from time to time by promoting private bills.

9 Section 12.

provisional order procedure for specific compulsory acquisitions. Unless an authorising Act provided any other procedure for selecting land the only alternative would be for the body authorised to acquire land to promote a private bill for any specific project and acquisition. Provisional orders, if authorised today, must still be made by a specified minister on the application of the acquiring body, and submitted to Parliament for confirmation, normally in batches of several at a time, in a provisional order bill. Each draft order must be given prior press publicity, and objections must be heard normally by a public local inquiry conducted by an inspector,[10] just as petitions under the Inclosure Act 1845 normally gave rise to objections which were investigated in a public local inquiry by an assistant Inclosure Commissioner. Should the minister concerned decide to proceed, he would make the provisional order, with or without modifications, and then it would be possible to challenge it again before Parliament. This further challenge would be by petition against the order, to be heard by a Select Committee on the Provisional Order Confirmation Bill in the same way as a petition against a private bill—which shows how limited advance from private bills to provisional orders was. It is true that a bill dealing with several projects at once might be cheaper in relation to each acquisition than a private bill, and its necessary sponsorship by a minister would certainly increase its chances of ready acceptance by Parliament as against a private bill's chances. But provisional order procedure is time-consuming.

## 3 HOW COMPULSORY PURCHASE ORDERS EVOLVED

A new advance was made when the need for Parliamentary confirmation was dispensed with. This came with the emergence of the 'compulsory purchase order', which dates from the era of Edward VII and Asquith, in the Housing, Town Planning, &c. Act 1909, and the Development and Road Improvement Funds Act 1909. A compulsory purchase order must be made or confirmed, with or without modifications, by whichever minister is appropriate to the purpose of the acquisition. There must be prior press publicity and a private hearing or a public local inquiry by an inspector into any consequent objections. This procedure resembles provisional order procedure, shorn of its Parliamentary stage. Its details differed from one authorising Act to the next, although the various procedures were more or less standardised. Eventually the Acquisition of Land (Authorisation Procedure) Act 1946 enacted the uniform code now substantially re-enacted in the Acquisition of Land Act 1981. Apart from certain special cases the 1981 Act code is now of general application when compulsory purchase orders are made. Even the special cases differ only in certain details, not in their main principles.

10 Local Government Act 1972, s 240.

There are, however, some compulsory purchase orders which need to be submitted by the appropriate minister to Parliament before they can come into effect. Each House has a period during which it can pass a resolution annulling the order, under the Statutory Orders (Special Procedure) Acts 1945 and 1965. This procedure applies to any order, though not by any means only a compulsory purchase order, the making of which any statute states is to be subject to 'special Parliamentary procedure'. In fact most of the remaining authorising Acts under which provisional orders were formerly prescribed for compulsory purchase of land have been subjected to a change, replacing provisional orders by compulsory purchase orders subject to special Parliamentary procedure.[11] Thus they continue to undergo Parliamentary scrutiny, but it is no longer necessary to submit them in a provisional order confirmation bill.

The modern position, therefore, is that four statutory codes contained in public general Acts provide for the four main parts of the compulsory purchase process.

First, the authorising Act in each case specifies which body or bodies can acquire land for what purpose, and whether the acquisition may be compulsorily made; and if so, whether land is to be selected for compulsory acquisition by means of a compulsory purchase order; and if so, whether the 1981 Act (replacing the 1946 Act) is to apply to that order. Special Parliamentary procedure may be prescribed as well.

Second, the 1981 Act governs the making of the compulsory purchase order, except in the special cases where a different code applies.

Third, the Act of 1965, modified in some respects by the Act of 1973, governs the actual acquisition procedure when each interest in land is to be acquired; although the alternative procedure in the Compulsory Purchase (Vesting Declarations) Act 1981, or any other procedure specially enacted in any particular case, may be used instead, in so far as it applies.

Fourth, the Act of 1961 governs the assessment of compensation for acquisition; except that compensation for depreciation of land is in fact governed by two brief provisions in the Act of 1965 and the leading cases which amplify those provisions, together with new provisions in the legislation of 1973.

Authorising Acts, which can be infinitely various, must be studied in their own right in each particular case, and on the whole are outside the scope of this book, which would otherwise become excessively bulky. But an exception is made in respect of statutes which authorise compulsory purchase for planning purposes,[12] since planning is specially closely related to compulsory purchase in regard to both procedure and

11 See ch 3 below.
12 See chs 11 to 13 below.

compensation. The standardised codes in the Acts of 1981, 1965 and 1961, together with the main variants upon them, are discussed in the chapters that follow.

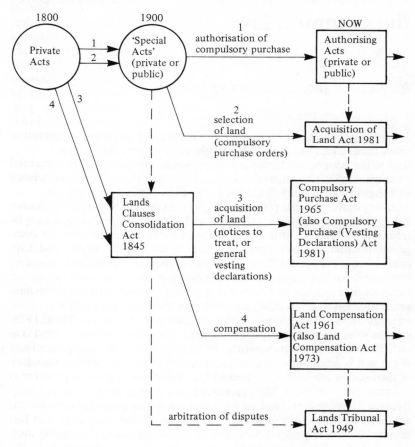

# Chapter 2

# Compulsory purchase, the courts and the common law

## A. Judicial interpretation of statutes

### 1 MEANING AND REASONABLENESS

Statutes are usually the beginning, not the end, of litigation. Attempts to word them clearly or comprehensively tend to provoke disputes which lead to the courts, not because human beings are perverse, but because clear wording makes them think they understand their rights more fully and they are keen not to be done out of them. It is not so much the uncertainty of the law that provokes litigation as an uncertainty whether the law applies to any given set of facts; and of course factual situations are infinitely various. Binding judicial precedent is not much help here. No previous situation is a completely factual 'precedent' for a later situation, probably not even if it is the same situation giving rise to another dispute. It is a truism that judicial precedent depends on the ratio decidendi of each relevant judgment, which is to say upon a process of abstraction and generalisation which will be more widely applicable the farther it is taken from the facts of the case in which each judgment was given. Thus it will no doubt be clear enough, if a judgment is lucidly expressed, what the ratio decidendi and consequently the binding rule of law happens to be. What will be much less clear in later cases of dispute is whether the facts of those cases are such as to make that rule of law applicable.[1]

Statutory provisions, like precedents, are rules or propositions of law. Because they do not need to be based on a reasoning process which depends on previously evolved propositions of law, they can, and for reasons of social policy often should, be more novel, extensive and arbitrary. But Parliament itself, unless either House is for some reason acting in a judicial capacity, will not have to interpret them even though it declared them. Individual or corporate subjects of the Crown have to interpret them, because they are law and ignorance of the law is not an

---

1 There is a similarity between equity and statutory branches of law: both involve problems of construction of wording. In each there is a temptation to regard the construction of words in a particular case as a precedent for the construction of the same or similar wording in another case, rather than merely a help in such construction. It is important to remember, as the courts have expressed it in many planning cases, that a right decision is 'a question of fact and degree' in all the relevant circumstances of each case.

excuse for its infringement. And the hierarchy of courts will have to interpret them also when each occasion arises.[2] This applies both in the fields of law which are based in the main on statute and in those which are based in the main on the principles of common law and equity.

Those branches of law which are based on common law and equity have been developed by the courts in their own atmosphere; and statutory changes, though often elaborate, are subordinated to this. Contract, tort and private land law are clear examples of such branches of law. But in relation to statutory provisions as such, the courts only have two basic doctrines to apply. These mark out the boundaries of the statutory jurisdiction rather than test its content, because Parliament is supreme and its policy is unchallengeable by the courts.[3] In relation therefore to the detailed wording of statutes, the principles of statutory interpretation apply, so that an answer can emerge to the question, 'What do these particular words mean?'[4] But in relation to the more generalised question, 'Is this factual situation, or this course of action, within the scope of the relevant statutory provisions?', it is the test of reasonableness which applies.

Thus in one dispute within the ambit of the law of housing a county court was held to have acted wrongly in varying a demolition order on a house by substituting a period of seven years for the period of ten weeks which the local authority had imposed as the time for compliance.[5] The Housing Act[6] had given the county court judge a wide discretion, not bounded by any maximum period, so there was no ground here for appeal based on rules of statutory interpretation. Yet the alteration was clearly unreasonable, and the Court of Appeal reversed it and restored the time limit which the local authority originally imposed in the demolition order.

## 2 ANALOGIES WITH THE COMMON LAW

The courts, then, can only apply the tests of reasonableness and statutory interpretation, which between them make up the ultra vires rule governing the lawfulness of functions carried out by statutory authorities and tribunals. But they need more than this to guide them when settling disputes in fields of law which are based on statute. Given that these fields are normally ones in which technical considerations are important,

2 Tribunals and public authorities must make decisions which *include* interpretations of the law. Appeals to the courts from those decisions must be substantially confined to points of law.
3 See *Edinburgh and Dalkeith Rly Co v Wauchope* (1842) 8 Cl & Fin 710; *Stockdale v Hansard* (1839) 9 Ad & El 1; *R v Graham-Campbell, ex p Herbert* [1935] 1 KB 594.
4 The so-called 'literal rule', 'golden rule' and 'mischief rule' all come down to the question of the meaning of particular words.
5 *Pocklington v Melksham UDC* [1964] 2 QB 673, [1964] 2 All ER 862.
6 Housing Act 1957, s 20.

how can reasonableness itself be established? Since the courts have the task of deciding, they naturally adopt reasoning processes which are familiar to them and which they consider suitable. In fact, by implication Parliament may be said to have invited this, having given the courts jurisdiction and no further instructions.

Therefore it need cause no surprise that the courts have developed rules by analogy with ordinary civil actions when deciding compulsory purchase disputes. 'A person seeking to obtain compensation under these Acts of Parliament must once and for all make one claim for all damages which can be reasonably foreseen;' this was the way in which Erle CJ, expressed his reasoning in 1863.[7] The word 'damages' in its ordinary common law context refers both to the wrongful act and to the compensation to be paid in respect of it. Applied here, by analogy, to compulsory purchase it refers both to the expropriation inflicted on the claimant and the compensation to be paid in respect of it. But since a multiplicity of proceedings is not desirable, a single award of 'damages' or compensation in any such case should as far as possible cover all heads of claim, notably for depreciation of land retained by the claimant as well as for land taken from him: the sum total is his 'true loss' consequent upon the compulsory purchase.

The component parts of such 'true loss' are none the less distinguishable from one another in such a case. The value of the land taken is essentially a question of purchase price: after all the law regards the transaction as none the less a purchase, though compulsory in nature. But the depreciation of any land not taken, though equally well a question of value, is essentially loss and not sale. So it can perhaps be said that purchase price compensation is clearly analogous to an agreed sale price under the law of contract, whereas depreciation compensation is analogous to damages in tort for nuisance.[8] Compensation for 'disturbance or any other matter not directly based on the value of land' is harder to deal with by analogy; but perhaps it may be thought of as bearing some resemblance to special as distinct from general damages, or to special contractual items to be quantified at a later stage contingently on whether and how they arise.[9]

Such reasoning by analogy only applies where payment has to be made for intra vires conduct. Being intra vires the authorising Acts, it is arguable that such conduct is lawful and thus not subject to a civil action for damages or to any alternative remedy.[10] The evolution of rules governing compensation for harm caused by such conduct must therefore depend not only on reasoning by analogy (or perhaps from quite

---

7 *Chamberlain v West End of London and Crystal Palace Rly Co* (1863) 2 B & S 617.
8 See chs 7 and 9.
9 See ch 10.
10 See *Hammersmith and City Rly Co v Brand* (1869) LR 4 HL 171; and *Kirby v Harrogate School Board* [1896] 1 Ch 437.

novel and separate bases if it could ever be shown that the courts might have any warrant for them) but also on whether the relevant statutory provisions could be interpreted to authorise, in a given set of circumstances, the payment of any compensation at all.[11]

On the other hand it might be argued in any case that harmful conduct could not be regarded as intra vires; if so, the authorising Acts would be irrelevant and a civil action for damages, or for some other suitable remedy, should lie, regardless of compulsory purchase powers being exercised. One notable illustration of this distinction occurred in *Metropolitan Asylum District v Hill*,[12] when a public authority proposed to build a smallpox hospital in pursuance of clear statutory powers to do this. Neighbouring owners succeeded in obtaining an injunction, because the use for this purpose of the land actually chosen would constitute a nuisance in relation to their land adjoining. The general statutory power did not make the particular proposal intra vires, because the discretion conferred by that power had to be exercised reasonably, and it would not be reasonable to choose a site detrimental to adjoining owners unless it could be shown that, because of the Act or of the circumstances, no better site was available.[13]

As Lord Atkinson said in *Lagan Navigation Co v Lambeg Bleaching, Dyeing and Finishing Co Ltd*:[14] 'If a public body have statutory powers which they may at will exercise in a manner hurtful to third parties or in a manner innocuous to third parties, that body will be held guilty of negligence, if they choose the former mode of exercising their powers and not the latter, both being available to them.'

Therefore it was very natural that Erle CJ should speak of 'damages' when referring to compensation payable in respect of a lawful activity. His use of the term 'damages' clearly imports an analogy, but not a precise one. In respect of purchase price compensation for land taken, and probably 'disturbance' compensation also, the closest comparison is perhaps to be drawn with a judgment at common law for a contract price to be precisely ascertained, under the terms of the contract, by valuation or arbitration:[15] '*id certum est quod certum reddi potest*'. The difference lies in the actual principles of assessment. In respect of depreciation compensation, the closest comparison is with a judgment at common law for damages in tort for nuisance; but, as will be seen, the analogy is far from exact, and compensation will be payable in some cases on a wider basis than damages for nuisance, and in other cases on a narrower basis, but

11  See *Atkinson v Newcastle Waterworks Co* (1877) 2 Ex D 441; *Hesketh v Birmingham Corpn* [1924] 1 KB 260; *Read v Croydon Corpn* [1938] 4 All ER 631; *Reffell v Surrey County Council* [1964] 1 All ER 743.
12  (1881) 6 App Cas 193.
13  See ch 9, for a critical view based on this case.
14  [1927] AC 226. But see ch 9, p 184, footnote 18.
15  See *Re Hopper* (1867) LR 2 QB 367.

never on a basis which is substantially the same even though the amount may be.[16]

## 3 ANALOGY WITH FREE MARKET SALES

The analogy with the common law goes much deeper than the question of rules evolved by judges, thrown back on their own resources by statute, when solving compensation disputes. The entire process of compulsory purchase itself rests on an analogy with common law. Indeed, virtually the only cause of difference is the element of compulsion; and so the factors which distinguish the process of compulsory acquisition from that of a sale of land by agreement at common law are traceable to the need for compulsion. It is true that the purpose of the acquisition must be intra vires; but so must any activity by a statutory body.

The closeness of the analogy can best be seen by working backwards. The final stage in a compulsory purchase or *expropriation* is normally the same as that in a sale by agreement, namely 'completion'. Title to the land is transferred to the acquiring body by a conveyance of the legal estate. This has been so thoroughly taken for granted that statutory provisions have only been thought to be necessary to deal with incidental matters, such as prescribing a standard form of conveyance, or authorising an acquiring body to complete unilaterally by executing a deed-poll in cases where landowners prove recalcitrant and refuse to convey. The Compulsory Purchase (Vesting Declarations) Act 1981 authorises the use of a 'general vesting declaration' which in effect telescopes the conveyance with the prior procedural stage of the 'notice to treat'; but this new procedure is expressly made to operate in the manner of a conveyance by deed-poll as applicable to a compulsory purchase.[17]

The end-product, at any rate in the form of a deed of conveyance, is virtually the same therefore in compulsory purchase as in a sale by agreement. But on tracing the process back to its earlier stages it is much easier to see what are the differences in procedure. Thus the prior stage in a sale of land by agreement is the contract. But in a compulsory purchase it is a 'notice to treat', at any rate where the acquiring authority do not use the new alternative mode of acquisition by vesting declaration which, as already stated, combines 'notice to treat' and conveyance in one.

A notice to treat is not in itself a contract.[18] It has important consequences which are discussed later; but what matters here is that the

16 See ch 9.
17 Compulsory Purchase (Vesting Declarations) Act 1981, s 8.
18 *Harding v Metropolitan Rly Co* (1872) 7 Ch App 154. See below, ch 14, pp 277 (the *Metrolands* case).

equivalent of an enforceable binding contract, as in a sale by agreement, does not exist in compulsory purchase until compensation has been fixed. Notice to treat and compensation together then constitute a contract, which is subject to completion in the ordinary way, as already described. This contract is enforceable, at least in theory, like any ordinary land contract.[19]

Before reaching the stage of a binding contract, the process of sale by agreement consists of negotiations or 'invitations to treat'. Before reaching the stage of a notice to treat, however, the process of compulsory purchase in Britain requires special authorisation, normally by means of a compulsory purchase order. Whereas the background of an effective private sale is the general common law, the background of a compulsory purchase is purely statutory. In the words of Lord Wilberforce in *Sovmots Investments Ltd v Secretary of State for the Environment*[20] 'Expropriation cannot take place by implication or through intention; it is authorised or not authorised. And to see which, it is necessary to construe the authority.'

But this difference, though striking, must not obscure the fact that when the machinery of compulsion has been effectively set in motion in any particular case the subsequent process of a compulsory purchase becomes as nearly as possible assimilated to that of a private land transaction. Not all private land transactions, however, are relevant here. The assimilation just mentioned is only to transactions which are assignments of *existing* rights (freehold or leasehold, legal or equitable) and not to those which are grants of *new* rights unless clear express statutory authority for any such grant exists in a particular case. Lord Wilberforce, in the speech referred to above, went on to say:

A power to acquire a right over land [ie to arrange that an owner's existing right in a given portion of land be transferred to the acquiring body] cannot authorise compulsion of an owner of land not being acquired [ie an owner whose existing right in a given portion of land is not, as such, intended to be transferred to that body] to grant new rights over that land; for the latter quite different words would be needed.[1]

The 'grant of new rights' would cover such matters as the creation of new easements and restrictive covenants and also of new leases, options and so forth; and it should make no difference in principle whether such a grant is express or implied.

In *Grice v Dudley Corpn*,[2] Upjohn J commented on the similarity between free and compulsory purchases:

19 *Grice v Dudley Corpn* [1958] Ch 329, [1957] 2 All ER 673 (below, p 59).
20 [1977] QB 411, [1977] 2 All ER 385.
1 For circumstances when new rights can in fact be lawfully acquired by compulsion, see ch 5 (below, p 98).
2 [1958] Ch 329, [1957] 2 All ER 673.

The relationship between the parties thus created by the service of the notice to treat has sometimes been described as a quasi-contract. It is, further, clear that where the parties have agreed upon the compensation, or it has been assessed, but not before, the remedy of specific performance is open to either side: see *Fry on Specific Performance* (6th edn) p 62. That state of affairs has sometimes been referred to as a Parliamentary contract.

The leading nineteenth-century authority for specific performance in these circumstances, *Harding v Metropolitan Rly Co*[3] in addition over-ruled a previous decision[4] that the remedy would be available on the strength of a notice to treat by itself.

The principles governing the relationship between the law of contract and statutory acquisitions of land under compulsory powers have recently been explained and applied by the Court of Appeal in *Munton v Greater London Council*.[5] In that case Newham London Borough Council compulsorily purchased the applicant's house and several others in the course of slum clearance under Part III of the Housing Act 1957. The applicant's surveyors accepted £3,400 (offered by the district valuer) 'subject to contract', the notice to treat having been served some time previously. A long delay followed but eventually the council took possession under a notice of entry.[6] The applicant demanded to have the price re-negotiated, and the district valuer duly raised it by 50%, to £5,100. 'But in the next few months' said Lord Denning MR, 'the property market collapsed'. The council therefore contested the figure of £5,100 and argued that the first figure of £3,400 was binding; but the Lands Tribunal and the Court of Appeal upheld the claim for £5,100.

Lord Denning MR accepted that, in a compulsory acquisition, 'the words subject to contract have no real application. But nevertheless they have, I think, the effect of preventing there being any firm agreement on the price. . . . It was only a provisional figure'. He pointed out that s 40 of the Law of Property Act 1925, which re-enacts the Statute of Frauds 1677 in requiring land contracts to be evidenced in writing before they can be enforced, has been held not to apply to *statutory* land acquisition.

That appears from *Pollard v Middlesex County Council*[7] when Parker J said: 'It is quite true that statutory agreements arising out of notices to treat are not within the Statute of Frauds, and that oral evidence of them may therefore be admitted'. This is followed in practice. Very rarely do the parties enter into an actual contract in writing. The [acquiring] authority serve a notice to treat. There is agreement on the price. Then the matter is completed by the conveyance and payment of the money.

3 (1872) 7 Ch App 154. See also *Re Cary-Elwes Contract* [1906] 2 Ch 143.
4 *Walker v Eastern Counties Rly Co* (1848) 6 Hare 594.
5 [1976] 2 All ER 815, [1976] 1 WLR 649.
6 Notices of entry are discussed below: ch 4, p 65.
7 (1906) 95 LT 870 at 871.

But service of the notice to treat is itself more than a mere negotiating move. 'It binds the [acquiring] authority to purchase and the owner to sell at a price to be ascertained: see *Mercer v Liverpool, St Helens and South Lancashire Rly Co.*'[8] So by using the phrase 'subject to contract', or any other wording showing that agreement is provisional only, either side can keep the question of assessment open, in which case the principle in *Birmingham Corpn v West Midland Baptist (Trust) Association (Incorporated)* will govern it.[9] But a *binding* agreement as to the price in a statutory land acquisition is enforceable as such, whether oral or written.

This point should be appreciated in the light of *Dutton's Breweries Ltd v Leeds City Council.*[10] In 1968 the local authority proposed to acquire, under the shadow of compulsion but by agreement, one of the company's public houses at a specified price, stating, however, that possession would not be needed for three years or so. In fact possession was not taken for eight years. The authority then asserted that they were still entitled to compel the company to convey the property at the price agreed in 1968, despite the inflation of land values in the intervening period. The Court of Appeal held that, because in the 1968 agreement the town clerk had stipulated that it was subject to a contract to be approved by himself, yet no such contract had been approved, there was in fact no contract. The authority's right to the property must therefore depend on the strict exercise of the statutory procedures for acquisition by compulsion. It followed that there had to be an up-to-date assessment of market value.

## 4 REQUISITIONING

It is important not to confuse compulsory purchase with requisitioning of land. The former is a part of the law of conveyancing; the latter has nothing to do with it. Although practical attention in cases of compulsory acquisition is normally focussed on the use to which land is to be put—usually public development, such as road construction, but sometimes a mere continuance of its existing use (eg for housing)—yet the heart of the matter legally is the transfer of title under compulsory modes of proceeding.

Requisitioning is, on the other hand, merely the transfer of the *use* of land without affecting its ownership. It is an unceremonious course of action and normally occurs only in wartime or some comparable

---

8 [1904] AC 461.
9 [1970] AC 874, [1969] 3 All ER 172. See below, ch 6, p 116.
10 (1981) 43 P & CR 160. The judge at first instance had held that there was an implied term in the original agreement for revision of the price in the event of a long delay; but the Court of Appeal held that the parties could not be taken to have implied any such thing.

emergency. The occupier of land is in effect paid compensation for being deprived of occupation by a public authority so that the property can be used for some urgent public purpose.[11] If the occupier is a tenant his leasehold obligations continue to bind him, and his liability to his landlord persists despite the fact that the requisitioning excludes him from the property until such time as it is released by the requisitioning authority.[12]

## B. Compulsory purchase disputes

### 1   LAW AND FACT

*Grice v Dudley Corpn* was an action brought for a declaration, and this kind of proceeding is one method by which a compulsory purchase dispute can come before the courts. This question of the way in which courts obtain cognisance of cases is important, because a detailed development of law in authoritative terms depends on there being judicial interpretations, as far as is possible, of the statutory provisions. But not all disputes are disputes of law, and it is only when they are that the courts are empowered to try them.

Compensation disputes, it should be noted, are chiefly disputes of fact, even if the elucidation of the facts in such cases is largely a matter of expert evidence such as should if possible be heard by a special, expert, tribunal. Under the Lands Clauses Acts, an expropriated owner had the choice of an arbitrator or a jury to settle disputed compensation.[13] An umpire chosen by two arbitrators or by the Board of Trade might act instead of an arbitrator.[14] Claims not exceeding £50 were to be settled by two magistrates.[15] If an owner was absent or untraceable, or failed to appear before a jury, compensation could be settled by 'an able practical surveyor'.[16] The jury or the magistrates seem to have acted like any normal court required to reach a decision after hearing expert witnesses. The arbitrator or umpire, however, is clearly to be regarded as a specialist tribunal; and before a specialist tribunal the central issues must still be issues of fact,[17] subject to this difference, that the expert evidence will be heard by an adjudicator who is himself an expert. As for the surveyor he,

11  See *Lewisham Borough Council v Maloney* [1948] 1 KB 50, [1947] 2 All ER 36 (Defence Regulations in the Second World War), and *A-G v De Keyser's Royal Hotel Ltd* [1920] AC 508 (Defence Regulations in the First World War).
12  See *Matthey v Curling* [1922] 2 AC 180.
13  Lands Clauses Consolidation Act 1845, s 23.
14  Ibid, s 27.
15  Ibid, s 22.
16  Ibid, s 58.
17  An arbitrator must decide points of law unless he feels it necessary to refer them to the High Court (see now Arbitration Act 1950, s 21 (1) (a)).

though an expert, did not in fact adjudicate but merely acted in an executive capacity when settling compensation; that is to say he produced a valuation, and not an arbitration between opposing claims.[18]

The issues of fact which were constantly processed through this ramshackle system threw up many issues of law relating to the assessment of compensation. Such issues of law would normally reach the courts through an 'action on the award'. This is essentially an action in contract,[19] the legal position being that, except where statute provides otherwise, an arbitration can only take place where two parties make an agreement to that end. In effect they contract out of their normal right to sue in the courts, in so far as they provide for settlement of disputes by arbitration; but because the overriding situation is contractual the courts take over where the scope of the arbitration agreement ends. Thus a party can 'bring an action on the award' in order to sue for an amount properly settled by an arbitrator, or to sue in respect of any breach of the arbitration agreement.[20]

Any of the old methods of settling an award of compensation could be dealt with in this way, even an award made by a jury. Thus the various questions of law as distinct from fact arising on the statutory provisions were liable to be decided by the courts and made applicable in future disputes in accordance with judicial precedent. As in all statutory subjects, case law tends to accumulate by way of interpretation of the statutes; and if Parliament does not like the legal propositions that emerge it can change them by fresh legislation.

## 2 OFFICIAL ARBITRATORS AND THE LANDS TRIBUNAL

The Acquisition of Land (Assessment of Compensation) Act 1919, did indeed change some of the propositions evolved by the courts: this will be discussed later. It also made a procedural change by substituting, for the various modes of assessment already described, one standard procedure of settlement of disputes arising over compensation. This comprised the setting up of a panel of official arbitrators, any one of whom

18 If surveyors are intended to 'hold the scales between vendor and purchaser' this may make their work in such a case an arbitration and not merely a valuation: *Boynton v Richardson* [1924] WN 262.

19 'The submission is an actual mutual promise to perform the award of the arbitrators': per Holt CJ in *Purslow v Baily* (1705) 2 Ld Raym 1039.

20 Alternatively, it became possible to take issues of law arising in arbitrations to the courts by 'stating a case'. The Common Law Procedure Act 1854, s 5, now re-enacted in the Arbitration Act 1950, s 21 (1) (b), gave power to an arbitrator to state his award in the form of a special case, which now goes to the High Court. An arbitrator's award, if undisputed and made under a written arbitration agreement, can normally be enforced as a judgment by leave of 'the High Court or a judge thereof' under the Arbitration Act 1950, s 26, which is easier and cheaper than bringing an action on the award. But this is purely a matter of enforcement.

would be available to adjudicate these disputes.[1] As before, questions of fact would be decided in accordance with ordinary and expert evidence; while questions of law would be decided in the same arbitration in accordance with the provisions of case law as well as statute, subject to the normal right of recourse to the courts themselves as already discussed.

The Lands Tribunal Act 1949, abolished the official arbitration procedure. It substituted adjudication by tribunal in compulsory purchase compensation disputes and many other matters as well. The Lands Tribunal is composed of lawyers (one of whom is President) and valuers, and 'any one or more of its members' can deal with any 'reference' which comes before it.[2] The arbitration concept, which is essentially contractual, is replaced by that of a modern tribunal, which is essentially statutory. Matters of law are taken to the courts, not by an 'action on the award', but by appeal against the tribunal's decision. The appeal lies direct to the Court of Appeal at the instance of 'any person aggrieved by the decision as being erroneous in point of law' (in other words on law only, not on fact or policy), and is by way of case stated.[3] Order 61 of the Rules of the Supreme Court prescribes a time limit of six weeks after the decision appealed against. Apart from this closely circumscribed right of appeal by case stated, any 'decision of the Lands Tribunal shall be final'.[4] But it is arguable that this restriction on appeals should apply, as in common sense and justice is surely right, to the *contents* of a decision and not to its *existence*. There is, in other words, a case for saying that to question whether there was jurisdiction for a purported decision of the Lands Tribunal, or to assert that it is inaccurate or forged, ought on principle not to be subject to such restriction at all. As will be seen later, similar considerations apply to the challenging of compulsory purchase orders.[5]

Most compulsory purchase disputes which become leading cases, and so play their part in the development of the law, arise over the question of compensation. Thus the earlier tendency for important questions of law in this field to emerge in court by way of an action on the award continues in the more modern form of an appeal from the Lands Tribunal by case stated to the Court of Appeal; and so ultimately, if the fight is a hard one, to the House of Lords, as in the celebrated case of *Birmingham Corpn v West Midland Baptist (Trust) Association (Incorporated)*,[6] which will be discussed in connection with compensation assessment procedure.[7] But

1 The 1919 Act, s 1.
2 The 1949 Act, s 3 (1).
3 Ibid, proviso to s 3 (4).
4 Ibid, s 3 (4).
5 See ch 3, p 51.
6 [1970] AC 874, [1969] 3 All ER 172.
7 See ch 6, p 116.

the legality of compulsory purchase proceedings could well be tested in relation to all manner of civil claims and perhaps even criminal proceedings. However, the most obvious alternative mode of action is to sue in the High Court for a declaration that a compulsory purchase order or a notice to treat, or both, should be treated as invalid. *Grice v Dudley Corpn* is a case of this kind. *Simpsons Motor Sales (London) Ltd v Hendon Corpn*, and *Capital Investments Ltd v Wednesfield UDC*, are other leading examples from recent years, which will be discussed later.[8]

## 3 EFFECT OF COMPULSORY PURCHASE ON CIVIL LIABILITY

It may thus happen that a dispute between two parties turns on a question of compulsory purchase even though neither of them is an acquiring authority. The action in *Hillingdon Estates Co v Stonefield Estates*[9] was for specific performance of a contract to buy land; and it succeeded despite the fact that a compulsory purchase order had been made which included that land. The impending compulsory transfer to the acquiring body was, in other words, treated as if it were a prospective sub-sale by the purchaser, who was therefore specifically liable to complete.

In *Baily v De Crespigny*,[10] the action was brought for damages for breach of a leasehold covenant, the plaintiff having leased land in Camberwell from the defendant with the benefit of a restrictive covenant against building on nearby land. The burdened land was compulsorily purchased by a railway company. Leaving aside the question whether or not the acquiring company could be held liable, the lessee proceeded on the basis of privity of contract to sue the lessor, presumably on the point that an assignor of a reversion[11] remains contractually liable for the breaches of covenant committed by his assignee, subject of course to his consequent right of indemnity against the assignee who is the cause of his troubles.[12] But the court very reasonably declined to treat the acquiring body as an assignee for the purposes of liability for breach of covenant; and it can be regarded as a general rule that a covenantor is *not* liable for the acts of an acquiring authority.[13]

8 See ch 4, p 59; ch 11, p 234, footnote 11.
9 [1952] Ch 627, [1952] 1 All ER 853.
10 (1869) LR 4 QB 180.
11 This would be equally true of an assignor of the lease.
12 Law of Property Act 1925, s 77 (1) (c).
13 The strict mutual liability of original parties to a lease is of course contractual; but the intervention of a compulsory purchase relieves them of that liability in regard to infringements forced on them by the compulsory purchase. This presumably has the effect of frustrating the contract in such circumstances. It negatives not only a party's direct liability but also a possible loss of his rights by waiver if the contractual breaches waived are committed in furtherance of compulsory powers, so that he has no choice in the matter: an example of this is *Piggott v Middlesex County Council* [1909] 1 Ch 134 (below, p 104, footnote 1).

In *Harding v Metropolitan Rly Co*[14] the court ruled that a body compulsorily acquiring a leasehold must undertake to indemnify the lessee against liability thereafter for breaches of covenant. The previous decision in *Baily v De Crespigny* might seem to have made this unnecessary. But later on, in *Matthey v Curling*,[15] the House of Lords held that leasehold covenants to pay rent and to deliver up premises at the end of the term are exceptions from the main rule, so that the lessee will remain liable and requires to be indemnified by the acquiring body in respect of such covenants.

## C. Statutory purchases by agreement

### 1 COMPULSORY POWERS IN THE BACKGROUND

In view of the hard feelings that the exercise of compulsion may be expected to cause, acquiring bodies will often try, as far as possible, to acquire land by agreement. Of course owners are usually aware that compulsory powers are available in the background, and therefore they often do sell voluntarily; but 'voluntary' in this context is very much a relative term. There are other situations, however, where authorising Acts only allow authorities to acquire land by agreement, and here a 'voluntary' sale is much more likely to be a genuine one. For example, local authorities may, under the Open Spaces Act 1906,[16] acquire land, by agreement only, for an open space or burial ground.

In either situation the ultra vires rule will apply. No statutory body can lawfully perform any function in the absence of statutory authority in respect of that function, not even on land it owns already. Nor can it acquire land by agreement for any function, any more than by compulsory purchase, unless there exists statutory authority to that effect. This is chiefly of concern to authorities themselves; but other people may be affected if they enter into contracts with statutory bodies and such contracts are made for purposes, or contain terms, which happen to be ultra vires, because such contracts cannot be enforced. For instance contracts whereby statutory bodies 'fetter' themselves, that is submit to an obligation not to exercise to the full their statutory powers, are ultra vires, regardless of the fact that they may save money or obtain some other benefit in return for restricting the scope of their discretion.[17]

14 (1872) 7 Ch App 154.
15 [1922] 2 AC 180. This case, however, concerned not compulsory purchase in the strict sense but a war-time requisition, and its applicability is therefore uncertain in this context.
16 Section 9.
17 *Ayr Harbour Trustees v Oswald* (1883) 8 App Cas 623; *William Cory & Son Ltd v City of London Corpn* [1951] 1 KB 8, [1950] 2 All ER 584; *Windsor and Maidenhead Royal Borough Council v Brandrose Investments Ltd* [1981] 3 All ER 38.

These pitfalls do not prevent acquiring authorities from obtaining land by agreement for their intra vires functions where compulsory powers exist. Section 3 of the Compulsory Purchase Act 1965 encourages this:

> It shall be lawful for the acquiring authority to agree with the owners of any of the land subject to compulsory purchase . . . for the absolute purchase, for a consideration in money, of any of that land, and of all estates and interests in the land.

Section 1 (3) states that 'subject to compulsory purchase' means that such purchase is authorised by a compulsory purchase order.

Thus it would be unwise for any such body to dispense with a compulsory purchase order, except in uncomplicated cases. If there is no compulsory purchase order, a selling owner may lawfully change his mind at any time before contracts are exchanged, however agreeable he may have shown himself up till then. If however a compulsory purchase order has been made, the acquiring authority can dispense with notices to treat (though they often do not), and other subsequent procedural steps and continue as in a purchase by agreement, secure in the knowledge that if a vendor ceases to be agreeable a notice to treat can still be served, so long as three years have not elapsed[18] since the compulsory purchase order came into effect.

If the vendor does enter into a binding contract he must keep to it. In *Crabb v Surrey County Council*,[19] the vendor's land was compulsorily purchased, with completion by registered transfer and payment settled as covering 'all items except disturbance'. This item was later assessed also, and the vendor gave a written receipt for its payment 'in full settlement of the disturbance claim'. Earlier an agreement had been entered into that the council would pay the vendor an extra stated sum, but only in the event of a planning permission, already applied for by the vendor to develop the land, being granted. It was, however, refused, and appeals were unsuccessful. The vendor asserted that the sum should still be included in his compensation, and made a claim for it before the Lands Tribunal. The council applied to have this claim struck out, and succeeded. The Lands Tribunal held that the arrangement was a binding contract, to the terms of which the vendor must be held. He could have sought specific performance if his planning application had succeeded.

---

18 Compulsory Purchase Act 1965, s 4. See below, p 60. Another possible type of situation is exemplified in *Dutton's Brewery v Leeds City Council*, discussed above (see p 27), where the vendors did not attempt to resile from the the acquisition but claimed successfully that the compensation agreed should be re-assessed; the authority were unable to resist this because the supposed (freely-agreed) contract was in fact non-existent.

19 (1982) 44 P & CR 119.

## 2   EXCLUSION OF COMMON LAW LIABILITY

It is the statutory nature of the acquisition which is significant, not the fact that the acquisition is, or is not, compulsory. It will be seen[20] that, where an acquisition is carried out compulsorily, no civil action can be brought in respect of the acquisition for the project which is lawfully carried out on that land and for which it was lawfully acquired. Instead there will be in many cases, though not in all, a right to compensation; and where there is no such right to compensation there is no remedy for any detriment which may be suffered. This principle which is obviously not without its controversial side, is founded on the decisions of the House of Lords in *Hammersmith and City Rly Co v Brand*,[1] and *Allen v Gulf Oil Refining Co*.[2]

Acquisition by agreement under statutory powers is dealt with in the same way. In *Kirby v Harrogate School Board*[3] land was acquired under statutory powers, by agreement, and in consequence of the acquiring body's project a restrictive covenant was infringed. In *Manchester, Sheffield and Lincolnshire Rly v Anderson*[4] the landlord's reversion to a leasehold was acquired under statutory powers by agreement, and in consequence of the acquiring body's project the landlord's covenant for quiet enjoyment of the premises by the tenant, whose interest had not been expropriated, was infringed. In both cases the court held that no action would lie; instead the aggrieved parties must assert their right, if any, to compensation.[5] Often a claimant will find it hard to establish a successful claim unless he can show that his enjoyment of a right such as an easement or restrictive covenant is interfered with— in other words a right over adjoining land not his own.

There is also the possibility that the vendor may be subject to some legal liability if there is a sale by agreement. This question arises where vendors are under some fiduciary duty in respect of the rights in the property vested in them, notably trustees, for sale or otherwise, tenants for life under strict settlements, and mortgagees. Their danger is that, since the acquiring authority, as will be seen, are under the same duty to pay compensation assessable according to the statutory rules, and no greater, where they purchase by agreement as they are when they purchase by compulsion, the persons to whom the vendor's fiduciary duty is owed[6] may argue that a higher amount would have been obtained

---

20 See ch 9.
 1 (1869) LR 4 HL 171.
 2 [1981] AC 101, [1981] 1 All ER 353
 3 [1896] 1 Ch 437.
 4 [1898] 2 Ch 394.
 5 But in *Bird v Eggleton* (1885) 29 Ch D 1012, it was held that when an acquiring body disposed of unwanted land which had been previously burdened by a restrictive covenant, the covenant revived.
 6 As far as the fiduciary duty of a mortgagee is concerned, an instructive contrast can be

on a sale by agreement to another purchaser and that this would have been a perfectly practicable choice to consider because the acquiring body did not exercise compulsion. To safeguard such vendors, the Land Compensation Act 1961, s 35, provides as follows:

The Lands Tribunal may on the application of any person certify the value of land being sold by him to an authority possessing compulsory purchase powers, and the sale of the land to that authority at the price so certified shall be deemed to be a sale at the best price that can reasonably be obtained.

This clearly does not apply where statute gives the acquiring body power to acquire solely by agreement. It only applies where acquisition by agreement occurs under the shadow of compulsory purchase powers.

3 STATUTORY PROVISIONS EXPRESSLY RELATING TO PURCHASE BY AGREEMENT

The Lands Clauses Consolidation Act 1845 contains a group of sections, 6 to 15, relating solely to purchase by agreement. It might be thought that since the authorising or special Act must have given power to acquire land for the acquiring body's project, the only further statutory authorisation necessary would be the power, if required, to purchase by compulsion. In point of fact most of the provisions in ss 6 to 15 relate to vendors under disabilities, such as those with limited freehold interests, trustees, executors, administrators, and corporations. Land vested in persons subject to such disabilities has now, however, been dealt with by reform of the general land law, so that there is customarily some person with sufficient power to dispose of it and the various beneficial interests are 'overreached'.[7]

Authorising Acts since 1845 have sometimes expressly applied the Lands Clauses Consolidation Act to cases where land can only be acquired by agreement, despite the fact that, in these as in compulsory purchase cases, the 1845 Act was apparently intended to apply automatically unless expressly excluded. As these are cases of acquisition restricted to agreement only, they commonly state that they incorporate the 1845 Act 'except the provisions relating to the acquisition of land otherwise than by agreement'. This seems to mean that ss 16 to 68 of that Act, including important compensation provisions, are excluded as being strictly confined to compulsory acquisitions. The sections (6 to 15) relating solely to purchase by agreement, referred to above, and various general provisions applicable both to compulsory acquisitions and to those by agreement, are, however, clearly intended to apply.

noted between the operation of s 35 of the 1961 Act and the principles applying to an ordinary case of sale by a mortgagee as exemplified in *Cuckmere Brick Co Ltd v Mutual Finance Ltd* [1971] Ch 949, [1971] 2 All ER 633.
7 Law of Property Act 1925, s 2.

Section 38 of, and the sixth Schedule to, the Compulsory Purchase Act 1965 specify certain of these authorising Acts which incorporate provisions of the 1845 Act in this way, and substitute corresponding provisions from the 1965 Act itself. But the 1965 Act provisions so applied do not extend to those sections in it which relate essentially to compulsory purchase as distinct from purchase by agreement, including in almost all cases the compensation sections. The important lesson to be drawn from this seems to be that if owners of land are willing to consider selling that land by agreement to an acquiring authority, at any rate where the latter are denied by their authorising Act the power to acquire compulsorily in any such case, they should take care to provide expressly for all reasonable stipulations in their favour that they require, especially where compensation is concerned. They should not be too ready to assume that there are statutory provisions, in the 1965 Act or elsewhere, which will imply into the contract of sale anything that they fail to insert into it themselves in express terms.

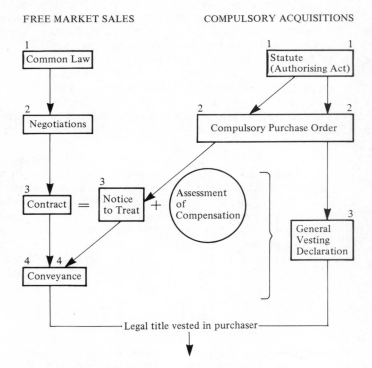

Chapter 3

# Compulsory purchase orders

## A. The nature and making of orders

### 1 ORDERS AS SUBORDINATE LEGISLATION

Under the normal system for compulsory purchase of land today, the legal provisions contained in the statutes themselves are general and not particular in scope. The procedural steps, and the documents embodying them, by which particular land is obtained by an acquiring authority are sub-statutory. They have to be executed in accordance with statute, but otherwise they seem executive rather than legislative in nature.

Compulsory purchase orders, however, are legislative. They change the law, not merely the position of the parties to any transaction. They do not compulsorily acquire land for the acquiring body from the previous owner; instead they change the law by proclaiming that it will henceforth be lawful on certain conditions for that to happen. The operative words in a typical compulsory purchase order are that the acquiring authority are 'hereby authorised to purchase compulsorily for the purpose of . . . the land which is described in the schedule hereto and is delineated and coloured . . . on the map prepared. . . .'[1]

A compulsory purchase order, therefore, is subordinate legislation, made or confirmed by a minister under statutory authority which must not be exceeded. It resembles bye-laws in that, if made by a local authority or other public body not the Crown, it requires ministerial confirmation. It is like a set of regulations in a statutory instrument if it is made directly, and not merely confirmed, by a minister. Whereas a statutory instrument is frequently the subordinate legislative counterpart of a public general Act, a compulsory purchase order, on the other hand, is the subordinate legislative counterpart of a private local Act. It is the direct modern descendant of the 'special Act' referred to in the Lands Clauses Acts because, like the 'special Act', it earmarks particular land to be subjected to the processes of compulsion.

The point may be pressed home by reference to the exceptional cases of compulsory purchase not authorised by this means.

---

1 See Compulsory Purchase of Land Regulations 1982 SI 1982/6 Schedule, Form No. 1, for the standard form of order.

## 2 COMPARISON WITH OTHER PROCEDURES

First, there is still the occasional possibility that specific land may be earmarked in the authorising Act itself. The Public Offices (Site) Act 1947 is a public general statute which authorised compulsory purchase of a particular site close to Westminster Abbey, specified in the Act by reference to a plan. Private local Acts may be thought to be more likely to specify land for compulsory purchase; but there is of course no reason why such Acts should not authorise compulsory purchase in general terms as so many public general Acts do. [2]

Second, the authorising Act may provide in general terms for the acquisition of land and allow the acquiring authority to proceed by a method not requiring further legislative sanction for specific acquisitions at all, even in the sense that a compulsory purchase order is legislative as suggested above. The Defence Act 1842,[3] s 16, empowers certain officers of the Crown to 'cause to be surveyed and marked out any land . . . wanted for the service of the Ordnance Department or for the Defence of the Realm', and this is the way such land is specifically earmarked. The Requisitioned Land and War Works Act 1945, s 35, even allowed the surveying and marking out to be dispensed with in cases where notice to treat was served before 1961; and the earmarking of the particular land then officially occurred for the first time in the notice to treat itself. It also dispensed in those cases with s 23 of the Defence Act 1842, which requires the consent of the Lord Lieutenant of the county,[4] and a warrant from the Treasury, before an acquisition can be made compulsorily (unless the enemy have actually invaded), compulsion being achieved under s 19 of the 1842 Act by two magistrates authorising the acquiring department to take possession of the land specified.[5] There were other statutes in the nineteenth century—and after—which enabled acquiring authorities to earmark particular land for compulsory purchase in this purely executive manner by surveying and marking out the sites required. The Admiralty, (Signal Stations) Act 1815, the Customs Consolidation Act 1853, and even the Coastguard Act 1925, made provision for selecting land in that way, without any legislative or sub-legislative procedure such as a 'special Act' or compulsory purchase

2 For example, the Metropolitan Paving Act 1817 (see p 39), the Liverpool Corporation Act 1966 (the authorising Act in *Grimley's* case: see ch 5, p 100), and numerous General Powers Acts promoted by the Greater London Council and other authorities.

3 See ch 1, p 6, for the royal prerogative in relation to defence. Where statute covers the same subject-matter as the royal prerogative, the latter is superseded: see *A-G v De Keyser's Royal Hotel Ltd* [1920] AC 508.

4 In *Hutton v A-G* [1927] 1 ch 427, it was held that the Lord Lieutenant acts in a purely administrative, and not a judicial capacity.

5 Compensation is payable for the price of the land taken, and also for 'injurious affection' ie depreciation) of land retained by the owner: *University College, Oxford v Secretary of State for Air* [1938] 1 KB 648, [1938] 1 All ER 69. See ch 9.

order. The Metropolitan Paving Act 1817,[6] a private local Act relating to London which is still at least partly in force, enacted that authorities responsible for the 'paving' of streets should select the properties they required for street widening or improvements; this purely executive process was subject only to control by the magistrates, in respect of assessment of compensation by a jury, and control by the Court of Chancery, in respect of disputes over title to land acquired.

Third, the authorising Act may still apply the nineteenth-century procedure of selecting particular land by 'provisional order', the forerunner of the modern compulsory purchase order. This procedure, unlike the purely executive method just described, is essentially legislative— elaborately and expensively so, which is why it has now been superseded in most cases. The kinds of compulsory acquisition or expropriation which still involve a provisional order include those undertaken for inclosures, under the Commons Act 1876,[7] for providing signal stations under the Lloyd's Signal Stations Act 1888, and for constructing light railways under the Light Railways Acts 1896 and 1912. The acquiring body must still apply to the minister specified in the relevant authorising Act to submit a provisional order to Parliament in a provisional order confirmation bill; and only if the bill is duly enacted can the acquiring body proceed.

## 3 HOW COMPULSORY PURCHASE ORDERS ARE AUTHORISED

To turn from these procedures to compulsory purchase orders is to turn from the exceptional to the normal case. The Local Government Act 1933 conferred a general power of compulsory purchase on various local authorities though it also empowered them[8] to select the particular land required by making provisional orders. But it went on to say[9] that compulsory purchase orders might be used instead where any later public general Act so authorised. There is now a standard procedure for making compulsory purchase orders, which the Acquisition of Land Act 1981 authorises any acquiring body to use if some other statute empowers them to to do so.[10] This Act of 1981 substantially re-enacts the Acquisition of Land (Authorisation Procedure) Act 1946, from which the procedure dates.

The Local Government Act, 1933 has been repealed and replaced by the Local Government Act 1972, s 121 of which enables 'principal

---

6 Known as Michael Angelo Taylor's Act.
7 See ch 1, p 16. The Second Schedule to the Statutory Orders (Special Procedure) Act 1945 converted some cases of acquisition by provisional order to special parliamentary procedure, described later in this chapter.
8 Sections 159, 160.
9 Section 161.
10 Section 1 (2) lists certain other Acts to which the standard procedure is applicable.

councils'[11] to purchase compulsorily any land, whether situated inside or outside their area for their functions, subject to minor exceptions, using the procedure laid down in what is now the 1981 Act. Since 1946 a great many statutes, chiefly but not exclusively public general statutes have applied that procedure to compulsory acquisitions by local authorities, government departments, statutory undertakers and public bodies generally, for a variety of functions of which the categories are never closed.

A typical example is s 9 (2) of the Police Act 1964, which states as follows:

The council of any . . . county or county borough (constituting a police area) may be authorised by the Secretary of State to purchase compulsorily any land which is required for the purpose of any of the functions[12] of the police authority for the county or county borough; and the Acquisition of Land (Authorisation Procedure) Act 1946, shall apply as if this subsection had been in force immediately before the commencement of that Act.

This provision shows clearly enough what is normally expected from an authorising Act in order to be able to apply the normal compulsory purchase procedure in modern times. First, it must specify the acquiring body or bodies; second, it must specify the purpose or purposes for which they may acquire land compulsorily; third, it must state which minister is to authorise such acquisitions, unless of course a minister is himself the acquiring authority; fourth, it must specify the mode of selecting the particular land in each case, and a reference to the Act of 1981 makes it clear at one stroke that (a) compulsory purchase orders are to be used for the selection and (b) the standard procedure is to be followed when making them.

Government departments are usually concerned more in confirming compulsory purchases by other bodies than in making their own. The relevant minister will be specified in the appropriate authorising Act, and is termed the 'confirming authority' as against the local council or other public body acquiring the land.[13]

11  These are county and district councils, London borough councils and the GLC. Compulsory purchase by district councils on behalf of parish and community councils is dealt with by s 125 of the 1972 Act and the Compulsory Purchase of Land Regulations 1982, SI 1982/6. All these authorities, including parish and community councils are empowered by s 16 of the Local Government (Miscellaneous Provisions) Act 1976 to demand on 14 days' notice that persons with rights in land give them information needed for the carrying out of their statutory function, relating to such land, subject to fines for wilful failure to comply.

12  In *Hazeldine v Minister of Housing and Local Government* [1959] 3 All ER 693, [1959] 1 WLR 1155 the Court of Appeal held that 'functions of the police authority' included provision of police housing.

13  1981 Act, s 7. Thus one obvious example of a 'confirming authority' is the Secretary of State for Education and Science in respect of acquisitions under the Education Act 1944. More often than not, however, the Secretary of State for the Environment is 'confirming authority'.

When ministers themselves acquire land compulsorily the authorising Act will be worded accordingly, as in the provision of the Police Act mentioned above, and confirmation is not required.

As for statutory undertakers,[14] a typical provision is s 9 of the Electricity Act 1947, under which the Minister of Fuel and Power may authorise any Electricity Board to purchase compulsorily any land they require for any purpose relating to the discharge of their functions; and the 1981 Act applies in succession to the 1946 Act. Water authorities may make compulsory purchase orders under the Water Act 1945, s 24, but may alternatively include authorisation for compulsory purchase in an order authorising construction works under s 23 (Water Act 1948, s 3 and Sch). Not only statutory undertakers but other public bodies enjoy compulsory purchase powers eg new town development corporations which have their own procedure under the New Towns Act 1981.

### 4 PROCEDURE FOR MAKING AN ORDER

Section 2 of the 1981 Act states: 'The authorisation of a compulsory purchase shall be conferred by an order (in this Act called a "compulsory purchase order")'. The substance of the 1981 Act code, except for acquisition by ministers, is contained in Part II (ss 10–15). It comprises the following main procedural steps: first, making the order in draft; second, publicising the draft order; third, dealing with objections; fourth, deciding whether the order is to be confirmed or rejected; fifth, publicising the order if it is confirmed.

Part II of the 1981 Act deals with orders made 'by local and other authorities', which may be regarded as the commonest kind. They are 'made', which means made in draft, in the 'prescribed form', describing the land to which they apply by reference to a map. The prescribed form is to be found in the Compulsory Purchase of Land Regulations 1982,[15] the Schedule to which sets out the form ('or a form substantially to the like effect') that must be used for each acquisition. Each standard form of order itself includes a schedule, in the nature of a table with columns for, respectively: the reference number of each property on the accompanying map; a brief description of each property; owners or reputed owners; lessees or reputed lessees; and occupiers, excluding tenants for monthly or lesser tenancies. If in lieu of payment other land is to be given in exchange for the land acquired, a second schedule to the order must list the 'exchange land'. The Second Schedule to the 1981 Act itself gives the option of incorporating in the order the 'Mining Code' formerly set out in ss 77 to 85 of the Railways Clauses Consolidation Act 1845, whereby the existing owner can continue to work minerals subject to adequate safeguards for the surface of the land.[16]

---

14 For a definition, see p 43.
15 SI 1982/6.
16 Part II of Sch 2 to the 1981 Act, which may be incorporated on its own, re-enacts s 77 of

Publicity is achieved by advertisement in the local press in two successive weeks,[17] and the Regulations have a prescribed form for this also, stating where in the locality the order and map can reasonably be inspected and specifying at least 21 days for objections. In addition, the owners, lessees and occupiers[18] referred to above are sent, in prescribed form, separate notices to the same effect. Notices must be served, either personally or by delivery to some other person at the premises, or by registered post or recorded delivery, upon each recipient, either by name or as 'owner' or 'lessee' or 'occupier' of the land (specifying it) if his or her name is not known, unless the acquiring authority fail to do so after suitable attempts, in which case similar notices are to be displayed instead on 'some conspicuous part of the premises'.[19]

Objections, unless the 'confirming authority' believes they can properly be dealt with when compensation is assessed, must be heard at a public local inquiry, the legal significance of which will be discussed later, or at a private hearing. The 'person who held the inquiry' or who conducted the hearing—meaning a Ministry inspector—makes his report, and the 'confirming authority' must consider this and the objections.[20]

The decision is then taken whether to confirm the order without modifications, with modifications, or not at all. This is essentially a policy decision. If the order is confirmed it becomes law; but 'special parliamentary procedure' applies in some cases, which will be discussed later.[1] Section 12 of the Tribunals and Inquiries Act 1971 obliges ministers to give reasons for decisions in matters where an inquiry has been or could have been held.

If the order is confirmed, a prescribed form of notice must be

the Railways Clauses Consolidation Act 1845, excluding mines and minerals from the acquisition unless specifically included or else necessary for 'the construction of the undertaking'; while Part III re-enacts the safeguards in ss 78–85 of that Act. The question of minerals may well affect value and compensation: see ch 7, p 130, also *Great Northern Rly Co v IRC* [1901] 1 KB 416.

17  1981 Act, s 11.
18  Ibid, s 12, which excludes tenants for a month or less (see *EON Motors v Secretary of State for the Environment and Newbury District Council*, (1981) 258 Estates Gazette 1300). In *Brown v Minister of Housing and Local Government* [1953] 2 All ER 1385, [1953] 1 WLR 1370, the court held that statutory tenants under the Rent Acts may be entitled to receive notice, as 'occupiers'. But s 12 (2) of the 1981 Act, re-enacting the Housing Repairs and Rents Act 1954, s 50 (1), has since enacted that they are not. And in *Grimley v Minister of Housing and Local Government* [1971] 2 QB 96, [1971] 2 All ER 431, the court held that there was no obligation to serve a notice on the owner of a property enjoying an easement over the property to be acquired. See ch 5, p 100.
19  1981 Act, s 6. Notices to corporate bodies are to be served upon their secretary or clerk, at their registered or principal office.
20  1981 Act, s 13. Section 14 states that extra land cannot be included unless all interested parties agree.
1  See p 53.

publicised in the local press, and separate notices to the same effect must be sent to the owners, lessees and occupiers who were notified previously. These notices must state where the order as confirmed, and the map, can reasonably be inspected.[2]

## 5 ACQUISITION BY BODIES OTHER THAN LOCAL AUTHORITIES

The procedure in Part II of the 1981 Act is not confined to local authorities. Statutory undertakers and other public bodies may be empowered by their authorising Acts 'as if (they) were a local authority'[3] to make use of that procedure when compulsorily purchasing land or they may simply be authorised to acquire land compulsorily, using either the compulsory purchase order procedure in the 1981 Act (or its 1946 predecessor) or else some other procedure specifically provided. Section 8 (1) of the 1981 Act defines 'statutory undertakers' as: (a) 'any person authorised by any enactment, to construct, work or carry on—(i) any railway, light railway, tramway, road transport, water transport, canal or inland navigation undertaking, or (ii) any dock, harbour, pier or lighthouse undertaking, or (iii) any undertaking for the supply of electricity, gas, hydraulic power or water', (b) the British Airports Authority or the Civil Aviation Authority, or (c) the Post Office or British Telecommunications, unless the context otherwise requires. The 'undertaking' of the British Airports Authority means its aerodromes.

The First Schedule to the 1981 Act adapts the procedure for making compulsory purchase orders to those made by ministers themselves. Each Minister prepares his order in draft, with a map, and after receiving the report of the inspector holding a public local inquiry into (or otherwise hearing) any objections, 'makes' the order himself, with or without modifications, if he sees fit to do so. But 'the form of the order shall be such as the Minister may determine'.[4] Subject to this, the procedure follows the pattern in the other cases, as already described.

# B. Inquiries and appeals

## 1 ADMINISTRATIVE CONTEXT OF INQUIRIES

The holding of the public local inquiry seems essentially to be an administrative fact-finding exercise, used by the minister's officials to help them decide between acquiring authorities and objectors when they disagree over the facts relating to a compulsory purchase situation. Local authorities and other public bodies do not hold public inquiries,

2  1981 Act, s 15.
3  For example, s 9 of the Electricity Act 1947. See p 41.
4  1981 Act, First Sch, para 1 (3).

presumably because they are not remote from the scene of dispute as the central government is. Their fact-finding is purely part of their administrative activity. Ministers have been authorised by various statutes, at least since Victorian times, to hold public inquiries in particular situations such as inclosure schemes,[5] though there seems to be no reason why they should not hold inquiries without statutory authority if they wish (as in the 'Crichel Down' affair).[6] This must be distinguished from the *duty* imposed on them by many statutes 'to afford a hearing' to objectors; and in these cases a public inquiry is one method of discharging this duty, though a private hearing is an alternative which many statutory provisions expressly allow. This choice indeed is given by the 1981 Act.[7]

A public inquiry, as distinct from a private hearing, bears a great, but superficial, resemblance to a trial. There will usually be two 'sides': authority *versus* objectors. Evidence will often be given by each 'side', and the witnesses giving this evidence will often be cross-examined. In a large inquiry counsel will often represent the parties, or some of them. But the outcome is not a judgment. The apparent 'judge', who is of course a Ministry inspector, makes his report after the inquiry is over; and after reading this report the minister makes his decision. This decision is essentially administrative, based, that is, on policy. He must take the relevant law and facts properly into account, but policy is the key.

In *Board of Education v Rice*,[8] Lord Loreburn LC said:

Comparatively recent statutes have extended, if they have not originated, the practice of imposing on departments or officers of State the duty of deciding or determining questions of various kinds. In the present instance . . . what comes for determination is a matter to be settled by discretion . . . but sometimes it will involve matter of law as well as matter of fact . . . In such cases the Board of Education will have to ascertain the law and . . . the facts, I need not add that . . . they must act in good faith and listen fairly to both sides . . . But I do not think they are bound to treat such a question as though it were a trial. . . .[9]

---

5  See ch 1, p 12 and 14.

6  See the report of the public inquiry held to investigate the affair: Cmnd. 9176 (1954). The subject matter of that inquiry would presumably now come within the purview of the 'Ombudsman': see Parliamentary Commissioner Act 1967, s 5.

7  Section 13 (2). The choice is made by the 'confirming authority'.

8  [1911] AC 179.

9  In *Wednesbury Corpn v Minister of Housing and Local Government* [1965] 1 All ER 186, [1965] 1 WLR 261, Lord Denning MR said, in similar vein, 'it cannot be regarded as if it were a lawsuit'. And in *Re London–Portsmouth Trunk Road (Surrey) Compulsory Purchase Order (No 2) 1938* [1939] 2 KB 515, [1939] 2 All ER 464, it was held that the acquiring authority need not give evidence at the inquiry, since the purpose was to afford a hearing for objections; but see p 47 below, for the modern Inquiries Procedure Rules.

## 2 NATURAL JUSTICE

When the decision has been taken—by the minister—any disappointed person, especially an objector, may wish to challenge it. The only way to do this, short of some political initiative, is to bring an action in the courts; and the normal method is to claim that the decision should be quashed or invalidated as contrary to law. An action for a declaration, or an application for an order of certiorari, in the High Court, is the choice in such cases. [10] If the inquiry is the source of grievance there will in effect be a claim that the minister's decision is unsound in law because he or the inspector mismanaged the hearing of objections. Since the procedure is really administrative it is hard to find a legal ground for challenge; but the courts have developed the doctrine that inquiries are a 'quasi-judicial' stage embedded in the administrative process, which means that their procedure must be governed by 'natural justice'. In *Errington v Minister of Health*,[11] Maugham LJ said, 'although the act of affirming (an) order is an administrative act, the consideration which must precede the doing of that act is of the nature of a quasi-judicial consideration'.

'Natural justice' comes down to two rules. The first is that whoever conducts the quasi-judicial proceedings must be free of bias. 'Justice should not only be done, but should manifestly and undoubtedly be seen to be done', as Lord Hewart CJ put it in *R v Sussex Justices, ex p McCarthy*.[12] The second is that both sides to a dispute should receive an adequate hearing over each disputed issue, which includes the right to argue against the opposing side's contentions though not to cross-examine the opposing side's witnesses.[13] Many unsuccessful attempts[14] have been made to invalidate ministerial decisions on this ground; but one that notably succeeded was *Errington v Minister of Health*, in which the inspector, having held a public inquiry, was sent subsequently to a discussion with local authority officers and listened privately to further arguments, the upshot being a ministerial decision in the local authority's favour. It is not suggested that this was the wrong decision, merely that a proper hearing was not afforded to the objectors in respect of some of the issues upon which the final decision rested. It was therefore quashed.

The issue of natural justice is an issue of law; though (unlike issues of law raised in the High Court by way of case stated) where the facts are already established, these will have to be put afresh to the court. This

10 See Professor H. W. R. Wade LLD *Administrative Law* chapter on 'Remedies'; and Professor P. Jackson *Natural Justice*.
11 [1935] 1 KB 249.
12 [1924] 1 KB 256.
13 Cross-examination is discussed below (p 47).
14 See, for example: *Re Manchester (Ringway Airport) Compulsory Purchase Order* (1935) 153 LT 219; *Frost v Minister of Health* [1935] 1 KB 286; *Offer v Minister of Health* [1936] 1 KB 40; *Horn v Minister of Health* [1937] 1 KB 164, [1936] 2 All ER 1299.

necessitates 'an application for judicial review, because the facts have to be placed before the superior court, and "the only way in which that denial of justice can be brought to the knowledge of this court is by way of affidavit" (see *R v Wandsworth Justices, ex p Read* [1942] 1 KB 281 at 283, [1942] 1 All ER 56, at 57, per Viscount Caldecote CJ)'.[15]

Another recent example of a breach of the rule of natural justice requiring an adequate hearing on a particular issue can be seen in a House of Lords case, *Fairmount Investments Ltd v Secretary of State for the Environment*.[16] The applicants' houses were included by the council of the London Borough of Southwark in a compulsory purchase order for slum clearance. The Inspector at the public inquiry, dealing with the question of unfitness for habitation laid considerable emphasis on worsening settlement of the foundation of these houses, an issue which was neither relied on by the local authority nor dealt with at the inquiry. This meant that, as Lord Russell of Killowen put it:

> Fairmount has not had . . . a fair crack of the whip. [Because that amounted to] a departure from the principles of natural justice it may equally be said that the [compulsory purchase] order is not within the powers of the [Housing] Act [1957] and that a requirement of the Act has not been complied with.

The order was quashed.

None of this alters the fact that, as Lord Diplock said in *Bushell v Secretary of State for the Environment*,[17] '. . . . the minister's ultimate decision is a purely administrative one . . . [and] what he does bears little resemblance to adjudicating on [an action at law] between the parties. . . . There is a third party who was not represented at the inquiry, the general public as a whole whose interests it is the minister's duty to treat as paramount.'

In *Ostreicher v Secretary of State for the Environment*,[18] Lord Denning MR said: 'An administrative inquiry has to be arranged long beforehand. There are many objectors to consider as well as the proponents of the plan. . . . The proper way to deal with [one party's request for an adjournment at a late stage] is to continue with the inquiry and hear all the representatives present; and then, if one objector is unavoidably absent, to hear his objections on a later day when he can be there. . . .' As to evidence in appeals against administrative decisions, '. . . it is not the practice to receive evidence by way of affidavits from both sides as

---

15 Per Robert Goff LJ in *R v Dorking Justices, ex p Harrington* [1983] 3 All ER 29.
16 [1976] 2 All ER 865, [1976] 1 WLR 1255.
17 [1981] AC 75 [1980] 2 All ER 608. The objectors alleged in vain that a refusal to allow them to cross-examine official witnesses at a motorway scheme inquiry was *ultra vires*. In a compulsory purchase inquiry, however, there is statutory provision for such cross-examination in specified circumstances discussed below (see p 49).
18 [1978] 3 All ER 82. The appellants claimed that there had been an unfair refusal to adjourn a public inquiry for their benefit.

to whether the inspector's conclusion was reasonable or not. Fresh evidence should not be admitted save in exceptional circumstances.'

On finance, the Court of Appeal commented in *Parker v Secretary of State for the Environment*[19] that expense is not an overriding point but one of the factors relevant to reasonableness. The comparative acquisition costs of the appellant's land and other land were, however, found to be very relevant in *Prest v Secretary of State for Wales*,[20] in which construction costs involved in a new sewage works were considered at the public inquiry, but not land costs; the Court of Appeal held that the failure of the inspector to take this factor into account, and the Secretary of State's refusal to do so thereafter, meant that the compulsory purchase order must be quashed.

A leading complaint of the objectors in *Bushell's* case (above) is that they were prevented from cross-examining the official side's witnesses. This was rejected emphatically. Lord Diplock said that there can be 'no obligation to disclose to objectors and give them an opportunity of commenting on advice, expert or otherwise. . . .'[1] The Court of Appeal stated in *George v Secretary of State for the Environment*,[2] that only in the most exceptional circumstances should cross-examination be allowed in proceedings relating to compulsory purchase orders, or in judicial review. Thus this principle applies to inquiries and to judicial proceedings.

## 3 INQUIRIES PROCEDURE RULES

The conduct of some, but not by any means all, public inquiries is now regulated not only by the all-embracing rules of natural justice but by statutory rules. Section 7A of the Tribunals and Inquiries Act 1958, inserted into the Act retrospectively by s 33 of the Town and Country Planning Act 1959, empowered the Lord Chancellor, after consultation with the Council on Tribunals, to 'make rules for regulating the procedure to be followed in connection with statutory inquiries held by or on behalf of ministers'. As a result of this the Compulsory Purchase by Public Authorities (Inquiries Procedure) Rules 1976[3] and the Compulsory Purchase by Ministers (Inquiries Procedure) Rules 1967[4] are now in force.

There are many kinds of inquiry not covered by such statutory rules. Yet since the essential code in the sets of rules which do exist is reasonably standardised, it is highly likely that administrative convenience will inspire most government departments to apply what is basically the same

**19** (1980) 257 Estates Gazette 718.
**20** (1983) 81 LGR 193.
 **1** [1980] 2 All ER at p 618.
 **2** (1979) 38 P & CR 609.
 **3** SI 1976/746 (made under the Tribunals and Inquiries Act 1971, s 11).
 **4** SI 1967/720.

procedure in the various kinds of inquiry, despite the absence of formal rules.

The Inquiries Procedure Rules of 1976 are expressed to apply to public local inquiries, and also to private hearings, held in connection with compulsory purchase orders being made under the standard procedure, though apparently not under any other procedure however closely similar.[5] The minister who is 'confirming authority', as discussed above, must give at least 42 days' written notice of the date of the inquiry to the acquiring authority and the 'statutory objectors', the latter being those owners, lessees and occupiers who have made (and not withdrawn) objections in consequence of being notified of the draft order.[6] The substance of their objections, and of others also if practicable, must be notified to the authority. If it is an inquiry and not a hearing there must normally be prior publicity in the local press and the public posting of notices near the land in question.[7]

The most important item in the Rules is the requirement that the acquiring authority serve a written statement of reasons, including any statement of views by a government department that they may be relying on, at least 28 days in advance of the inquiry on all statutory objectors; and they must afford a reasonable opportunity to inspect and copy the maps, plans and other documents they are going to put in evidence.[8] Thus the objectors know what official case they will have to meet, just as the parties to a civil action at law will know from the pleadings what case will be presented against them

This safeguard of justice certainly adds to the 'quasi-judicial' quality of a public inquiry. So does the right to appear,[9] given by the Rules to the authority and objectors though not confined to them if the 'appointed person'—the minister's inspector—sees fit to allow other persons a hearing. The inspector has a wide discretion as to the conduct of the inquiry, and is not bound by the detailed rules of evidence and procedure which apply in the courts so long as he observes the rules of natural justice. But the acquiring body have the right to begin and to make the final reply. They may also amend their written statement of reasons, if the inspector so allows, 'so far as may be necessary for the purpose of determining the questions in controversy between the parties'. But if so he must adjourn the inquiry or otherwise allow the statutory objectors to adjust themselves to any such change in the case they have to meet; and he may recommend how any additional costs, incurred by reason of the change, shall be borne. Statutory objectors may also apply to the minister in writing, at least 14 days before the inquiry, for a representative of

5 Rule 2. See p 57 below.
6 Rule 4 (2).
7 Rule 4 (1), (3).
8 Rule 4 (4).
9 Rule 5. There seems to be no general *duty* to appear. See footnote 9 to p 44 above.

any government department whose views have been included in the written statement of reasons to attend the inquiry for examination and cross-examination concerning those views, so long as 'the merits of Government policy' are left severely alone.[10]

The inspector may, and if requested by the authority or a statutory objector, must, inspect the land in question after the inquiry, at a time specified during the inquiry. Representatives of the authority and the statutory objectors are entitled to go with him.[11] He then makes his report in writing to the minister. After this point the quasi-judicial aspect of the proceedings fades away, except that if the minister differs from any recommendation made by the inspector because he disagrees over a finding of fact, or receives new evidence, expert or otherwise, or considers a new issue of fact, he must give the parties 21 days' written notice before making a decision. They may in that interval make written representations about the matter or, in the case of new evidence or a new issue of fact, ask for the inquiry to be reopened.[12]

Subject to this the minister is responsible for having his decision, with reasons, given in writing to the parties involved, together with a copy of the inspector's report.[13] He may, under s 250 of the Local Government Act 1972, make orders as to the payment of costs, including 'the costs incurred by him in relation to that inquiry'; and it is ministerial practice since 1965 to award to *successful* objectors their costs against the acquiring authority, quite apart from the question, discussed above, of liability for the costs of any adjournment or alteration, as recommended by the inspector.[14]

As for compulsory purchases by ministers themselves, the Inquiries Procedure Rules of 1967, apply substantially the same procedure for public inquiries and private hearings as the Rules of 1976 do in the case of local authorities, except of course that the minister himself in effect combines the two rôles of acquiring body and 'confirming authority'.

## 4 'PRECLUSIVE CLAUSES' AND CHALLENGE IN THE COURTS

It might be thought that there should be a general right to apply to the courts to invalidate any compulsory purchase order on a relevant point of law, for example that it is ultra vires because it does not come within the powers conferred by any authorising Act, or that proper statutory procedure has not been complied with. The present legal safeguards over

---

**10** Rules 6 and 7.
**11** Rule 8.
**12** Rule 9.
**13** Rule 10.
**14** See Ministry of Housing and Local Government Circular no. 73/65, dated 1 December 1965.

public inquiries, though essentially concerned with natural justice and statutory rules of procedure, are part of the general law. In *O'Reilly v Mackman*[15] the House of Lords stressed that the fundamental principle is the distinction between public law and private law cases. In the former there has to be a 'filter' to prevent actions being pursued by 'busybodies and cranks';[16] applicants must therefore show, as the Supreme Court Act 1981, s 31, puts it: 'sufficient interest' (or locus standi)—ie reasonable justification for seeking remedies against a public authority. These remedies are the common law 'prerogative orders' of certiorari, prohibition and mandamus, plus injunctions and declarations. The procedure in these cases, known as 'judicial review', is laid down in the Rules of the Supreme Court, Ord 53.

It should also be noted that even if an official decision appears to be intra vires it may still be quashed on the *Wednesbury*[17] principle—ie that, viewed objectively, it is in itself so unreasonable in all the circumstances that *no* reasonable authority could have arrived at it.

But statutes sometimes exclude 'judicial review' in favour of more specialised procedures. Part IV[18] of the Acquisition of Land Act 1981 provides that 'any person aggrieved' can make application to the High Court to challenge a compulsory purchase order 'on the ground that the authorisation of a compulsory purchase thereby granted is not empowered to be granted under this Act or [the relevant authorising Act] . . .'—ie substantive ultra vires—or for some flaw in procedure—ie procedural ultra vires.[19] Such an application may be made on the ground that the requirements of the Tribunals and Inquiries Act 1971, or subordinate legislation made under it, have been infringed. Application can only be made to the court within six weeks of the publication of the notice which states that the order has been made or confirmed. The court may quash the order if satisfied that it is ultra vires in its substantive terms, or that any procedural default has 'substantially prejudiced' the applicant.[20] Subject to his limited right of application to the court within six weeks, a compulsory purchase order made under the 1981 Act 'shall

15 [1982] 3 All ER 1124. See also *Cocks v Thanet District Council* [1982] 3 All ER 1135.
16 Per Warner J in *Barrs v Bethell* [1982] 1 All ER 106 at 120.
17 *Associated Provincial Picture Houses Ltd v Wednesbury Corpn* [1948] 1 KB 223, [1947] All ER 680.
18 Sections 23–27.
19 Section 23. On comparable wording in Sch 3 to the Housing Act 1957, see *Fairmount Investments Ltd v Secretary of State for the Environment* (above, p 46), where an order was 'not within the powers of the Act' because of a breach of the rules of natural justice. For a case of substantive ultra vires see *Meravale Builders Ltd v Secretary of State for the Environment* (1978) 36 P & CR 87, in which a compulsory purchase order purporting to be made under Part V of the Housing Act 1957 (which relates to the provision of council housing) was quashed because its purpose was to acquire land for a new road intended to be part of the general highway network in the locality (ie its provision was not reasonably incidental to the provision of council housing).
20 1981 Act, s 24.

not . . . be questioned in any legal proceedings whatsoever'.¹ It 'becomes operative' when the notice of its making or confirmation, referred to above, is first published;² but this does not apply where 'special parliamentary procedure' is used.³

Statutory restriction of challenges in the courts was investigated by the House of Lords in *Anisminic Ltd v Foreign Compensation Commission*.⁴ A 'preclusive clause', as Lord Wilberforce termed it, governed determinations by that Commission of claims for compensation under the Foreign Compensation Act 1950, in these terms: 'The determination . . . shall not be called in question in any court of law.' But as Lord Reid said: 'It is one thing to question a determination which does exist; it is quite another thing to say that there is nothing to be questioned'—in other words to 'call in question' an official decision presupposes that the decision truly exists, and it must be distinguished from arguing that a purported decision is a 'nullity'. Lord Pearce pointed out that, if this were not so, 'the court . . . could not even enquire whether a purported determination was a forged or inaccurate order'.⁵ By a majority of three to two their lordships held that the determination could be challenged at law, and declared invalid if shown to be ultra vires.

In *Anisminic* the terms of the 'preclusive clause' in the Act of 1950 ruled out legal challenge altogether. This is more drastic than most 'preclusive clauses', which do at least allow the customary six weeks' period for such challenge that compulsory purchase orders are subject to, as described above. The question arises whether an official decision subject to the kind of 'preclusive clause' which is qualified by a six weeks' period of challenge can be quashed in the same way as the unqualified kind of 'preclusive clause' exemplified in *Anisminic*. In an earlier leading case, also decided in the House of Lords and also by a majority of three to two, *Smith v East Elloe RDC*,⁶ a compulsory purchase order was challenged on the ground that it had been made in bad faith. The challenge was not made within the six weeks' period of the 'preclusive clause'; but it was argued that bad faith or fraud took the case outside the scope of the clause. But the majority refused to make the distinction.

The Court of Appeal has distinguished *Smith v East Elloe RDC* from the *Anisminic* case, one reason being that the latter was not a case on a compulsory purchase order. In *Routh v Reading Corpn*⁷ Salmon LJ, having referred to the *East Elloe* case, said that 'it should have been apparent that if there was anything in the point that the compulsory

---

1 Ibid, s 25. 'Judicial review' is thus excluded.
2 Ibid, s 26. See p 42 above.
3 See below, pp 53–57.
4 [1969] 2 AC 147, [1969] 1 All ER 208.
5 At [1969] 1 All ER 237.
6 [1956] AC 736, [1956] 1 All ER 855.
7 (1970) 217 Estates Gazette 1337.

purchase order was a nullity it was imperative to take proceedings in the court . . . within six weeks'. Unless the House of Lords overrules this, *Anisminic* will be confined to cases where a 'preclusive clause' is unqualified, or at any rate where the six weeks' challenge period is not available under it.

In *R v Secretary of State for the Environment, ex p Ostler*,[8] the Court of Appeal followed the *East Elloe* case and distinguished the Anisminic case when upholding an appeal against a decision of the Queen's Bench Divisional Court to quash a compulsory purchase order. Objectors to a previous compulsory purchase order (concerning land required for an inner relief road at Boston, Lincolnshire) had withdrawn their objections on getting a secret assurance that a side road would subsequently be widened to give better access to their property. When later the compulsory purchase order for this subsequent project was published, the applicant claimed that he would have objected to the first scheme had he known that it would have led to the second; but the inspector at the inquiry rejected this as irrelevant and the second order was confirmed. More than six weeks later the applicant heard of the secret assurance given to the first objectors and applied for an order of certiorari to quash the second order. Lord Denning MR, distinguished the *Anisminic* case on the grounds that: (*i*) the statute there gave no right of challenge at all, not a limited right; (*ii*) the decision there challenged was was made by a truly 'judicial body'; (*iii*) the decision there was itself challenged, not the process of arriving at the decision. Whether (*ii*) and (*iii*) are distinctions of substance is perhaps arguable.[9]

Public law remedies, whether given in the course of 'judicial review' or of restricted statutory appeals under 'preclusive clauses', are always at High Court's discretion,[10] never available as of right. In this they resemble the equitable and statutory remedies of injunction and declaration in private law actions, but not the common law remedy of damages in such actions which is available as of right.

A case in which a compulsory purchase order was duly challenged within the six weeks' period was *Webb v Minister of Housing and Local Government*.[11] The order there was made in respect of land required for a

8  [1977] QB 122, [1976] 3 All ER 90.
9  See the judgment of Walton J in *Graddage v London Borough of Haringey* [1975] 1 All ER 224, [1975] 1 WLR 241 (and other cases therein cited), holding that an official order which was plainly ultra vires on its face could be disregarded as a nullity and need not even be challenged in court. The House of Lords has, however, stressed that it is only safe to disregard official orders in the plainest cases: *London and Clydeside Estates Ltd v Aberdeen District Council* [1979] 3 All ER 876. If the alleged invalidity is arguable, a court must decide.
10  This was stressed by the Queen's Bench Divisional Court in *R v Aston University Senate, ex p Roffey* [1969] 2 QB 538, [1969] 2 All ER 964 and by the Court of Appeal in *R v Herrod, ex p Leeds City Council* [1976] 1 All ER 273.
11  [1965] 2 All ER 193, [1965] 1 WLR 755.

local authority's 'works scheme' for a sea wall under the Coast Protection Act 1949. The scheme, like the order, was subject to a six weeks' preclusive clause. A challenge in the High Court was made within six weeks of the Minister's confirmation of the order but not within six weeks of his confirmation (which occurred earlier) of the works scheme. Yet the challenge to the order, being within the time limit, was held by the majority of the Court of Appeal to make it possible to challenge the scheme, not purely on its own account but as a ground for quashing the order: it was the scheme which was at fault, not the order as such. This appears to mean that where a project comprises two official stages it will be treated as one whole process, at any rate as regards the question of applying the preclusive clause.[12]

In *London and Westcliff Properties Ltd v Minister of Housing and Local Government*,[13] a local authority proposed to purchase compulsorily a tenement block in order to redevelop the site; and the Minister, as 'confirming authority', confirmed the compulsory purchase order. But the local authority had made a bargain with the freeholders that, if the latter would undertake and pay for the redevelopment project, the authority, in return, would acquire only the leasehold and, having done so, would release it to them for a nominal consideration. This purpose was duly disclosed in the order itself. But s 26 (4) of the Town and Country Planning Act 1959[14] requires the Minister's express consent to a disposal of compulsorily purchased land for less than market value; and the leaseholders challenged the order on the ground that it openly purported to disregard this rule. The High Court accepted their argument and quashed the order, even though the minister who should have expressly consented to the proposed disposition at the nominal price, but did not, was the same as the minister who confirmed the order in terms which proclaimed that very intention.

## C. Procedure for orders in special cases

### 1 SPECIAL PARLIAMENTARY PROCEDURE

Not all compulsory purchase orders under the 1981 Act procedures can be made effective simply in consequence of a minister's decision. This is because some are subject to 'special parliamentary procedure', to understand which it is necessary to consider, first, what that procedure consists

---

12 It should be noted also that an application to quash a compulsory purchase order, provided it has been made within the six weeks' time-limit, can be amended after that time limit has expired: *Hanily v Minister of Local Government and Planning* [1951] 2 KB 917, [1951] 2 All ER 749.
13 [1961] 1 All ER 610, [1961] 1 WLR 519.
14 On this, see ch 4, p 78.

of and, second, what kinds of order are subject to it. Special parliamentary procedure applies to many kinds of order, but in this connection it is of course only compulsory purchase orders that need to be considered.

The statutes governing this matter are the Statutory Orders (Special Procedure) Acts 1945 and 1965. The orders to which any statute passed since 1945 applies them 'shall be of no effect' until laid before Parliament in accordance with their provisions.[15] A compulsory purchase order governed by any such provision must first go through the procedure previously described, up to the point where the relevant minister would confirm it. That minister must then give three days' notice in the *London Gazette* that he will lay it before Parliament. A period of 21 days after the order has been so laid is then allowed for the presentation of petitions against it. Such petitions as are certified as being 'proper to be received' are reported to both Houses of Parliament, specifying whether they are 'of general objection', meaning totally hostile, or 'for amendment', meaning partially hostile.[16]

After this report there is a 'resolution period', again of 21 days, during which the order will become void if *either* House resolves to annul it. If there are no petitions and no resolution to annul, the order will 'come into operation' at the end of the 'resolution period' (unless a later date is specified in it). But if there are petitions they 'shall stand referred to a joint committee of both Houses', so long as no resolution to annul is passed; but either House may resolve that a 'petition of general objection' shall not be referred to a joint committee, in which case if there are no other petitions which are so referred the order will 'come into operation' as stated.[17]

Where any petition is referred to a joint committee of both Houses that committee can report that the order 'be not approved' if the petition is one of 'general objection'. The committee can however report the order either with or without amendment (that is, approving it) in respect of either kind of petition. If reported 'without amendment' the order will come into operation at once (unless a later date is specified in it). If reported 'with amendment' it will come into operation when the minister so determines; but if he still wishes it to come into effect 'without amendment', or if the joint committee reported that it 'be not approved' but he wishes it to go forward nevertheless, he must promote a Bill to that effect, rather as if the old style 'provisional order' procedure were being used. Such a Bill will be treated as a public Bill which has reached its report stage in each House.[18]

15 Act of 1945, s 1. It may be noted that s 8 and Sch 2 substituted special parliamentary procedure for provisional orders in certain specified cases.
16 Ibid, ss 2, 3 (The 1965 Act substituted 21 for 14 days).
17 Ibid, s 4.
18 Act of 1945, ss 5 and 6.

Compulsory purchase orders which are subject to special parliamentary procedure may be specified under any authorising Act; but the cases which need to be considered here are provided for in the 1981 Act itself, in Part III.[19] It should be noted that compulsory purchase orders governed by special parliamentary procedure 'come into effect', if they do, in accordance with that procedure, not in accordance with the 1981 Act, s 26, as referred to earlier.[20]

Special parliamentary procedure applies to a compulsory purchase order under these provisions if the land to be taken comprises 'an ancient monument', unless the Secretary of State is himself the acquiring authority or certifies that the authority have given him an undertaking to observe suitable conditions protecting the land.[1] The 1981 Act also applies special parliamentary procedure to an order if the land to be taken belongs to a local authority, or has been acquired by statutory undertakers for the purposes of their undertaking,[2] or belongs inalienably to the National Trust, and they maintain an objection to the order.[3]

Where the land to be taken has been acquired 'for the purpose of their undertaking' by statutory undertakers, not only does special parliamentary procedure apply if they maintain an objection to the order, but they also have the right, during the period for objecting to the order, to make a representation to the 'appropriate Minister' (ie the Secretary of State[4]) that the land (or any part of it) is in fact being *used* for that purpose or that an interest in it (or any part of it) is *held* for that purpose. The object in doing this is that such land must then be excluded from the compulsory purchase order, unless the 'appropriate Minister' certifies that serious detriment to the undertaking will not occur, either because the statutory undertakers will be able to make use of other land in place of the land taken or because circumstances are such that no replacement land is needed. This will protect, where necessary, any railway, water, gas, electricity or other such installations threatened with compulsory purchase.[5]

Special parliamentary procedure also applies[6] where the land to be

---

19 Sections 16–22. Part III does not, however, apply to any order confirmed by Act of Parliament under the Statutory Orders (Special Procedure) Act 1945, s 6 (1981 Act, s 27).
20 See above, p 51.
1 1981 Act, s 20.
2 Ibid, s 17. Acquiring authorities for this purpose are: the Greater London Council, the Common Council of the City of London, the councils of counties, districts, London boroughs or the Isles of Scilly; statutory undertakers; the National Coal Board; or any other body duly specified in an order to be made by the Secretary of State. 'Statutory undertakers' are as defined in the 1981 Act s 8, referred to above (see p 43).
3 1981 Act, s 18.
4 Ibid, s 8 (3).
5 Ibid, s 16.
6 Ibid, s 19 (1).

taken is 'part of a common,[7] open space, or fuel or field garden allotment'[8] unless the Secretary of State certifies either (a) that other land, not less in area, is to be available in exchange and will be 'equally advantageous' to the public and to any commoners and others with rights in the land taken, and subject to equivalent rights for their benefit, or (b) that the land taken is not more than 250 square yards, or that it is needed to widen or drain (or partly to widen and partly to drain) an existing highway and no land is needed in exchange to benefit the public or any commoners or others with rights in it. A compulsory purchase order may accordingly provide for discharging any such land, when acquired, from such 'rights, trusts and incidents' and attaching them to the land given in exchange. But in these cases the certificate must not be given unless the Secretary of State has first publicised his intention to do so, allowed 'all persons interested to make representations and objections', held a public inquiry if 'it appears to him to be expedient so to do', and considered the representations and objections and the report of the inquiry, if any.[9]

Certificates granted by a minister under any of the provisions of Part III of the 1981 Act must be published in the local press 'as soon as may be' by the acquiring authority.[10] They can be challenged in the High Court within six weeks, in the same way as compulsory purchase orders themselves, but only on the ground of procedural default. If satisfied of this, the court may quash them, wholly or in part.[11]

A dispute which illustrates the workings of these special parliamentary procedure provisions occurred in *Middlesex County Council v Minister of Housing and Local Government*.[12] Two local authorities were competing for the same land. One of them duly prepared and publicised a compulsory purchase order. The time given for making objections was five weeks. Over eight months later, the public inquiry began. Two days before that, the second local authority, which was also preparing for compulsory purchase, succeeded in buying the land by agreement, and then attempted to prevent the rival authority's order from becoming

---

7  This includes any land subject to be enclosed under the Inclosure Acts 1845–1882, and any town or village green. (Ibid, s 19 (4).

8  The meaning of 'fuel or field garden allotment' is (ibid) 'any allotment set out [as such] under an Inclosure Act'.

9  1981 Act, s 19 (2), (3). This procedure must not be confused with that for *inclosing* a common (see ch 1, p 11) or for expropriating commoners (see ch 4, p 77). In *Wilson v Secretary of State for the Environment*, [1974] 1 All ER 428, [1973] 1 WLR 1083, a certificate concerning the exchange of part of a village green was quashed because the green was misleadingly described, with the result that prospective objectors, being thrown off the scent by this procedural default, were 'substantially prejudiced'.

10  1981 Act, s 22. They 'became operative' at the date of first publication: ibid s 26 (see above p 51 for the application of s 26 to compulsory purchase orders themselves).

11  Ibid, ss 23, 24. Apart from this they 'shall not . . . be questioned in any legal proceedings whatsoever': ibid, s 25.

12  [1953] 1 QB 12, [1952] 2 All ER 709.

effective. The minister confirmed that order none the less, whereupon the second authority challenged it on the ground that, since the land had now become the property of a local authority (themselves), special parliamentary procedure ought to apply; the minister and the first authority denied this. The Court of Appeal held that, for land to be regarded as local authority land for the purposes of special parliamentary procedure, it must already be owned by that authority at the time for making objections; therefore any objection, made by the party as owner at a time after the period for objections has ended, cannot be regarded as 'duly made'. The challenge by the second authority was therefore not 'duly made'; and the minister's confirmation of the order, without resort to special parliamentary procedure, was upheld.

## 2 ORDERS NOT MADE UNDER THE ACQUISITION OF LAND ACT 1981

There are various authorising Acts which specify compulsory purchase orders as the mode of earmarking particular land, but unlike the general run of such Acts require a special procedure of their own to be used and not the standard procedure contained in the Act of 1981. These separate procedures do not vary from the standard procedure to any fundamental extent, but rather in points of detail. Because they differ from the standard procedure, however, it seems that the Inquiries Procedure Rules do not apply to them.[13]

The Housing Act 1957, Part III, which deals with slum clearance, prescribes, for the making of compulsory purchase orders in such a case, the procedure set out in the Third Schedule to that Act. The New Towns Act 1981 prescribes separate procedures for compulsory purchase, in various situations, of land required for new towns, set out in the Fourth and Fifth Schedules to that Act. Other separate procedures for making compulsory purchase orders are to be found in the Second Schedule to the Water Act 1945, the Eighth Schedule to the Water Resources Act 1963, the Second Schedule to the Pipe-lines Act 1962, and the Fifth Schedule to the Forestry Act 1967. But all these codes now provide that the subsequent procedure, after a compulsory purchase order has come into operation, will be governed by the same provisions as apply when an order has been made under the standard procedure, namely those contained in the Compulsory Purchase Act 1965. They will be examined in the next two chapters.

13 See p 47.

# Chapter 4

# Compulsory purchase conveyancing

## A. Notice to treat

As soon as a compulsory purchase order has come into operation, attention shifts to the Compulsory Purchase Act 1965, because this statute contains the main provisions governing the actual acquisition of particular properties under compulsory powers. This part of the law could perhaps be termed 'compulsory purchase conveyancing'. The end in view is the same as in private conveyancing by agreement, namely the vesting of the property—normally the full unincumbered legal estate, freehold with vacant possession—in the purchaser. The abnormal features of this kind of conveyancing derive from the fact that no choice remains to the vendor, for the public interest demands that the purchaser not only gets the land but makes a particular use of it afterwards, and that justice must be regulated through compensation.

### 1 PURPOSE OF THE NOTICE

The first step in the classic procedure—as distinct from an alternative procedure, introduced later—is the 'notice to treat'. Section 5 (1) of the 1965 Act states as follows:

When the acquiring authority require to purchase any of the land subject to compulsory purchase, they shall give notice[1] (hereafter in this Act referred to as a 'notice to treat') to all the persons interested in, or having power to sell and convey or release, the land, so far as known to the acquiring authority after making diligent inquiry.

In very broad terms it can be said here that the recipients will be freeholders and leaseholders, although further details of this matter will appear in the next chapter. The 'notice to treat' must specify the land to which it relates, 'demand particulars' of the recipient's rights in the land and his claim in respect of them, and express willingness 'to treat for the

1 In *Hewitt v Leicester City Council* [1969] 2 All ER 802, [1969] 1 WLR 855, a notice to treat sent through the post by recorded delivery was returned marked 'gone away'. The Court of Appeal held that this did not count as 'service' at all; so that service could not be deemed 'to have been effected', at the time when it would have been likely to be 'delivered in the ordinary course of post', under the Interpretation Act 1889, s 26. A fresh notice was duly received later by the owner's agents.

purchase of the land' and consider compensation for 'damage which may be sustained by reason of the execution of the works'.[2]

Unlike the broad sweep of the compulsory purchase order, the notice to treat must relate to a particular transaction, whereby the acquiring body deal with a particular landowner. It might be termed a compulsory negotiation, as distinct from an 'invitation to treat' in the language of the law of contract. It is not a contract in itself, but coupled with a settled figure for compensation it becomes one. Salmon LJ said in *West Midland Baptist (Trust) Association (Incorporated) v Birmingham Corpn*:[3]

It is not until compensation is agreed or assessed that the equitable title in the land passes to the party who has served the notice to treat. Either party can then—but only then—obtain specific performance, the one to have the legal title conveyed to him on payment of the price, the other to have the price paid on conveying the legal title.

## 2 ABANDONMENT AND INVALIDITY

Taking as read, for present purposes, the question of compensation, it is worth stressing how close the analogy with contracts is meant to be. Not that an acquiring body will ever resort to an action for specific performance, because it has statutory powers of compulsion that are more effective. It is scarcely more likely that vendors will do so, because in those cases where appreciable delay occurs, the urge of the landowner seems to be to invalidate the purchase and keep the land, if possible, rather than to hasten its sale.

In *Grice v Dudley Corpn*,[4] for example, the defendant corporation obtained a compulsory purchase order in 1938, under the Public Works Facilities Act 1930, and served notice to treat on the owner of the land in question early in 1939. After some delay and disagreement the war intervened. By 1951 the corporation had totally revised its plans as far as the particular land was concerned, dropping the original plan for street widening and a new market hall and substituting what Upjohn J called 'general redevelopment'. After disputes over the price payable, the owners of the land in 1955 issued a writ in the High Court for a declaration that the notice to treat was no longer valid. Upjohn J laid down certain rules of law, based on an analysis of earlier cases. First, the notice to treat must be enforced in 'a reasonable period', and will only be enforceable beyond such a period if the delay is explained and such enforcement 'is equitable . . . in all the circumstances of the case'.

---

2 Compare the Lands Clauses Consolidation Act 1845, s 18. The law *assumes* that compensation is payable: 'the intention to take away property without compensation is not to be imputed to the legislature unless it is expressed in unequivocal terms' (*Belfast Corpn v O D Cars Ltd* [1960] AC 490, [1960] 1 All ER 65). But see ch 15, *passim*.

3 [1968] 1 All ER 205 at 216.

4 [1958] Ch 329, [1957] 2 All ER 673.

Second, the acquiring body 'may evince an intention to abandon' the rights conferred by the notice to treat. Third, 'this court has an inherent jurisdiction . . . at the instance of the Attorney General on behalf of the public or of a person damnified, to restrain the further exercise of . . . powers not in accord with the special Act. These three propositions . . . tend to merge one into the other . . . for unequivocal acts of abandonment seldom arise.' The judge summed up the situation by saying, 'It seems to me that the original scheme is dead. . . . Accordingly, it seems to me, on the facts, that this order has been abandoned.' Even if that were not strictly correct it would 'be most inequitable, after this long delay, to allow (the corporation) any further time in which to retrace their steps. . . . I propose to make a declaration that the notice to treat is no longer of validity or legal effect, and I shall declare that the defendants have no powers under, or by virtue of, the compulsory purchase order to acquire the plaintiff's premises or any part thereof.'

It should be noted that the court did not claim to invalidate the actual compulsory purchase order, which apart from anything else seems to have applied (as in many other cases) to a larger area than just the property subject to the notice to treat in this dispute. The judge treated the *order*, in this particular context, as 'abandoned', at any rate in equity, and held the *notice* to be invalid. The latter is the essence of the decision: the notice *is* invalid; the order is only *treated* as being abandoned, and only in this particular context. In theory a new, valid, notice to treat might then be served. In this case, and in practice in most cases, such a step would be ineffective because of s 4 of the 1965 Act, which says 'The powers of the acquiring authority . . . shall not be exercised after the expiration of three years from the date on which the compulsory purchase order becomes operative'. It was held in an early case, *Marquis of Salisbury v Great Northern Rly Co*,[5] that the service of notice to treat, in relation to any land, counts as sufficient exercise of compulsory purchase powers to satisfy this provision.[6] Conversely the service of a notice to treat more than three years after the order has taken effect would be of no avail; and in *Grice v Dudley Corpn* the defendants could not, in the judge's words, 'retrace their steps' for this reason quite apart from any question of equity.

These issues were also raised in *Simpsons Motor Sales (London) Ltd v Hendon Corpn*.[7] The plaintiffs sold second-hand cars on 'the North Road site' adjoining Burnt Oak Broadway, Hendon. In July 1952, the defendants obtained a compulsory purchase order, under Part V of the Housing Act 1936, for council housing on this land; and within a month notice to

5  (1852) 17 QB 840; also *Tiverton and North Devon Rly Co v Loosemore* (1884) 9 App Cas 480.
6  1845 Act, s 123, corresponding to s 4 of the 1965 Act.
7  [1964] AC 1088, [1963] 2 All ER 484.

treat was served. There followed a long delay when, for financial and policy reasons, the corporation reconsidered its plans; and in fact the plaintiffs took a hand and tried to persuade them to make use instead of the 'Colindale' site nearby. In 1959 the plaintiffs issued a writ claiming that the notice to treat was no longer effective. Ultimately they appealed unsuccessfully to the House of Lords, where Lord Evershed took up the three grounds of challenge enunciated by Upjohn J in *Grice's* case: namely, delay; abandonment; and ultra vires: and he added the fourth which also emerged in that case, namely contravention of rights in equity.

Lord Evershed held, first, that there was no evidence of ultra vires proposals for use of the land outside the purposes of the Housing Acts. Second, he held that the corporation were not in the circumstances 'guilty of inanition or procrastination', the reasons for delay, as explained above, being a sufficient justification of it. Third, he held that there was no abandonment: 'again I think the question substantially one of fact'. The authority may show an intention to abandon a compulsory purchase, and the owner may accept this, whereupon 'the quasi-contractual relationship which the notice to treat has caused to come into existence is then determined. I also accept . . . that the private owner might not be willing to accept the abandonment but could proceed to enforce his claim under the notice to treat; and in that event it would not be open to the local authority to rely upon their own wrongful act of abandonment to defeat the private's owner claim. But nothing of that kind occurred in the present case'. Fourth, he held that there was no equitable right—no bad faith 'nor . . . anything which could fairly be called misconduct or abuse of powers'—that the owners could rely on to defeat the compulsory purchase.[8]

## 3 CONSEQUENCES OF AND WITHDRAWAL FROM THE NOTICE

Section 6 of the 1965 Act provides that, if the recipient of a notice to treat does not, within 21 days of service, submit his claim for compensation to the authority or 'treat' with them, or if both sides do not agree over the amount of compensation, 'the question of disputed compensation shall be referred to the Lands Tribunal'. This last provision can be exercised unilaterally, like bringing an action in a court, by the authority or the landowner giving notice of reference to the registrar of the Lands Tribunal under Rule 16 of the Lands Tribunal Rules 1975.[9] Thus once a notice to treat has been served, the acquiring authority can be compelled to proceed, subject to certain exceptional cases to be explained shortly. It is not necessary for the owner to apply to the High Court for a prerogative order of mandamus, though it would no doubt be granted if needed. An

8 Contrast *Sydney Municipal Council v Campbell* [1925] AC 338.
9 SI 1975/299.

early case in which mandamus was granted, to compel an acquiring body to proceed after serving notice to treat, is *R v Hungerford Market Co, ex p Davies*.[10] If compensation is assessed and the authority delays again, the owner can then sue for specific performance of what by that time will constitute an enforceable contract.

The owner will only be able to resist a notice to treat unilaterally by bringing an action to invalidate it on one of the grounds discussed in *Grice's* and *Simpson's* cases. The authority will likewise be bound by the notice to treat, and unable to escape from it unilaterally, unless there is occasion to withdraw it in certain specified cases. Thus the 'special Act'—which in modern terms means either the authorising Act or the compulsory purchase order—may allow withdrawal.

Section 31 (1) of the Land Compensation Act 1961, allows the authority to withdraw a notice to treat served on any owner of particular land within six weeks of receiving a claim for compensation from him or from any other owner of the same land on whom a notice has been served. Section 31 (2) of that Act allows the authority to withdraw any notice to treat served on such owners if one of them has failed to submit in good time a notice of claim, provided that the authority do so 'at any time after the decision of the Lands Tribunal on his claim but not later than six weeks after the claim has been finally determined', unless they have entered into possession of the land.[11]

Claims must reach the authority in time to enable them to make a proper offer'.[12] The price of withdrawal is payment of compensation for the resulting loss and expenses incurred by the recipient of the notice, but not in respect of the period after the time when the Lands Tribunal considers 'a proper notice of claim should have been delivered'.[13]

In *Methodist Church Purposes Trustees v North Tyneside Metropolitan Borough Council*,[14] it was held that a 'proper notice of claim' must be delivered within 'a reasonable time' (ie the six-week periods referred to above do not apply) and must include a quantified amount as the sum claimed; but that provisional amount can be amended later when the relevant valuation facts become better known.

One other possibility of withdrawal seems to be implicit in s 8 (1) of the Act of 1965, under which a notice to treat in respect of part of a property can be met by a statement that the recipient is 'willing and able to sell the whole'. The procedure in such cases will be discussed more fully later;[15] but it is relevant to note that, by implication, an authority unwilling to

10  (1832) 4 B & Ad 327.
11  The date when the claim is 'finally determined' depends of course on whether there is an appeal to the Court of Appeal, or indeed a further appeal to the House of Lords.
12  1961 Act, s 4 (1) (b) (see ch 6, p 123).
13  Ibid, s 31 (3).
14  (1979) 38 P & CR 665.
15  See ch 5, p 102.

take the whole, and not permitted under s 8 (1) to take part, is entitled to withdraw altogether from taking the land. This was decided, under the corresponding provisions of the Act of 1845,[16] in *King v Wycombe Rly Co*.[17] If the notice to treat withdrawn in this way included other land, at any rate land of the same owner, the entire notice can still be withdrawn, as in *Thompson v Tottenham and Forest Gate Rly Co*.[18]

### 4 FIXING THE INTERESTS TO BE ACQUIRED

It used to be thought that compensation had to be assessed as at the date of the notice to treat—a very questionable proposition since appreciable delays often ensue and the period may be one of inflation. This fallacy has now been exploded, and the present law will be discussed later.[19] But it was also assumed that the notice to treat fixes the interest to be acquired; and this is inevitable, because there is a separate notice for each owner being expropriated. It has been held that if a landlord who received a notice to treat later granted a lease for three years to his tenant, who had hitherto held under a weekly tenancy, the new lease was not compensatable: *Re Marylebone (Stingo Lane) Improvement Act, ex p Edwards*.[20] But existing estates and interests in land can be dealt with after the notice to treat.[1]

The underlying principle is given statutory expression in the Acquisition of Land Act 1981.[2] This says that the assessment of compensation in accordance with the Land Compensation Act 1961 (discussed in Part II of this book) is subject to the following requirement. The Lands Tribunal must ignore 'any interest in land, or any enhancement of the value of any interest in land, by reason of any building, erection, work done or improvement or alterations made, whether on the land purchased or on any other land with which the claimant is, or was at the time of the erection, doing or making of the building, works, improvement or alteration, directly or indirectly concerned', if 'satisfied that the creation of the interest, the erection of the building, the doing of the work, the making of the improvement or the alteration, as the case may be, was not reasonably necessary *and* was undertaken with a view to obtaining

---

16 Section 92.
17 (1860) 28 Beav 104.
18 (1892) 67 LT 416.
19 See ch 6.
20 (1871) LR 12 Eq 389.
1 In *Cardiff Corpn v Cook* [1923] 2 Ch 115, a leasehold was being expropriated. The owner claimed a moderate figure for compensation (a nil value for the lease, and £550 for disturbance); but before the authority decided upon it, the lease was assigned, and the assignee submitted a revised claim comprising £3,375 value for the lease. The court held that the assignment and the submission of a revised claim were both perfectly permissible, and that the assignor's own claim for disturbance remained valid also.
2 Section 4. The Housing Act 1957, Sch 3, contains a similar provision. Merger is *not* forbidden (see below, p 94).

compensation or increased compensation'.[3] It is important to note that both these factors must be proved before the interest or the enhancement in value is ignored.

Yet it should be remembered also that if a new interest (probably a tenancy) is created, the value of that interest will in principle be balanced by a corresponding decrease in value of the interest out of which it was created, being now in reversion or otherwise subject to it.[4]

## 5 THE CONVEYANCE

As in private conveyancing, the ultimate stage in the transfer of land is a conveyance of the legal title to the purchaser, by registered or unregistered conveyance depending on whether the land lies in a locality where compulsory registration is in force.[5] Because this stage is virtually the same as in a sale of land by agreement little is said about it in compulsory purchase legislation. Section 23 of the 1965 Act, however, states, 'The costs of all conveyances of the land subject to compulsory purchase shall be borne by the acquiring authority'. It also provides that conveyances may be in the form prescribed by the fifth Schedule, or in similar form, 'or by deed in any other form which the acquiring authority may think fit'.[6] This liability for costs does not extend to collateral

3 In *Banham v London Borough of Hackney* (1970) 22 P & CR 922, the acquiring authority asserted this principle—in vain—where the expropriated owner of a house had previously had a weekly furnished tenant but had served notice to quit which was not contested. Tenanted, the property had a market value of £3,000; with vacant possession it was £3,750. The Lands Tribunal (the President: Sir Michael Rowe QC) rejected the argument that the extra £750 was unjustified (after all, both figures had been agreed as genuine market valuations). He thought the sum represented what a purchaser might well offer a tenant in return for quitting. But see Land Compensation Act 1973, s 50: below, p 91.

4 *Ex p Edwards* (above) might still apply if a new lease is granted bona fide more than three years after the compulsory purchase order—ie too late for notice to treat to be served on the lessee: Compulsory Purchase Act 1965, s 4 (above, p 60). Authorities commonly serve notice to treat well within the three-year limit but tend to delay matters thereafter (as in the *Grice* and *Simpson* cases discussed above: see pp 59–61) and such an application of *Ex p Edwards* might well encourage them further in so doing.

5 See *Crabb v Surrey County Council* (1982) 44 P & CR 119.

6 As to costs, at one time the question arose whether they should be an itemised taxation of costs or a solicitor's all-in scale fee. The Solicitor's Remuneration Order 1883 (as amended), r 11, excluded the scale fee, for compulsory acquisitions. The Solicitors' Remuneration (Registered Land) Order 1955 did not. In *Re West Ferry Road, Poplar, Re Padwicks Estate* [1955] 2 All ER 638, [1955] 1 WLR 751, the acquiring authority claimed that the latter order should be construed as excluding the scale fee for registered land also, so that an itemised taxation of the vendor's costs could be obtained; they argued that uniformity and justice required this. The Court of Appeal rejected the claim, on a straight basis of interpretation of the relevant provisions. But on 1 January 1973 the Solicitors' Remuneration Order 1972 came into effect, which prescribed that, in place of scale fees previously authorised for non-contentious business, solicitors should henceforth charge 'such sum as may be fair and reasonable in all the circumstances'. Thus the scale fee was eventually dispensed with after all.

transactions, such as apportionments of rent under s 19 of the 1965 Act when part only of leasehold land is compulsorily purchased.[7]

## B. Entry upon land

### 1 RIGHT TO ENTER AND NOTICE OF ENTRY

In private conveyancing under the ordinary principles of the common law it is the execution of the conveyance of the legal estate that entitles a purchaser to go into possession. In compulsory purchase the same applies, which means that possession cannot normally be taken by the acquiring body at the date of the notice to treat: they must wait until completion, which itself will not normally occur until the compensation has been settled and is to be paid. Payment, conveyance and entry into possession should all coincide. Under a general visiting declaration, to be discussed below, the legal title passes at the date when the declaration is specified to take effect, and the right to take possession coincides with the vesting. In all these cases the right to take possession is subject to the rights of any actual tenants who are not being expropriated and whose interests are being allowed to terminate at common law or are being expropriated later.

Section 11 (1) of the 1965 Act—which, however, does not apply when general vesting declarations are used—empowers an acquiring authority to serve on the relevant owner, occupier and lessee 14 days' 'notice of entry' by virtue of which they can enter into possession of any land in advance of payment of compensation, provided that they have already served notice to treat. But if they do this, 'any compensation agreed or awarded for the land of which possession is taken shall carry interest at the rate prescribed under s 32 of the Land Compensation Act 1961,[8] from the time of entry until the compensation is paid, or is paid into court in accordance with this Act'. A similar right to serve 14 days' 'notice of entry' at any time after service of a notice to treat exists in relation to leasehold interests excluded from the scope of a general vesting declaration.[9]

---

7 *Re Hampstead Junction Rly Co, ex p Buck* (1863) 1 Hem & M 519.
8 See ch 6, p 125, for interest from the date of the award.
9 Compulsory Purchase (Vesting Declarations) Act 1981, s 9. See below, p 68. The Compulsory Purchase Act 1965, s 11 (3), gives a general right to serve 3 to 14 days' notice for entry on land before acquisition, for the purpose of surveying, or 'probing or boring to ascertain the nature of the soil and of setting out the line of the works', on payment of compensation for any damage (disputed assessments being referred to the Lands Tribunal). For local authorities, the Local Government (Miscellaneous Provisions) Act 1976, s 15, prescribes a more detailed procedure for such surveys (including boring to investigate subsoil and minerals, and aerial surveys); the procedure provides for advance notification to owners, objections (by statutory undertakers), compensation for damage, and fines for obstruction.

Schedule 3 to the 1965 Act prescribes an alternative procedure for gaining entry—or rather preserves it, since like the procedure for notices of entry it is a re-enactment in substance of provisions contained in the Act of 1845. Disadvantageous and cumbersome by comparison, it is unlikely to be much used today. Under it the acquiring body can indeed enter without serving notice, but only after first obtaining the consent of 'each person interested in or entitled to sell and convey the land'— presumably the owner of every subsisting legal estate in it—or, if such consent is not forthcoming, only after first paying the compensation into court and also tendering to the owner a bond for that amount, including interest.

This then, is the sequence of events in a straightforward case involving land where there is one owner-occupier and no other person owns any freehold or leasehold in law or equity: notice of the compulsory purchase order; then notice to treat; and then, if the acquiring authority are in a hurry, notice of entry, all served on the same party and in that order.

But if the land is let to (say) a tenant on a yearly tenancy the notice to *treat* need only be served on the landlord; whereas the notice of *entry*, though it must be served on both the landlord and the tenant, is really aimed at the latter and is the only formal warning which he need receive that the acquisition is in fact going ahead.[10]

Where an acquiring body reach the point of taking physical possession, either by actual entry or by having the right to do so (by virtue of the conveyance of the legal title, or in consequence of serving notice of entry in advance of such conveyance) they must accept the disadvantages of this as well as the advantages. 'Entry' makes them occupiers. In *Harris v Birkenhead Corpn*[11] the defendants compulsorily purchased a house as part of a slum clearance project. They served notice of entry on both the landlord and the tenant. The tenant moved out and the house remained vacant for some months, during which time it was vandalised. The plaintiff, aged four-and-a-half, wandered in and fell from a broken window. It was held that the authority were 'occupiers' for the purposes of occupier's liability in the tort of negligence, because although they had not yet taken physical possession of the house they had become free to do so under the notice of entry.

In *Cohen v Haringey London Borough Council*,[12] property subject to a compulsory purchase order was sold, but the owner ignored letters from the acquiring authority, who, as a result, served notice to treat and notice of entry on the wrong person. They then entered and took possession, and discovered the error, whereupon they re-served the notice to treat and notice of entry on the right person. The validity of this action was

10   To achieve emphasis at the expense of strict accuracy, it might be said that, where land is let, notices to treat are for landlords but notices of entry are for tenants.
11   [1976] 1 All ER 341, [1976] 1 WLR 279.
12   (1980) 42 P & CR 6.

challenged but the Court of Appeal upheld it. Retrospective service of notices is thus intra vires if reasonable in the circumstances, subject to the overriding three-year time-limit for notices to treat.[13]

## 2 ENTRY, EXPROPRIATION AND DISPOSSESSION

Care must be taken in compulsory purchase cases to distinguish between expropriation and dispossession. The former is the essence of compulsory purchase: it consists of forcing an unwilling freeholder or leaseholder to sell his freehold or leasehold to the authority. But if he is a landlord he holds in reversion, not possession, and so is not being dispossessed. If he is a freehold or leasehold owner-occupier he will be both dispossessed and expropriated. If he is a tenant, however, he may well be dispossessed without being expropriated, if the authority acquire his landlord's interest and are then able to terminate his tenancy, or prevent its renewal, in accordance with the law of landlord and tenant. If he is a short-term or periodic tenant who has sublet he may well be got rid of without being either expropriated or dispossessed.

If notice of entry is served on an owner-occupier it does not affect the fact that he is being both expropriated and dispossessed; though of course it brings forward the time of his dispossession and causes interest to become payable in consequence. But if notice of entry is served on an occupying tenant who would otherwise have been turned out at common law, then he is not being merely dispossessed but expropriated as well.

If an acquiring authority should serve notice to treat on a landlord, but not on his tenant occupying the land on a periodic tenancy, and compensation is then assessed and paid to the landlord, the implication of s 11 (1) of the 1965 Act is that notice of entry no longer needs to be considered. If the authority then wish to enter quickly before the tenancy can be terminated by notice to quit or effluxion of time, can they do so? Section 20 of the 1965 Act, discussed in the next chapter, seems to imply that they can require a yearly or lesser tenant to give up possession at any time; but it is assumed in practice that, if there is no termination at common law, a notice of entry should still be used.

## 3 ENFORCEMENT OF POSSESSION; ILLEGAL ENTRY; RATE DEFICIENCY

If the owner or occupier or any other person refuses to give up possession of land upon which an acquiring body are entitled to enter, or hinders them from entering on or taking possession of it, s 13 of the 1965 Act provides that 'the acquiring authority may issue their warrant to the sheriff to deliver possession of it to the person appointed in the warrant to receive it'. The costs of this procedure are to be paid by the recalcitrant party, and deducted from any compensation payable to him;

13 Under the Compulsory Purchase Act 1965, s 4 (see above, p 60).

alternatively if necessary the amount may be distrained for. On the other hand, the acquiring body or any of their contractors may happen to enter upon land before the right to do so has arisen, in which case s 12 of the 1965 Act provides that the acquiring body 'shall forfeit to the person in possession of that land the sum of ten pounds in addition to the amount of any damage done to the land by entering and taking possession'. This amount is recoverable summarily as a civil debt in a magistrates' court, subject to appeal to the Crown Court; and if after it 'has been adjudged to be forfeited under this section' the unlawful possession continues, a further forfeit of £25 a day is payable, but proceedings to recover it must be taken in the High Court. These forfeits[14] are not however payable if the compensation agreed or awarded has already been paid, in good faith, to the wrong person provided that the acquiring body reasonably believed that he was entitled to it.

When the acquiring body do take possession, they may under s 27 of the 1965 Act 'from time to time, until the works are completed and assessed to rates, be liable to make good the deficiency in the several assessments for rates by reason of the land having been taken or used for the purposes of the works'. This liability depends on whether, at the time of taking, it is 'land which is liable to be assessed to rates'. The relevant time is 'when the compulsory purchase order became operative'; but in any urban local authority area only half the deficiency is to be made good. The liability, however, can be expressly excluded by the compulsory purchase order, and does not apply at all to acquisitions under the Housing Act 1957.

## C. General vesting declaration

### 1 STATUTORY AUTHORITY FOR QUICK VESTING

Such is the traditional procedure. Recent statutes, however, have introduced an alternative procedure, which telescopes into one stage the two separate stages of the notice to treat and the conveyance. This one stage is a 'general vesting declaration'. Certain statutes pioneered the new procedure in special cases, but it was made of general application by the Town and Country Planning Act 1968, the provisions of which have been re-enacted in the Compulsory Purchase (Vesting Declarations) Act 1981. Section 1 (2) of the latter Act applies the procedure to 'any Minister or local or other public authority authorised to acquire land by means of a compulsory purchase order'. The provisions setting out this procedure are an adjunct to the general procedural code in the Act of 1965.

The advantages of the new procedure are such that one would expect it to be used in most cases from now on. Yet not only may there still be

14 The amounts have not been changed since they were originally enacted in 1845.

circumstances in which its use will be inconvenient or impossible so that notices to treat must be used instead, but it seems that, even apart from these, acquiring bodies often actually prefer to continue using notices to treat. This may be related to the fact that the acquiring authority's option to withdraw from the acquisition during the interim period between notice to treat and conveyance, in certain circumstances, is not open to them if they use a vesting declaration, because if they do there is no such interim period.

## 2 GENERAL VESTING DECLARATION PROCEDURE

Any acquiring authority as defined in s 2 of the Compulsory Purchase (Vesting Declarations) Act 1981[15] may take advantage of the procedure, provided that it has received its authorisation from a compulsory purchase order. It will be recalled that the order 'becomes operative' when the authority gives notice that it has been made or confirmed, to the particular landowners concerned and to the public in general.[16] This notice, or any separate later one provided that no notice to treat has been served, must explain the procedure for 'general vesting declarations' in a set form, and invite every owner of land—that is to say the land covered by the order and not included in any notice to treat—'to give information to the authority making the declaration in the prescribed form with respect to his name and address and the land in question'.[17] It must also specify the earliest date when the general vesting declaration can be executed, which will be two months ahead, or longer; but an earlier date can be chosen if all occupiers of land concerned agree to this in writing.[18]

The acquiring authority may then 'execute' the general vesting declaration 'in the prescribed form vesting the land in themselves from the end of such period as may be specified in the declaration. . . .'[19] This is a period which must be *not less* than 28 days after the date on which the service of notices of the making of the general vesting declaration has been completed. The date at the end of that period is called the 'vesting date'. These notices must be served, in a prescribed form, on every occupier of the land in question, apart from land subject to certain excluded tenancies, and on anyone else 'who has given information' as

15  Any minister or other public authority to whom s 1 (2) of the Act applies, as stated above on p 68.
16  Acquisition of Land Act 1981, s 26. See ch 3, p 51.
17  Compulsory Purchase (Vesting Declarations) Act 1981, s 3.
18  Ibid, s 5 (which takes care to provide, however, that where 'special parliamentary procedure' applies and compulsory purchase orders 'become operative' under that procedure (if at all) and not under the Acquisition of Land Act 1981, s 26—see above, p 54—general vesting declarations 'shall not be executed' until such compulsory purchase orders 'come into operation').
19  Ibid, s 4.

invited, 'specifying the land and stating the effect of the declaration'.[20]

The notice in which the intention of making the general vesting declaration is disclosed must be registered in the local land charges registry.[1] If, as is common, it also serves as the notice of the coming into operation of the compulsory purchase order, it is important to remember that such registration is only required by virtue of the general vesting declaration and not of the compulsory purchase order; so that if a notice of the making of a compulsory purchase order does not state that a general vesting declaration is to be made, either because a decision has been taken solely to use notices to treat or because no decision on the point has yet been taken, then that notice does not have to be registered.[2] There is no question of registering *notices to treat* as local land charges. But an attempt has been made to argue that they should be registered as ordinary land charges at the Land Registry, on the ground that they are estate contracts: *Capital Investments Ltd v Wednesfield UDC*.[3] This was rejected on the obvious ground that notices to treat are not in themselves contracts, as discussed earlier.[4]

Thus the sequence of procedural steps is as follows:

(1) Making or confirming the CPO (Compulsory Purchase Order).
(2) Service (and registration) of notice proposing use of GVD (General Vesting Declaration) (whether or not the same as the notice that the CPO has been made or confirmed).
(3) Execution of the GVD (not less than two months later).
(4) Service of notice that GVD has been executed and will take effect on a specified date not less than 28 days later.
(5) Vesting of the legal title to the land in the acquiring authority on that specified date, referred to as the 'vesting date'.

Prescribed forms can be found in the Compulsory Purchase of Land Regulations 1982[5] for the statement explaining the general vesting declaration procedure which must be included in the notice in step no. (2) above, for the declaration itself (step no. (3)), for the notice stating that the declaration has been made and what its effect is (step no. (4)), and for the giving of information as requested in the notice in step no. (2). The first three are to be used by the acquiring authority and the last one by the landowners concerned.

20 Ibid, s 6.
1 Ibid, s 3 (4).
2 The compulsory purchase order itself does not have to be registered; although s 11 (1) of the Land Commission Act 1967, which was enacted in connection with the general vesting declaration procedure which that Act made standard form for compulsory acquisitions by the Land Commission, required that compulsory purchase orders made by the Commission should be registered in this way.
3 [1965] Ch 774, [1964] 1 All ER 655.
4 See p 24, above.
5 SI 1982/6. See reg 5, and Sch (forms 8, 9 Part I, 9 Part II, and 10).

## 3 WITHDRAWAL, SEVERANCE AND LIMITATION

When a general vesting declaration has been duly executed its effect will be the same as if the authority had conveyed the land in question to itself unilaterally, by deed poll.[6] The cases in which this is done are provided for in the 1965 Act, and will be discussed below; but they are special cases, whereas the new procedure is intended to be of general application. It will, of course, also have the same effect as if a notice to treat had been served on all the landowners concerned;[7] and the main significance of this is that the parties should begin at once to negotiate compensation if they have not done so already. The right of the authority to withdraw from a notice to treat, however, clearly should not normally apply because that right, which presupposes that the conveyance has not been executed, is by way of a special concession available to acquiring authorities between the notice to treat and the conveyance but not later. Since the general vesting declaration is notice to treat and conveyance in one, the appropriate time for exercising the right of withdrawal—which in any case is not so much the consequence of a notice to treat as a move to escape its consequences—is in fact telescoped out of existence.[8]

The rights of withdrawal in relation to compensation claims, therefore, are expressly stated not to apply.[9] Withdrawal by agreement presents no problems. Withdrawal by virtue of the authorising Act or compulsory purchase order might in theory present problems, but seems unlikely to arise in practice. There remains the question of withdrawal where the authority wishes to take part only and the owner resists on the ground that they should take all or none: that is to say a case where 'severance' is proposed and resisted. Here the right of withdrawal is expressly *preserved* as part of the general procedure for dealing with such cases, which will be discussed later; it is sufficient at this point to say that, if the authority do withdraw, the interest of the landowner in question 'shall not vest in the acquiring authority by virtue of the general vesting declaration'.[10] Presumably as a result of this there will be an equity to compel rectification of the general vesting declaration.

Similarly, the 1965 Act procedure to gain entry on land, by means of a 'notice of entry' served by the authority, does not apply:[11] though

---

6 Compulsory Purchase (Vesting Declarations) Act 1981, s 8. (See below, pp 74 to 77, for conveyances by deed poll).

7 Ibid, s 7 (this does not apply to persons on whom an actual notice to treat has for some reason already been served, nor to holders of excluded tenancies on whom notice to treat may need to be served as discussed below).

8 As to title deeds, see ibid, s 14.

9 Ibid, s 7 (3).

10 Ibid, Sch 1, para 6. (see ch 5 for the general procedure).

11 Ibid, s 8 (3).

liability for compensation is made to arise as if possession of the land had been gained in that way.[12] The question of entry on land has already been discussed earlier in this chapter.

A limitation period prohibits references of compensation disputes to the Lands Tribunal later than 'six years from the date at which the person claiming compensation, or a person under whom he derives title, first knew, or could reasonably be expected to have known, of the vesting of the interest'.[13] Special provisions deal with rents and rent charges,[14] absent and untraced owners,[15] recovery of compensation overpaid and other mistaken payments,[16] and urban development corporations.[17]

## 4   EXCLUDED TENANCIES

A difficult and important question relating to general vesting declarations is that of excluded tenancies. Where land is let to tenants there will clearly be complications absent from those cases where owner-occupied land is acquired. In the general law of compulsory purchase, to be discussed later, it will be seen that leaseholds, whether fixed-term or periodic, of which the term is a year or less, are normally excluded from compulsory purchase; so that the acquiring body need only acquire the landlord's reversion and (since statutory protection of tenants does not prevail against compulsory purchase) wait until the tenancies end by notice to quit or effluxion of time.[18]

This system applies to general vesting declarations; and the Compulsory Purchase (Vesting Declarations) Act 1981[19] refers to such tenancies as 'minor tenancies'. Thus the general vesting declaration, just like ordinary private conveyances, not only vests the legal estate in the purchasers but gives them thereby the right to take physical possession of land subject to the rights of tenants who are not being bought out. But the Act also refers to a category of leasehold which it terms a 'long tenancy which is about to expire'. A tenancy of this kind is one 'granted for an interest greater than a minor tenancy, but having on the vesting date a period still to run which is not more than ... such period, longer than one year, as may ... be specified in the declaration. ...'[20]

This is to give the acquiring authority a choice. Where land is subject to a tenancy they can either acquire that tenancy, in which case they get

12  Ibid, s 10 (for entry, see p 65, above).
13  Ibid, s 10 (3).
14  Ibid, Sch 1, Part II.
15  Ibid, s 10 (2).
16  Ibid, ss 11, 13.
17  Sch 2. See Local Government, Planning and Land Act 1980, Part XVI.
18  See ch 5, pp 87–90.
19  Sections 2, 9.
20  Section 2 (2) of the Act.

possession of the land (assuming that there is no sub-tenancy in force) at the price of paying compensation, or avoid paying such compensation, in which case they must wait until the tenancy comes to an end. Where a general vesting declaration is not being used, the authority will either serve or refrain from serving a notice to treat, depending on whether or not they think they can afford to wait or to acquire. But where a general vesting declaration is used, the authority will acquire, and must pay compensation for, all freehold and leasehold interests greater than 'minor tenancies' unless they specify leaseholds with stated periods, longer than a year, to run, which will then be excluded from the declaration. They will not buy out any such leasehold, and possession will be delayed so long as that leasehold lasts as the price of economising on compensation.

Yet if the possession of the land in question becomes urgent they can serve a notice to treat in respect of any such tenancy excluded from the general vesting declaration. This applies not only to any 'long tenancy which is about to expire', as specified by them in the declaration, but to any minor tenancy as well. Having served a notice to treat they can then go on to obtain possession by serving a 'notice of entry' in the same manner as under the 1965 Act—and this also will be discussed later, when it will be seen further that a special problem arises over compensation when notice to treat is served in respect of a minor tenancy.[1]

General vesting declarations apply generally since 1968 the procedure previously applied to the Land Commission and to local authorities acquiring land 'for planning purposes'. In the latter case such authorities could only proceed in this way as a matter of urgency and with ministerial consent; and the name given to the procedure was 'expedited completion'. The Town and Country Planning Act 1968 repealed the provisions enacting it.[2]

# D. Unwillingness or inability to sell

The conveyancing in compulsory purchase is complicated in certain cases which receive special attention in the 1965 Act. On the whole these provisions apply to notices to treat and general vesting declarations alike, but where this is not so the differences will be pointed out. There are owners who are recalcitrant, absent or under a disability, and there are persons with incumbrances such as mortgages, rentcharges and rights of common.

1  See ch 5, p 89, below.
2  Eleventh Schedule. For 'planning purposes", see ch 11. 'Expedited completion' was provided by the Town and Country Planning Act 1962, ss 74–76.

## 1   RECALCITRANCE

Section 9 of the 1965 Act provides that if the owner of any land being compulsorily purchased fails or refuses to make title or convey the property or otherwise complete the transaction, the acquiring authority may pay the compensation into court, giving all reasonably available details of the recalcitrants and their interests. The authority may then vest the legal title to the land in themselves unilaterally by deed poll 'containing a description of the land in respect of which the payment into court was made, and declaring the circumstances under which, and the names of the parties to whose credit, the payment into court was made'. The court is the High Court, which may invest or otherwise deal with the money by virtue of the powers conferred on it by s 6 of the Administration of Justice Act 1965, and distribute it as it thinks just when the various recalcitrant owners lay claim to it. A general vesting declaration, if used, would seem to have exactly the same effect and consequences as a deed poll. The recalcitrants may go further in their resistance and try to prevent the authority taking possession of the land: the remedy for this was discussed earlier in this chapter.[3] Payment into court seems to be appropriate where there are rival as well as recalcitrant claimants; only the court can decide between disputing claims.

## 2   DISABILITY

The First Schedule to the 1965 Act contains a procedure for use when owners are under a disability because they are corporations, tenants for life or in tail, trustees for charitable or for other purposes, or merely persons entitled to the rents and profits of the land. In fact, however, these provisions have been included purely out of caution. They derive from the Act of 1845,[4] but since then there have been major reforms in the law whereby land held by or for the benefit of such persons or bodies has been made readily marketable, provided always that set procedures are followed, either by those persons or bodies themselves or by other persons or bodies in whom the legal estate has been vested or who have been given control over it. The sale and conveyance of land compulsorily purchased in such cases can be carried out in the normal way and the compensation money paid or applied similarly in return for it. If the procedure in the First Schedule ever does need to be used, the money should be paid into court (or possibly to trustees specially appointed). The land must then be conveyed by the persons in whom it is vested, regardless of disabilities, failing which the acquiring body can vest it in themselves by deed poll, and the money is then paid out as is just. Nevertheless the Local Government Acts, the Companies Acts, the Law

---

3  See p 67, above.
4  Sections 7 to 9. These were important at the time.

of Property Act 1925, the Settled Land Act 1925, the Charities Act 1960, and various other statutes provide for all these cases nowadays. Section 42 (7) of the Law of Property Act 1925 says as follows:

Where a purchaser has power to acquire land compulsorily, and a contract, whether by virtue of a notice to treat or otherwise, is subsisting under which title can be made without payment of the compensation money into court, title shall be made in that way unless the purchaser, to avoid expense or delay or for any special reason, considers it expedient that the money should be paid into court.

In other words, the procedure now contained in the First Schedule to the 1965 Act should not be used if it can possibly be avoided.

## 3 ABSENCE

The Second Schedule to the 1965 Act deals with cases where an owner is abroad or 'cannot be found after diligent inquiry has been made'. The authority must pay the compensation into court, and may then convey the legal estate in the land to themselves by deed poll.[5] If the absent owner reappears he must then apply to the court to have the money paid out. If he objects to the compensation assessment he can apply to the Lands Tribunal to re-assess it; and if he succeeds in obtaining more the authority must pay his costs as well as the additional money, whereas if he fails the costs remain in the discretion of the Lands Tribunal.[6]

# E. Incumbrances and omissions

There remains the question of land incumbered by mortgages, rent charges or rights of common. Payment into court can be made; but the 1965 Act envisages direct payments where possible, and if necessary the execution of a deed poll. How easements and other such rights are dealt with is discussed in the next chapter.

## 1 MORTGAGED LAND

Mortgages are dealt with, partly in accordance with general principles, partly under ss 14 to 17 of the 1965 Act. The authority can (and in principle should) serve notice to treat on both the mortgagor and the mortgagee and have the compensation settled jointly with both of them,

---

5 For an example of this kind of situation, which occurs rarely, see the Lands Tribunal decision in *Peltier and Caddle v Manchester Corpn* (1974) 29 P & CR 262 (joint owners, one absent in the USA, whereabouts unknown: the other not entitled to claim payment of half the compensation awarded by the Tribunal, without recourse to the High Court). For joint tenancy see *Williams v British Gas Corpn*, below, ch 5, p 86.

6 These provisions are unnecessary where a general vesting declaration vests the interest in the acquiring authority: Compulsory Purchase (Vesting Declarations) Act 1981, s 10 (2).

either by agreement or by reference to the Lands Tribunal; but disputes over the parties' respective rights may well be taken to the courts. If the mortgage debt exceeds the value of the land being acquired, s 15 in any case authorises the acquiring body to proceed in this way, paying compensation into court and executing a deed poll if necessary. Section 14 authorises them if they wish to pay off the mortgage direct, with six months' notice or interest in lieu, and have the mortgagee's interest conveyed to them; if the mortgagee is unwilling they can pay the money into court and execute a deed poll; but in any case they will obviously make use of this section only if the value of the land exceeds the mortgage debt. The mortgagor's equity of redemption can then be purchased in the ordinary way.

If only part of a mortgaged property is being taken—in other words there is a 'severance'—the acquiring body may pay the mortgagor and disregard the mortgage. If the portion of land required by the authority will be less in value than the full amount owing under the mortgage, but the mortgagee regards the remainder as insufficient security or is in any case unwilling to release the portion of land the authority wish to take, he may require them, by s 16, to proceed in the same way as under s 15. The authority will then pay the compensation to him—or if necessary into court, and execute a deed poll—including any payment in respect of severance, or other special matters. If the portion of land required is greater in value than the mortgage debt, it would seem that the mortgagee can insist on being included in the compulsory purchase proceedings anyway, even though the authority would presumably be more willing to deal with a mortgagor in such circumstances. There is in fact general authority for the right of any mortgagee to receive a notice to treat: *Martin v London, Chatham and Dover Rly Co*,[7] and this applies to equitable as well as legal mortgagees. Under all these statutory provisions, if the date for repayment of the mortgage was postponed, any consequent loss in respect of the expenses of reinvestment and loss of a favourable rate of interest by the mortgagee must also be compensated.

## 2 RENTCHARGES

Where the land acquired is subject to a rentcharge, s 18 of the 1965 Act provides as follows. The amount of compensation payable for release of the rentcharge is to be settled by the Lands Tribunal, in the event of a dispute. If only part of the land is acquired, the landowner as well as the person entitled to the rentcharge takes part in the proceedings; and the rentcharge may be apportioned, or else restricted so as to apply exclusively to the part of the land not compulsorily purchased provided that the person entitled to it is satisfied that this will still provide adequate security. Details must be given in a memorandum of release

7  (1866) 1 Ch App 501.

endorsed on the instrument creating the rentcharge if it is tendered to the acquiring body; and they also have the power, if necessary, to pay compensation money into court and execute a deed poll releasing the land acquired from the rentcharge.

With some exceptions, the Rentcharges Act 1977 phases out existing rentcharges over the next 60 years, and in general prohibits the creation of new ones.

### 3 RIGHTS OF COMMON

Where land acquired is subject to rights of common, the commoners as well as the freeholders—whether or not he is lord of the manor—will be entitled to compensation, since their rights can hardly continue as against the acquiring body and must therefore be expropriated.[8] The procedure for doing this is contained in the Fourth Schedule[9] to the 1965 Act. The acquiring body may convene a meeting of all persons with common rights, if as is likely these cannot be ascertained more directly. Prior press publicity and the posting of notices is necessary. The meeting may then appoint a committee of up to five persons to negotiate compensation with the acquiring body; and all those with common rights will be bound thereby. In default of agreement with the acquiring body the amount is to be assessed by the Lands Tribunal. The acquiring body need not concern themselves about the apportionment between the various commoners, but are entitled to pay the compensation to the committee, or any three of them, and get a good discharge. If there is no effective meeting or committee of the commoners the Lands Tribunal acts on their behalf.

The freeholder or lord of the manor must convey the land to the acquiring body when the compensation is paid or tendered to him, and the conveyance vests the freehold in them; or if necessary they can pay the compensation money into court and execute a deed poll. They will be entitled then to take possession, subject however to the rights of common until these have been extinguished on payment of compensation to the commoners; if necessary that money also can be paid into court. The authority can then execute a deed poll freeing the land from all the rights of common.

### 4 INTERESTS OMITTED FROM PURCHASE

It may be that an acquiring authority take possession of land in ignorance of some estate or interest which they should have expropriated. If so, s 22 of the 1965 Act protects them from an action for trespass[10] provided that

8 On the question of how common land can have been included in the compulsory purchase order in the first place, see ch 3, p 56.

9 Applied by s 21.

10 '. . . the acquiring authority shall remain in undisturbed possession of the land.'

within six months they make good this default, paying not only the capital value of the interest but also mesne profits where appropriate. The assessment may well take longer than six months; but presumably it is sufficient to make an offer, and if necessary refer the matter to the Lands Tribunal, within that time. No notice to treat is needed, but the appropriate conveyance will have to be made.

# F.  Disposal and appropriation of land acquired

The general statutes governing compulsory purchase do not contemplate the re-sale or other disposal of land acquired, except for the Act of 1845, which contains provisions for the sale of 'superfluous lands'.[11] These provisions, however, have habitually been excluded in recent years and have been ignored by the 1965 Act in its selection of those provisions of the 1845 Act which it regards as appropriate for re-enactment in modern conditions. It seems to be largely a matter of chance what statutes do make express provision for disposal of land. Section 123 of the Local Government Act 1972 makes general provision for the leasing, sale and exchange of local authorities' land. Sections 23 and 26 of the Town and Country Planning Act 1959 purport to relax statutory requirements which exist for ministerial approval of any disposal of land by local authorities and related bodies such as river authorities and statutory water undertakers.

The general provision in these sections, that such ministerial consent is no longer needed, is subject to sweeping exceptions. Thus if such land was acquired by any such authority under compulsory powers it still cannot be appropriated to a different purpose (s 23 (2) (b)) without ministerial consent, nor disposed of if it has not been so appropriated (s 26 (2) (b)), without such consent; nor can any such land be disposed of without ministerial consent for less than market value (s 26 (4)); and there are other categories of exception. But the extent of the power of disposal of land acquired by public bodies[12] does not seem to have been greatly tested in the courts up to the present time.[13]

Appropriation to another purpose is akin to both acquisition and disposal, the only real difference being that it is a transfer from use for

---

11  Sections 127 to 132. A right of pre-emption is given first to the original owners, and then to neighbouring owners, if these sections apply. See *London and South Western Rly Co v Gomm* (1882) 20 Ch D 562; also ch 2, p 34, footnote 5.

12  See ch 11, p 235, below, in respect of land held 'for planning purposes'.

13  A curious recent case is *Laverstock Property Co Ltd v Peterborough Corpn* [1972] 3 All ER 678, [1972] 1 WLR 1400. It is an object lesson in how to dispose of public authority land unwisely. In *Great Western Rly Co v May* (1874) LR 7 HL 283, the House of Lords held that land required under the 'all or nothing' rule (see pp 101–104, below) can be disposed of as 'superfluous lands'. But, as stated above, the 'superfluous lands' provisions are now normally excluded from compulsory purchases.

one statutory purpose to use for another statutory purpose of the same authority—which means in practice a *local* authority since local authorities are multi-purpose authorities. Ministerial consent is normally needed.[14] Any consequential interference with private rights over such land should, on principle, be compensatable but not subject to restraint by injunction, just as if the land had been acquired instead of appropriated. Indeed, if there is appropriation (or acquisition) 'for planning purposes', the Town and Country Planning Act 1971, s 127,[15] makes express provision to that effect.[16]

**14** Town and Country Planning Act 1959, s 23 (1) (b); Local Government Act 1972, s 122.
**15** On this, see ch 11, p 238, below.
**16** For appropriation, see *Dowty Boulton Paul Ltd v Wolverhampton Corpn (No 2)* [1976] Ch 13, [1973] 2 All ER 491. Yet that decision was contradicted by another: *Earl of Leicester v Wells-next-the-Sea UDC* [1973] Ch 110, [1972] 3 All ER 77. In both cases the appropriation was for housing. The *Dowty Boulton Paul Ltd* case in effect treats appropriation in the same way as acquisition (which would seem to be the logical and sensible approach) but the *Earl of Leicester's* case unfortunately does not.

# Chapter 5

# Land taken

## A. Land ownership in law and equity

### 1 MEANING OF 'LAND'

It is one of the dangers of the study of any branch of law that the complexity of legal rules and procedures distracts from the subject-matter, or perhaps distorts its importance. So here: the discussion of the statutory and conveyancing procedures in compulsory purchase almost makes the student forget to ask what it is that is being compulsorily purchased.

The problem is the same as in private land law. What in fact is 'land'? It is very different from corporeal chattels—moveable objects—in that the physical substance cannot be picked up and used. If this appears to be happening, it is really the produce of the land which is picked up and used—soil, minerals, crops—not the 'land' itself. The ownership of land is in truth a territorial concept. A 'landowner' is a person officially recognised as having certain rights of authority and control within certain boundaries, however constricting the boundaries and however limited the rights. Within a given set of boundaries there is a general right to control; but superimposed on it there can exist many special rights *'in alieno solo'* which detract from it. The general right to control can itself be divided in terms of time, or it can be perpetual; and in addition the benefits which normally exist inseparably from these various rights can be separated from them and as a result can be enjoyed independently of them in equity.

Chattels, and intangible rights such as the goodwill of a business,[1] are not subject to compulsory purchase. If they are destroyed, or their owner is deprived of them for some other reason, then the authority will normally have to pay him damages, or disturbance[2] compensation, depending on whether the loss was caused avoidably or unavoidably.

Soil, minerals, crops, fixtures (including buildings) are part of the land so long as they remain attached to it, on general principles of common law; compulsory purchase passes their ownership to the acquiring authority along with the land to which they are attached, just as in a free

1 See *Bailey v Derby Corpn*, discussed below in ch 10, p 204.
2 See below, ch 10.

80

market transaction. But an owner has a choice in the matter, which the acquiring body must accept—he can sever fixtures and the like, and sell the land free of them or sell them to the authority, unsevered, as part of the land.[3]

If fixtures, crops and so forth are not severed it is possible to arrange that they are dealt with by means of a separate valuation. Timber is often dealt with in this way.[4] Presumably neither party can compel the other to make a separate valuation, or to resist it, unless the Lands Tribunal as a question of valuation decides that it would be unreasonable to do otherwise. Obviously a separate valuation must not be a mere contrivance to increase compensation.

An acquiring authority in a normal case will wish to obtain the perpetual right to full control of land without any subtraction of the benefits whether in terms of present or future control, or of enjoyment as distinct from control, or of separate rights *in alieno solo*. They will wish to obtain the unincumbered legal fee simple absolute in possession, with vacant possession. If this state of affairs does not exist over any particular land it will be because separate rights of enjoyment or control—leases, easements, equitable interests—have come into existence as against the legal freehold; and the authority will wish to buy them all out together and so reconstitute the unincumbered legal fee simple absolute in possession, with vacant possession. Cases will be considered where acquiring bodies do not need or wish to do this, or where they cannot do it.[5] But normally acquiring bodies do not desire to share the control and enjoyment of the land they acquire with any other landowner of whatever kind. It is a practical problem in every case whether they can achieve that aim, or need to achieve it, and how they achieve it.

Section 7 (1) of the Acquisition of Land Act 1981 interprets 'land', 'in relation to compulsory purchase under any enactment', as including 'anything falling within any definition of the expression in that enactment'. In other words, look up the authorising Act. Section 1 (3) of the 1965 Act has an essentially similar interpretation. Some authorising Acts contain such a definition and some do not. The Land Compensation Act 1961 (not an authorising Act) has a more detailed definition than most, namely 'any corporeal hereditament, including a building as defined by section, and includes any interest or right in or over land and any right to water'; while 'building', as defined, 'includes any structure or erection and any part of a building as so defined, but does not include plant or machinery comprised in a building'. The definitions of 'land' and

---

3  See *Gibson v Hammersmith and City Rly Co*, discussed below in ch 10, p 208. If he severs fixtures etc. he can then obtain compensation for consequential loss in value reasonably and naturally incurred in respect of them.

4  See *Re Hasluck, Sully v Duffin* [1957] 3 All ER 371, [1957] 1 WLR 1135.

5  See later in this chapter, in relation to leaseholds, easements, etc. See also *London and Westcliff Properties Ltd v Minister of Housing and Local Government* (ch 3, p 53).

'building' in the Town and Country Planning Act 1971 are very similar to those in the 1961 Act.[6]

Statutory definitions of 'land', therefore, give little, if any, help. This is not surprising because in truth it is not 'land' which is compulsorily purchased but *rights* in land, just as in free market property transactions. A compulsory purchase, even of an unencumbered owner-occupied freehold with vacant possession, has no effect whatever on the physical nature of any land. What it does do is enable an authority wishing to carry out some public works project to do so on the land selected for that project because the requisite property rights are in the authority's hands and in no others. Timing of the work is then a matter for that authority.

Decided cases establish that authorities can normally expropriate freeholds and leaseholds, in law and in equity, under their standard compulsory purchase powers. Yet this is nowhere expressly stated. The cases treat it as implicit in the statutes. In addition, authorities cannot obtain lesser rights, except such as are appurtenant to freeholds or leaseholds as 'dominant' or 'benefited' land, unless the contrary is expressly authorised in some relevant statute.

What expropriation strictly achieves is: (1) in respect of a legal freehold, the compulsory conveyance of the title to that freehold; (ii) in respect of a legal leasehold, the compulsory assignment of the title to that leasehold; (iii) in respect of equitable freeholds and leaseholds, the compulsory transfer of the right to those interests. In practice equitable interests are merely extinguished on payment of their value to their owners; and the separate benefit conferred by each one is merged back into the legal estate from which it was derived. Merger is also the fate of legal leaseholds and reversions, unless there is some exceptional reason for retaining them as separate entities.[7]

If land is owned in separate but adjacent parcels, there may be a dispute as to whether these should be aggregated or be considered separately. In *Rothera and Goddard v Nottingham City Council*,[8] two groups of cottages fronting on to the same road were compulsorily purchased. They had all been in one ownership at one time, but eventually the group of even-numbered and the group of odd-numbered cottages respectively devolved under two separate trusts under the terms of a will. The titles to both groups were eventually re-united in the same trustees. It was established that, taken together, the two groups would have a higher market value than the aggregate of values of the two groups treated separately. It was held that, because of the separate trusts, they must be treated separately. In view of what was said by Lord Watson in

---

6 The Land Compensation Act 1973 does not contain any definition of 'land'.
7 It seems clear that there is no distinction, for compulsory purchase purposes, between registered and unregistered land.
8 (1980) 39 P & CR 613.

the House of Lords in *Cowper-Essex v Acton Local Board*, which is discussed in a later chapter, it may be that this ought to be reconsidered.[9]

## 2 EQUITABLE INTERESTS

Acquisition of an unincumbered and undivided legal fee simple absolute in possession, with vacant possession, is the standard procedure. If legal ownership is split into a freehold reversion and one or more leaseholds, any or all of these may be acquired except, in the normal case, leases or tenancies for a term, fixed or periodic, of a year or less. If the beneficial interest in land is enjoyed separately in equity under a trust or settlement, as in the case of life interests and entails, infants' interests and other equitable rights, the normal conveyancing practice under the Settled Land Act 1925 and the Law of Property Act 1925 applies as it would in any private transaction, and so the legal estate is conveyed to the purchasing authority while the separate equitable interests are 'over-reached'. But commercial equitable interests not subject to over-reaching are entitled to be acquired and paid for in their own right, so long as they amount to equitable freeholds and leaseholds. This means that estate contracts, including options, and equitable mortgages, charges and liens are to be compensated for; but restrictive covenants and equitable easements and profits à prendre are not. Rights created in equity by propriety estoppel will no doubt be compensatable also, provided that they are rights in the freehold or in a leasehold.[10]

In *Rogers v Kingston-upon-Hull Dock Co*,[11] a yearly tenant had obtained under an agreement with his landlord an option either to remove buildings put up by him as tenant or to receive a proportion of their value by a charge on the land, should his tenancy be determined in less than 20 years. On compulsory purchase his tenancy came to an end by notice to quit after seven years. Thus there was no question of expropriating a legal leasehold interest; but the tenant's charge represented an equitable leasehold interest extinguished by the acquisition, and compensatable in respect of the 13 years still remaining out of the 20 covered by the agreement.[12]

In *Oppenheimer v Minister of Transport*,[13] the claimant held an option

---

9  See below, ch 9, p 179. That case concerned injurious affection; but the principle seems generally applicable.
10  The equity in such cases arises from conduct, not contract, though the underlying idea is that an obligation exists in either situation. See *Crabb v Arun District Council* [1976] Ch 179, [1975] 3 All ER 865, and cases therein cited.
11  (1864) 5 New Rep 26.
12  The claimant's charge, enforceable against his landlord, represented a share in the value of the property which in consequence reduced the value to the landlord. Compulsory purchase compensation had to reflect this.
13  [1942] 1 KB 242, [1941] 3 All ER 485. Such options are estate contracts. But the right to serve a notice desiring to acquire the freehold reversion to a long lease of a house under

to purchase the freehold of fields being acquired for a trunk road in Berkshire. This was an equitable freehold interest extinguished by the acquisition, and so compensatable.

In *Blamires v Bradford Corpn*,[14] trustees of a will were empowered to allow the testatrix's son to occupy business premises for as long as he wished at a specified weekly rent. The son duly exercised this option; subsequently the defendant corporation compulsorily purchased the property under the Housing Act 1957. The High Court held that the option created an equitable lease for the plaintiff's life,[15] when exercised, and was compensatable on that basis. As an estate contract, like other options and equitable leases by agreement, it ought to have been registered as a Class C (iv) land charge,[16] but was not. This, however, did not take away the right to compensation. Land charge registration is only necessary to protect an interest from being overridden by a transaction that inherently purports to disregard that interest or to take effect on a basis inconsistent with it. Or it might be put a little differently by saying that the doctrines of notice, and registration in lieu of notice, exist only for the necessary protection of bona fide purchasers for value without that notice. Either an acquiring authority with statutory powers are not to be put in this category (except where claimants do not come forward and so are unascertained for that reason) or else the owner of the equitable interest has in any case, notice or no notice, lost his essential equitable remedy of specific performance because that is inconsistent with the compulsory purchase.[17] The claimant can in fact demand only his proper share of the market value purchase price compensation; and since (and in so far as) he is an ascertained party, there is no justification for refusing it to him.

In *Hillingdon Estates Co v Stonefield Estates*,[18] the position is slightly less obvious. That decision on the face of it amounts merely to this, that a compulsory purchase order does not prevent a court from awarding specific performance of a contract to sell land. But the implications which follow from the decision, quite consistently with the other cases

the Leasehold Reform Act 1967 is not an option, or any other property right, and so is not compensatable: *Johnson v Sheffield City Council* (1982) 43 P & CR 272. Actual service of such a notice, however, would create a property interest in equity.

14 [1964] Ch 585, [1964] 2 All ER 603.
15 By virtue of Law of Property Act 1925, s 149 (6), this took effect as a lease for 90 years determinable on the tenant's death.
16 For this, see now the Land Charges Act 1972, s 2 (4).
17 He could thus only be entitled to a sum of money equivalent to damages for breach of the agreement to grant him the lease. The equitable lessor *would* have been liable to pay this sum had he received from a purchaser without notice a price representing the full value of the property with vacant possession. The sum would have represented the value of the equitable lessee's interest. When paid as compulsory purchase compensation it goes direct from the acquiring body to the equitable lessee, and does not reach him via the lessor in the form of damages.
18 [1952] Ch 627, [1952] 1 All ER 853. See above, p 31.

discussed above, are as follows. The property has already, by virtue of the contract, passed to the purchaser in equity; so that, if the compulsory purchase were fully completed before the prior private transaction, the purchaser under that transaction would have his equitable freehold (or leasehold) expropriated. Whereas, if the prior private transaction were fully completed first, the legal right to the land as well as the equitable would be taken from the private purchaser, instead of remaining outstanding in the private vendor and being taken directly from him.

More recently, the decision of the Court of Appeal in *D H N Food Distributors Ltd v Tower Hamlets London Borough*[19] shows that for the purpose of compulsory purchase compensation no less than for other purposes the law gives recognition to equitable interests such as those arising out of contractual licences (or other licences where the licensor's right of revocation is restricted), and likewise those existing under a trust. An equitable right, like a legal estate, is therefore compensatable on the basis that it is an asset of which the acquiring body are depriving its owner, who should receive its capital value in recompense.

## 3 THE TOTALITY OF OWNERSHIP

These equitable rights, separately compensatable, should not be regarded as additional burdens for the acquiring authority. Their true significance is that of separate parts of the totality of ownership, which in cases such as those just described are paid for separately instead of together. Thus if the unencumbered legal fee simple absolute in possession, with vacant possession, in Blackacre has a market value of £100,000, there should not in principle be any addition to this figure if separate rights are carved out of this undivided totality of ownership. If therefore a leasehold interest worth £70,000 has been created just before the compulsory purchase order, the market value of the freehold reversion should be £30,000; or if an option worth £51,000 has been granted, the legal freehold as it now is, incumbered by that option, is worth only £49,000. If an outright contract of sale has come into existence, the entire capital value of the land has passed to the purchaser and the vendor's right in it survives as a purely nominal one, accompanied by his substantive right against the purchaser under the contract, on a personal basis, to receive the contract price—which may or may not coincide with the compulsory purchase compensation at 'market value' payable to the private purchaser by the authority acquiring from him. The same principle gives similar results where the land is mortgaged.

It would be wrong to assert that the undivided totality of value of an unincumbered legal freehold with vacant possession will be exactly the

**19** [1976] 3 All ER 462, [1976] 1 WLR 852. The compensation in dispute was that payable for disturbance (see below, ch 10, p 199).

same figure as the sum of separate compensatable interests in that same land. For example the market value of commercial premises such as a shop is often actually *less* unlet than let: but that is only because of a general assumption in practice that the last thing the landlord wants in such a case is possession. The departure of the commercial tenant, in other words, is normally not an opportunity to 'marry' possession with the reversion and so aggregate the value of both; it is merely an unwelcome hiatus in the flow of revenue derived from having a thriving tenant in occupation. But it is a different matter if the landlord actually wants to take possession and to become an owner-occupier, in order either to run his own business on the property or redevelop it.

The assessment of value of any interest in land, for compulsory purchase purposes or otherwise, is a task for a valuer, not a lawyer; and a valuer may well find that special factors have to be taken into account in various different situations. But broadly speaking there is, for legal purposes, an overall value of land which will be shared out when lesser interests in that land are created, leaving a residue for the legal freeholder which may be no more than nominal in some cases. In short, it should make comparatively little difference to an acquiring authority whether the ownership of the land is subject to lesser interests or not.

One point which must be stressed here arises from the fact that lesser freehold rights (like leaseholds, discussed below[20]) are capable of being created and terminated, and so differ from *legal* freehold title ('fee simple absolute in possession') which is perpetual ownership without beginning or end. Compulsory purchase of legal freehold is unambiguous, because it can only mean compulsory transfer of the existing right and can never involve either compulsory creation or termination of that right. But lesser freeholds, which can only exist in equity, always arise by individual creation and are often of limited duration as well. In practice this is more likely to cause problems in relation to commercial equitable freeholds, including options and other interests founded on contingent contracts as well as those estate contracts which are not contingent. The point at issue here in regard to lesser freeholds—namely, can they be compulsorily *created* as distinct from being compulsorily transferred?—also arises for leaseholds, which are examined separately below. Acquiring bodies will not normally relish such complications; but sometimes they might wish to act in this way, and the rule is that they cannot do so in the absence of clear statutory authorisation.

It may be noted here that in *Williams v British Gas Corpn*,[1] the Court of Appeal held that because the claim property was owned by joint tenants, unless all of them claimed together the claim must fail. The claim was for depreciation under the Land Compensation Act 1973, Part I,[2] but the principle would seem to be generally applicable.

## 4 SQUATTERS

It often happens that a person with title to land, by virtue of which he has the right to possession, acquiesces in its possession by some other person without such right—ie a trespasser—and the latter intentionally treats the land as if in fact he has a right to it, which makes him what is usually called a 'squatter'. After (normally) 12 years of such 'adverse possession' the rightful owner's title is extinguished under the Limitation Act 1980. But even before that time the 'squatter', though liable to ejection if proceedings are brought by the true owner, is entitled to resist any third party who attempts to deprive him of the land. 'Squatter's rights' are thus 'good against the whole world', except for the rightful owner during the 12-year limitation period, and the intentional possession thus gives the squatter a right to the land which all persons must respect (except the true owner) from the very outset. This includes acquiring authorities. Hence if the rightful owner does not appear, the squatter will be able to claim that compulsory purchase compensation is payable to him. This contention was upheld by the Privy Council in *Perry v Clissold*.[3]

# B. Leaseholds and licences

## 1 DISTINCTION BETWEEN TERMS EXCEEDING, AND NOT EXCEEDING, A YEAR

If any of the land subject to compulsory purchase is in the possession of a person having no greater interest in the land than as tenant for a year or from year to year, and if that person is required to give up possession of any land so occupied by him before the expiration of his term or interest in the land, he shall be entitled to compensation for the value of his unexpired term or interest in the land, and for any just allowance which ought to be made to him by an incoming tenant, and for any loss or injury he may sustain.

This important provision, contained in s 20 (1) of the 1965 Act, regulates the acquisition of fixed term or periodic tenancies for a year or less. It is curious because it takes for granted an assumption, made and acted on by the courts, that such tenancies are not in the normal case to be compulsorily purchased at all. The acquiring body should obtain the legal estate or estates in reversion, and then serve notice to quit as a private landlord would. Clearly this will normally suit an acquiring authority,

---

2 See below, ch 9, p 187.
3 [1907] AC 73. Presumably, however, the authority will be well advised to pay the compensation into court, leaving the 'squatter' to apply for it, if there is any possibility of the true owner appearing and laying claim to it (see above, ch 4, p 75).

rather than have to go through all the procedural stages of expropriation merely to acquire an interest which will come to an end before they are likely to want to go into physical possession; and indeed they may well adopt the same policy towards appreciably longer leaseholds if they are in no hurry.

Presumably tenancies at will (and at sufferance) come within s 20, though in practice it is obvious that no compensation would be payable to such tenants since there is no length of term to which they are entitled. But on the instantaneous termination of their interests such tenants will normally have the status of licensees, with a right to a period of notice which is reasonable in all the circumstances before they can be required to depart (on pain of being trespassers thereafter). The position of licensees is discussed below.[4]

The crucial time under s 20 is the date when the authority require to go into physical possession. If this is so soon that a tenancy for a year or less cannot be left to determine at common law, the section applies to the situation. It follows that a notice to treat can be served in respect of a lease of over a year, that no action need be taken until the lease has less than a year to run, and that the authority can then serve a notice of entry and take possession and pay compensation under s 20, which they could not have done before: authority for this is the decision in *R v Kennedy*.[5]

It has been held that in such a case there is no need to serve a notice to quit upon a periodic tenant even though that is essential to terminate his interest at common law. The alleged ground for this is that entry (not notice of entry) impliedly has the effect of a notice to quit so that the 'unexpired term or interest in the land' (s 20) is valued as continuing until the date on which a valid notice to quit, if served when entry actually occurred, would have taken effect (*Greenwoods Tyre Services Ltd v Manchester Corpn*).[6] The reasoning is doubtful, there being no obvious statutory or common law authority for it. Compulsory purchase statutes empower authorities to *acquire* rights, not to terminate them. Termination can therefore only occur under the existing rules of common law varied by the relevant statutes such as those relating to the law of landlord and tenant. Nevertheless the approach adopted in the *Greenwoods Tyre Services Ltd* case is likely to be followed in practice for the sake of convenience.

If, however, a general vesting declaration is executed this vests the legal title in the acquiring body automatically except for tenancies for a year or less and longer leases which are specified; the older procedure can then be used in respect of these, starting with a notice to treat however

---

4  See p 95.
5  [1893] 1 QB 533. (Discussed further in ch 6, p 120, below).
6  (1971) 23 P & CR 246. The main substance of the valuation of such an interest—domestic or trade disturbance (see ch 10)—must therefore be assessed in relation to that period of time.

short the tenancy, if the authority cannot wait until they determine. But apart from this, 'a notice to treat . . . is not a necessary preliminary step. On the other hand . . . it is perfectly proper for the acquiring authority to give such a notice if it thinks fit . . .', in order to give advance warning and obtain details of claims.[7]

*Newham London Borough Council v Benjamin*, from which the foregoing quotation comes, is the leading modern case on this subject. The claimant had a lease with less than a year to run. The acquiring body served a notice to treat on him as well as on his landlords. He argued that this entitled him to have compensation assessed regardless of when they would take possession. The Court of Appeal rejected this claim. Lord Denning MR said that

the whole subject of the legislation was to put short tenancies on a special footing because they were short. Even if [the tenant] is given notice to treat, it only means that compensation is to be assessed 'in the manner directed by the said Act . . .', ie in accordance with [s 20].[8]

Consequently he was not entitled to any compensation unless actually required to give up possession before his interest came to an end.

By contrast, in *Runcorn AFC v Warrington and Runcorn Development Corpn*[9] notice to treat was served on a leaseholder with two and a half years to run, followed by eight weeks' notice of entry when there remained less than a year to run. The Lands Tribunal rejected the authority's argument that s 20 applied, because that point is to be settled by reference to the notice to treat—which fixes the interest to be acquired—not the notice of entry—which is merely concerned with enabling an authority to take physical possession before acquiring title.

If a valid notice to quit all or part of an agricultural holding is served on the tenant *after* an acquiring authority have agreed to buy out the landlord or have served (or are deemed to have served) notice to treat on the latter, and because the land is required for a non-agricultural use by the acquiring body the tenant cannot resist the notice to quit (whether it is served by the original landlord or by the authority in their rôle as assignee landlord),[10] s 59 of the Land Compensation Act 1973 now gives the tenant a choice. This is, either to let the notice to quit take effect in the ordinary way, or to go out of possession as if he were being expropriated by notice of entry so as to bring into play s 20 of the 1965 Act. If he elects to follow the latter course he must give written notice of his election to the authority, and then give up possession on or before the date of termination under the notice to quit. He can claim compensation

7 *Newham London Borough Council v Benjamin* [1968] 1 All ER 1195 at 1200, per Widgery LJ (as he then was).
8 Ibid at p 1199.
9 (1983) 45 P & CR 183.
10 On this, see *Dawson v Norwich City Council* (1978) 37 P & CR 516.

as if dispossessed by notice of entry on the day before the date of termination.

## 2 CREATION, TERMINATION AND INCIDENTS OF LEASEHOLDS

A matter about which very little authority exists is the question whether compulsory powers can lawfully be exercised in regard to leaseholds not by procuring their transfer to acquiring bodies but by allowing the latter to create new leaseholds for their own benefit or to extinguish old leaseholds which they do not want.

The latter course of action is something they appear to be doing all the time; but this is (in law) an illusion. If leaseholds come to an end in a compulsory purchase what in fact happens in legal terms is either (a) acquiring bodies transfer leaseholds to themselves and continue in the role of tenants themselves or, more usually, merge the leaseholds into the reversions they acquire at the same time from the landlords, or (b) acquiring bodies acquire reversions alone and then, as new landlords, turn out the tenants within the terms of the law of landlord and tenant by notice to quit or otherwise—which in strict theory means ensuring that there is no renewal of the tenant's contractual term. Extinguishment of easements and other rights *in alieno solo* is another matter, and is discussed below.[11]

The former course of action, the creation of new leaseholds, is lawful but only when expressly authorised by sufficiently clear statutory wording. These cases are exceptions to the general rule which is otherwise, as Lord Wilberforce made clear in *Sovmots Investments Ltd v Secretary of State for the Environment*.[12] The question of creation of new rights by virtue of compulsory powers, however, extends more widely than leaseholds, and is discussed below, in connection with easements and other rights *in alieno solo*.[13]

A landlord's reversion is a 'bundle of rights' which includes the benefit of the tenant's covenants (and the converse is true of the landlord's covenants in relation to the tenancy). In *Leek v Birmingham City Council*[14] the Lands Tribunal stressed that the benefit of a tenant's covenant to repair was 'a genuine property right of the landlord' and must be taken account of in valuing the claimant's freehold reversion. Conversely, in *Khan v Birmingham City Council*[15] the Court of Appeal held that, since the vendor's property was tenanted when it was acquired, he could not claim compensation as if he enjoyed vacant possession.

11 See p 100.
12 [1977] 2 All ER 385 at p 393 'A power to acquire a right over land cannot authorise compulsion of an owner of land . . . to grant new rights over that land. . . .'—see above, ch 2, p 25.
13 See p 98.
14 (1982) 44 P & CR 125.
15 (1980) 40 P & CR 412. See below, ch 6, p 122.

## 3 STATUTORILY PROTECTED TENANTS

Statutory protection of tenants does not prevail against compulsory purchase, no matter whether acquiring bodies expropriate the tenants direct, or displace their landlords. The statutes do not expressly say this, but it is implicit in their provisions.

As regards residential tenants, the Rent Act 1977 provides, in s 14, that local authorities and other bodies providing public housing are exempt from control, and in s 98 that a court may make an order for possession of a dwelling if satisfied that this is reasonable and that suitable alternative accommodation is or will be made available to a protected or statutory tenant of it. Section 144 of, and the Ninth Schedule to, the Housing Act 1957 used to provide that in statutory acquisitions of land generally the 'undertakers' must not enter into possession until the Secretary of State had approved a scheme for rehousing, or decided that none was needed, where 30 or more residents were displaced; but these provisions were repealed by the Land Compensation Act 1973 and replaced by a more broadly conceived set of rules for rehousing, which are considered in chapter 10.

The availability of other premises, whether provided by themselves or some other authority, for rehousing an expropriated residential occupier—that is to say one from whom the freehold or leasehold of his home is being compulsorily purchased—has in the past been treated by some acquiring bodies as a factor which offsets the extent of his interest, so that they would reduce his compensation accordingly. Section 50 of the Land Compensation Act 1973 now prohibits this. With regard to the landlords of residential tenants being rehoused on compulsory purchase, s 50 conversely prohibits the payment of any item of compensation attributable to an increase in value of the reversion by reason of the tenant's departure, provided that the tenancy existed at the date of the actual or deemed notice to treat. These provisions are not confined to statutorily protected dwellings. It should be noted that it is generally to an acquiring authority's advantage financially that premises being acquired are tenanted, whether statutorily protected or not, rather than owner-occupied, for reasons discussed below in connection with business premises.[16]

In regard to business tenancies, protected under Part II of the Landlord and Tenant Act 1954 (as amended), Lord Denning MR, in *Benjamin's* case discussed above, referred to this aspect of the claimant's position as follows, in relation to the legal position at that time (ie before 1973).

It is true that, apart from the compulsory acquisition, he would have been entitled to apply for a new tenancy. Parliament, however, has enacted that his

16 See p 94.

compensation under [s 20 of the 1965 Act] is to be assessed without regard to his right to apply for a new tenancy [see s 39 (1) of the Act of 1954]. It expressly says that he is to be no worse off than if his landlord intended to demolish the premises or wanted them for his own business [see s 39 (2)], in which case he would have been compensated by being paid twice the rateable value [see s 37 (2) of the Act of 1954].[17]

Section 39 (1) of the Act of 1954 was repealed by s 47 of the Land Compensation Act 1973, which now provides that a business tenant is to have the benefit of his statutory protection taken into account when compulsory purchase compensation is assessed. Conversely the landlord's compensation must be assessed on the basis that he holds the reversion to a protected and not an unprotected tenant. The substance of the protection is the tenant's right to apply to the court for a new tenancy; and the three possible outcomes of such an application are that (i) the tenant will get a new tenancy, unless the landlord successfully opposes this either (ii) on a ground which arises from the tenant's shortcomings or (iii) on a ground which does not so arise—for example a genuine practicable intention to redevelop the property. Outcome (i) means that the tenant gets the benefit of protection directly, by staying on; outcome (iii) means that he gets the benefit in money form, as compensation for not staying on; outcome (ii) means that he gets the benefit in neither form, because he is undeserving.

If only the landlord of business premises is expropriated, and not the tenant, the acquiring authority are normally put on the same footing as that landlord. In principle they would be able to defeat the tenant's claim for a new tenancy because the purpose of their acquisition will involve redevelopment. This is not a purpose that the expropriated landlord could have relied on. Section 47 of the 1973 Act requires it to be assumed (contrary to reality) that neither the authority nor any other body with compulsory purchase powers are acquiring the property. Therefore there is no ground left for dispossessing the tenant under the 1954 Act,

---

17 Sections 57 and 58, of the Landlord and Tenant Act 1954, empower government departments to issue certificates to landlords and superior landlords who are public bodies, stating that in the public interest, or for reasons of national security, the use of land let must be changed by a stated date. Such certificates (which must not be issued without first affording to the tenants affected a chance to make representations) will operate to prevent the grant of new business tenancies, subject to the payment of compensation under s 37 of that Act, as already mentioned. In *R v Minister of Transport, ex p W H Beech-Allen Ltd* (1963) 16 P & CR 145, a local authority requiring land for a road-widening scheme made a deal with the leaseholder, who was their own tenant nearing the end of his business tenancy, that they would exclude the land from the compulsory purchase order if the tenant would concede the leasehold to be now no more than a yearly tenancy. The authority then applied for, and got, a s 57 certificate, for use in opposing the tenant's claim for a new tenancy. The tenant applied to the Queen's Bench Divisional Court for certiorari to quash the certificate. The court held the issue of the certificate to be intra vires s 57, and not in breach of the agreement with the authority.

and the market value of the landlord's interest falls accordingly. If, however, the landlord already had independent grounds for opposing the grant of a new tenancy when his own expropriation supervened, the market value of his reversion should (in principle, at any rate) be the higher for it. In either case, however, the question of granting a new tenancy may still lie some way in the future if the tenant has a contractual term with time still to run, and it will be all the more likely that (short of liability to forfeiture, which defeats the tenant's protection in any case) there will be no prospect of the landlord's recovering possession. If therefore the authority choose to expropriate the landlord and not the tenant in such circumstances, they need only pay for his reversion a market value price which recognises the tenant's position as being pretty securely protected: in other words comparatively little. But they will not have got possession.

If, however, the authority expropriate the business *tenant*, or take possession of the property under a notice of entry or some analogous procedure, they must compensate him accordingly. Compensation for the tenant's interest, like the landlord's, goes on the footing that the tenant is protected, as s 47 prescribes. As before, the threat of compulsory purchase, involving redevelopment as it must normally do, has to be disregarded as a prospective reason for dispossession under the 1954 Act; so that unless the existing landlord has an independent ground for recovering possession the tenant must be compensated as being fully protected.

In theory, therefore, s 47 of the 1973 Act pushes the tenant's compensation up and pulls the landlord's compensation down, by the same factor. Since the 1954 Act is to apply on the basis of the tenant's being protected against dispossession, the position is as if the landlord or the tenant or both, as the case may be, were assigning their interest to the acquiring body. The capital value of the landlord's reversion will clearly be lower on the open market if it relates to a fully protected tenancy. Yet there need not be a corresponding increase in the capital value of the tenancy. That value is likely to be minimal because the rent under the tenancy will be a market rent (even though controlled) which means that substantially all the value of the premises goes to the landlord. An assignee of the tenancy will not be disposed to pay a significant sum to the assigning tenant on top of the market rent which will be payable to the landlord, and security of tenure does not affect this. (On the other hand, scarcity and demand may sometimes give such tenancies a market value notwithstanding the obligation to pay a full market rent.) It is only when a leasehold has been granted for appreciably less than a market rent that it constitutes an asset commanding any market value on assignment in the way that a freehold does. When leaseholds at market rents are expropriated, the bulk of the compensation payable is 'disturbance', which will be discussed in ch 10, rather than capital value.

It follows from this that although the change in the law of leasehold compensation made by the 1973 Act apparently benefits tenants at the expense of landlords, in substance it benefits *acquiring bodies* at the expense of landlords. It is therefore of advantage to acquiring bodies that commercial properties being compulsorily purchased should be currently let to protected tenants rather than owner-occupied. Conversely, when compulsory purchase threatens any property currently let the landlord and tenant are well advised to agree on a merger or surrender so that it will be owner-occupied by the time the acquisition takes place.[18]

A similar state of affairs prevails in regard to farm land. In *Rugby Joint Water Board v Shaw-Fox*,[19] Lord Denning MR reviewed this area of the law as it stood before 1973 and referred to an earlier decision, *Minister of Transport v Pettit*.[20]

In that case we considered the compensation payable to the tenant of a farm on its compulsory acquisition. The majority of this court held that the tenant would get only small compensation because his compensation would have to be assessed on the basis that he could be turned out on 12 months' notice. That decision is in full accord with the Agriculture (Miscellaneous Provisions) Act 1968. Section 42 of that Act provides, in effect, that the tenant's compensation shall be assessed on the basis that he has to go on the expiry of 12 months' notice to quit.[1] (But it is to be noticed that he gets compensation for disturbance under s 9 of that Act, which would be a sum equal to four years' rent.)

The Master of the Rolls went on to say that since a farm tenant without a lease comprising a fixed term for a long period 'only gets small compensation', it must follow that his landlord 'should get large compensation on the basis that at the end of the 12 months he would get vacant possession'. But that is no longer the law.

Section 48 of the Land Compensation Act 1973 now makes a corresponding change for agricultural holdings to that made by section 47 for business tenancies. There are of course differences of detail. Whereas statutory protection for business tenants takes the form of enabling them to apply for new tenancies under the Act of 1954, the Agricultural Holdings Act 1948 protects farm tenants by giving them, after any contractual term is over, a yearly tenancy in respect of which a notice to quit cannot be served by the landlord except on grounds that, very

18  It should further be noted that if property is not in unified owner-occupation it is more difficult to attribute any development value to it over and above the existing use value. On this, see below, ch 8.

19  [1971] 2 QB 14, [1971] 1 All ER 373. The subsequent appeal to the House of Lords is not now relevant.

20  (1968) 20 P & CR 344.

 1  The Agricultural Holdings (Notices to Quit) Act 1977 provides that 12 months is to be the minimum length of a notice to quit for farm tenants, subject to a general right enjoyed by a tenant to retain possession in the absence of any valid reason to turn him out as specified in those provisions.

broadly, correspond with those on which an application for a new business tenancy can be resisted. As in cases of business protection, a farm tenant dispossessed for reasons not arising from any default on his part is compensated for losing his security of tenure; though of course a tenant who is in default is not thus compensated. To this 'disturbance' compensation payable by the landlord under the Act of 1948, s 9 of the Agriculture (Miscellaneous Provisions) Act 1968 adds another sum, also payable by the landlord to the departing tenant, of four times the yearly rent 'to assist in the reorganisation of the tenant's affairs'.[2]

Section 48 of the 1973 Act now requires the compensation payable to expropriated farm landlords and tenants to be assessed on the footing that the possibility of serving a notice to quit, or the fact that a notice to quit has actually been served even if the tenant has already departed as a result of it, must be disregarded if the only justification for the notice is the fact that the land is required for use by an acquiring authority. This repeals s 42 of the Act of 1968 referred to by Lord Denning MR in the passage quoted above, and reverses its effect. But s 12 of the Act of 1968, which applies to cases of compulsory purchase the provisions of s 9 concerning payment for 'reorganisation of the tenant's affairs', remains in force. Therefore to avoid duplication any amount due under that section to the departing tenant from the acquiring authority must be deducted from the expropriation compensation also due from them to the tenant. Yet if his compensation would have been *larger* but for s 48 of the 1973 Act he must get that larger sum (and see p 89, above for his choice under s 59).[3]

In theory, therefore, 'large compensation' now goes to farm tenant's and 'small compensation' to farm landlords, instead of the reverse before 1973 as stated by Lord Denning MR. But the general comments made above about business tenancies apply also to farm tenancies; so that it is acquiring authorities rather than farm tenants who will profit from the reduction of payments to landlords under s 48.

## 4 LICENCES

In principle it might be thought that licences are altogether outside the scope of compulsory purchase. As far as the common law is concerned this is probably true. But in recent years the law relating to licences has been developed in such a way as now to make clear that a great many equitable interests arise out of licences, for example interests by way of

---

2 On this, see below, ch 10, p 215.

3 Often, an acquiring authority will come to an agreement with the tenant as to terms on which he will leave of his own accord. See *Wakerley v St Edmundsbury Borough Council* (1978) 38 P & CR 551, in which there was a deed of surrender of a farmer's agricultural tenancy to the authority as his new landlord, in consideration of a licence for him to continue to occupy and farm and retain the profits of farming; the Court of Appeal upheld his entitlement to the benefit of these profits.

equitable estoppel and constructive trusts.[4] Such rights are presumably equitable freeholds and leaseholds. The equitable principles underlying these rules are concerned with total or partial restriction of the licensor's right to revoke. If therefore they do not have the effect of clearly allowing revocation within a year or less, s 20 of the Compulsory Purchase Act 1965 (see above, p 87) presumably cannot apply.

## C.  New rights and rights less than full occupation

### 1 BENEFITS, BURDENS AND NEW RIGHTS

It has been shown above that as a general rule acquiring authorities cannot insist on obtaining rights in land in the form of newly-created interests such as new legal or equitable leases, or new equitable freeholds (such as options). Nevertheless they will be able to insist on such grants if it can be shown that clear express statutory authority exists for this. Such authority has been rare in the past, but is now becoming more common. Linked with this is the problem of rights '*in alieno solo*' such as restrictive covenants, easements, profits à prendre and other servitudes. Three distinct possibilities need to be considered. Is land being compulsorily acquired which has an easement appurtenant to it as a *dominant* tenement? Or is land being compulsorily acquired which is subject to an easement as a *servient* tenement? Or is a new right in land being compulsorily acquired purely as an easement or some other right less than full freehold or leasehold occupation *usque ad coelum et ad inferos*?

To take the last question first, the cases establish that a new right less than full occupation cannot be taken compulsorily over land unless an authorising Act clearly so provides. If a railway or road is to pass across land by a viaduct or a tunnel, the acquiring authority must still acquire the land in full occupation unless there is clear statutory authority to the contrary. An example of a case in which such authority existed for the compulsory acquisition of a stratum of land below the surface, for an underground railway, is *Metropolitan Rly Co v Fowler*,[5] in which Lord

---

4 See *DHN Food Distributors Ltd v Tower Hamlets London Borough* [1976] 3 All ER 462, [1976] 1 WLR 852. Other leading cases on equitable proprietary estoppel included: *Plimmer v Wellington Corpn* (1884) 9 App Cas 699; *ER Ives Investment Ltd v High* [1967] 1 All ER 504; and *Salvation Army Trustee Co v West Yorkshire Metropolitan County Council* (1980) 41 P & CR 179. See above, p 83, and below, ch 16, p 308.

5 [1893] AC 416. In spite of this decision the legislation (normally private Acts) which authorises such acquisitions usually refers to the taking of 'easements or rights' (or similar terminology). In *Knott Hotels Co Ltd v London Transport Executive* (1975) 31 P & CR 294, the Lands Tribunal again stated that to take a stratum of land for a tunnel is a compulsory purchase in the full sense and is not the mere acquisition of an 'easement' or similar 'right'. In this case the British Transport Commission Act 1955 not only spoke of 'easements or rights' but actually forbade the acquiring authority to 'acquire compulsorily under the powers of this Act any part of the scheduled lands'—ie the lands

Ashbourne said: 'The railway company took more than an easement, they took an interest in land—taking a practically perpetual right of exclusive possession in the tunnel'. Consequently they were liable to pay land tax. Another example is *City and South London Rly Co v St Mary Woolnoth*.[6] But lack of such authority prevented the compulsory acquisition of a stratum below the surface in *Sparrow v Oxford, Worcester and Wolverhampton Rly Co*[7] and of a newly-created easement in *Pinchin v London and Blackwall Rly Co*.[8] If authority does exist to obtain a substratum then a notice to treat must be served: *Farmer v Waterloo and City Rly Co*.[9] As for easements, it must be remembered that if a tunnel were an easement there might be difficulty in identifying its dominant tenement.

The House of Lords has recently emphasised this principle in terms which show that it extends to any new grant, including grants of full occupation as in legal or equitable leaseholds and equitable freeholds such as options and other estate contracts.[10] The facts of the case in question, however, relate to easements. The dispute in this case, *Sovmots Investments Ltd v Secretary of State for the Environment*[11] concerned the property known as Centre Point, at St Giles Circus in London, a development (completed in 1967) consisting of a very tall office block and a connecting bridge linking this to the 'Earnshaw wing' comprising a four-storey commercial building with a flat roof ('podium') supporting on stilts a six-story residential block designed for 36 maisonettes.

The fact that Centre Point remained virtually unused caused considerable public controversy, and in 1972 Camden London Borough Council made a draft compulsory purchase order to acquire the residential block for council housing under Part V of the Housing Act 1957. The essence of the dispute lay in this, that the acquisition would transfer the residential block to separate ownership by the authority, but that such ownership would be useless in practice without easements of access, services and support.

The authorising Act (the Housing Act 1957) did not give the necessary express authority for compulsory creation of easements. The Secretary

along the route of the Victoria Tube Line in London. Obviously this wording was intended to prevent acquisition of properties *at surface level* (other than for stations, etc). But since compulsory acquisition of strata of subsoil is indeed compulsory acquisition of 'part of land', the compulsory purchases for the Victoria Tube Line (and other such projects) were strictly ultra vires; and the Tribunal so held; though for practical purposes the parties required this legal point to be disregarded and their valuation dispute settled as if the law were otherwise, which the Tribunal agreed to.

6 [1905] AC 1.
7 (1852) 2 De GM & G 94.
8 (1854) 5 De GM & G 851.
9 [1895] 1 Ch 527.
10 See the words of Lord Wilberforce quoted in ch 2 (above, p 25).
11 [1977] QB 411, [1977] 2 All ER 385.

of State (and his inspector) took the view that implied authority existed under the rule in *Wheeldon v Burrows*.[12] This rule justifies the implied inclusion (for a purchaser's benefit), in a deed of conveyance which makes no mention of them, of potential easements (as at the time of the conveyance) which are 'continuous and apparent' or 'necessary to the reasonable enjoyment of the property'. The rule applies to free market sales by agreement; the question is whether by analogy with such sales it applies to compulsory acquisitions also.

At first instance Forbes J disagreed with the Secretary of State and quashed the compulsory purchase order. The Court of Appeal agreed with the Secretary of State and restored the order. The House of Lords, by a majority of four to one, disagreed with the Secretary of State and restored the decision of Forbes J to quash the order. Lord Edmund-Davies quoted Lord Parker of Waddington in *Pwllbach Colliery Co Ltd v Woodman*:[13] 'The law will readily imply the grant or reservation of such easements as may be necessary to give effect to the common intention of the parties . . .'; but he denied that this can apply to compulsory acquisitions because 'there is no common intention between an acquiring authority and the party whose property is compulsorily taken from him, and the very basis of implied grants of easements is accordingly absent'. (Whether this is true of agreed sales under the shadow of compulsion is not known.)

## 2 AUTHORISATION OF ACQUISITION BY THE CREATION OF NEW RIGHTS

Even while the *Sovmots* case was still before the House of Lords, Parliament passed the Local Government (Miscellaneous Provisions) Act 1976. Section 13 of and Schedule 1 to this Act make it lawful, where an authorising Act empowers any *local authority* to compulsorily purchase land, for a compulsory purchase order made thereunder to provide that this may be done by the acquisition of a 'new right'. Such rights are 'rights which are not in existence when the order specifying them is made'. The order must therefore specify such a right. Nothing is said by way of limiting the meaning of 'new right' beyond the definition just quoted; so although easements and similar rights are probably envisaged as the most likely kind of 'new right' which will be wanted in practice, yet newly created tenancies are not excluded, nor is anything said by way of excluding equitable interests.

Compensation is expressed to be payable in these cases for 'injurious affection' of other land of the same owner.[14] If the 'new right' relates to land within the scope of the law concerning 'material detriment',[15] the

12 (1879) 12 Ch D 31.
13 [1915] AC 634, at p 646.
14 See ch 9 for 'injurious affection'.
15 See below, p 103.

owner will be entitled to require the authority to acquire his 'interest in the whole of the relevant land' and not merely the 'new right', if 'material detriment' can be established. After notice to treat is served for acquiring a 'new right', the local authority can serve notice of entry 'for the purpose of exercising that right' (which is deemed to have been created when the notice to treat was served).[16]

There were already a great many statutes authorising the taking of new rights. These are usually rights analogous to easements rather than true easements, there being in most cases no genuine dominant tenement.[17] Statutory rights of this kind are as a rule termed 'wayleaves'. Common examples involve pipe-lines for sewers, water-mains, gas and oil, and electricity cables whether in underground conduits or carried above ground on pylons. The acquisition or retention of this kind of right over land has been held, in *Padfield v Eastern Electricity Board*,[18] to be capable of amounting to compulsory purchase. But a true compulsory purchase leads ultimately to the execution of some form of conveyance of the property to the acquiring body, which is unlikely to be the case when all that is needed is to give the authority a compulsory power to place a pipe or cable in or over private land.[19] The practical question is financial, namely that the landowner subjected to the compulsion should be entitled to receive proper compensation. In principle this ought probably to be regarded as the equivalent of depreciation compensation rather than of a purchase price; but in practice the problems of assessment usually lead to reliance upon a standard tariff of a given amount of money for a given length and width of land used, depending on how effectively the necessary interference with the property, whether for installation or for maintenance, can be (and is) made good.

## 3 RIGHTS WHICH ARE NOT INTERFERED WITH

As for existing easements, the law appears to be that, if a dominant tenement is compulsorily acquired, the rights appurtenant to it are acquired with it, as in ordinary private conveyancing. If a servient tenement is compulsorily acquired the rights over it are not acquired but either left undisturbed or else disturbed at the cost of paying compensation for 'injurious affection'. The acquisition of dominant tenements presents no problems. The acquisition of servient land is more likely to give rise to trouble in practice because it is there that the easements and other servitudes actually subsist.

16 Presumably notice to treat is to be served on whichever person (leaseholder or free-holder) has title by virtue of which he could have granted the 'new right' voluntarily instead of compulsorily.
17 Such as the Highways Act 1980, s 250 (compulsory acquisition of 'rights' by highway authorities).
18 (1971) 24 P & CR 423.
19 See the *Knott Hotels Co Ltd* case (above, p 96).

In *Grimley v Minister of Housing and Local Government*,[20] an acquiring authority prepared a compulsory purchase order for an acquisition under a private Act, and included one half of a building comprising two semi-detached houses, each half of which enjoyed the customary easement of support over the other. The second applicants, as owners of the half *not* included in the order, objected to not being served with notice of the order in respect of the easement of support they enjoyed over the half that was so included,[1] claiming to come within the scope of the words 'every owner, lessee and occupier . . . of any land comprised in the order' as stated in the relevant statutory provisions.[2] This claim was alleged to be justified in its turn by the wide definitions of 'land' contained in those provisions, including the private Act, especially since the latter expressly included 'any easement'.

The application was made to the High Court, Queen's Bench Division, to quash the compulsory purchase order. The judge refused,[3] saying that the only question here was whether the second applicants were 'the owners of land within the relevant statutory provisions . . . they qualify as owners of land, if at all'. He pointed out that 'owner' is a term defined in the relevant provision as meaning a person 'entitled to dispose of the fee simple', and also said, 'I do not think that the context or subject does require me to suppose that land includes rights over the same land, any more than it requires me to hold that "owner of land" means "owner of the rights over that land"..' But the right of support would remain.

### 4 RIGHTS WHICH ARE INTERFERED WITH

The failure of the person entitled to an easement over the land being compulsorily purchased to make good his claim, in *Grimley's* case, to be regarded as an 'owner' is in line with several Victorian cases, although strictly these related to notices to treat and not to compulsory purchase orders. Thus in *Duke of Bedford v Dawson*,[4] it was held that interference with an easement over land taken could not be an 'entry' upon 'land' as far as the easement was concerned. A similar decision was reached in relation to a restrictive covenant over land taken, in *Kirby v Harrogate School Board*.[5]

Where easements, restrictive covenants and other such legal or equitable rights over land are interfered with, the proper remedy is

---

20 [1971] 2 QB 96, [1971] 2 All ER 431.
1 At the stage of the compulsory purchase order, the normal assumption is that easements etc. over the land to be acquired will *not* be interfered with. Whether this assumption is right or wrong will only become apparent after the land has actually been acquired. But see above, ch 4, p 77, for rights of common.
2 See now the Acquisition of Land Act 1981, s 12.
3 John Stephenson J (now LJ).
4 (1875) LR 20 Eq 353.
5 [1896] 1 Ch 437 (see ch 2, p 34).

compensation. Had the interference not been authorised by the statutory powers conferred upon the acquiring body, they would be liable in tort or in contract (in relation to easements and covenants respectively) to damages or an injunction. The statutory authority is held to negative this liability, but compensation has been held to be payable instead for the 'injurious affection' suffered. But if the exercise of statutory powers could be carried out by a choice of more than one mode, for example in relation to actual siting of any building or works, any particular choice giving rise to more harm than some other particular choice is regarded as perverse and negligent, and actionable in tort accordingly, presumably on the basis that, as an unjustified exercise of a choice it lies outside the statutory authority which would otherwise apply to it. The siting of a smallpox hospital was held to be actionable in tort for that reason in *Metropolitan Asylum District v Hill*;[6] this was an ordinary case of private nuisance, but had the interference been with an easement or covenant the same reasoning would apply.[7]

This power, in general terms, to interfere with easements, covenants and such rights subject to payment of compensation but free of liability at common law, seems wide enough for most purposes relating to compulsory purchase. Nevertheless s 127 of the Town and Country Planning Act 1971 expressly authorises any interference with 'any easement, liberty, privilege, right or advantage annexed to land and adversely affecting other land, including any natural right of support', subject to payment of compensation for injurious affection on the same basis as in compulsory purchase generally. But this provision only applies to works on land 'acquired or appropriated by a local authority for planning purposes, whether done by the local authority or by a person deriving title under them'; and 'planning purposes' seems to relate only to purposes within the scope of the planning Acts.[8]

# D. Severance of land

## 1 ALL OR NOTHING, OR ONLY PART

To take a stratum of land is ultra vires unless the authorising Act clearly allows it; but to take any part of an owner's land divided territorially is normally intra vires, without need of such authorisation. This is so whether the division, or 'severance', of an owner's land is indicated in the

---

6 (1881) 6 App Cas 193.

7 On this see ch 9, pp 169, 185.

8 On this see ch 11, p 230. If the acquiring body are a local authority they may already hold the land they need though for a different statutory purpose. To use it for a new purpose they must *appropriate* it, and that change of use may result in the infringement of some right over it, such as a restricitve covenant. See above, ch 4, p 79, footnote 16.

compulsory purchase order or whether it does not appear until a particular notice to treat or vesting declaration is so framed as to bring it about.[9] The possible circumstances of severance are infinitely various; but two common varieties occur when part of a frontage is taken for road widening, and when a new road or railway is constructed through farm land or other open country.

Whether or not the proposed 'severance' has appeared in the compulsory purchase order itself, the owner to be expropriated can in certain cases challenge it at the stage of the notice to treat or general vesting declaration, the former by virtue of s 8 (1) of the Act of 1965, the latter by virtue of the Compulsory Purchase (Vesting Declarations) Act 1981.[10] The procedure in these two sets of provisions, in the cases to which they apply, is basically the same. The authority demands part of the owner's land; the owner retorts 'all or nothing'. The authority may decide to take all, in which case the acquisition goes forward on that footing; or they may decide to take nothing, in which case if they have served an actual notice to treat they must signify an intention to abandon it, as in *Thompson v Tottenham and Forest Gate Rly Co*,[11] when the acquiring body expressly served a notice to that effect. Or they may decide to insist on taking part only, in which case the Lands Tribunal must settle the dispute unless the owner gives way.

An owner cannot by this procedure resist severance of all lands but only those in which the sale of part 'of a house, building or factory or of a park or garden belonging to a house', is demanded. There is now, however, a comparable procedure for farm land, under the Land Compensation Act 1973, which will be described below.

The Lands Clauses Consolidation Act 1845, s 92, allowed owners to resist a severance of 'any house or other building or manufactory' in all cases. But various statutes cut down this right, before the Act of 1965, re-enacting earlier provisions,[12] cut it down generally in the way to be described (ie in terms of 'material detriment').

No procedural steps are specified in the 1965 Act; but if a general vesting declaration is used the Compulsory Purchase (Vesting

---

9  Whatever area the compulsory purchase order covers, the basic rule is that the authority may acquire any separate part of it from time to time as the need arises.
10  Section 12 and Sch 1.
11  (1892) 67 LT 416. See p 63.
12  In *Genders v LCC* [1915] 1 Ch 1, the right to resist severance was limited under a private Act to any acquisition which would 'take or interfere with the main structure'. It was held that 'interfere with' must mean something other than 'taking' part of the actual building. So to acquire the forecourt of the building (a chapel) for street widening in such a way as to come within nine inches of the centre steps, leaving a steep drop to the street, counted as 'interference', especially since it would necessitate carrying out works to give a new usable access. Therefore the owners could compel the authority to take the whole, if they wanted to take any of the property at all.

Declarations) Act 1981[13] requires 'a notice of objection to severance' to be served normally within 28 days of the notice that the general vesting declaration will take effect. The authority then have three months in which to serve notice that the 'deemed notice to treat' is withdrawn, or to serve notice that all the land is to be included in the vesting declaration, or to refer the dispute to the Lands Tribunal. If no action is taken within three months, withdrawal is deemed to have taken place in respect of the owner's land.

## 2 'MATERIAL DETRIMENT'

The Lands Tribunal, should the dispute be referred to it, must only decide in the authority's favour if it finds that the part demanded can be taken, '(a) in the case of a house, building or factory, without material detriment, or (b) in the case of a park or garden, without seriously affecting the amenity or convenience of the house'.[14] Section 58 of the Land Compensation Act 1973 now requires the tribunal to take into account not only the land remaining but the land to be acquired, its proposed use and, if the acquisition is for works to be carried out on the land to be acquired and other land as well, the use of that other land and the works as a whole.

This question of the presence or absence of 'material detriment' seems to be essentially one of fact; but it is probably true to say that the factual assessment is one which must be made by the mind of a valuer, with an eye to value and marketability so as to provide some sort of objective test rather than the subjective opinion of the owner or any other person. The question is, will the severance seriously affect, not a particular person, but the generalised concept of a purchaser as reflected in 'the market'? The importance of this approach to the whole problem of compensation will emerge later, in Part II of this book. In *Ravenseft Properties Ltd v Hillingdon London Borough*[15] the authority in question were empowered to acquire from the property known as the Old Bank House at Uxbridge the greater part of its garden, including the rear access, leaving merely the building itself and a little of the curtilage. They served notice to treat accordingly. The owners in reply required them to take the whole. The Lands Tribunal upheld the owner's claim, on the facts of the case, but pointed out that it is not enough for this purpose merely to prove depreciation because, if it were, severance compensation (see ch 9) would be redundant.

The wording of these provisions needs to be handled with some care and flexibility. It has been held that business use does not prevent a

13 Section 12, Sch 1.
14 Ibid. The 1965 Act s 8 (1), which applies in other cases, has similar wording. For apportionment of rent on severance, see s 19 of that Act.
15 (1968) 20 P & CR 483.

building from being a 'house'.[16] A block of offices has been held to constitute a 'building': *Greswolde-Williams v Newcastle-upon-Tyne Corpn*.[17] A complex of separate buildings constituting a hospital has been treated as a 'house': *Governors of St Thomas's Hospital v Charing Cross Rly Co*.[18] In *London Transport Executive v Congregational Union of England and Wales*,[19] a private Act empowered the plaintiffs to compulsorily purchase land by using the old procedures in the Lands Clauses Consolidation Act 1845, including s 92. They sought a declaration in the High Court that s 92 did not apply to their proposed acquisition of 'back land' adjoining the defendants' church in Streatham. Goulding J held that the church premises were a 'building', that the premises including the 'back land' must be considered as a whole, and that the defendants were therefore entitled to require the plaintiffs to take all or nothing for the enlargement of their adjoining bus garage though the plaintiffs required nothing more than the 'back land'.

A lessee may object to the taking of part without committing his lessor: *Pulling v London, Chatham and Dover Rly Co*:[20] so an authority may be faced with the possibility of taking a larger amount of a given piece of land leasehold than freehold, or (no doubt) vice versa. If they do acquire more land leasehold than freehold they will be liable on the covenants in the lease in respect of that land of which the freehold has not been taken, as in fact they would in any case where only a leasehold is acquired: *Piggott v Middlesex County Council*.[1]

Where a local authority propose to acquire compulsorily a 'new right' in land under the Local Government (Miscellaneous Provisions) Act 1976,[2] and the land comes within the cope of the above rules, the owner may correspondingly compel the authority to take his 'interest in the whole of the relevant land' and not merely the 'new right', if the Lands Tribunal is satisfied as stated above. The compulsory purchase order and notice to treat will then be taken to authorise acquisition on this basis.

16 *Ravenseft Properties Ltd v Hillingdon London Borough* (1968) 20 P & CR 483.
17 (1927) 92 JP 13.
18 (1861) 1 John & H 400.
19 (1978) 37 P & CR 155.
20 (1864) 3 De GJ & Sm 661.
1 [1909] 1 Ch 134. In this case the local authority compulsorily acquired the front portion of an old house, adjoining a road they wished to widen, from the freehold landlord. They then went into possession of the entire property. It was held that they had, by doing this, stepped into the tenant's shoes and taken over his liability to the freeholder for the upkeep of the rear portion. Since they had demolished the entire building, and let the site to a sub-tenant who removed the topsoil from the garden, the court enforced forfeiture of the authority's leasehold (ie all except the frontage) and also awarded damages against them. The forfeiture relieved them of the embarrassment of continuing to hold the unwanted lease of the rear part.
2 Section 13 and Sch 1, see above, p 98.

## 3 SEVERED FARM LAND[3]

The definition of 'material detriment' just discussed is designed to apply
to built-up and not unbuilt land other than parks and gardens. The
obvious category of property left out of this definition is farmland, or at
any rate the open land of farms as distinct from farmhouses and other
farm buildings as such. The Land Compensation Act 1973 has now
supplied an equivalent protection, using not the 'material detriment'
concept but a rather more specific one expressed in the words: 'not
reasonably capable of being farmed'. When an acquiring body, most
notably the Department of Transport when building motorways, and
other highway authorities building new roads, acts to acquire part only of
a farm, the farmer may wish to resist by adopting the 'all or nothing'
approach; and this new procedure is available accordingly. The principle
is the same as that of 'material detriment', but there is considerable
difference in detail.

Sections 53–57 of the 1973 Act contain the new procedure, or rather
two new related procedures. A distinction is drawn between (i) claimants
with an interest greater than a lease for a year or a yearly tenancy, which
includes all leaseholds beyond that length and freeholds as well, and (ii)
claimants with an interest *not* greater than a lease for a year or a yearly
tenancy.

Section 53 provides that, if any acquiring body should serve a notice to
treat on any person in respect of agricultural land whose interest is
greater than yearly, whether or not he is in occupation, but the notice
applies to part only of the 'agricultural unit', the recipient may within
two months serve a counter-notice requiring them to buy in addition his
interest in the whole of *any other land* within the *same* unit which he also
holds under an interest greater than yearly. But he has to assert that the
'other land' is 'not reasonably capable of being farmed' even together
with 'other relevant land', if any, which means (*a*) further land in the
same 'agricultural unit' in which he does *not* hold an interest greater than
yearly, *or* (*b*) land in a different 'agricultural unit' in which he *does* hold
such an interest. Neither the 'other land', nor the 'other relevant land' (if
any) must be currently subject to a notice to treat.

The counter-notice, a copy of which should be sent to any other person
with an interest in the 'other land' to which it relates, may, after a two
months' period allowed for both sides to reach agreement, be referred,
by either side, to the Lands Tribunal (s 54), which must decide whether
the claim that the 'other land' cannot reasonably be farmed is justified. If
the counter-notice is upheld, or accepted without challenge, the authority are deemed to have served a notice to treat for the 'other land' which
cannot be withdrawn; but the claimant can withdraw the counter-notice

3 See also the 'blight notice' provisions in ch 13, pp 257, 261, below.

within six weeks after compensation is assessed. The assessment must exclude 'new' development value.

If the interest is a lease this means that the authority will be saddled with a landlord in respect of the 'other land', and they may offer to surrender the lease to him. In default of agreement within three months over reasonable terms they must refer the question to the Lands Tribunal, which must then settle them, disregarding any special provisions in the lease itself. The landlord is deemed to accept the surrender one month thereafter. The authority are empowered to farm the land if necessary.

Section 55 provides that there shall be a slightly different but parallel procedure if the farm is held under an interest not greater than a lease for a year or a yearly tenancy. The law of agricultural holdings being what it is, in the majority of cases this interest will in fact be a yearly tenancy. The procedure takes effect this time not on notice to treat but on notice of *entry*. Where notice of entry is served in respect of part of an agricultural holding, upon an occupier whose interest is no greater than yearly, he may serve a counter-notice within two months claiming that the rest of the holding—ie the farm, in so far as it is comprised within that interest—is 'not reasonably capable of being farmed', even together with 'other relevant land', if any, which means (*a*) land within the *same* 'agricultural unit', or (*b*) land occupied by him at the date when the notice of entry is served, under an interest *greater* than yearly, in some other 'agricultural unit'. Neither the rest of the holding nor the 'other relevant land' (if any) must be currently subject to a notice of entry.

The counter-notice, a copy of which must be sent to the claimant's landlord, signifies that the claimant elects to treat the notice of entry as covering the entire holding, though not of course any 'other relevant land'. Either side may, after a two months' period allowed for both sides to reach agreement, refer the counter-notice to the Lands Tribunal (s 56), which must decide whether the claim is justified. If the counter-notice is upheld, or accepted without challenge, the notice of entry is deemed to apply to the entire holding, provided that the claimant gives up possession of every part of it within a year. The authority will be deemed to have taken possession on *the day before* the expiry of the year (or other period) of the claimant's interest which was current when the counter-notice was accepted or upheld. This should avoid problems of calculation relating to fractions of periods in regard to assessment of the compensation for that part of the land.

It is possible, in fact highly likely, that the unwanted part of the agricultural holding which an acquiring body may be compelled to take in this kind of case is not land of which they wish to obtain the landlord's interest. They may not even have been authorised to do so. It is therefore provided that neither they nor the claimant shall be liable to the landlord in respect of the transfer if it should conflict with the terms of the lease or tenancy. Moreover the landlord is to have legal possession at once of the remainder of the holding deemed included, by this procedure, within the notice of entry; and the tenancy is terminated when the claimant has given up possession, without prejudice to prior rights and liabilities— which, on the tenant's side, are in fact transferred to the authority.

The acquiring authority thus obtain *possession* from the tenant of the part of the farm they want and also the part they do not want; but whereas they also get the *ownership* of the part they want it is very unlikely that they get (or need) the ownership of the part they do not want. The tenant relinquishes both parts while the landlord unless he is at the same time successfully applying the procedure under ss 53-54 described above, is having the occupation of the part the authority do *not* want thrust upon him in addition to the reversionary ownership which he already holds by virtue of being the landlord. In such a situation the landlord is being compelled to become the unwilling owner-occupier of the unwanted part of that farm. But if the tenant in a given case can prove that the part not wanted cannot be reasonably farmed, it is up to the landlord to take advantage of that fact; because such a contention is either valid or not valid quite independently of tenancies and reversions. The only genuine difference is likely to arise if the landlord has other land available nearby and the tenant has not, being land which, when conjoined with the unwanted part of the farm, produces a unit which *is* capable of being reasonably farmed.

Disputes over amounts payable are to be settled by the Lands Tribunal. Any increase in value of the unwanted part of the farm which accrues to the landlord is to be set off against the compensation due to him for the part of the farm that is wanted and therefore taken. If the landlord thinks he should get compensation for deterioration of the holding under s 58 of the Agricultural Holdings Act 1948, he must serve his claim on the acquiring authority within three months after the tenancy is terminated.

There are other statutory procedures analogous to service of a notice of entry. Section 57 of the 1973 Act requires any acquiring authority wishing to use them in obtaining part of a farm to serve notice of intention to do so on the occupier, who will thereupon be able to take advantage of the procedure under ss 55 to 56 just described.

There is also the situation described earlier in this chapter where, under s 59 of the 1973 Act, the tenant of an agricultural holding, whose interest is not greater than yearly, receives a *notice to quit* in the course of a compulsory purchase of the land, and is thereupon empowered to require instead that he be expropriated, rather than dispossessed by whoever is his landlord. If this situation arises in regard to part and not the whole of any farm, s 61 empowers any tenant in such a case who elects to be expropriated, to serve notice on the acquiring authority that the remainder of the farm cannot be reasonably farmed on the basis prescribed by s 55. But he can only do this if his election under s 59 is made within two months of the notice to quit, or of the relevant decision of the Agricultural Land Tribunal if later. The authority may accept the notice to take the remainder of the farm, within two months; if not, the tenant may refer the matter to the Lands Tribunal within two months after that. Within 12 months after a successful notice is accepted or upheld the tenant may give up possession of the part not required. The acquiring authority are then deemed to have gone into occupation, under a notice of entry, upon the day before the expiry of the year (or other period) of the tenancy current when the notice was accepted or upheld. The rest of the procedure, including that relating to the unloading of possession of the unwanted land on to the landlord, is that which is applicable under ss 55 to 56, as already described.

## 4 FRAGMENTED LAND

Where an extensive area of land is owned, normally farmland or any other sizeable country estate, although urban land is not of course ruled out, one form of severance which often occurs is where a road or railway cuts a swathe leaving separated portions of the owner's land on either side. Since this may leave parts of land useless to the owner though not taken from him, and maybe greatly reduce or even destroy the economic viability of the whole, and since as will be seen compensation payable must cover depreciation of land not taken as well as the value of land which is taken,[4] it may well be cheaper for the acquiring body to provide connections between the severed portions of land. It does not seem that there is a general compulsion on them to do this, although express provisions to provide such bridges, tunnels or other 'accommodation works', as they are called, were enacted in the Railways Clauses Consolidation Act 1845.[5] Even where there is no statutory compulsion, however, the alternative might be to pay virtually the whole value of any depreciated land in many cases—for instance where it is deprived of all access from a public highway, or its size or shape or both make it virtually unmarketable and so generally useless—in which case it would make more sense to buy the land outright.

Section 8 (3) of the 1965 Act states that if any authorising Act imposes a duty of making a connection with severed lands for the owner's benefit, the acquiring body may choose to buy any such piece of severed land (even if the owner would prefer to keep it and be given a connecting bridge or tunnel) either if the price would be less than the cost of the accommodation works or if the piece of land is less than half an acre, provided in either case that the owner has no other land adjoining it. Section 8 (2) states that if any such severed pieces of land are left, of less

4  See ch 9, p 175, below.
5  Sections 16, 68.

than half an acre, the owner may compel the acquiring body to buy any of them, provided that land is 'not situated in a town or built upon',[6] and provided also that the owner has no other land adjoining the severed fragment 'into which it can be thrown so as to be conveniently occupied with it'. If there is such other land the owner's only power is to compel the acquiring body to incorporate the severed fragment into it at their own expense.

6  Lands not continuously built upon, though near a railway station, were held to be 'not situated in a town', in *London and South Western Rly Co v Blackmore* (1870) LR 4 HL 610.

# Part two

# Compulsory purchase compensation

# Chapter 6

# Nature and assessment of compensation

## A. Money for land

### 1 THE LUMP SUM

'A person seeking to obtain compensation under these Acts of Parliament must once and for all make one claim for all damages which can be reasonably foreseen'. So said Erle CJ in *Chamberlain v West End of London and Crystal Palace Rly Co.*[1] In similar vein, Sir Wilfred Greene MR said, 'The truth of the matter is that . . . the sum to be ascertained is in essence one sum, namely, the proper price or compensation payable in all the circumstances of the case', in *Horn v Sunderland Corpn.*[2]

In a simple case, where a particular piece of land is acquired in its entirety, this means that what the landowner loses in land value he must get back to the equivalent amount in money: the compulsory acquisition of a property worth £10,000 is compensated for by a money payment of £10,000. If half a property worth £10,000 is acquired, the owner must be left at the end with £10,000 composed of £5,000 in land value and £5,000 in compensation money, in place of his former £10,000 in land value. But, as will be seen, there are likely to be many cases where (say) half of a property worth £10,000 is taken, at a purchase price compensation of £5,000, but the remainder, for any of various reasons, has a depreciated value proportionately less than half—say for example two fifths—so that to preserve the owner's total asset of £10,000 an additional sum of compensation must be awarded (if the rules so allow). In such a case the owner's original £10,000 in land value will have become £10,000, composed of £4,000 in land value, £5,000 in purchase price compensation, and £1,000 in additional compensation. But the proper claim will not be for two sums; it will be for 'one sum' (as Sir Wilfred Greene MR said) of £6,000, being a total assessed under two 'heads' of compensation.[3] There are, however, other cases again where owners do not get their loss made up in full, and the reasons why this is so will be critically explained in the following chapters.

---

1 (1863) 2 B & S 617.
2 [1941] 2 KB 26, [1941] 1 All ER 480.
3 In fact there are more than two; but 'disturbance' is treated from the legal standpoint as part of the purchase price of the land taken (see ch 10, p 197).

## 2 VALUATION AND LAW

The assessment of compensation, as a detailed process, is a matter for valuers and not for lawyers. It is thus a question of fact, but expert fact needing to be proved by the testimony of expert witnesses who, in this context, must be valuers. A valuer's status is not in itself a matter for a court; but status may well affect the credibility of a particular valuer's evidence in any particular case, in the eyes of lawyers as well as of other valuers. On the other hand there are other factors which may carry more weight in a particular case, such as an individual's professional experience, or the internal consistency or lack of it in an individual's evidence.

The tribunal which will normally need to make assessments of this kind is the Lands Tribunal,[4] which must apply the law as well as adjudicate questions of ordinary and expert fact, whether the sitting member of the Tribunal is a lawyer or a valuer. Before it will appear: (i) the valuer for the claimant—or a barrister or solicitor if legal points of any importance are at stake, or perhaps the claimant in person, or even a friend if the Tribunal so allows—and (ii) the valuer for the authority, or else the District Valuer (who is an official of the central government) or one of his subordinates if the authority lack a valuer of their own.

But the assessment of value of land for the purposes of compensation must always conform with the legal rules governing this matter[5] in addition to being carried out with reasonable technical competence. Ignorance of the law excuses no-one who breaks it, layman as well as lawyer, so the valuer needs to be aware of the relevant legal rules as well as the relevant rules of valuation. Nevertheless, in respect of the law, valuers and other laymen will defer to the advice of lawyers and the decisions of the Lands Tribunal will be subject to review by the Court of Appeal and the House of Lords. The Lands Tribunal and the practitioners will take the routine questions of law in their stride; but they will be ready to see the more difficult problems, for which no authoritative precedents exist, go to the Court of Appeal and the House of Lords for decision.

The relationship of law to valuation was brought into focus by the Privy Council in an Australian compulsory purchase case, *Melwood Units Pty Ltd v Commissioner of Main Roads*,[6] by stating that the application of wrongful *valuation* principles is not merely a valuation issue but an issue of *law*.

---

4 See p 122, below.
5 Other legal questions may be relevant also, for example the question whether a right to compensation may be assigned. In *Dawson v Greater Northern and City Rly Co* [1905] 1 KB 260, the Court of Appeal held that it could be. There was a compensation *agreement* in that case; but it must be remembered that a *compulsory* purchase is not the less a land transaction for being compulsory. The right to compensation, once it has come into existence, is a 'chose in action'.
6 [1979] AC 426, [1979] 1 All ER 161.

# B. The time of assessment

## 1 THE SPURIOUS RULE AND HOW IT EVOLVED

Easily the most striking illustration of this has occurred in relation to a problem of basic importance: at what date is compensation to be assessed? It will be remembered from an earlier discussion in this book that the Victorians displayed a very nonchalant attitude towards assessing compensation.[7] Forty-eight sections of the Lands Clauses Consolidation Act 1845, are devoted to the procedure for obtaining compensation. None deals with the principles of assessment. The various procedures resolved themselves into two groups: those where valuation experts presided (decision by arbitrator, umpire, 'able practical surveyor') and those where they did not (decision by jury, or magistrates): and it may be that in practice the more complex assessments tended to be made by one of the procedures in which a valuation expert presided.[8] Whether that was so or not, the law assumed that rules of assessment were a question of valuation expertise only, and were not in need of any legal formulation. The courts soon found that this was a mistake; but Parliament did not concede the point until 1919.[9]

It was clear from the beginning that the issue of the notice to treat is the procedural stage at which the interests to be acquired are fixed. The fixing of such interests is the very point of serving a notice to treat. They can change hands by assignment after that date; but if they come into existence after that date they will be ineffective to increase the burden of paying compensation which rests on the acquiring authority.[10]

In a straightforward case the date of service of the notice to treat was as a rule conveniently acceptable also as the date for assessing compensation, but only in so far as no disagreement existed. In other words this might well be a convention but was not suited to being a rule because it had not been framed to meet a difficulty. Had there been any appreciable inflation, difficulties would have arisen soon enough; but this was not a feature, apparently, of the Victorian scene, nor of any later scene until the Second World War. During this long period the convention slowly hardened into an apparent rule of law, accepted not only by valuers but by practising lawyers and the courts themselves. The Court of Appeal referred to it in 1941, in the leading case of *Horn v Sunderland Corpn*, as if it went without saying. As late as 1968, no less a person than Lord Denning MR is reported as observing, in *Newham London Borough*

7 See ch 1, p 15, above.
8 But the jury procedure was available, complexity or no complexity, if either side held back from negotiation.
9 Acquisition of Land (Assessment of Compensation) Act 1919.
10 See ch 4, p 63.

*Council v Benjamin:* [11] 'if the compensation falls to be assessed under the general "notice to treat" provisions . . ., then it is to be assessed at once as at the date of the notice to treat. . . .' From this it is apparent that 'at once' and 'at the date of the notice to treat' could be stated together without any suspicion of inconsistency. But the attention of the court was not in reality being directed, in anyone's mind, to this point at all, which had nothing to do with the dispute in the *Benjamin* case.

## 2 THE JUDGMENT IN PENNY V PENNY

The same comment can be made of the famous leading case from which the purported rule was derived, *Penny v Penny*, decided in 1868. The decision in that case was carefully analysed by the House of Lords in the case which exploded this mythical rule, *Birmingham Corpn v West Midland Baptist (Trust) Association (Incorporated).* [12] Lord Morris of Borthy-Gest in the latter case described how in *Penny v Penny*,

a testator had certain leasehold premises in which he carried on business with two of his sons. By his will he left the leasehold premises to his executors on trust to permit the two sons to occupy the premises so long as they or one of them continued to carry on the business and paid a certain rent. . . . On 8 May 1866, the Metropolitan Board of Works served on the executor a notice to treat. . . . The executor sent in a claim. A notice to treat was also served on the two sons who were continuing to carry on the business. They also sent in a claim. The executor's claim went before a jury. The jury gave an award . . . of a sum . . . assuming a rack rent and disregarding the right of the two sons to occupy the premises. The claims of the two sons were referred to arbitration and an amount was awarded them. . . . It included a sum for trade compensation and a sum for their interest in the leasehold. . . . It seems clear that it would not have

11 Chapter 5, p 89. See also *Hewitt v Leicester City Council* [1969] 2 All ER 802, [1969] 1 WLR 855, in which the Court of Appeal held that a notice to treat was not 'served' when it came back through the post to the acquiring authority marked 'returned undelivered' and 'gone away'. It was in fact 'served' on the claimant's agents seven months later. Lord Denning MR said: 'this is important because the value of the property is normally to be ascertained as at the date of the service of the notice to treat'.

The Court of Appeal gave judgment in that case on 31 March 1969. The same court (differently composed) had given judgment on 27 October 1967, in the *West Midland Baptist (Trust)* case (see below) in terms which had seriously questioned the 'rule' that value is assessed as at the date of the notice to treat. In *Wilson v Liverpool City Council* [1971] 1 All ER 628, [1971] 1 WLR 302, the same court refused to allow claimants, who had not challenged assessment as at the date of notice to treat before the Lands Tribunal, to change their minds and do so on appeal. Lord Denning MR said 'They must have seen the judgments given in this court in October 1967, long before the Lands Tribunal entered on this reference'. Alternative valuations as at the different dates should therefore have been asked for, now prescribed in the Lands Tribunal Rules 1975, r 54 (3); and see below (footnote 18 on p 125). It is therefore surprising that the judgments in *Hewitt's* case did not take the same question into account. The court came perilously near penalising a party in one case for doing what it had itself done in another.

12 [1970] AC 874, [1969] 3 All ER 172.

been right to require the board to pay both sums in full. In the result the court held that the two sons were entitled to retain their award but that the executor's claim should be dealt with afresh. . . . The sons had their right to be in the premises at a low rent. The executor had the residue of a lease which could be valuable, but in arriving at a valuation, it would be wrong to disregard the fact that so long as the sons exercised their rights, the executor's interest was worth less than the full and fair value of the property itself. . . .

In other words the decision in *Penny v Penny* was that the two compensation claims were in terms inconsistent with one another, in that part of the value of the compulsorily purchased property would be paid twice over unless the executor's claim were reduced to take account of the sons' claim. The court's attention was concentrated upon this issue; and the question of the proper date of the assessment, for which the case has been supposed to be the leading authority, had so little to do with the ratio decidendi that whatever was said about it was not merely obiter but so casual and unconsidered as to be virtually per incuriam.

Sir William Page-Wood VC pointed all this out. But one sentence has been taken from his judgment as reported in the Law Reports and has been the foundation of statements that valuations are to be made as at the date of notices to treat. . . . The report does not set out the actual date when possession was taken but I would infer that there was no long delay after the dates of the notices to treat. The house and premises were being acquired so that a road could be constructed from Blackfriars to the Mansion House. . . . No question arose . . . concerning any possible variations in value as between any of the dates. What the Vice-Chancellor was so clearly and logically laying down was that the acquiring board must not be made to pay twice over. . . . Then follows this passage: 'That is not at all the scheme of the Act. The scheme of the Act I take to be this: that every man's interest shall be valued, *rebus sic stantibus* just as it occurs at the very moment when the notice to treat was given'.

This statement quoted by Lord Morris from the judgment of Sir William Page-Wood[13] is the celebrated passage which comprises the alleged rule in *Penny v Penny*. Yet its choice by posterity (valuers and lawyers alike) is highly selective, as Lord Morris carefully makes clear.

The case is not only reported in the Law Reports. It is also reported as follows: 37 LJ Ch 340; 18 LT 13; 16 WR 671. It is, I think, significant that in each one of these reports the reference is not to 'the very moment when the notice to treat was given' as in the Law Reports but to the moment of valuation. Thus in 16 WR at p 673, are the words:
'The scheme of the Act I take to be this: that every man's interest should be taken *rebus sic stantibus* just as it occurs at the very moment when the valuation is to be made'.
In 37 LJ Ch at p 344, the sentence is given:
'The scheme of the Act was that every man's interest must be valued *rebus sic*

13 [1969] 3 All ER at pp 185–86 (quoting (1868) LR 5 Eq at p 236).

*stantibus* just as it occurred at the very moment when the valuation was to be made. . . .'

In 18 LT at p 14, the sentence is given:

'I consider the scheme of the Act of Parliament to be that every man's interest shall be valued *rebus sic stantibus* just as it occurs at the moment when a valuation is to be made'.

The reporters were in each case different.[14]

It might be added that the only thing we can be reasonably certain that the judge actually said in *Penny v Penny* was '*rebus sic stantibus*'.

### 3 THE CORRECT RULE AND HOW IT WAS ESTABLISHED

Since the Second World War, inflation has pursued its course un-checked, and it was merely a question of time before the absurdity and injustice of the non-existent rule in *Penny v Penny* gave rise to scandal. In the *West Midland Baptist* case, notice to treat was deemed to have been served on 14 August 1947, the property in question being 'the People's Chapel' in the central area of Birmingham. Acquisition was for the purposes of redevelopment of the area, a project involving many com-plications and much delay. Ultimately the site was vested in the corpora-tion, and both sides agreed that 30 April 1961, should be taken as the date when the building of a new chapel on a new site could reasonably have begun. Assessment of compensation as in 1961 gave an agreed figure of £89,575. But the corporation claimed, in reliance on *Penny v Penny*, that the date of assessment must be taken as the date of the deemed notice to treat in 1947; and assessment as in 1947 gave a much lower figure, £50,025. Lord Morris observed that: 'it would, I think, be a shocking thing if any principle of law could be invoked leading to the result that the trustees who had to spend nearly £90,000 were only to receive about £50,000. . . .'[15] No doubt the payment by the corporation of the difference between the lower and the higher sums might have been disallowed by the district auditor, or at the suit of an angry ratepayer, as illegal expenditure;[16] and it was therefore to be expected that the corpor-ation would wish to test the matter before a superior court. But why, in the face of a decision by the Court of Appeal that the higher sum was correct, the corporation thought it fit to pursue the matter to the House of Lords is not so clear. It is true that the members of the Court of Appeal were not unanimous in condemning the 'rule' in *Penny v Penny* whole-heartedly in general terms; and indeed all that they strictly needed to do in the *West Midland Baptist* case was to condemn it in relation to one type of compensation claim, the 'equivalent reinstatement' variety to which the claim in that case belonged. It is also true that the House of Lords

14  Ibid, p 186.
15  Ibid, pp 181–82.
16  See ch 1, p 12, above.

might have reversed the decision of the Court of Appeal. Fortunately the House of Lords provided the whole-hearted condemnation which the Court of Appeal did not quite succeed in achieving.

As for deciding positively upon an appropriate time at which the land should be valued, there emerged a difference of possibilities. In the *West Midland Baptist* case itself the mode of compensation was what is known as 'equivalent reinstatement'. Lord Reid identified the correct date as being the date when the reinstatement becomes reasonably practicable; and, as stated above, it was agreed on both sides in this case that 30 April 1961, should be so regarded. But in the normal case of purchase price compensation Lord Reid said as follows:

> No stage can be singled out as the date of expropriation in every case. Sometimes possession is taken before compensation is assessed. Then it would seem logical to fix the market value of the land as at that date and to take actual consequential losses as they occurred then or thereafter provided that the dispossessed owner had acted reasonably. But if compensation is assessed before possession is taken, taking the date of assessment can, I think, be justified because then either party can sue for specific performance and the promoters obtain a right to the land, as if there had been a contract of sale at that date.[17]

There was general agreement with this proposition that the date of taking possession, or the date of the assessment itself, whichever is the sooner, should be the date of valuation. In *W and S (Long Eaton) Ltd v Derbyshire County Council*[18] it was applied to the case of a purchase notice (which is undeniably a compulsory purchase) in circumstances when market values had in fact not risen but fallen after the (deemed) notice to treat. The Court of Appeal held that the 'date of the assessment', if this takes the form of an award by the Lands Tribunal, is the last day of the hearing before the Tribunal. But if the Court of Appeal remits a case to the Lands Tribunal for re-hearing, market value is to be assessed as at the day (or last day) of the original Lands Tribunal hearing.[19]

### 4 THE RULE FOR LEASEHOLD

The choice of the date of the notice to treat, being normally too early, has thus clearly been exposed as unjust at least to freeholders. But there is an apparent divergence from this in the case of leaseholders, at any rate in some circumstances; and it may well be that a belief in the suitability of

---

**17** [1969] 3 All ER at p 180. On specific performance, see ch 4, p 59, above. The decision meant overruling *Phoenix Assurance Co v Spooner* [1905] 2 KB 753, a first-instance judgment in which it was held that compensation must be assessed as at the date of notice to treat despite the fact that the buildings had subsequently been burned down while still the property of the vendor, who had thereupon obtained payment for their loss under a fire insurance policy.

**18** (1975) 31 P & CR 99. For purchase notices and blight notices (which if accepted or upheld involve a *deemed* notice to treat), see below, chs 12 and 13.

**19** *Hoveringham Gravels Ltd v Chiltern District Council* (1978) 39 P & CR 414.

an early assessment date for the benefit of leaseholders influenced many practitioners in favour of the imaginary rule in *Penny v Penny*. Clearly, the later the date of assessment, the shorter the time the lease will have to run, and so the less will be the value of a lease for calculating compensation. The question here is, what is the most just approach to the problem?

In *R v Kennedy*,[20] a railway company served a notice to treat on a leaseholder, the lease having a number of years to run. They took no further action in respect of the lease directly, but instead reached an agreement with the lessor (in this case the Crown, owner of the freehold) who proceeded to exercise a 'break clause' in the lease whereby the lessor could give the lessee a mere three months' notice to terminate. Shortly after, the railway company, which was acquiring the freehold by agreement, took possession of the land. The tenant claimed the value of the full residue of his term as at the date of the notice to treat, which it was pointed out occurred before the operation of the 'break clause'. The court rejected this claim, saying: 'Nothing was done under that notice to treat'; all that was in fact acquired from the tenant was a residuary period of less than three months.

In *R v Kennedy* the court evaded the issue of whether or not the notice to treat fixed the date for valuing the claimant's interest. Instead it held that no action had in fact been taken under the notice to treat, but that expropriation took place, using what is now the procedure in s 20 of the Act of 1965, of a tenancy which had already been transformed into one with a year or less to run.

The issue of valuation as at the date of the notice to treat was once again evaded in a more recent leading case concerning a leasehold, namely *Holloway v Dover Corpn*.[1] The property in this case was a bakery let to a tenant on a lease due to expire in 1954. Notice to treat was deemed to be served in 1949. No action had been taken by the corporation to get possession by the date of expiry of the lease, and the tenants remained in occupation thereafter under the statutory protection for business tenancies conferred by Part II of the Landlord and Tenant Act 1954. In 1957 the corporation at length acquired the freehold reversion from the landlords, and by virtue of holding the reversion then served notice, as landlords, terminating the protected tenancy and opposing the grant of a new tenancy on the grounds that the premises were to be demolished and redeveloped in accordance with their scheme for comprehensive development of the area. The corporation conceded that they, now being landlords, should pay to the tenants the statutory compensation under s 37 of the Landlord and Tenants Act, namely a sum equal to twice the rateable value. But the Lands Tribunal, on the application of the

20 [1893] 1 QB 533.
 1 [1960] 2 All ER 193, [1960] 1 WLR 604.

tenants, held that compulsory purchase compensation was also payable, in respect of the lease valued as at the date of the deemed notice to treat in 1949. The Court of Appeal, however, found in favour of the corporation that no interest had in fact been compulsorily acquired from the tenants at all, their tenancy having already come to an end in accordance with the law of landlord and tenant. 'The truth is, that in the event there never was any expropriation'.

Valuation as at the date of the notice to treat would not necessarily work out to the tenant's advantage in every case, even if it were a genuine rule of law. In *Square Grip Reinforcement Co (London) Ltd v Rowton Houses Ltd*[2] the boot was on the other foot. The plaintiffs held office premises under two leases, each containing a 'break clause'. The acquiring authority served notices to treat shortly before the 'break clauses' could have been acted on by the landlords, but took no action for over a year. The tenants objected to having compensation assessed as at the date of notice to treat, though Danckwerts LJ was satisfied that it was 'the normal rule', and 'very well settled'. He added, speaking of the typical tenant,[3] that

it suits him to have the value assessed at the earliest possible date, since a term of years is a wasting asset. In the present case, the only reason for the tenant's desire to have the assessment at a later date—after March 17, 1963—is because after that date the landlords could no longer bring the term to an end on September 17, 1963, whereas at any previous time before March 17, the value presumably is diminished by the possibility of a notice to determine the term on September 17, 1963. But the tenant, in his contentions, is faced with the difficulty of finding some other date appropriate for the assessment of the value. . . . I have looked carefully at the other cases which were cited to me and I cannot find in any of them anything which compels me to depart, in the present case, from the normal rule for the assessment of compensation.

Now 'some other date appropriate' has been found, thanks to the *West Midland Baptist* case, and the 'normal rule' has gone. The tenants do not seem, in the *Square Grip Co* case, to have argued for the main principle on these lines, but merely to have alleged that 'the true facts of the relationship between the tenants and the landlords could be properly

---

2 [1967] Ch 877, [1966] 3 All ER 996.
3 *Cardiff Corpn v Cook* [1923] 2 Ch 115, must be a case of an *a*typical tenant, in that he fixed the value of his leasehold interest at nothing, regardless of the date of valuation or notice to treat, and claimed solely for 'disturbance'. But the acquiring authority dallied too long in face of this golden opportunity, apparently thinking up arguments to get the better of the disturbance claim. While they were still thinking, the lease was assigned to the sub-tenant of part of the premises. He promptly made a new sub-lease of the part he did not occupy, and then submitted a revised claim in respect of the head lease taking into account the profit rent in respect of the new sub-lease and the value of his own occupation, all of which when capitalised came to £3,375. The court held that there was no legal objection either to this revised claim by the assignee or to the continued assertion of the disturbance claim (£550) by the assignor.

ascertained' at the date of entry rather than at any other time; but the taking of physical possession is only one significant factor out of several. To avoid having to deal with contradictory propositions for leaseholds arising from the vagaries of 'break clauses' and other contingent elements, it is preferable to apply to leaseholds as well as freeholds the rules laid down by the House of Lords in the *West Midland Baptist* case, namely that compensation is to be assessed, whatever the interest expropriated, as at the date of the assessment itself, or of taking possession of the land if sooner, or (in 'equivalent reinstatement' cases) the date when the reinstatement becomes reasonably practicable. Thus, as far as it is possible to do so, the problem of uncertainty and the problem of inflation are solved together.[4]

## C. Reference to the Lands Tribunal

### 1 THE REFERENCE, AND EXPERT WITNESSES

Section 6 of the Act of 1965 provides that:

If a person served with a notice to treat does not within 21 days from the service of the notice state the particulars of his claim or treat with the acquiring authority in respect of his claim, or if he and the acquiring authority do not agree as to the amount of compensation to be paid by the acquiring authority for the interest belonging to him, or which he has power to sell, or for any damage which may be sustained by him by reason of the execution of the works, the question of disputed compensation shall be referred to the Lands Tribunal.

This, as was pointed out at the beginning of this chapter, must include all damages that can be reasonably foreseen, the compensation being as far as possible a single lump sum.

Section 1 of the Land Compensation Act 1961 states similarly that compulsory purchase compensation disputes are to be referred to the Lands Tribunal,[5] and that the same applies where the dispute is over apportionment of rent under a lease of land of which only part is being acquired. An acquiring authority can in theory be forced by a prerogative order of mandamus to proceed, if dilatorily, to make the statutory assessment of disputed compensation; but in practice nowadays it suffices to give notice of reference to the Registrar of the Lands Tribunal.

4 As to the assessment of landlords' reversions, see *Leek's* and *Khan's* cases, above, ch 5, p 90.
5 The Lands Tribunal (set up by the Lands Tribunals Act 1949) began its work in 1950, replacing the panel of official arbitrators who had previously determined compensation disputes (see above, ch 2, p 29). Section 3 of the Lands Tribunal Act 1949 authorises the Lord Chancellor to make rules governing procedure before the Tribunal. Those currently in force are the Lands Tribunal Rules 1975, SI 1975/299, as amended by the Lands Tribunal (Amendment) Rules 1977, SI 1977/1820 and 1981, SI 1981/105, and the Lands Tribunal (Amendment No. 2) Rules 1981, SI 1981/600.

Section 2 of the 1961 Act limits the number of expert witnesses before the Tribunal to one on either side; but as an exception to this one additional witness on either side may be heard in relation to a compensation claim for the value of minerals, and another on either side in relation to a claim for disturbance of business; and the Lands Tribunal may in any case waive the limitation to one if it thinks fit.[6]

## 2 SEALED OFFERS, COSTS AND GENERAL PROCEDURE

Costs of compensation hearings before the Tribunal are within its discretion, which is normally, but not necessarily, exercised on the basis of awarding an owner his costs against the acquiring authority unless they themselves offered more than the Tribunal awarded.[7] Either side may also choose to make an unconditional offer to accept, or pay, as the case may be, a particular sum.[8] If this is not accepted and the dispute has to be adjudicated by the Tribunal the offer, if persisted in, must be a 'sealed offer', meaning that it is given to but not disclosed to the Tribunal. Having declared the award, the Tribunal then ascertains the amount of the 'sealed offer'; and if it appears that the offer is as favourable to the side that did not accept it as the award is, or more so, then the side that made the offer must be awarded their costs against their opponents unless the Tribunal considers special reasons exist to order otherwise. This rule only applies to costs incurred after the making of the offer.[9]

Before a claimant can take advantage of the 'sealed offer' rule he must have delivered to the acquiring authority, 'in time to enable them to make a proper offer', a written notice of the amount claimed.[10] This 'must state the exact nature of the interest in respect of which compensation is claimed, and give details of the compensation claimed, distinguishing the amounts under separate heads and showing how the

---

6 In the Report of the Committee on the Use of Valuers in the Public Service (Cmnd 5518) it was stated that until recently the average interval between the date of listing a case for hearing in the Lands Tribunal and the actual date of hearing was seven months. Procedure, however, has been expedited, and this gestation period can now be as little as three weeks. (See *Simpson v Stoke-on-Trent City Council* (1982) 44 P & CR 226).

7 Lands Tribunal Rules 1975, r 56 (as amended). The Registrar of the Tribunal may make recommendations as to who pays costs in proceedings heard by him, subject to a right of appeal to the Tribunal within ten days. But see *Hood Investment Co Ltd v Marlow UDC* (1963) 15 P & CR 229. In *Pepys v London Transport Executive* (1974) 29 P & CR 248, the Court of Appeal went so far as to treat the claimant, who was awarded no compensation, on the same footing as an unsuccessful plaintiff in a civil action for damages, against whom costs should therefore be awarded in full, regardless of the fact that an underground stratum of the claimant's property had in fact been taken (see below, ch 9, p 177).

8 Land Compensation Act 1961, s 4 (1), (3).

9 Ibid, Lands Tribunal Rules 1975, r 50. The 'sealed offer' procedure is similar to that which applies when a defendant to a civil action offers a sum in settlement of a claim against him for damages and pays it into court.

10 See ch 4, pp 61–62.

amount claimed under each head is calculated'. If the claimant fails to comply, the Lands Tribunal must award to the acquiring authority their costs against him 'so far as they were incurred . . . after the time when in the opinion of the Lands Tribunal the notice should have been delivered', unless the Tribunal considers there are special reasons to order otherwise.[11] This rule applies whether or not either side makes a 'sealed offer'.

Mention has been made of the provision that 'disputed compensation shall be referred to the Lands Tribunal' if a claim is not submitted, or negotiations are not begun, within 21 days of the actual or deemed service of notice to treat, and also of the more flexible requirement that a claim must be submitted to the acquiring authority 'in time to enable them to make a proper offer' if the claimant is to avoid the likelihood of being saddled with both his own and the acquiring authority's costs thereafter. Reference to the Tribunal (unless by consent it is to sit as an ordinary arbitrator) must be made formally. If there are several interests in the same land and several notices to treat the acquiring authority may require the Tribunal to consolidate the proceedings and hear the claims together.[12]

The registrar to the Tribunal must register the reference and send a copy of the notice to the other party or parties to the dispute.[13] Proceedings go forward in much the same way as in the trial of an action at law.[14] Except when acting, by consent, as an ordinary arbitrator the Tribunal sits in public—unless the claimant asks or agrees that an oral hearing be dispensed with—and it may inspect the land in question. If a case 'calls for special knowledge' the President may appoint an assessor or assessors.[15]

The Tribunal usually receives evidence by oral testimony (though it can receive affidavits); and 'a party may appear and be heard in person, by counsel or solicitor, or, on obtaining leave of the Tribunal . . ., by any other person. . . .' The claimant normally begins.[16] Provision is made for the ordering of discovery of documents, for the holding of interlocutory proceedings and pre-trial reviews, and for the disposal by 'a member or members of the Lands Tribunal selected by the President for that purpose' of preliminary points of law (not to be confused with appeals on points of law to the Court of Appeal by way of case stated).[17]

11 Land Compensation Act 1961, s 4 (1), (2).
12 Ibid, s 3.
13 Lands Tribunal Rules 1975, rr 16, 17. (The notice 'shall not be given before the expiration of 28 days from the date of service or constructive service of the notice to treat or (where no notice to treat is served or is deemed to be served) of the notice of claim': r 16 (3)).
14 Ibid, Part VII (rr 31 to 62).
15 Ibid, rr 33, 33A, 34, 35.
16 Ibid, rr 39, 44, 52.
17 Ibid, rr 40, 45, 45A, 49.

Decisions of the Tribunal 'shall be given in writing, together with a statement of the Tribunal's reasons for its decision' unless the Tribunal considers that an oral statement of decision and reasons will be appropriate instead.[18] The Tribunal may award interest on the compensation payable, from the date of the award but not earlier, at the same rate as a court could award on a judgment debt.[19]

## D. Deferred or advance payments

Because compensation must be claimed 'once and for all ... for all damages which can be reasonably foreseen' it is payable in the normal case, like damages at law, in a lump sum; while the implication seems clear that further loss can, in principle,[20] be claimed separately later on if it was not reasonably foreseeable, always assuming that such a thing could be satisfactorily proved. There was a power, seldom used in practice, for payment to be made for compulsory purchase by means of an annual rentcharge, 'secured in such manner as may be agreed between the parties' (and enforceable, upon default for 30 days or more after any payment due is demanded in writing, by proceedings in High Court, or by distress and sale of goods and chattels of the acquiring authority) for a vendor disposing of the fee simple.[1] This has now been repealed by the Rentcharges Act 1977.

Of more importance perhaps in modern circumstances is the possibility of paying compensation partly in advance. Until recently there was no statutory provision for this; though circular No. 15/69 of the Ministry of Housing and Local Government recommended acquiring authorities 'to give sympathetic consideration to requests for such

18 Ibid, r 54. 'Where an amount awarded or value determined by the Tribunal is dependent upon the decision of the Tribunal on a question of law which is in dispute in the proceedings, the Tribunal shall ascertain, and shall state in its decision, the alternative amount or value (if any) which it would have awarded or determined if it had decided otherwise on the question of law' (r 54 (3)).

In *Wilson v Liverpool City Council* (see footnote on p 116, above), the appellant did not ask the Tribunal to state alternative awards despite the fact that the law relating to the claim had been thrown into considerable doubt by the Court of Appeal's decision in the *West Midland Baptist (Trust)* case some time before. Lord Denning MR said: 'It is, of course, within the jurisdiction of (the Court of Appeal) to remedy errors made in point of law by a tribunal of first instance. . . . But it is a matter for the discretion of the court'. The discretion was not exercised on this occasion because the claimant had failed to use the alternative award procedure. Claimants and authorities alike should therefore take this procedure seriously.

19 Ibid, r 38 (applying s 20 of the Arbitration Act 1950). See *Weeks and Weeks v Thames Water Authority* (1979) 39 P & CR 208 (a case on injurious affection), in which the Lands Tribunal described it as 'curious' that it could not award interest to cover an earlier period notwithstanding that a claimant had been 'kept out of his money'.

20 *Re Ware and Regent's Canal Co* (1854) 9 Exch 395.

1 Compulsory Purchase Act 1965, s 24.

payment in advance', at any rate where general vesting declarations were being used. One difficulty which might be overcome in this way was 'the fact that an owner would be deprived of the title to his property, and might thereby be hindered in raising finance for the purchase of alternative accommodation' in many cases in which a general vesting declaration is used, because it transfers the legal title to the land much sooner than under the older procedure by notice to treat with subsequent conveyance.[2] The circular pointed out that an authority can recover any over-payments of compensation made in the course of an acquisition occurring by may of a general vesting declaration. Such over-payments must have been made in respect of undisclosed incumbrances or lack of title to the land or part of it. Disputes over the amount or apportionment of compensation involved are to be settled by the Lands Tribunal; and the amount as settled 'shall be recoverable as a simple contract debt in any court of competent jurisdiction'.[3]

Statutory authority for the payment of compensation in advance is now available in s 52 of the Land Compensation Act 1973. Claimants may demand this from an acquiring authority who have already either taken possession or, in the case of a dwelling acquired for council housing, served a notice allowing its occupier to remain in residence. The amount is 90% of the compensation as either agreed or (in default of agreement) estimated by the authority. If it is later found to have been incorrectly estimated the amount wrongly paid becomes repayable on demand. Payment is to be made within three months after the taking of possession or of the demand for payment, whichever is later. No advance, however, is payable if the land is mortgaged and the principal of the loan is more than 90% of the compensation; while if the principal is 90% or less, the amount of any advance payment must be reduced by whatever sum is necessary to secure the release of the mortgage. An advance payment under s 52 must be registered as a local land charge; and if the land is afterwards disposed of, or leased, by the recipient of the compensation the acquiring authority can 'set off' the amount of the advance against whatever further compensation (if any) may then become payable to a different claimant.

In *Simpson v Stoke-on-Trent City Council*,[4] the claimant sought a

---

2 Payment in advance must not be confused with *acquisition* in advance, that is to say acquisition 'notwithstanding that the land is not immediately required' (Town and Country Planning Act 1959, ss 46 and 48, relating to 'town development' and trunk roads respectively; and see also New Towns Act 1981, s 10, for wide powers of acquisition by new town development corporations).

3 Compulsory Purchase (Vesting Declarations) Act 1981, s 11, re-enacting Town and Country Planning Act 1968, Third Schedule, paras 10 to 15.

4 (1982) 44 P & CR 226. It was stated that, in addition to paying up to 90% in cases coming under s 52, the authority in this case also operated a 'local scheme' under which they would agree to pay up to 75% to claimants still occupying (for good reasons) the property being acquired. For disturbance compensation, see below, ch 10.

'bridging loan' to finance the purchase of another house on the compulsory purchase of his previous one, and claimed the interest payable on that house as an item of disturbance compensation. The Lands Tribunal refused to award it, saying that he could have sought an advance payment under s 52 and having failed to do so he could not fairly unload the resulting financial burden on to the acquiring authority.

# Chapter 7

# Market value

## A. The general concept

### 1 NEED FOR STATUTORY INTERVENTION

The question of market value is a paradox which lies at the heart of the law of compulsory purchase of land. 'Market value' as a concept means a purely natural phenomenon, namely a price-level reached between buyers and sellers bargaining with the minimum of artificial constraints: in theory without any such constraints. But this condition of the 'free market' is the very opposite of the condition of a compulsory purchase, which is ex hypothesi a situation of constraint. Therefore to say that compulsory purchase compensation is to be assessed at 'market value' is to say that a state of affairs is to be visualised in terms of its direct opposite.

This problem did not appear pressing, at least to Parliament, before 1919, the assumption being that although there might well be difficult disputes over compensation, they would be such as any competent valuer could solve without special guidance from the law. This did not prevent disputes from reaching the courts, and the courts had to evolve various rules of law to settle them. These rules, being required for the purposes of a branch of law based on statute, depended first of all on the twin principles of statutory interpretation and reasonableness. But they were helped out by the application of common law doctrines on the footing that, since compulsory purchase involves the sale of land with compulsion added, the law of contract must also be relevant.

The results produced by judicial reasoning did not give full satisfaction to the guardians of the public purse, who felt that the courts had opened the door to a certain amount of overcharging. The sudden increase of state intervention in the life of the community, caused by the First World War, made the question seem urgent; and statutory rules for the assessment of compensation were imposed by Parliament in the Acquisition of Land (Assessment of Compensation) Act 1919. These rules have been added to since 1919; and they have themselves been subject to judicial interpretation, a fate that can happen to any statute. They have not claimed to cover every detailed problem of compensation; and in any case they did not conflict with every aspect of the rules previously developed by the courts. As a result we now have a comprehensive statutory framework of principles for purchase price compensation, with details partly to be found in the statutory rules and partly contained in judicial decisions. It will be convenient to take the present statutory framework of principles as a basis, and relate to it the detailed points of law derived both from the statutory provisions and from the cases.

## 2 THE OBJECTIVE APPROACH AND THE POINTE GOURDE RULE

By virtue of s 9 of the Land Compensation Act 1961 there must be disregarded any depreciation of 'the relevant land' attributable to the fact that 'an indication has been given', in the current development plan or otherwise, that it 'is, or is likely, to be acquired by an authority possessing compulsory purchase powers'—no reduction of compensation, in other words, is allowed for the acquiring authority's benefit simply because the acquisition is compulsory. It will be seen, from the 'willing seller' principle to be discussed shortly, that this provision may not be strictly necessary; it was no doubt put in to make assurance doubly sure. In any case it is consistent with the general concept of 'market value' in compulsory purchase by being (a) just, and (b) artificial. 'Relevant land' simply means (in effect) the land being acquired, and no other.

Presumably all that was intended was that the acquiring body should not be heard to argue: 'Had we not come along, you could have sold your land on the open market for £ (x+y). But this compulsory purchase by us means that no other buyer is interested any longer. Therefore the price must be reduced to only £x.' However the courts have decided that s 9 is more 'flexible' than that.[1]

The converse[2] of this rule is not enacted, presumably because it is not necessary. But there is said to be a closely related rule, laid down by the Judicial Committee of the Privy Council in *Pointe Gourde Quarrying and Transport Co v Sub-intendent of Crown Lands*.[3] The Crown compulsorily acquired land in Trinidad which was needed for constructing a United States naval base during the Second World War. The owners added to their claim for the market value of the land, an additional item of compensation in respect of the stone produced by their quarry on the land. They argued that the stone was particularly valuable for the naval base, saving the need to transport other stone from further afield—presumably this reasoning applied alike to stone already quarried and

1 See below, p 134.
2 Meaning *increase* in value due to the prospect of compulsory acquisition. This, like depreciation, is a question of valuation fact; it must not be confused with the pre-1919 practice of adding 10 per cent to the value of land if an acquisition was compulsory, which was not a question of fact but virtually a question of law (or at any rate, of custom) (see the 1961 Act, s 5, rule (i): p 136, below).
3 [1947] AC 565.

stone to be quarried in the future. This head of claim was rejected. It was only relevant to the particular project of the acquiring authority, not to the general market value of the land, because no other purchaser of the land would have been interested in paying more by reason of the fact that the stone was useful for the proposed naval base. There was no general demand for the *land* from persons wanting to use the *stone*, only from persons wanting to use the land which in its existing state comprised the quarry. Persons needing the stone would want to buy it on its own as produce, not to buy the land that produced it. The general demand from potential quarry operators was reflected in the general market value figure already referred to, which was not disputed.[4]

The apparent principle in this case is usually expressed by saying that no additional amount of compensation is payable if it relates solely to the scheme or project for which the acquiring authority needs the land. In *Wilson v Liverpool City Council*,[5] the acquiring authority compulsorily purchased land for a council housing scheme. As soon as it was known that the compulsory purchase order had been confirmed, an adjoining owner sold some land to a private developer for £6,700 an acre. Lord Denning MR said: 'That value was an enhanced value because seller and purchaser knew of the scheme; and knew that the council would install sewage works, and so forth, of which the developer could take advantage.' The Land Tribunal assessed compensation at a figure of only £4,600 an acre for the land compulsorily purchased, although both areas of land were comparable for valuation purposes. They disregarded the difference in values between the two figures as 'an increase in value which is entirely due to the scheme underlying, the acquisition', as Lord MacDermott put it in the *Pointe Gourde* case.[6] The Court of Appeal not only upheld the decision that this principle should apply to the current case, but also approved the view of the Lands Tribunal that it should apply whether or not 'the scheme is precise and definite'. The council's scheme was not settled in detail until later; but the Lands Tribunal thought that 'a prospective purchaser . . . would have known well enough . . . what the (council's) scheme was . . . at the very latest . . . when the compulsory purchase order was confirmed'.

Lord Denning MR commented: 'A scheme is a progressive thing. It starts vague and known to few. It becomes more precise and better known as time goes on. Eventually it becomes precise and definite, and known to all. Correspondingly, its impact has a progressive effect on values. At first it has little effect because it is so vague and uncertain. As it becomes more precise and better known, so its impact increases until it

---

4  On the question of minerals, see ch 3, p 41, above.

5  [1971] 1 All ER 628, [1971] 1 WLR 302, discussed in the previous chapter with regard to the date for the assessment of compensation (see p 116, footnote 11).

6  [1947] AC 565 at p 572; note that the difference had nothing to do with the difference between 'existing use' value and development value, discussed in ch 8, below.

has an important effect. *It is this increase, whether big or small, which is to be disregarded as at the time when the value is to be assessed.'*

It is very doubtful whether the *Pointe Gourde* principle is either sound or just. Its application in the *Wilson* case seems unfair: why should one owner get less per acre than his neighbour for comparable land, merely because he sold under compulsion and his neighbour did not? The decision in the *Pointe Gourde* case is correct enough in itself, because the actual item of claim in dispute was attributable to an inconsistency of reasoning, as shown above.[7] But it is unsound to refer to a particular inconsistency in terms of a general principle expressed as 'an increase in value which is entirely due to the scheme'. What should be disregarded as a matter of principle is not 'increase in value' (which is ex hypothesi imaginary anyway) but the fact of compulsion. This, though ex hypothesi extremely real, is inevitably quite incompatible with the concept of 'market value'; and the law depends entirely on 'market value' because there is no other objective test available at present, and objectivity is vital. The so-called *Pointe Gourde* rule,[8] therefore, not only differs from the true rule—the 'willing seller' rule (see p 136, below)—but distracts attention from it.

The objection to the alleged *Pointe Gourde* principle is that its effects are erratic, as the *Wilson* case shows. A more remarkable example is *Jelson Ltd v Blaby District Council.*[9] Land outside Leicester was chosen in the 1930s as the site of a possible new road. In the 1950s private housing development was allowed on surrounding land except for a strip where the new road was expected to go. Then the road scheme was abandoned. The landowners applied for planning permission for housing development; but the narrowness of the strip and the proximity of the houses built nearby made such development unacceptable and permission was refused. A purchase notice[10] followed, and the local authority was compelled to buy the land.

The proceedings then became a dispute over compensation. What was the market value of this land? The value of its existing use as a strip of grassland was negligible. Its development value for housing (or anything else), as will be seen in the next chapter, depends on planning permission and market demand both being available.[11] It was possible that developers would wish to acquire the strip if planning permission were

---

7 To argue as the claimant did in the *Pointe Gourde* case is rather like saying that the market price of a farm as a going concern includes not only the land, the goodwill and the equipment but also the retail value of all the produce into the bargain. The point at issue was expressed admirably by Lord Moulton in his statement quoted below, in ch 10 (see p 206, below).

8 A valuation rule if it were genuine, yet its origin is legal.

9 [1978] 1 All ER 548, [1977] 1 WLR 1020.

10 See ch 12, below, for purchase notices.

11 See below, ch 8, p 150—the *Camrose* case.

forthcoming, but this is problematical. Planning permission had been refused, but it might be assumed. As is explained in the next chapter, the Court of Appeal held that it could *not* be assumed.[12] This meant that development value was ruled out and only existing use value could be claimed: a harsh result but in clear accordance with the law.

The case came back to the Lands Tribunal to fix compensation in accordance with that decision. The Tribunal, and on appeal the Court of Appeal, held that *Pointe Gourde* principle *required development value to be paid*—the very item excluded by the Court of Appeal in the first decision. The principle, it was said, requires a decrease, as well as an increase, in value to be disregarded if it is 'entirely due to the scheme underlying the development'. Disregarding a decrease means allowing an increase. To reinforce the decision it was held also that s 9 of the 1961 Act (described above) produced the same result.

The Court of Appeal decision overturned the former Court of Appeal decision (which was in no way impugned) relating to the same matter. That s 9 applies seems doubtful, because the disputed strip was not 'indicated' as being earmarked for compulsory purchase. This is the very reason why the purchase notice was used. As for *Pointe Gourde*, this reminds us that there can never be a 'scheme underlying' a purchase notice. Finally, the sum arrived at as being development value presupposed that the land in dispute was a mathematical fraction of the surrounding land already developed, and not what it was in reality, a strip too inconvenient to build on by virtue of its shape.

The decision can plausibly be defended on the ground that it merely allowed the claimants to recover some development value of which the adverse terms of the planning decision had deprived them. The answer to that is that Parliament has expressly legislated against giving compensation for such adverse planning decisions, so that the decision ran counter to statute, which is scarcely just to the local authority or the public.[13]

Contrasting with the *Jelson* case is *Birmingham District Council v Morris and Jacombs*,[14] also a decision by the Court of Appeal. The landowners were granted planning permission to develop an area of land conditionally upon their leaving a small portion for vehicle access. There was in fact alternative access, and instead of using the small portion of land as the condition required they applied for further permission to develop it. Naturally this was refused; and they then served a purchase notice, which was upheld. Again, the dispute centred on the distinction between a small figure for existing use value (as access to developed land) and a

---

12 See below, ch 8, p 164—the *Jelson* case (first dispute).
13 Compensation for adverse planning decisions generally is discussed below, in chs 15 and 16.
14 (1976) 33 P & CR 27. See also *Myers v Milton Keynes Development Corpn*, discussed in ch 8 (below, p 151).

large figure for residential development value. The *Pointe Gourde* principle was not applied, and it was held that the alleged 'diminution' from the large to the small figure did not result from the 'scheme', so that the small figure was the proper one.[15] Ormrod LJ said: 'This so-called principle . . . in fact consists of a single sentence taken out of Lord MacDermott's speech giving the opinion of the Privy Council in the *Pointe Gourde* case. . . . That is now said to be a principle. This seems to me to be another example of the widespread tendency to isolate a statement or sentence in a judgment of, or a speech in, the House of Lords and call it a principle, with all the consequential difficulties that arise'.[16]

Once again, it is to be observed that all talk of a 'scheme' is beside the mark because the relevant compulsory acquisition—the purchase notice—was not for the purpose of any scheme of the acquiring authority. It will be seen later (in ch 13) that purchase notice acquisitions are deemed to be 'for planning purposes' under Part VI of the Town and Country Planning Act 1971, whereas the development value in question in the *Morris and Jacombs* case and the *Jelson* case related to the private development on the adjoining land.

It will be noticed that the *Pointe Gourde* rule is said to require valuers to 'disregard an increase' or 'disregard a decrease', as the case may be, if such an item of alleged value is solely attributable to the 'scheme'. In disputes such as the *Wilson* case it was necessary to 'disregard an increase'; and nothing was said about s 9 of the 1961 Act. This implies that an increase must *not* be disregarded because it says that a decrease *must* be disregarded if 'attributable' to the compulsory purchase. Yet in disputes such as the *Jelson* case s 9 and the *Pointe Gourde* rule appear to work in harmony in that both point to 'disregarding a decrease'.

But presumably *Pointe Gourde* and s 9 ought to be in harmony always or not at all. That they should coincide in half the cases and conflict in the other half hardly makes sense. Moreover the decisions embody other weaknesses. Considering *Pointe Gourde* requires attention to be focussed on the 'scheme'; yet s 9 is concerned not with the 'scheme' (if any) but with the compulsory purchase itself. A purchase notice does not occur for furtherance of any 'scheme' whatever, but merely in consequence of a need to preserve a claimant from injustice.

Further complications occur when 'marriage value' is involved, as in *Trocette Property Co Ltd v Greater London Council*.[17] The claimants held a lease, with 11 years to run, of a cinema. The respondents were at one and the same time the local planning authority and the freeholders; and they refused (as freeholders) to grant a new lease to facilitate redevelopment of

---

15 The facts of this case should be compared and contrasted with those of the *Adams & Wade* case discussed in ch 12 (below, p 244).
16 (1976) 33 P & CR at p 38.
17 (1974) 28 P & CR 408 (on marriage value see below, p 141).

the site, because (as planning authority) they thought it might be wanted at some date for a new road. This denied to the claimants any 'marriage value' which might have accrued to their leasehold by way of a share of development value likely to arise if the leaseholder and freeholder had agreed to join forces and redevelop. The claimants successfully served a purchase notice, and persuaded the Court of Appeal that 'marriage value' should be included in the compensation. Section 9 and *Pointe Gourde* worked together, it would seem, to induce the Court to 'disregard' the 'decrease' caused by loss of the 'marriage value'. Yet the acquisition had in fact come about because of the purchase notice, and not because of any 'scheme' for a new road, since that road was merely a possibility at some future time. This meant that the Court had to concentrate on s 9 rather than *Pointe Gourde*. Section 9, it appears, is 'flexible', by virtue of the words 'attributable' and 'indication' which it contains. With this 'flexibility' should be contrasted the meticulous approach of the Lands Tribunal to the question of indicating what statutory functions the land is acquired for under a purchase notice, as displayed in *Hyatt v Dover Corpn.*[18]

The *Pointe Gourde* doctrine has been accepted without comment by the Privy Council in *Melwood Units Pty Ltd v Commissioner of Main Roads.*[19] This and the other leading cases all show that, whatever its origins, the doctrine's use today is largely (though not entirely) attuned to development value. The 'increase' and 'decreases' commonly tend in practice to be inclusions or exclusions of development value. The law relating to this aspect of market value is considered in the next chapter.

## 3 'COMPARABLES' AND OTHER 'MARKET VALUE' FACTORS

It has become reasonably apparent at this stage that 'market value' is very definitely a generalised concept, not a particular phenomenon. What any particular purchaser pays for land, whether at public auction or by private treaty, is not of itself 'market value': though of course as a matter of practical convenience it is natural enough for valuers to use the phrase in this sense. It will, however, be very relevant *evidence* upon which a finding of 'market value' should be based.

The best way to understand 'market value' is to imagine going to an experienced and competent valuer and asking him for his advice as to the

---

**18** (1951) 2 P & CR 32. See below, ch 12, p 246.
**19** [1979] AC 426, [1979] 1 All ER 161. Note that, in Lord Russell's opinion: '. . . it is plain that in assessing compensation for compulsory acquisition a tribunal is not required to close its mind to transactions subsequent to the date of [acquisition]: they may well be relevant . . . to a greater or lesser degree. . . .' The Australian term for compulsory purchase which readers of the reports of the *Melwood Units* case will no doubt bear in mind, is 'resumption'—ie the land is being 'resumed' (at least in theory) by its original owner at common law, the Crown.

likely price which he would expect a particular property to fetch *if it were to be sold.*[20] Recent previous prices will probably help him to arrive at a figure, whether they were given for the same land or for comparable land. They may not necessarily be consistent with one another, since evidence does not always present itself in the most helpful form. If so, it may well be necessary to look carefully for special factors which suggest an explanation for any discrepancy, even if all that can be discovered is a difference in the individuals concerned.

One factor may be that allegedly 'comparable' values arrived at for other properties may have been fixed in an agreed settlement and not in an expert adjudication by the Lands Tribunal. If there is a lack of proper advice, such figures may be too low. In *Xerri and Shanks v Enfield London Borough Council,*[1] Sir Michael Rowe QC, then President of the Lands Tribunal, commented on this problem. 'This Tribunal has said on more than one occasion that the danger . . . is a real one, though it seldom carries with it any stigma of unfair conduct by a District Valuer or his officers; but the Tribunal has also said that if settlements of this kind *are* to be disregarded, there must be evidence clear and positive to prove that they were on too low a basis.'

There are other possibilities. In *IRC v Clay and Buchanan,*[2] assessment had to be made of the market value of a house for tax purposes. It had been sold to its present owner not long before, who wanted it in order to extend an adjoining nursing-home. The previous owner sold for £1,000, having earlier refused to put it on the market for £750 which was the current price-level for comparable houses. Whatever might be thought of suggesting £1,000 in advance as the market value being a *prospective* figure for some possible use, in this case £1,000 was an *actual* figure already paid. The Court of Appeal therefore rejected arguments that the current value was not £1,000 but £750. The conclusion to be drawn from this case seems to be that, whereas 'market value' is a generalised figure which a valuer should put forward by way of professional advice in relation to a prospective sale, an actual particular price, already paid in fact, is proper evidence to be taken into account by the valuer in reaching such a figure. This may be subject perhaps to a rule that any such price should be disregarded if for some reason it is unreliable, for example if it is not genuine but was arrived at in a collusive transaction.

---

20  In the related field of estate duty valuation, Ungoed-Thomas J said in *Re Hayes's Will Trusts, Pattinson v Hayes* [1971] 2 All ER 341 [1971] 1 WLR 758: 'It has been established time and again . . . that there is a range of price, in some circumstances wide, which competent valuers would recognise as the price which "propery *would fetch* if sold in the open market".'
1  (1966) 18 P & CR 117.
2  [1914] 3 KB 466.

# B. The six main rules of valuation

Section 2 of the Act of 1919, now re-enacted with slight changes of wording by s 5 of the Act of 1961, laid down six rules to govern the assessment of market value. They may be regarded as the basic rules, because they are concerned solely with land being acquired, without apparently considering other land either as affecting, or being affected by, the land acquired, from the standpoint of value. But, as will be seen,[3] depreciation for land not acquired is also in many cases to be covered by compensation, in addition to purchase price compensation for land acquired. Section 5 provides, 'Compensation in respect of any compulsory acquisition shall be assessed . . .', and this wording seems wide enough to cover depreciation of land retained as well as payment for land acquired. The section also speaks of compensation for any matter 'not directly based on the value of land'. If this formula is applied, the conclusion seems to follow that depreciation as well as purchase price compensation requires payment to be 'directly based on the value of land'; and this by implication, suggests that s 5 must apply equally to both kinds of compensation.

## 1 RULE (*i*)

The first of the six rules is: 'No allowance shall be made on account of the acquisition being compulsory', which Lord Denning MR has described[4] as being 'directed to the added sop (which was in the old days always given in these cases) of 10 per cent to soften the blow of compulsory acquisition. Rule (*i*) disallows that 10 per cent'. The 10% rule was evolved as a matter of custom and accepted by the courts: notably in *Re Athlone Rifle Range*,[5] in which the custom was upheld in principle although an attempt to get 20% was rejected. Whether any such allowance should be allowed, or (as now) not allowed, is a policy question. Whether a flat rate of 10% in all cases would be anything other than purely arbitrary is a separate question of principle.[6]

## 2 RULE (*ii*)

The second rule of s 5 is the most important: 'The value of land shall, subject as hereinafter provided, be taken to be the amount which the land if sold in the open market by a willing seller might be expected to realise.' The first comment on this statement is that it clearly treats the marketing of the land in question as a notional transaction, distinct from

3  Ch 9.
4  In *Harvey v Crawley Development Corpn* [1957] 1 QB 485, [1957] 1 All ER 504.
5  [1902] 1 IR 433.
6  It may well be that the 10% allowance was intended to cover prospective development value. If so, it is understandable but still arbitrary.

the actual compulsory purchase—especially if the compensation to be assessed is for depreciation and not as a purchase price. The seller is not really 'willing', because either the acquisition is fully compulsory or else it is made by agreement but under compulsory powers. Each valuer concerned is, in other words, required to give his professional advice on a *likely figure* just as he would in a free sale, bearing in mind that the 'freedom' of this sale is notional, not actual.

The next comment is that payment of purchase price compensation (and probably of compensation for depreciation also) relates to the land in question as a capital asset at the time of assessment, not to its produce, income or future profits regarded as separate entities. The question of produce has been touched on already in the *Pointe Gourde* case. Prospective profits of a building developer were excluded from compensation in *Wimpey & Co Ltd v Middlesex County Council*,[7] but it will be seen later that loss of profits currently being earned by an existing business, and loss of 'goodwill', which is the value of a business as a capital asset, are compensatable under the heading of 'disturbance'.

The third comment is that there must obviously be a willing buyer as well as a willing seller; though of course the acquiring authority can be regarded as a more-than-willing buyer, which is why rule (ii) troubles to refer only to the seller. But it should be pointed out that there are cases where there is no likelihood of any buyer being 'willing' to buy at the lowest price at which the seller is 'willing' to sell. This is the situation which brings rule (v) into play—the 'equivalent reinstatement' rule discussed below.

The wording of rule (*ii*) is very similar to wording in the Finance (1909 to 1910) Act 1910 which was interpreted in the *Clay and Buchanan* case already referred to. There, 'in the open market' was held to imply that land is 'offered under conditions enabling every person desirous of purchasing to come in and make an offer'. A 'willing seller' is 'one who is a free agent', not 'a person willing to sell his property without reserve for any price he can obtain for it'. A price which the land is 'expected to realise' implies a reference to 'the expectations of properly qualified persons who have taken pains to inform themselves of all the particulars ascertainable about the property, and its capabilities, the demand for it, and the likely buyers'[8]—in short, the professional opinions of competent valuers. It may be further deduced that although the free nature of the particular acquisition must be notional, the state of the market taken into account is actual.[9]

---

7 [1938] 3 All ER 781. For 'goodwill' see ch 10, p 202, below.
8 *IRC v Clay and Buchanan* [1914] 3 KB 466 (Swinfen Eady LJ and Cozens Hardy MR).
9 Restrictions applying to the property must be taken into account: *Corrie v MacDermott* [1914] AC 1056. If the property consists of licensed premises the value of the licence, including whether or not it is in suspense, must be duly taken into account also: *Tull's Personal Representatives v Secretary of State for Air* [1957] 1 QB 523, [1957] 1 All ER 480.

Particular care is, however, needed in cases of severance. Whether this may occur at all is a question already discussed in chapter 5; while the payment of severance compensation, in regard to land retained by its owner after other land is in fact severed from it under compulsory powers, is discussed later in chapter 9. But the problem here is the effect of severance on the market value of the land actually taken. To put it bluntly, can the acquiring authority achieve an advantageous reduction of compensation by taking a substantial part of an owner's land which has a disproportionately low value in isolation, instead of taking it all?

For example they may decide that they can make do with 99 out of a total of 100 acres, the remaining acre constituting the sole access to the 99, so that the latter have only a derisory value on their own;[10] the fact being that the authority happen already to have another piece of land of their own which will provide an alternative access. The answer is that they cannot. If the owner's 99 acres currently enjoy a viable access through his remaining acre, the market value of the 99 must remain undiminished precisely because that access is available.[11] On the other hand, the owner may have 99 acres, not without any access at all, which is unlikely, but without an access which will be adequate if the land is to be capable of effective development and enjoy any corresponding development value (as discussed in chapter 8). If so, the full market value for development is not payable merely because the authority already have such an access available to them independently; instead it is only to be paid subject to a deduction representing what the owner would himself have had to pay in order to obtain the access necessary to carry out development.[12]

If because of its special historic or architectural character property has been 'listed' by the Secretary of State for the Environment under s 54 of the Town and Country Planning Act 1971, any depreciation in value attributable to that fact is to be disregarded to the extent that permission must be assumed to be available for any works of alteration or extension, except in so far as he has already refused permission for them (or granted conditional permission merely); but no such permission is to be assumed

But the prospect of rehousing the occupier of residential property is irrelevant to the question of his compensation and must be disregarded, whether as an argument for decreasing his compensation (if any) or for increasing his landlord's; Land Compensation Act 1973, s 50 (see above, ch 5, p 91).

10   Usually referred to as 'accommodation land'. Another aspect of the same problem is the question of separate but adjacent parcels of land. If their value in the aggregate is different from the aggregate of their separate values, what is their 'market value'? As to this, see Lord Watson's statement of principle in *Cowper-Essex v Acton Local Board* (below, ch 9, p 179).

11  *Earl Fitzwilliam's Wentworth Estates v British Railways Board* (1967) 19 P & CR 588.

12  *Stokes v Cambridge Corpn* (1961) 13 P & CR 77.

for any demolition unless involved with carrying out marginal development under Schs 8 and 18 to and s 278 of the 1971 Act.[13]

## 3 RULE (iii)

The third rule of s 5 provides:

The special suitability or adaptability of the land for any purpose shall not be taken into account if that purpose is a purpose to which it could be applied only in pursuance of statutory powers, or for which there is no market apart from the special needs of a particular purchaser or the requirements of any authority possessing compulsory purchase powers.

Before the objective 'willing seller' rule was enacted in 1919, the courts had already applied it or something like it. At any rate they said that 'value' meant value to the seller. The Judicial Committee of the Privy Council so held in a Canadian case, *Cedar Rapids Manufacturing and Power Co v Lacoste*;[14] and Eve J, expressed the same view in *South Eastern Rly Co v LCC*.[15] Earlier, in an unreported case[16] in which a water authority required land adjoining a lake for the purpose of water-supply installations, it was held that an enhanced value could properly be attached to the land in consequence of the authority's purposes, and they must therefore pay more for lakeshore land than any normal market purchaser could have been expected to offer. But even so the increased value must be attributable to a market in relation to their project, not merely to their particular need in respect of that project. Again, in *Re Lucas and Chesterfield Gas and Water Board*,[17] the fact that the purchaser's purpose depended on statutory powers was said not to invalidate the attribution of additional value; but it was held that the determining factor is whether there is a genuine market not the need of the authority to carry out particular project for which the land is acquired.

There is no rule that a 'market' must necessarily consist of more than one buyer; and the truth of this will be seen below when 'marriage value'

---

13 Town and Country Planning Act 1971, s 116, amended by Town and Country Amenities Act 1974, s 6. For marginal development value see below, ch 16.

14 [1914] AC 569. See also *Vyricherla Narayana Gajapatiraju v Revenue Divisional Officer, Vizagapatam* [1939] AC 302.

15 [1915] 2 Ch 252. Note the formulation of the principle by the Judicial Committee of the Privy Council in *Fraser v City of Fraserville* [1917] AC 187 at 194: '. . . the actual value to be ascertained is the value to the seller of the property in its actual condition at the time of expropriation with all its existing advantages and with all its possibilities, excluding any advantage due to the carrying out of the scheme for which the property is compulsorily acquired'.

16 *Manchester Corpn v Countess Ossalinsky* (unreported, but tried in the High Court in April 1883—see next footnote).

17 [1909] 1 KB 16. The report contains extracts from the *Ossalinsky* case just mentioned, in which Grove J is in fact shown to have been enunciating the basis of the modern doctrine, though the award of higher compensation in the case itself was not disturbed.

of land is discussed. Indeed there will frequently be several 'markets' for a given piece of property, some wide, some narrow. The vendor will wish to sell in the market which commands the highest price, however wide or narrow it may be, in other words whether there are a hundred buyers or merely one. But if there are no genuine buyers at all then clearly there is no market.

The key words of the third rule are, therefore, 'no market'. Also, if a 'purpose' (prospective use of land) cannot be achieved without statutory powers, this is to be left out of account on the same footing as the absence of a 'market'. And if demand for the land in question is evinced only by a particular purchaser's special needs', or by a project which cannot be achieved except by a public body with compulsory powers under an authorising Act, then there is no effective 'market'. It is often said the the *Clay and Buchanan* case led to the inclusion of the words 'special needs of a particular purchaser'. But the wording of the rule seems to relate to a potential acquisition, whereas the acquisition under dispute in that case had already taken place.[18]

A similar problem may arise where there is (say) farmland, or industrial or commercial land, which is likely to have more attraction for a neighbouring owner—to enable him to extend his property—than for a newcomer in the same line of activity. But what if there are two such owners, the rule above referring only to 'a particular purchaser'? Perhaps the best answer is that a general purpose such as farming, or commercial or industrial activity, commands a generalised market demand, and is to be distinguished from 'special needs'. The attraction of the property in this case would be essentially a question of its position and not its condition. If so, a valuer might properly advise its owner as prospective vendor, that its 'market value' was higher by virtue of its likely attraction for any neighbouring owner.[19]

A comparable case came before the Court of Appeal in *Lambe v Secretary of State for War*.[20] Here the special attractiveness was that of a landlord's reversion in the eyes of a sitting tenant. The latter would pay more than any other purchaser, who would only be obtaining an investment; and a valuer could properly advise the vendor of the reversion that the 'market value' would in fact be the higher amount obtainable from a sitting tenant. This argument, like the similar argument based on special

18  The Lands Tribunal has emphasised the particularity of the 'particular purchaser', saying that: '. . . the effect on value of the demand of a particular purchaser is quite different from the effect on value of the demand of a particular class of purchaser; the phrase 'a particular purchaser' clearly indicates the singular, and cannot include the plural without altering the meaning' (*Frank Boot Stores Ltd v City of London Corpn* (1971) 22 P & CR 1124 at 1132). In other words, the context excludes the normal rule under the Interpretation Act 1978 that the singular embraces the plural and vice versa.

19  This could only be a generalised factor, subject to any evidence of interest from actual neighbouring owners, as in the *Clay and Buchanan* case, above (p 135).

20  [1955] 2 QB 612, [1955] 2 All ER 386.

attraction for neighbouring owners, might seem doubtful on the ground that the prospect is not sufficiently generalised to amount to a 'market', and the particular neighbour or sitting tenant may not be sufficiently interested or well-off to purchase in the actual circumstances. But a 'market of one' can be genuine.

This higher market value attributable to the special advantages of combining a lease with a reversion, or two neighbouring properties, or the like, is often termed 'marriage value'. One of the benefits which may flow from it is the possibility of realising development potential in the land, because this is normally something which is best achieved by an owner-occupier of a unified site. Development value is discussed in the next chapter. An example of such a situation has however been commented on already.[1]

The court accepted the argument for the higher amount in *Lambe's* case and rejected the acquiring authority's claim that it was excluded by the 'special suitability' rule.[2] Now, it may well be that a valuer is justified in advising a vendor to aim at receiving the higher figure, even if it turns out afterwards that the special purchaser was not forthcoming. But the acquiring body in *Lambe's* case were themselves the sitting tenant. Had they bought the reversion alone, presumably they need only pay for it as an investment.[3] If so, then by the same reasoning an acquiring authority will only have to pay a higher figure for land which has a special attraction for a neighbouring owner if they are themselves such a neighbouring owner. The difference between what is actual, and has happened, and what is potential, and might happen, ought to be taken fully into account. As Lord Robertson said in *Bwllfa and Merthyr Dare Steam Collieries (1891) Ltd v Pontypridd Waterworks Co*[4] '. . . it is natural that the compensation should be assessed once and for all, and by estimate. But . . . as in this instance facts are available they are not to be shut out'.[5]

The acquiring authority in the *Pointe Gourde* case at first attempted to apply the 'special suitability' rule when resisting the owner's claim, referred to earlier, for additional compensation in respect of the availability of stone for the proposed naval base. The Judicial Committee of

1 The *Trocette Property Co Ltd* case: see above, p 133.
2 Parker LJ said: 'The expression "special suitability or adaptability of the land" in rule (3) is . . . clearly referring to the quality of the land. . . . The fact that the sitting tenant may be prepared to pay more than an investor in order not to be turned out does not clothe the land with special suitability, within that rule, the value of which is to be ignored' ([1955] 2 QB 612 at p 619). Note that 'special suitability' governs 'the special needs of a particular purchaser'; therefore once 'special suitability' was held not to apply to the acquiring body's purpose the fact that they were a 'particular purchaser' (if they were) could not help them.
3 For leaseholds and reversions generally, see ch 5, pp 87–95. See in particular p 90: value of the benefit of covenants (*Leek v Birmingham City Council*).
4 [1903] AC 426.
5 See *LCC v Tobin*, ch 10, p 203.

the Privy Council, although finding for the authority on the grounds already explained, held that exclusion of value for 'special suitability' did not apply to the special suitability of products of the land, but only of the land itself.

## 4   RULE (*iv*)

The fourth rule of s 5 excludes any item of value depending on the use of any of the property 'in a manner which could be restrained by any court, or is contrary to law, or is deterimental to the health of the occupants of the premises or to the public health'. Disputes do not seem to have arisen over this rule; but its relevance to the question of 'site value' compensation for 'unfit houses' will be considered at the end of the next chapter.

## 5   RULE (*v*)

The fifth rule of s 5 is of great practical importance:

Where land is, and but for the compulsory acquisition would continue to be, devoted to a purpose of such a nature that there is no general demand or market for land for that purpose, the compensation may, if the Lands Tribunal is satisfied that reinstatement in some other place is bona fide intended, be assessed on the basis of the reasonable cost of equivalent reinstatement.

Section 45 of the Land Compensation Act 1973 states that a claimant can choose to have his premises treated as being within this rule if they comprise a dwelling currently or last occupied by a disabled person and modified for his use.

The rule applies when the property taken is such that no-one is likely to buy it on the open market for more than a nominal sum, whereas the owners on expropriation lose an asset they cannot expect to replace without buying other land at a market price which is likely to be anything but nominal. Church premises are a typical example of property for which the 'equivalent reinstatement' rule is appropriate, as for example in the *West Midland Baptist* case already discussed, in which a chapel was compulsorily acquired. Lord Reid observed: 'The date on which reinstatement might reasonably have begun was the date by which they could have made contracts for the rebuilding work which would have determined its total cost.'[6]

As with the 'material detriment' rule, the Lands Tribunal is given a discretion, and it is unlikely that an appeal to the Court of Appeal could succeed unless the Tribunal's exercise of discretion in a particular case were plainly unreasonable. Notable decisions in which the Tribunal has exercised its discretion against 'equivalent reinstatement' include *Edge Hill Light Rly Co v Secretary of State for War*,[7] where the finding was that

6   [1969] 3 All ER 172 at 174.
7   (1956) 6 P & CR 211.

reinstatement was not bona fide intended, and *Festiniog Rly Co v Central Electricity Generating Board*,[8] where the finding was that the cost of reinstatement would be disproportionately high in relation to the value of the concern expropriated.[9]

'Devoted to a purpose', however, must be interpreted reasonably and not too narrowly. In *Aston Charities Trust Ltd v Stepney Borough Council*,[10] it was held that the premises of a charitable trust did not cease to be 'devoted to the purpose' of the trust merely because war-time bomb damage obliged the trust to give up using most of the premises and to let part of it for storage. In *Zoar Independent Church Trustees v Rochester Corpn*[11] the Court of Appeal held, by a majority, that 'devoted' will cover a case in which premises are temporarily out of use or used temporarily, occasionally or partly for any purpose other than their primary purpose. Although the premises acquired in this case comprised a ruinous chapel of which the congregation had dispersed, one of the trustees acquired new premises and set up a new trust for a new church with a new name but similar worship. The true test was held to be whether the purpose of the original chapel was to be reinstated, and on the facts the claimants were entitled to say that 'reinstatement in some other place is bona fide intended'. As for the question whether the original premises 'would continue to be' devoted to their purpose but for the acquisition, this must be considered as at the time of the notice to treat; and in this case the original chapel was still in use at that time in circumstances which suggested that the use was likely to continue.

Whether reinstatement cost is reasonable depends on the facts of each case. The replacement of monumental Victorian architecture by a modern functional construction often makes it difficult to decide on what is in truth 'equivalent' or comparable.[12]

---

8  (1962) 13 P & CR 248.

9  But see *Nonentities Society Trustees v Kidderminster Borough Council* (1970) 22 P & CR 224, *Manchester Homeopathic Clinic Trustee v Manchester Corpn* (1970) 22 P & CR 241, and *Sparks v Leeds City Council* (1977) 34 P & CR 234, in which equivalent reinstatement claims were upheld in respect of a theatre, a clinic and a political club respectively. There was no market demand for these, and there was a genuine and reasonable intent to reinstate them elsewhere. But in *Wilkinson v Middlesbrough Borough Council* (1981) 45 P & CR 142, the Court of Appeal held that use of premises for a veterinary practice was not 'a purpose of such a nature that there is no general demand or market': ie special factors relating the marketability of veterinary *practices* must not be applied to the marketability of the *premises*.

10  [1952] 2 QB 642, [1952] 2 All ER 228.

11  [1975] QB 246, [1974] 3 All ER 5.

12  What is unstated in relation to rule (*v*) is the question of 'prospective development value'. This is discussed in the next chapter; but it can be pointed out here that the nominal value of a building devoted to a special purpose can only be understood in the sense of value in relation to its existing use. If (as will be more fully explained in the next chapter) the site is attractive to developers, *and* planning permission for lucrative development exists or can be assumed, *and* the consequent market price (allowing for

## 6 RULE (*vi*)

The sixth and last rule of s 5 is, like the first, purely negative: 'The provisions of rule (*ii*) shall not affect the assessment of compensation for disturbance or any other matter not directly based on the value of land.' It may be deduced from this that depreciation of land, whether as 'severance' or 'injurious affection', is unlike 'disturbance' a matter 'directly based on the value of land' and therefore covered by rule (*ii*).[13]

# C. Neighbouring land

### 1 JUSTIFIABLE AND UNJUSTIFIABLE ASSUMPTIONS

The law leaves to valuers the difficult question of assessing value in each particular case. Unfortunately valuers often disagree, especially when representing opposing clients. A fertile source of disagreement lies in the fact that, not only is 'market value' in compulsory purchase a notional thing, but all valuations are notional to the extent of the assumptions that have to be made. The 'market' is a continuing thing, and interest largely centres on its future workings. Assumptions, based on sound professional experience, knowledge and technique, have to be made by every valuer.[14] A valuer has to decide what factors are relevant to the continuing value of a property and their relative importance one with another, what other properties if any are comparable and in what respects, and what allowances if any ought to be made for new factors which have yet to make their appearance. Various tables of figures for calculation purposes, and other external aids to assessment, are available to a good valuer as the tools of his trade; but he relies on his personal judgment, and uses, rather than leans on, these external aids.

It follows from this that there is plenty of scope for dispute about the assumptions any valuer makes; and Parliament has thought it necessary, in ss 6 to 8 of the 1961 Act, to restrict those which may be made as between one piece of land and another, in addition to stipulating in the six rules of s 5 the assumptions that may or may not be made when land is valued per se.

Section 6 and the First Schedule deal with the case where the acquiring authority are taking the claimant's land and other land together for some

demolition costs) is high enough to exceed the 'equivalent reinstatement' figure for compensation, then the development value figure and not the 'equivalent reinstatement' figure ought to be the right one. There is, however, also the question of 'disturbance' and the principle in *Horn v Sunderland Corpn* (see ch 10, p 200, below).

13 See ch 10, p 196, below.
14 See the comments (ch 8, p 164, below) on the reasoning of the House of Lords in *Margate Corpn v Devotwill Investments Ltd*.

public project involving development. In this diagram, the claimant's land is B.

It may be conceivable to a valuer that if B were *not* being acquired, the actual or prospective carrying out of the project on A might well (if beneficial) raise the value of B or (if objectionable) lower it. This is purely notional, because B is ex hypothesi being acquired, which is why the compulsory purchase compensation is in fact being assessed. Also, the boundary between A and B is irrelevant to the authority and their project, though it is clearly not irrelevant to the claimant. It is accordingly provided that no notional increase or decrease in value of B (the 'relevant land') is to be made on this assumption, *unless* the authority's project could reasonably be conceived as being carried out on A in *other* circumstances not involving acquisition by the acquiring authority.

As a rule, land A is the remainder of the land comprised in the compulsory purchase order.[15] But where land B is in 'an area of town development',[16] or an area of comprehensive development', as defined in the current development plan,[17] or within the area of a new town (or an extension of one),[18] land A will be not only any other land included in the compulsory purchase but any other land in the relevant area. That being so, the notional increase or decrease in value of B to be disregarded is that which could not reasonably be envisaged in the absence of the comprehensive development or of the designation of the new town or its extension, or of the town development, as the case may be.

Section 51 of the Land Compensation Act 1973 provides a further refinement in a case where land B is within the area of a new town, or an extension of one, designated for providing, as one of its main purposes, houses or 'other facilities' in relation to some specific public development. This particular 'public development', which can be any existing or proposed development project carried out under statutory powers by a government department, statutory undertakers or any body of persons authorised to borrow money with ministerial consent[19] and which need

15 Section 6 (3). More rarely it will be, instead of a compulsory purchase order, a special Act or provisional order, or in defence acquisitions (where this procedural stage is absent) the notice to treat (see ch 3, p 38, above).
16 Defined in s 1 (1) of the Town Development Act 1952.
17 See below, ch 11, for comprehensive development (now 'action areas').
18 Designated by an order made under s 1 of New Towns Acts 1965 or 1981.
19 A new airport, or a tunnel under the Channel, are possible projects which could bring s 51 into play.

*not* be within the designated new town area, has to be specified by the Secretary of State[20] 'in relation to that area' between the time when the new town order has been published in draft and the time when it is finally made. The notional increase or decrease in value of B which is to be disregarded will then include any 'which is attributable to the carrying out or the prospect of the public development specified.' Suppose the government plans to create a new port, and to build a new town nearby. Compensation for compulsory purchase of land for the new town must not be adjusted for any notional increase or decrease in the value of the land taken, attributable to activities on other land in the new town, unless it could be reasonably envisaged even if there were *neither* the new town *nor* the new port.[1]

Section 6 came up for consideration in *Davy v Leeds Corpn*.[2] Slum clearance was carried out by the respondent corporation by means of compulsory purchase, to be followed by clearing and redeveloping the site. The appellant claimed that his land, included in the area to be compulsorily purchased, would be notionally increased in value as land B in the above diagram, by what was to happen on the surrounding land A. 'Instead of buying a site with houses in a bad condition around it, (a willing buyer) would be buying a site in an area which was bound to be cleared and available for development.' The question was whether the clearance (which, by virtue of s 6 (3) of the 1961 Act, is to be regarded as development) was likely in other circumstances to be carried out in the absence of compulsory purchase by the authority. The appellant claimed that it was likely, because the Housing Act 1957 prescribed two methods of slum clearance, and only one of them involved compulsory purchase. But the respondent corporation argued 'that there never had been a practical possibility of private developers redeveloping the land under consideration'; and the Court of Appeal and House of Lords held that this contention was established. As a matter of practicability, therefore, there never was any likelihood of slum clearance except in consequence of the authority's acquisition; and so the appellant failed to obtain enhanced compensation.[3]

## 2 'SET-OFF' AND SUBSEQUENT ACQUISITIONS

Section 7 and the First Schedule provide for 'set-off' in certain cases, that is to say a deduction from compensation. The justification is that the

---

20  In a direction given by order in the form of a statutory instrument subject to annulment by either House of Parliament.

1  So if a notional increase or decrease in that value can be reasonably envisaged even in the absence of the new town, it must still be disregarded if it is attributable to the new port.

2  [1965] 1 All ER 753, [1965] 1 WLR 445.

3  It is often said that these provisions cover the same subject-matter as the alleged *Pointe Gourde* doctrine discussed earlier in this chapter. But they relate strictly to neighbouring land, whereas the *Pointe Gourde* doctrine (as defined) does not.

claimant, in addition to 'the relevant land' compulsorily acquired from him, has 'other land contiguous or adjacent' to it which he retains, indicated in the accompanying diagram as C.

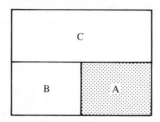

Thus the claimant originally owned B and C together; but the acquiring authority are taking A and B. This means that the claimant's retention of land is actual, and not merely notional as in s 6. If the land retained, namely C, is genuinely depreciated, it will be a question of claiming 'injurious affection' compensation. This is examined in chapter 9. Section 7 deals with the converse situation, which is that C genuinely increases in value by what is done on A and B. If this increase in value is attributable to the actual or prospective carrying out of the authority's project of development, it must be 'set-off' against the compensation payable in respect of B, provided that, and in so far as, it 'would not have been likely to be carried out' in other circumstances not involving acquisition by the acquiring authority. If the 'relevant land', B, is in an area of comprehensive development, or of a new town (or extension) or town development, the authority's development giving rise to the increase in value of C may be of any land in that area including B itself; but the set-off must not be made unless the development 'would not have been likely to be carried out' if that area had not been so declared. It should be noted that this is only a question of 'set-off' against compensation, so that an increase in value of C exceeding the compensation for B is not 'set-off' as far as that excess is concerned; and also that the 'set-off' must only be made if, as in *Davy's* case, there is no practicable possibility of the development giving rise to the increase being carried out in other circumstances.

The claimant must own land B and land C 'in the same capacity', which means beneficially, or as personal representative or trustee,[4] alike for each piece of land. Section 8 (5) provides that the 'set-off' prescribed by s 7 is not to be made if alternative 'set-off' provisions apply by virtue of a local enactment or of certain specified public general Acts. If the local enactment restricts the increase in value so 'set-off' to the 'existing use' of land (a term which will be explained later), this restriction must be disregarded.

4 Section 39 (6) of the 1961 Act.

Section 8 is chiefly concerned with two further situations, in which the acquiring authority make a subsequent acquisition of land for the same project. The first is where the land C is itself subsequently acquired. The second is where the land C is still not acquired but other land, D, which the claimant owns, or which a person deriving title from him owns, is

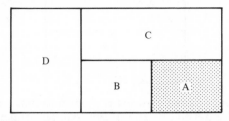

subsequently acquired. If there has previously been a 'set-off' under s 7 or one of the other enactments referred to above, the increase in value thus taken into account must not be 'set-off' twice over should land D be acquired; but on the other hand it must not be ignored, as if s 6 required it to be disregarded, should land C itself be acquired. Conversely, if a depreciation of land C has been compensated as 'injurious affection' it must not be ignored, as if s 6 required it to be disregarded, should land C be acquired; and presumably also it is not to be compensated twice over should land D be acquired. The point is that if land C has as greater or lesser value by virtue of the first acquisition, that change in value is genuine and must be so regarded; on the other hand it is a once-for-all change, to be met by a once-for-all compensation or 'set-off' and not more than one.

### 3  KEEPING ASSUMPTIONS WITHIN BOUNDS

These difficult rules are enacted chiefly for the purpose of guiding valuers in the lawful exercise of their professional skills. It is not difficult even for valuers to misinterpret them, especially s 6. This may be due to a misunderstanding of the true purpose of such provisions. Section 6 is intended as an instruction to valuers not to make a special kind of assumption or notional calculation which, whatever justification might be advanced in its favour, would distort the 'market value' calculation to be made in accordance with the fundamental provisions contained in s 5. It is true that valuers inevitably make assumptions; s 6 is meant to restrain them from making too many.

An illustration of this difficult matter is afforded by the decision of the Lands Tribunal in *Halliwell and Halliwell v Skelmersdale Development Corpn.*[5] The unsuccessful claimant, admitting that he must not make assumptions, in regard to a new town, which are forbidden by s 6, argued

5  (1965) 16 P & CR 305.

that it 'must carry with it the implicit requirement that there should be substituted such development as would have been likely to have been carried out apart from that designation (as a new town)...'. In other words, it must be assumed that the designation and subsequent building of the entire new town from 1961 to 1965 must be totally ignored, leading to a further assumption, to 'fill the gap' during those years, that some alternative development would have occurred giving an enhanced value to the claimant's land. The fallacy here is that s 6 does *not* require anyone to ignore what has happened, especially the provision of a whole new town. It merely requires the exclusion, in a calculation, of any gain or loss supposedly attributable to any *kind* of development which would not occur but for the particular project—in this case the new town. (It would have to be the *kind* of development rather than the particular development because although, say, houses would probably have been built in a given area, the *identical* houses actually built would presumably not have been built in other circumstances.) The Tribunal adopted the statement that there is '... no requirement ... that we must assume facts different from what they were.... There is only a requirement to adjust the compensation...'; and this is surely right.

Sections 10 to 13 of the 1961 Act set out rules for special cases. These are so highly specialised and limited in their application that an account of them would be out of place in this book, except for the 'site value' provisions of the Second Schedule as applied by s 10. The question of 'site value' for 'unfit houses' under the 1961 Act and the Housing Acts will, however, be briefly dealt with in the next chapter.

# Chapter 8

# Development value

## A. Market demand and planning control

### 1 THE MARKET AND THE PROSPECT OF DEVELOPMENT

'In 1952, some of our great cities were congested and overpopulated. In order to relieve the congestion, Parliament passed the Town Development Act 1952. The overspill was to be siphoned off to the smaller towns (which)...were given compulsory powers to acquire land for the purpose. Basingstoke was one of the towns selected to receive an influx from London...A goodly portion of the land they required, namely 550 acres, was owned by the Viscount Camrose and the Hon. Michael Berry. The Basingstoke Council agreed to buy this land.... Mr Hobbs, a member of the Lands Tribunal, sat to fix the price....

Out of the 550 acres, the council are taking 383 acres for residential purposes. One hundred and fifty acres are near to the present town. Mr Hobbs fixed their value at £291,400. But 233 acres are much further away. Mr Hobbs fixed their value at £95,000. The landowners...say that, in putting the value at £400 an acre, the tribunal treated the 233 acres as agricultural land, ignoring the fact that it is to be valued on the footing that it has planning permission. I cannot accept this criticism. Even though the 233 acres are assumed to have planning permission, it does not follow that there would be a demand for it. It is not planning permission by itself which increases value. It is planning permission coupled with demand.

This statement is taken from the judgment delivered by Lord Denning MR in *Viscount Camrose v Basingstoke Corpn.*[1] It provides valuable judicial recognition of the fact that 'market value' of land is composed of more than one element—'development value' as well as 'existing use value'—and also of the fact that 'development value' in turn depends on the co-existence of two things, market demand for the land for development purposes and planning permission, actual or assumed, for such development. Land being in short supply in this country, it is usually not difficult for a valuer to assume that market demand exists for any prospective development of land for which planning permission is under consideration. But it is certainly possible to envisage such permission being sometimes available for land for which there is no market demand; and this will be the case where appreciable areas of land are all at once earmarked for new town or town development as in the *Camrose*

1 [1966] 3 All ER 161. This case also dealt with industrial development.

case itself. There is here no market demand, in as much as the land is still remote from any existing urban development which provides commercial facilities and good communications, roads, sewers, water supply, gas and electricity. This is not a question of arbitrary rules, but of relevant facts, to be taken into account as any valuer would properly take them, while disregarding the acqiring authority's own project of development.[2]

A very similar case to *Camrose* is *Myers v Milton Keynes Development Corpn*.[3] Lord Denning MR referred to the earlier case and then said as follows: 'In the present case the question of fact to be answered can, we think, be best formulated in this way: on 18 March 1970[4] what price would a willing seller be prepared to accept, and a willing purchaser to pay, for the Walton Manor estate, if there had been no proposal for a new town at Milton Keynes; and if the prospects of development on and in the neighbourhood of the Walton Manor estate had then been such as they would have been if there had been no proposals for a new town'.[5] The case was then remitted to the Lands Tribunal 'for reconsideration in the light of the law as we have tried to expound it'. Shortly afterwards the corporation applied for 'elucidation of the Court of Appeal's judgment', and were told (contrary to the decision of the Lands Tribunal in the meantime) that there was no exhaustive list of assumptions on which the assessment should be based.[6] The court directed that one further expert witness should be called on each side to give evidence of value on the basis of whatever assumptions might be acceptable,[7] subject to cross-examination (and, if convenient, to the prior exchange of proofs of evidence). But Lord Denning MR in effect touched on the basic point at issue when he referred to the question whether, 'if there had been no scheme, this land would probably have remained open countryside'.

The legal approach is no doubt an over-simplification in the eyes of valuers; but as far as the law is concerned, the proper analysis of land value seems to be threefold. There are, in other words, three elements of value which, when aggregated in a proper case, go to make up the market price of land. But not all the three elements of value are present every time. They can be expressed as the 'existing use' value of land, the value of the prospect of development over and above the existing use, and the total cost of such development if carried out (including the developer's

2 See ch 7, pp 134–135, above.
3 [1974] 2 All ER 1096, [1974] 1 WLR 696.
4 The date when notice to treat was served.
5 'But with this one additional circumstance, that the purchaser had an assurance that in March 1980 or thereafter, if he applied for planning permission to develop the Walton Manor estate or any part of it for residential purposes—in a manner not inconsistent with the development corporation's proposals—he would be granted it'.
6 Supposedly confined as a matter of law to those mentioned by the Court of Appeal as a matter of illustration until the 'elucidation' was provided.
7 But contrast this with what is said about the attitude of the courts to the making of assumptions later in this chapter (see pp 163–166, below).

profit). Thus a paddock, if a market demand exists only for the land in its 'existing use', may have a value of (say) £1000. If on the facts a market demand can be shown to have arisen for that paddock as a building plot for a house, a 'prospective development' value of (say) an additional £19,000 may then be added: total development value, £20,000. If the house is built (permission having been granted for this) the total cost of this development may be (say) £30,000; grand total after development, £50,000. It does not matter whether or not the land is sold before development. No-one is likely to sell the finished product for less than £50,000, even if the owner does his own development and therefore has no need to expend £20,000 to buy the site as a building plot.

Further, this basic process may be repeated as often as is practicable, in many different forms. Thus a site with a house on it in the middle of a town, with its 'existing use', in its developed state as a house, commanding a figureof £50,000, may be in demand for further development by conversion to offices. The 'prospective development value' for this may be (say) an additional £40,000: total development value, £90,000. The actual cost of the development constituting this conversion may be (say) £20,000: grand total after the conversion development, £110,000.

The process can be expressed diagrammatically.

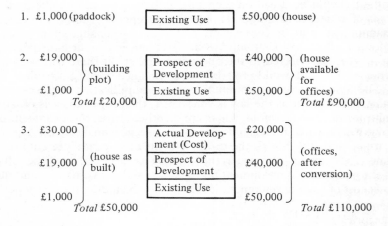

It will be noticed that stage (3) in the first process of development is at the same time stage (1) in a subsequent process of development. But it will be noticed also that stage (2) in any process of development sees the property in exactly the same physical state as stage (1). It is this lack of difference in physical terms that presents the most teasing problem in the assessment of compulsory purchase compensation, namely, should land be treated as having an 'existing use' value only, or should it be treated as having a 'prospective development' value on top of 'existing use' value to give an over-all development value? If the latter is right, what prospective development should be taken into account?

It is well known that the value figure representing the prospect of development, or 'development potential', although a perfectly genuine component in the market value of the property, is also often an elusive one. Essentially it is what remains after a process of elimination, either (i) by deducting the existing use value from full market value of the property in its current state, or (ii) by deducting from the anticipated full market value of property after it is developed both (a) the full actual cost of development and (b) the existing use value of the property before the occurrence of that development. The residue may be a positive figure or it may be nil.

## 2 PLANNING CONTROL AND 'HOPE VALUE'

Before the days of planning control, this was a valuation problem to be solved simply by ascertaining any relevant evidence of market demand for development of the land. But nowadays, whatever the demand, no purchaser will pay a development price unless the necessary planning permission is forthcoming. Either factor alone—market demand, planning permission—is not enough to raise the price of land above 'existing use' value; this was the basis underlying Lord Denning's judgment in the *Camrose* case. In that particular dispute it was the existence of market demand which, unusually, raised the legal issue. In most cases it is the existence of the necessary planning permission. If an effective planning permission does exist, then to that extent there is no problem, so long as proper account is taken of market demand. But in a normal case the possibility of development is often only a potential question, at the time when particular land becomes subject to compulsory purchase. The question must then be: for what development *could* the owner have sought permission; and can it now be taken into account, or not?

When planning control on the present scale was introduced in 1947, there was an easy answer because the Town and Country Planning Act of that year simply expropriated for the state's benefit all prospective development value, except for the value of 'Third Schedule' development. This, as will be seen later, consists of a group of carefully defined categories merely marginal to the 'existing use'.[8] Many complications ensued, but for compulsory purchase at least, the result was straightforward. The Town and Country Planning Act 1954, however, restored 'prospective development' value to owners (if they succeeded in getting planning permissions) but mysteriously failed to take account of compulsory purchase, as a result of which vendors were paid development value in private transactions but not in compulsory ones. The discontent

---

8 Now 'Eighth Schedule' development. See ch 16, p 316, below.

that this caused at length gave rise to the Town and Country Planning Act 1959, which restored development value to vendors in compulsory purchase transactions, and the relevant provisions were re-enacted in the Act of 1961.

The position, therefore, is that market demand for development must be proved, and planning permission must exist *or be assumed to exist*, in order to justify a claim that any land possesses development value. But purchasers are in fact often prepared to hazard money on the possibility that permission might actually be granted sooner or later even if it has not been granted yet. If so, land for sale will be valued as having 'hope value' on top of existing use value. This usually amounts to little; but it is sometimes substantial. In *Watkins v Kidson*,[9] the claimant in 1962 inherited 22 acres of farm land near Brackley, in Northamptonshire, valued then for estate duty at £1,581. Also in 1962 Northamptonshire County Council published proposals for an eventual planned increase of the town of Brackley. But no planning permission for development of those 22 acres yet existed when in 1972 the appellant sold them to a developer for £264,000 and was in consequence assessed to capital gains tax; though such permission had been applied for and was afterwards granted. At that time development value was included in capital gains taxation. In the Chancery Division of the High Court Fox J rejected the appellant's claim that the absence of planning permission in 1972 took him out of the scope of the relevant taxing provisions.[10] The amount in this case assessed to the tax (£258,961) can be regarded as 'hope value' on a large scale (or in other words development value on a speculative basis); but often it differs little from existing use value.[11]

## 3 SEVERED LAND

It is accordingly necessary in a modern compulsory purchase to make 'assumptions as to planning permission' to discover whether purchase price compensation should include 'prospective development' value on top of 'existing use' value, the latter being payable in any event unless there is special reason to the contrary.[12] But there is a difficulty. These

9 [1977] 3 All ER 545. And see the *Vyricherla* case (above, p 139).
10 Finance Act 1965, Sch 6, para 23 (1) (b). For this taxation and the general question of taxing 'betterment', see below, ch 14.
11 As in the *Camrose* case. See above, p 150.
12 Until their repeal by ss 86 and 101 of the Land Commission Act 1967, Part IV and the Third Schedule to the Act of 1961 used to provide for additional 'prospective development value' compensation to be paid to an expropriated owner if, within *five years* after completion, such additional value was created by a later planning decision in respect of the land taken. The decision had to relate to development other than that involved in the scheme or project for which the land had been compulsorily purchased; but the additional compensation was not payable in any case if the land were within the area of a new town or town development or comprehensive development (see ch 11). The amount payable was the difference between the value already paid to the expropriated

'planning assumptions' are only applicable to the land which is actually being acquired, referred to in the Act as 'the relevant land', and not to any land retained by its owner but subject to depreciation by 'severance' or 'injurious affection'. Superficially, the answer to this objection is for planning permission actually to be sought by the owner for development of the land *retained*. This course of action is perfectly possible in respect of that land. It would, of course, be completely futile in respect of the land being acquired, since the local planning authority cannot be expected to consent to any development on it inconsistent with that intended by the acquiring body. On the one hand, the true purpose would be to ascertain proper compensation, not to carry out actual development. On the other hand a planning permission would, at least in theory, open the way to actual development.

It is essential not to lose sight of the fact that market demand is the basis of development value, notwithstanding the alleged relevance of the *Pointe Gourde* doctrine. In the *Melwood Units* case[13] referred to in the previous chapter, it was agreed that the whole of a large urban site in Brisbane enjoyed market demand for 'drive-in shopping centre' development. When the site was bisected and depreciated by a road scheme the Privy Council upheld, in principle, the owners' claim that development value, for 'drive-in shopping centre' use, should be included in their compulsory purchase compensation. There would have been planning permission, but for the road scheme. As to demand, the only valuation evidence that was closely relevant was the fact that the major portion of the site remaining after its division was soon privately sold for development of that very same kind, and at a high price; this was pretty cogent evidence, even on its own, of the existence of genuine market demand. Yet the *Pointe Gourde* doctrine was also pressed into service to buttress the decision. Supporting the evidence of market demand for development, the doctrine merely seems redundant; had it supported some other conclusion it would have been at variance with the market evidence.

Unfortunately the taking of part of an owner's land will put an end to its capacity for development as a whole. An actual project of development suitable for what is left may well be disproportionately insignificant compared with what might have been suitable for the whole area if it had not been 'severed'. Development value of the part of land taken and the

owner and the higher value in consequence of the new decision; and claims had to be made within six months of that decision.

A leading case under these provisions was *Enfield London Borough v Lavender Garden Properties Ltd* [1968] 2 All ER 401. Allotments bought for £625 an acre existing use value were transferred by purchase notice to the local authority for £20,000 an acre housing development value. Under Part IV of the 1961 Act another £5,000 an acre were added.

**13** [1979] AC 426, [1979] 1 All ER 161. See p 134 above and p 177 (ch 9) below. (For other cases involving main roads (see p 164, below).

part of land retained respectively would thus consist of two or more separate amounts separately arrived at, and in the aggregate likely to total much less than the development value appropriate to the land as a whole, because of comparative lack of demand for development of smaller areas.

A comparable situation arises where a number of small properties separately owned, say houses in an area of town redevelopment, are all acquired together. Here the separation exists *before* the compulsory acquisition, not as a consequence of it: indeed the acquisition is probably intended to aggregate all these sites for a comprehensive project of development. Nevertheless compensation is assessable separately for each separate owner; and once again development value is small because of the lack of demand for development of small areas.

The fair solution would be to aggregate the small sites, for the purpose of assessing development value, to the same extent that they are to be aggregated for the purposes of the acquiring authority's project of development itself, and then divide the resulting development value rateably among the small owners. Certainly, the owners of small sites comprised in a larger area to be compulsorily purchased should in any case consider aggregating their holdings of their own accord, for this reason. The same applies to tenants and reversioners, and possibly to dominant and servient owners, incumbrancers, and legal and equitable owners.[14]

Where an acquisition 'severs' a larger area of land, the 'planning assumptions' ought not to be restricted to the 'relevant land', which is the land being acquired, but ought to be applicable to the entire area, land taken and land retained alike. Then purchase price, 'severance' and 'injurious affection' compensation, and 'set-off' as well, could all be assessed on a uniform basis. But the law on this is uncertain.

# B.  Statutory assumptions as to planning permission

## 1  ACTUAL AND ASSUMED PERMISSIONS

The main statutory provisions which authorise the making of planning assumptions are contained in ss 14 to 16 of the Act of 1961. Section 14 (1) states that 'such one or more of the assumptions . . . as are applicable to the relevant land or any part thereof shall be made in ascertaining the value of the relevant interest'. All other factors which are relevant to a proper valuation, such as market demand for development or for existing use, are still relevant, so long as they do not conflict with the statutory provisions.

Any assumptions as to planning permission made by virtue of these

---

14  But see above, ch 4, p 63 (Acquisition of Land Act 1981, s 4).

sections do not automatically require it to be assumed that other planning permissions will be refused; although it may well be relevant that a 'certificate of appropriate alternative development' (to be discussed later) states in a particular case that some specified development could not reasonably be permitted. But in any case no *planning* assumption can be made unless some statutory provision authorises it.

As for actual existing planning permissions, these are effective to justify development value quite independently of all 'assumptions'. There could in fact be several planning permissions, actual or assumed, which are available concurrently.[15] In a normal case they will be alternative, and not cumulative, in their effect upon development value. Thus if an actual or assumed permission justifies adding £1,000 prospective development value for housing, and another justifies adding £2,000 prospective development value for shops, the proper development value will be the higher of these amounts, £2,000, but not their sum, £3,000. A purchaser interested in developing the land for housing will pay a price enhanced by £1,000; a purchaser interested in developing the land for shops will pay a price enhanced by £2,000; and the vendor will sell to the latter; but no purchaser will have any incentive, on the known facts, to pay the vendor a price enhanced by £3,000.

Section 15 authorises the assumption of planning permission for the acquiring authority's development; but since there is unlikely to be appreciable market demand for development of the kind that most public authorities will wish to carry out, there will be little increase in the value of the land as a result of this, except perhaps where housing development is intended.[16] In addition, planning permission may be assumed for 'Eighth Schedule'[17] development, which, as described above, is strictly marginal to the 'existing use' of property. In valuation terms this 'existing use development' is most probably taken into automatic consideration by valuers in any valuation of property on an 'existing use' basis. The only time when 'Eighth Schedule' development permission cannot be assumed is when it has in fact already been restricted by an actual planning decision (which, though perfectly possible, is not usual) and compensation in respect of the loss of value resulting from such a restriction has become payable.

15 See *F Lucas & Sons Ltd v Dorking and Horley RDC* (1964) 17 P & CR 111.
16 In *Myers v Milton Keynes Development Corpn* (see above, p 151) the Lands Tribunal said that there is a clash between this (or perhaps any) assumption and the *Pointe Gourde* rule. It is respectfully suggested that there is no clash. All that an assumption does is to settle the question of planning permission. But, as Lord Denning MR said in the *Camrose* case (see p 150, above) development value also requires demand; and the true point at issue in the *Myers* case was whether a demand would exist in the absence of the acquiring body's project.
17 Schedule 8 to the Town and Country Planning Act 1971 (see ch 16, below). This replaces Sch 3 to the Town and Country Planning Act 1947, to which s 15 (3) of the 1961 Act actually refers.

## 2 RELEVANCE OF THE DEVELOPMENT PLAN

The planning assumptions which are most useful to owners in the normal case are, however, those depending on local planning authorities' development plans. Section 16 provides that planning permission may be assumed for proposed development which, in the current development plan, is specifically indicated for the relevant land, or is a reasonable project of development for some use within a *general* category 'zoned' for an area which includes the relevant land.

Specific indication is reserved, as a rule, for public development such as roads and schools, which are not likely to interest purchasers in general and not therefore likely to encourage market demand. But the general categories of development for which land is customarily 'zoned' in development plans comprise, in broad terms, the following: residential, commercial and industrial development. These are varieties of development which do attract appreciable market demand among private developers; and they can therefore be regarded collectively as 'lucrative' development.

They can also be regarded as being virtually the only categories of land *use* (whether involving development or not) which can be thought of as having a wide and general market value. Agricultural *use* is another general category; but it does not have much significance in the context of market demand for *development* and cannot, therefore be regarded as 'lucrative'. In the *Camrose* case discussed at the beginning of this chapter, the claimants were not content to accept 'agricultural value' for their land so long as they thought they had a chance to establish a right to residential or industrial *development* value.[18] Agricultural value is largely a matter of existing use. Indeed the use of any land in its existing state for agriculture or forestry does not, under planning law, involve 'development' at all; and agricultural development as such is largely a question of agricultural building operations, which are normally no more than peripheral to the process of agriculture—except perhaps where 'factory farming'[19] is taking place.

Section 16 authorises planning permission to be assumed for development, 'lucrative' or otherwise, if the relevant land is in an area 'zoned' for one or more uses and the proposed development is for such a use. But the test which must be satisfied is specific as well as general. Not only must the land be in a 'zone' for the particular use for which the development is proposed, but in addition it must be 'development for which planning

---

18  For another aspect of this matter, see the leading case of *Horn v Sunderland Corpn* (ch 10, p 200, below).

19  The question whether broiler-houses and other such 'factory farming' buildings are agricultural or industrial has caused difficulties in recent years in relation to rating. Only if essentially agricultural in their use would they be entitled to exemption from rates and so share the benefits of 'agricultural de-rating'. The Rating Act 1971 now grants them this exemption.

permission might reasonably have been expected to be granted in respect of the relevant land. . . .' For example, planning permission cannot be assumed for housing development, even in an area 'zoned' for housing, if the relevant land is too small or too narrow to be suitable, or liable to flooding or subsidence, or is for any other proper reason of fact or policy unfit for development of this kind.[20] If the relevant land is included in an 'area of comprehensive development'[1] planning permission may be assumed for development for any one of the 'planned range of uses' for the entire area, provided that 'planning permission might reasonably have been expected to be granted' for that development had there been no such 'area of comprehensive development'. If any development has in fact already been carried out in that area at the date of the actual or deemed notice to treat, in accordance with the plan, it must be assumed also that such development has not occurred.[2]

When deciding whether permission for notional development under all these planning assumptions 'might reasonably be expected to be granted', the reasonableness to be taken into account includes the question whether any conditions, and if so which ones, would be attached to the permission.[3] Similarly it must be decided whether permission would be deferred. In any case it must always be assumed that 'no part of the relevant land were proposed to be acquired by *any* authority possessing compulsory purchase powers'.

If the relevant land is in an area 'zoned' for any 'lucrative' use or uses, namely those 'of a residential, commercial or industrial character', or an 'area of comprehensive development', which in this context almost certainly amounts to the same thing, then the way is open for the owner to lay claim to an appreciable element of prospective development value, subject of course to the reasonable suitability of the particular land to particular development suggested. But the current development plan may not be so favourable to the owner's land. It may indicate the land as the site of particular development of some other kind, or it may include it in a 'green belt' or it may not make any provision for it. In the latter case

---

20 In *Provincial Properties (London) Ltd v Caterham and Warlingham UDC* [1972] 1 QB 453, [1972] 1 All ER 60, the Court of Appeal accepted that certain land on a hill, though 'zoned' as residential, should stay undeveloped for amenity. No permission to build could be assumed. The claimants argued that if the *general* test in s 16 indicates planning permission the *specific* test is concerned with detail only. This is wrong. Both tests apply to permission as a whole.
1 See ch 11, p 228, below.
2 This is because the plan for the entire area must be disregarded.
3 Particular factors not serious enough to be treated as inconsistent with planning permission altogether may nevertheless raise important questions of planning detail. See for example *Eardisland Investment Ltd v Birmingham Corpn* (1970) 22 P & CR 213, where it was held that account must be taken of the existence of a tree preservation order, the significance of which was quite independent of that of the development plan when it came to assessing a compensation figure which would include development value.

it will remain 'white' on the map. 'White land' is most likely to be farmland or other rural land which the local planning authority wishes to remain in its undeveloped state.

## 3 CERTIFICATES OF APPROPRIATE ALTERNATIVE DEVELOPMENT

If this is the case, Part III of the 1961 Act (ss 17 to 22), as amended by s 47 of the Community Land Act 1975[4] in regard to applications made since 12 December 1975, gives an owner of any interest in land being compulsorily acquired[5] a sporting chance none the less to lay claim to prospective development value. He does this by applying to the local planning authority[6] for a 'certificate of appropriate alternative development'. The acquiring authority may also apply for one of these certificates, but their incentive to do so is not likely to be so great. No application, however, may be made if a dispute over compensation has already been referred to the Lands Tribunal, unless with the written consent of the other party to the dispute or with leave from the Tribunal. The Secretary of State for the Environment has power to regulate, by development order, the procedure governing 'certificates of appropriate alternative development'; and under this power was made the Land Compensation Development Order 1974,[7] which needs to be read in conjunction with Part III of the 1961 Act.

Any application for one of these certificates '(a) shall state whether or not there are, in the applicant's opinion, any classes of development which, either immediately or at a future time, would be appropriate for the land in question if it were not proposed to be acquired by any authority possessing compulsory purchase powers and, if so, shall specify the classes of development and the times at which they would be so appropriate; (b) shall state the applicant's grounds for holding that opinion; and (c) shall be accompanied by a statement specifying the date on which a copy of the application has been or will be served on the other

---

4 Continued by the Local Government, Planning and Land Act 1980, s 121 and Sch 24, despite the repeal by that Act of the Community Land Act.

5 Section 22 of the 1961 Act makes it reasonably clear that the land must be subject to a compulsory purchase order or private Act authorising its acquisition, or to a purchase or 'blight' notice (for these, see ch 12 and 13, below), or to an agreement for purchase under statutory powers, if this procedure is to be used.

6 This will be the London borough council (or the City Corporation) in Greater London: London Government Act 1963, s 24. Elsewhere it will normally be the district council as 'district planning authority'. But if the application specifies development which appears to be a 'county matter', it must go on to the county council as 'county planning authority'. The Local Government Act 1972, Sch 16, as amended by the Local Government, Planning and Land Act 1980, Schs 14 and 34 broadly provides that 'county matters' are mineral workings of various specified kinds, development in a National Park, and any other matters which may be additionally prescribed.

7 SI 1974/539.

party directly concerned'.[8] The local planning authority must, between 21 days and two months after that date, issue the certificate specifying the class or classes of development for which permission, in their opinion, 'would have been granted' in the absence of compulsory purchase, whether or not subject to any conditions or to deferment, or alternatively that *no* development, other than any involved in the acquiring authority's project, could be envisaged. The latter is commonly termed a 'nil certificate'. Any class or classes of development approved in a certificate need not be the same as specified by the applicant; nor need they necessarily be in accordance with the development plan.[9]

The local planning authority must serve on the other party a copy of the certificate they issue to the applicant. A county planning authority must also serve a copy on any district planning authority in whose area the land is situated, and vice versa.[10] If they do not agree with the development suggested in the application, or with any written representations made to them by the applicant or the other party, they must include with the certificate a written statement of reasons together with information about how an appeal may be made against the certificate.[11] If 'any person appearing to them to have an interest' in the land makes a written request for the applicant's name and address, the date of application, and a copy of the certificate, the authority must furnish these.[12]

Appeal may be made against an unfavourable certificate either by the owner of the interest in land to which it relates, or by the acquiring authority. If no certificate is issued within two months, or such longer period as the parties and the local planning authority agree to in writing, a right of appeal arises as if a certificate were issued opposing any development other than that of the acquiring authority.[13] The time for appeal is one month. It is made to the Secretary of State for the Environment by notice in writing, a copy of which must be sent to the other party and to the local planning authority.[14]

Within one month after the notice of appeal, or longer if the Secretary

8  1961 Act, s 17 (3), as amended (see footnote 4, p 160, above).
9  1961 Act, s 17 (4); Land Compensation Development Order 1974, art 3 (2).
10  1961 Act, s 17 (9); 1974 Order, art 3 (4). Similar but special arrangements apply to Greater London.
11  The inclusion of this information is mandatory and its omission invalidates the certificate: *London and Clydeside Estates Ltd v Aberdeen District Council* [1979] 3 All ER 876 (this was a decision of the House of Lords on parallel provisions in Scots legislation).
12  1974 Order, arts 3 (3), 5.
13  1961 Act, s 18 (1), (4). The local planning authority's duty is to issue a *valid* certificate, not an invalid one. If a certificate is in fact issued but is invalid, then no certificate has in law been issued, as happened in the *London and Clydeside* case (see above, footnote 11). Although after two months the applicant in that case could have appealed to the Secretary of State, this legal issue of validity was pursued instead.
14  1974 Order, art 4 (1), (2).

of State allows, the appellant must furnish him with a statement of the grounds of appeal and a copy of the original application and of the certificate (if any), or else 'the appeal shall be treated as withdrawn'.[15] The Secretary of State, who must first provide a hearing before an inspector for the parties and the local planning authority if either party so desires, is to consider the matter entirely de novo. Accordingly he 'shall either confirm the certificate, or vary it, or cancel it and issue a different certificate in its place, as he may consider appropriate'.[16]

The validity of the Secretary of State's decision 'shall not be questioned in any legal proceedings whatsoever', except by an application within six weeks of it to the High Court by 'any person aggrieved' or the local planning authority. The grounds of challenge can be either that the decision is ultra vires the 1961 Act (as amended) or that 'any of the requirements of (the Act) or of a development order or of the Tribunals and Inquiries Act 1971 . . ., or rules made thereunder have not been complied with in relation to it. . . .' The court may quash the decision if satisfied that it is ultra vires 'or that the interests of the applicant have been substantially prejudiced by a failure to comply with the said requirements. . . .' A 'person aggrieved' will in practice almost certainly be either the owner or the acquiring authority since the term appears to mean a person suffering a direct financial detriment from the offending decision.[17]

It will be discussed later how the reasonably incurred expenses of making a compensation claim can be included in the amount claimed. From this it might be thought that the cost of an application for a certificate of appropriate alternative development should be included, since the purpose of the application is to discover if the 'market value' of land acquired includes certain development value. Yet in *Hull and Humber Investment Co Ltd v Hull Corpn*,[18] the Court of Appeal held that the cost of a successful appeal over a certificate was incurred in 'increasing' compensation, rather than in establishing the true amount of it, and so was not an 'expense'.

It is most important to remember the limitations of this 'section 17 certificate' procedure. In the first place it should be invoked only when a compulsory purchase, or purchase under statutory powers, is actually

15  Ibid, art 4 (3), (4).
16  1961 Act, s 18 (2), (3).
17  1961 Act, s 21 (as amended). In *Philips v Berkshire County Council* [1967] 2 QB 991, [1967] 2 All ER 675 (a highway case), a local authority were held to be a 'person aggrieved' as a result of an unfavourable decision of a court whereby they were 'left with a legal burden' that otherwise they 'would have discharged'. The local *planning* authority, however, receive a separate mention in s 21 because they cannot in this context be a 'person aggrieved'; *R v Dorset Quarter Sessions Appeals Committee, ex p Weymouth Corpn* [1960] 2 QB 230, [1960] 2 All ER 410.
18  [1965] 2 QB 145, [1965] 1 All ER 429.

under way.[19] In the second place it is applicable only to land not 'zoned' for industrial, commercial or residential uses, or combinations of such uses, or comprehensive development.[20] In the third place it is relevant only to the assumption of planning permission and not to the existence of actual market demand. Thus in one case a certificate was issued stating that permission for office development would have been granted for land being compulsorily purchased under a blight notice.[1] The acquiring body denied that appreciable *market demand* existed for development of the particular site, because of its proximity to a site where an 'offensive trade' was carried on. The Lands Tribunal, in assessing the compensation, upheld this contention and, despite the certificate, restricted the compensation price to existing use value and a little 'hope value'.[2]

## 4 THE COURTS' ATTITUDE TO THE MAKING OF ASSUMPTIONS

Disputes over the inclusion of development value in the 'market value' of land usually raise technical questions of valuation rather than law. After all, it must not be forgotten that, despite all the involved references to development and planning permissions in the various statutory provisions discussed in this chapter, the only question at stake is, what should be the amount of compensation payable? Not actual development but only the *value* of development is under consideration here. There are, however, one or two leading cases which should not be overlooked.

In *Re Croydon Development Plans* 1954 *and* 1959, *Harrison v London Borough of Croydon*,[3] the provisions of s 16 of the 1961 Act, relating to planning assumptions based on 'zoning', came under discussion. The defendant corporation compulsorily purchased properties belonging to the plaintiff. The development plan showed the land as included in an area 'zoned' for 'shopping and other business'. The plaintiff applied on a procedure summons to the High Court, Chancery Division, for a declaration that planning permission for *office* development should be assumed. The defendants suceeded in persuading the judge to set aside the summons for absence of jurisdiction because, as Pennycuick J said, the issue was 'a hypothetical question of fact'—specialised fact of exactly the kind that a valuation tribunal, namely the Lands Tribunal, should determine—and not a legal issue as a disputed construction of s 16 would have been.[4]

---

19 It is not certain that this limitation on use is strictly adhered to in practice. On this point, see s 22 of the 1961 Act and footnote 5 on p 160, above.
20 1961 Act, s 17 (1).
1 For blight notices, see below, ch 13.
2 *Bromilow v Greater Manchester Council* (1975) 31 P & CR 398. The offensive trade was a 'bone-works'. Contrast with this case *Grampian Regional Council v Secretary of State for Scotland* [1983] 3 All ER 673, [1983] 1 WLR 1340, HL. For 'hope value' see above, p 153.
3 [1968] Ch 479, [1967] 2 All ER 589.
4 The section directs the valuer as to the *kind* of assumption he is to make in relation to the

*Jelson Ltd v Minister of Housing and Local Government*[5] was a decision bringing to an end the earlier phase of the dispute which reappeared in *Jelson Ltd v Blaby District Council*, involving the *Pointe Gourde* doctrine, which was discussed in the previous chapter.[6] The plaintiffs owned land near Leicester through which a ring road had been planned to run. They were granted planning permission to develop the land by building housing estates, except on the narrow strip of land where the ring road was to go, which was about 146 feet wide. The plan for the ring road was then abandoned; but although compulsory purchase for road purposes was no longer intended the plaintiffs promoted an 'inverse compulsory purchase' by means of a purchase notice (to be discussed in a later chapter). To do this they had first to undergo an adverse planning decision leaving the land 'incapable of reasonably beneficial use in its existing state', which duly came to pass when in 1964 they applied to develop the strip of land for housing. Permission was refused on the ground (not surprisingly) that such development would 'result in an arrangement of gardens and garages which would spoil the outlook from the fronts of a large number of existing houses to an unacceptable degree'. The land being thus virtually useless, the way was open for the purchase notice, the confirmation of which had the effect of a deemed notice to treat by the rural district council.

Argument then shifted to the compensation. The strip of land, having been 'sterilised' by the abortive ring road scheme, did not enjoy any advantageous 'zoning' under s 16 of the 1961 Act. Consequently the owners applied for a certificate of appropriate alternative development under s 17. A 'nil certificate' was issued. All appeals, up to and including the Court of Appeal, failed. Lord Denning MR pointed out that the planning assumptions, if any, are to be made as if the land 'were not *proposed* to be acquired'; and this phrase is interpreted in s 22 so as to depend, in this kind of case, on a deemed notice to treat having occurred. The assumptions must be made therefore at that date and not earlier. In this case the adjoining land had already been developed for housing by that date,[7] and the relevant factual situation therefore justified a finding that development of the strip of land could not reasonably have been permitted.

In *Margate Corpn v Devotwill Investments Ltd*[8] it was the planning

terms of the development plan; but it does not do his work for him by stating exactly what *specific* assumptions he is to make in regard to the particular property under consideration. The distinction drawn by Pennycuick J could have been drawn with advantage by the House of Lords in the *Devotwill* case (see next page).

5  [1970] 1 QB 243, [1969] 3 All ER 147.
6  See above, p 131.
7  The fact it was development on the adjoining land to the exclusion of the strip was not the fault of the owner but of the public authorities concerned (though this is not compensatable—see ch 15). For s 22, see p 160, footnote 5, above.
8  [1970] 3 All ER 864.

assumptions in s 16 of the 1961 Act that were in issue. The respondent company held land in Birchington, Kent, alongside a congested main road. The appellant corporation refused them planning permission to develop for housing, on the ground that the land might be needed for the purposes of a relief road. As a result, the company successfully put forward a purchase notice, as in *Jelson's* case; but unlike that case the land was in an area 'zoned' for residential use. The corporation argued before the Lands Tribunal that the present congested main road must be taken into account, so that only a modest scheme of housing development could have been contemplated. But the company argued that because the relief road was intended it must be assumed that a consequent reduction of traffic congestion would occur, thus justifying a fuller scheme of housing development and so a higher development value. The company succeeded before the Lands Tribunal and the Court of Appeal, but the House of Lords ordered the dispute to be remitted to the Lands Tribunal for reconsideration.

Lord Morris of Borth-y-Gest stated that the company's case depended on the making of an assumption about a future relief road which, though accepted by the Lands Tribunal and Court of Appeal, was not required by any statutory provision. He therefore declared it to be erroneous in law. Yet the art of valuation in any case involves making assumptions, because value is to a large extent governed by future prospects which must in turn be largely, though not entirely, governed by assumptions. It is true that the Act of 1961 compels the making of certain express assumptions; but it does *not* prohibit all others—in fact it could scarcely do so without making the valuation process next to impossible. Not assuming the relief of traffic congestion amounts, for valuation purposes, to assuming that traffic congestion will not be relieved. Some assumption here is clearly unavoidable, quite apart from the provisions of s 16.

Lord Morris remitted the case to the Lands Tribunal 'for new consideration of the lines that I have indicated'. These lines, which will be touched on in a moment, were set out in some detail. But it is submitted that, lacking any statutory basis, they could only be suggestions. Any choice of them, or others, by the Tribunal would have to be made on the basis of reasonable expert valuation opinion; and although factual evidence would have to be considered, a great many assumptions would have to be made as well—especially as the main exercise must, by virtue of s 16, be a notional one. In addition, the matters suggested by Lord Morris involve complex and extensive planning questions, such as it might well be necessary to consider before reaching a planning decision on an actual project of development, but hardly before reaching a notional one for the purposes of assessing compensation. 'Were there some other ways (of dealing with traffic congestion)?... Was there a housing shortage which presented an urgent and serious problem?... All the many relevant facts and circumstances would have to be considered before answer could be given'. It is hard to escape the conclusion that the Lands Tribunal was given the task of making a great many more extra-statutory valuation assumptions than before.[9]

## C. Cleared site value

The distinction between development value and existing use value must not be confused with another distinction which is frequently met with, but is more specialised, being confined strictly to houses, namely that which is drawn between the value of a site plus the house on it and 'cleared site' value. The phrase 'full market value' tends to be used both of full development value and of value of site plus house, and this increases the likelihood of confusion. 'Cleared site' value, however, is only used in relation to property which comprises a house that is 'unfit for human habitation' within the meaning of s 4 of the Housing Act 1957. The distinction may be brought into focus most effectively by considering that 'cleared site value' and the value of site plus house alike may need to be regarded as comprising, according to circumstances, either an existing use value or a development value, at least in theory. And in a case already discussed in another context, *Davy v Leeds Corpn*,[10] it was common ground that slum houses were to have a 'cleared site' value only: the dispute centred on whether site value should be enhanced notionally by the prospect of redeveloping adjoining land or whether (as was in fact held in that cae) s 6 of the 1961 Act prevented this.

Cleared site value, which is chiefly applicable to slum clearance purchases under the Housing Act 1957, is a survival from the days before planning control, planning assumptions and the present statutory rules for assessing 'market value'. All of these should now suffice to ensure that proper compensation is assessed for slum houses—notably rule (*iv*) of the six rules in s 5 of the 1961 Act. This, it will be remembered, requires any item of value to be disregarded if it relates to a use of property which is contrary to law or detrimental to health. It is also noteworthy that the whole point of the 'cleared site' concept is that its value is assumed to be without question *less* than the value of site plus house.[11] Indeed the Housing Acts contain elaborate rules for making a

9   There is a hidden distinction at the root of this difficult matter. It is between a statutory assumption *as to planning permission*, which is purely notional and a question of law, and an assumption as to factual occurrences. Valuers must continually make assumptions as to facts, particularly future facts, because that is what 'the market' is all about. This distinction, though hidden, in fact gave the Lands Tribunal no trouble in this case; but it led the House of Lords into treating valuers' assumptions as to relevant facts as if they were not a question of expert fact but a question of law. See p 163, footnote 4, above.

10   See ch 7, p 146, above.

11   Note, for example, *Northwood v LCC* [1926] 2 KB 411, a case where the value to

variety of payments to bring site value compensation in deserving cases partly or wholly *up* to the value of site plus house. Yet for redevelopment purposes a house, as distinct from its site, especially an unfit house, is likely to be a liability and not an asset, representing a figure *lower* than cleared site value by the amount of the prospective cost of its demolition. Accordingly the Second Schedule to the 1961 Act provides that in such a case the compensation payable is not to *exceed* the value of site plus house. In spite of this, the provisions for bringing up site value to the value of site plus house have been extended,[12] instead of being abolished; and the Second Schedule itself provides that the minimum compensation of an unfit house shall, if it is owner-occupied, be its gross value for rating.

The Second Schedule also enacts that cleared site value compensation may be applied to certain other cases in addition to ordinary slum clearance, namely acquisitions under the Planning Acts, for new towns and town development, and for council housing where the authority is the Greater London Council. The local authority which is housing authority for the area concerned submits an order to this effect to the Secretary of State not later than the compulsory purchase order (or the deemed notice to treat), with corresponding procedure for publicity and the hearing of objections. It should be noted that an objection to site value compensation must be made at this stage, and not later. To dispute the unfitness of a house at the time of the assessment of the compensation is too late.[13]

licensed premises of the justices' licence was left out of account because the property was being acquired at 'cleared site value'. (See also ch 7, p 137, footnote 9, above).

12 See the Housing (Slum Clearance Compensation) Act 1965, ss 1–2, and the Housing Act 1969, ss 65–68 and Sch 5. The sum needed to bring 'site value' up to the market value of site plus house, in accordance with these provisions, must be reduced by a proportion corresponding to any actual proportion of the house not used as 'a private dwelling'. It was argued that this means use as a private dwelling *by the claimant and no-one else* (ie not by a tenant): *Hunter v Manchester City Council* [1975] QB 877, [1975] 2 All ER 966. But this narrow interpretation was rejected.

13 Housing Act 1957, s 59 and Third Schedule. For further details, see *West's Law of Housing* (4th edn, 1979 and supplement). On the meaning of 'house' see *Quillotex Co Ltd v Minister of Housing and Local Government* [1966] 1 QB 704 [1965] 2 All ER 913.

# Chapter 9

# Severance and injurious affection

## A. Depreciation and actionable nuisance

### 1 EFFECTS OF STATUTE ON NUISANCE SITUATIONS

The law of compulsory purchase obliges landowners to submit to being parties to a contract, but it ought not to follow that they must in addition submit to being victims of a tort. Nevertheless this, or something like it, has come about in many cases, partly as a result of confused judicial thinking in the nineteenth century, and partly as a result of the inadequacies of the compulsory purchase statutes then and now. The Land Compensation Act 1973 was passed to deal with these inadequacies, though it has only gone part of the way to curing them.

The tort to which some landowners may have to submit, in effect even if the fact is not officially admitted, will be private nuisance, or public nuisance privately actionable on proof of special damage.[1] Noise, vibrations, smells and fumes are familiar examples of nuisance in this context. Interferences with easements, as by blocking an access road, obstructing ancient lights or withdrawing support from a building entitled to be supported, are other important examples. Blocking a public road so that access thereby to private premises is obstructed is public nuisance privately actionable on proof of special damage.[2] Infringement of a restrictive covenant is strictly a breach of contract and not a tort; but in as much as this involves a right over land being interfered with, the wrongdoing is closely analogous to a private nuisance and indeed is susceptible to remedy at common law and in equity in essentially the same way. Whether liability for an 'escape' under the rule in *Rylands v Fletcher*[3] is to be regarded in the same light is not clear; but if it is right to hold that statutory bodies are free of liability for what would otherwise be an actionable nuisance, which is based on fault, a fortiori it should be right to hold them free of liability in cases where that liability is strict—ie independent of any fault.

The point at issue here is not whether the event causing damage

---

1 See textbooks on tort generally in regard to private and public nuisance.
2 *Wilkes v Hungerford Market Co* (see p 184, below).
3 (1868) LR 3 HL 330. But there may be special statutory provisions governing the 'escape' itself, eg the Railway Fires Acts 1905 and 1923.

satisfies the tests for establishing civil liability in nuisance at common law. That is essentially an objective question of whether in the circumstances the plaintiff's enjoyment of land has been unreasonably interfered with. The relevant point is this: granted that such interference has actually occurred, and is therefore actionable, is that right of action taken away by virtue, and merely by virtue, of the statutory authorisation conferred upon the body controlling the offending land?

The statutes did not, and still do not, deal expressly with this question, an omission which is totally unjustifiable. As a result the courts were landed with the problem, which Parliament let go by default, and they produced an unsatisfactory answer to it. They did lay down a rule, for which *Metropolitan Asylum v Hill*[4] is a leading authority, that a purported exercise of statutory powers is ultra vires if exercised unreasonably, as when a smallpox hospital is proposed to be built on a site close to houses when it could be put on some more remote site; in which case the proposed activity is said to be unlawful *because it is a nuisance*. Unfortunately there has been confusion of thought arising from a failure to distinguish between the statute which confers powers in general terms— the authorising Act—and the statute, or sub-statutory decision, which selects particular land, whether involving the exercise of compulsory powers or not. The logic of *Hill's* case seems to be that the authorising Act gives no assistance to the statutory body if the decision selecting *particular* land involves a nuisance.

The question of remedies is important. In tort a defendant, if liable, may be restrained by an injunction or subjected instead to the financial sanction damages. The latter is, in effect, compensation for actually doing the wrongful act, as against being restrained from doing it, and is obtainable by a successful plaintiff as of right at common law, whereas an injunction is a discretionary remedy obtainable in equity. For example, in *Ough v King*[5] the successful plaintiff to an action in nuisance (interference with an easement of light) was denied an injunction but awarded damages to cover the depreciation to her property which the nuisance had caused. A court's discretion could easily be exercisable in this way wherever statutory land acquisitions depreciate adjoining land.

Unfortunately there exists the leading case of *Hammersmith and City Rly Co v Brand*[6] where premises were depreciated because of vibrations caused by trains on a railway newly constructed nearby—a clear prima facie case of nuisance.[7] Now, in *Hill's* case, the choice of particular land was held to be unlawful precisely because it gave rise to a nuisance. Yet in *Brand's* case, the nuisance was recognised—and brushed aside.

---

**4** (1881) 6 App Cas 193 (see ch 2, p 23, above).
**5** [1967] 3 All ER 859, [1967] 1 WLR 1547.
**6** (1869) LR 4 HL 171.
**7** A leading case in private nuisance involving noise and vibrations is *Sturges v Bridgman* (1879) 11 Ch D 852.

The choice of land for the railway in *Brand's* case came directly under an Act of Parliament—the 'special Act' for that particular undertaking. In *Hill's* case just as in *Brand's* case, the selection of land was dependent on statutory authority; but unfortunately the purchase of land by agreement under a general authorising Act bears a less obviously statutory appearance than an Act which is a 'special Act'. Yet it must not be forgotten that compulsory purchase orders, though only sub-statutory, were expressly stated to be part of the 'special Act' in recent compulsory acquisitions; moreover they are the part which selects the particular land. Acquisitions which statutory authorities make purely by agreement and without compulsion do not even need a compulsory purchase order for the purpose of selecting particular land. But that does not make them less subject to statutory authorisation and the 'ultra vires' rule. Therefore the approach later adopted in *Hill's* case, if correct, should by the same token have been adopted in *Brand's* case also. But it was not; unfortunately *Brand's* case has been taken as belonging to the mainstream of the law governing compulsory purchase compensation while *Hill's* case has been regarded as irrelevant to compensation.

## 2 THE SCOPE OF STATUTORY AUTHORISATION

It had been contended in *Brand's* case that bodies acquiring land under statutory powers were not entitled to commit a nuisance thereon unless the statute clearly authorised them to do so. In the House of Lords this view was unanimously rejected, even though it had been accepted by Baron Bramwell in the court below. Lord Chelmsford took the view that it is not necessary for a statute to authorise the commission of what would otherwise be a tort: the authorisation to carry out the statutory purpose is apparently sufficient to justify any tort if it can be regarded as unavoidable. He put it this way: '. . . we do not expect to find words in an Act of Parliament expressly authorising an individual or a company to commit a nuisance or to do damage to a neighbour . . . if such locomotives cannot possibly be used without occasioning vibration . . . it must be taken that power is given to cause that vibation without liability to an action'. And Lord Cairns, though dissenting on the eventual decision, agreed on this point, saying, '. . . I have, therefore, no hesitation in arriving at the conclusion that no action would be maintainable against the railway company'.[8]

8  The weakness in their Lordships' reasoning is that the relevant statutes are not concerned in the slightest with the *practicability* of the acquiring body's project either in principle or in detail, so that whether trains must vibrate or not is altogether beside the point. Statutes are necessary, in the public interest, in order to give two privileges to the acquiring authority: (i) power to act as a corporate body, as distinct from a fluctuating group of individuals or even a partnership; (ii) power to take land from unwilling proprietors. Item (i) means that the individuals promoting the project need not put their entire personal fortunes at risk, and will find it easier to tap other people's; item (ii)

The later decision of the House of Lords in *Hill's* case suggests that in theory—though scarcely in practice—the selection of the actual site of the railway could have been cancelled by injunction because it would involve a nuisance to neighbours. But their Lordships in *Brand's* case bluntly took the view that the nuisance, though clear, was not actionable at all, because it was 'necessary'; and although a distinction may be drawn between the two cases on the ground that re-siting was impracticable in *Brand's* case, the decision in that case does not seem to have been considered on such a basis. Anyway the claim in that case was made ex post facto for money compensation; it was not made in advance for an injunction as in *Hill's* case.

The House of Lords recently reaffirmed its approach to this matter in *Allen v Gulf Oil Refining Co.*[9] A private Act had given compulsory purchase powers to the defendants, enabling them to construct an oil refinery. The plaintiffs, whose adjoining houses were dwarfed by the refinery, sued in nuisance and negligence seeking injunctions to restrain use of the refinery which depreciated their premises by fumes, vibrations, noise, flames and fears of explosion. Reversing a majority decision in the plaintiffs' favour by the Court of Appeal, their Lordships held that there was no entitlement even to damages let alone injunctions. Lord Roskill said that 'the lesser private right must yield to the greater public interest.' Admittedly the defendants 'must . . . exercise [their] powers without negligence . . . meaning reasonable regard for the interests of others.' But the defendants were held not to be at fault in this respect. As to compensation, Lord Edmund-Davies said: 'the absence of compensation clauses from an Act conferring powers affords an important indication that the Act was not intended to authorise interference with private rights'; but 'the indication is not conclusive'. It was not treated as 'conclusive' in this case. Despite proof of nuisance the plaintiffs were denied legal redress.

An injunction being a discretionary remedy, the view could easily have been taken that, whenever a choice of particular land under statutory powers (whether by compulsion or by agreement) could not practicably be altered, a court awarding an injunction would be exercising its discretion improperly. But this would merely withhold an unsuitable remedy; it would not deny that there was an actionable wrong. Compensatory damages at common law should be available as of right. As the law stands, statutory compensation is in fact payable in many cases, but by

means that they will get all the land *they* reasonably want, regardless of what its owners reasonably want. It ought to follow that if what the promoters also reasonably want is to depreciate land by vibrations, smoke or what not, instead of taking it outright, they should pay accordingly, by damages at common law if there is no separate provision for compensation under statute, just as they pay for taking land outright.
9 [1981] AC 101, [1981] 1 All ER 353.

no means in all; while on the authority of *Brand's* case liability in tort is negatived altogether. [10]

This right to compensation has been spelled out by the courts from certain provisions of the Lands Clauses Consolidation Act 1845, which have been expressly and indefinitely prolonged in their effect by the Compulsory Purchase Act 1965. The effectiveness of this right to compensation is, however, impaired by the fact that those provisions were not designed to bear the burden of interpretation put upon them. As Parliament did not attend to the problem, the courts attempted to make up for the omission by reading into the statutory provisions a right to compensation which was not there. Making law by benevolent misinterpretation is even less efficient than making law by fictions. The upshot was the emergence of *two* kinds of compensation for depreciation. One was rather more generous than the right to common law damages for nuisance, but was applicable only to a limited class of cases. The other was so much less generous that it often resulted in no compensation at all, as in fact happened in *Brand's* case itself. These rules, being arbitrary, led to injustice.

### 3  WHAT THE 1845 ACT SAID

A study of the Act of 1845, from which these rules were derived, suggests that there was no intention on the part of Parliament to enact two kinds of compensation. Sections 16 to 68 of that Act are grouped under the general heading of 'the purchase and taking of lands otherwise than by agreement'. They are procedural, and not concerned with principles of assessment. Their only references to land which is depreciated instead of acquired are as follows.

Section 18 requires a notice to treat to refer to: 'compensation to be made to all *parties* for the damage that may be sustained by them by reason of the execution of the works'. 'Parties' refers to 'all the parties interested in', or empowered to convey, 'the lands which . . . (the acquiring body) are authorised to purchase or take'—but no others. Thus compensation for 'damage' is not an independent matter but purely incidental to acquisition.

Section 21 provides that if 'any such party' (referring back to s 18) fails to negotiate for, or to agree upon, compensation, including that payable 'for any damge that may be sustained by him by reason of the execution of the works', the procedure 'hereinafter provided' is to be applied.

The next references differ according to different procedures provided for by the Act of 1845. Section 22 refers to claims for compensation not exceeding £50, which in default of agreement must be 'settled by two justices', including cases of 'lands . . . injuriously affected by the works'.

---

**10** It is important to note that this abrogation of liability in tort is not expressed by statute but has been inferred by the courts.

Section 23, however, refers to 'compensation claimed or offered in *any such case*'—which can only refer back to s 22—exceeding £50; here the procedure must be arbitration or, failing that, a jury. The words in s 22 governing these two provisions do not appear to subordinate 'injurious affection' to the 'taking' of lands, so that 'injurious affection' here could be quite independent of expropriation. But it is highly unlikely that a distinction was intended; certainly there is no express wording drawing such a distinction or even referring to one. Throughout the 1845 Act the assumption seems to be merely that 'the parties' who are, collectively, to be *expropriated* are to be compensated for 'injurious affection' caused by carrying out the acquiring body's 'works' on the land authorised to be taken, regardless of whether the injury arises on land taken from the 'party' claiming or from a different 'party' in the collective group.[11] The only clear implication seems to be that the claimant in such a case is retaining some land, which suffers, and is not being expropriated from all his property in the immediate vicinity.

The Act of 1845 further assumed that an arbitrator or umpire (ss 25 to 37—now repealed by the Compulsory Purchase Act 1965) did not require to be told how to assess compensation, but that a jury did (ss 38 to 57—also repealed). Thus s 49 required the jury, if used, to 'deliver their verdict separately' for sums, if any, payable respectively for the land taken and for 'compensation for the damage . . . to be sustained by the owner of the lands by reason of the severing of the lands taken from the other lands *of such owner*, or otherwise injuriously affecting such other lands . . .'. Here, without prior warning, 'severance' appears as a special variety of 'injurious affection'. What still seems reasonably clear, however, is that injurious affection was considered only in regard to an owner from whom some land has been taken. The implied distinction is between an owner from whom some land has been taken and an owner from whom *no land has been taken*. It is, however, not the distinction (which was developed later and lasted until ended in 1973) between injurious affection arising respectively on land taken from the claimant and on land not taken from the claimant, regardless in the latter case of whether he had in fact had other land taken from him or not.

After a group of sections (58 to 62) providing for the assessment of compensation by an 'able practical surveyor' in the absence of the landowner, there follows a section, 63, which appears parallel to s 49, except that whereas s 49 applied to juries, s 63 applies to 'the justices, arbitrators or surveyors, as the case may be'. It requires, in lieu of words prescribing a separate verdict in the case of a jury, that 'regard shall be had . . . not only to the value of the land to be purchased . . . but also the

---

11 Contrast with this (a) the later situation exemplified in *Edwards v Minister of Transport* (below, p 180) and (b) the modern situation resulting from the enactment of Part I and s 44 of the Land Compensation Act 1973 (below, pp 181, 186–192).

damage, if any, to be sustained by the owner of the lands by reason of the severing of the lands taken from the *other* lands *of such owner*, or otherwise injuriously affecting such other lands . . .', which from 'sustained' onwards uses identical language to that of s 49.

Finally, after four more ancillary sections, comes the all-important s 68. It begins by postulating an owner who 'shall be entitled to any compensation in respect of any lands . . . which shall have been taken for or injuriously affected by the execution of the works, *and for which the promoters of the undertaking shall not have made satisfaction . . .*'. It then prescribes the procedure to be used for assessment. The point of the section is reasonably clear, namely to deal with cases where land is taken by acquiring bodies before compensation is assessed, let alone paid, the situation then being such that an acquiring body, having succeeded in getting land without having to pay for it first, may perhaps lack any urgent incentive to settle up. Accordingly owners are empowered to compel the making of the assessment without delay. The all-important words 'shall be entitled to any compensation' must therefore refer back to previous provisions in the Act, particularly s 18, which make it clear what must be paid for. The words '*shall have been* taken for or injuriously affected by' in s 68 contrast with 'land *to be* purchased', and 'damage, if any, *to be* sustained' in s 63. Certainly no intention exists in the wording of s 68 to set up a new head of compensation for a kind of loss not otherwise dealt with.

Nevertheless that is just what the courts did interpret s 68 to mean. This is partly because Parliament did not make clear provision for cases of injurious affection arising on land not taken from the claimant, or at any rate occurring to a claimant from whom no land was taken. But more important, it is because of the clear belief of the courts (especially of the House of Lords in *Brand's* case) that Parliament must be deemed to have impliedly authorised the commission of nuisances with impunity by acquiring bodies, which would have meant that many landowners were left defenceless before serious or even total cases of depreciation of their property.

The most extreme possible injustice stemming from this could have arisen from (say) the acquisition of neighbouring property to that of a landowner in circumstances such that a private right of way constituting the only access to his land became totally blocked by the acquiring body's project. Since he lost no land he would not come within the scope of the Act of 1845, unless s 68 (or any other section) were interpreted so as to confer a right to compensation in his kind of case, regardless of what violence this would require to be done to its wording. And, thanks to *Brand's* case, he would be deemed to have been deprived of all remedy in nuisance by virtue of the statutory powers conferred upon the acquiring body. Everyone must judge for himself whether the interpretation of s 68 of the Act of 1845 was justifiable in these circumstances, and whether (in theory or practice or both) the courts ought instead to have refrained from such a course and allowed an extreme case of injustice to lead to an outcry, and so perhaps to reform.

# B. Depreciation resulting from taking the claimant's land

### 1 PLUGGING THE GAP IN COMPENSATION

Section 63 of the 1845 Act uses the words '. . . severing . . . or otherwise injuriously affecting . . .'. Here, if anywhere, is the legal source for the terms 'severance' and injurious affection' in use today. They are not defined in any enactment. What should be noted is that s 63 regards 'injurious affection' as a wider concept, and 'severance' as a subordinate category. In this sense, therefore, severance is one kind of injurious affection. Such usage is still met with nowadays; but it is more usual to regard the two terms as different, though closely related, and of equal standing. Injurious affection in its modern sense is virtually private nuisance which is not actionable by virtue of the reasoning in *Brand's* case, but which may be compensatable (and in some circumstances is in fact compensatable beyond the scope of private nuisance). It is depreciation of land caused by what happens on other land. Severance is depreciation of land by virtue of its own inadequacy after being cut off from other land previously held with it. Injurious affection in its older sense, embracing severance, is in fact the Victorian term for 'depreciation' in general—or at any rate depreciation caused by some act or process other than mere effluxion of time.

Section 63, though not repealed, is re-enacted in s 7 of the Compulsory Purchase Act 1965:

> In assessing the compensation to be paid by the acquiring authority under this Act regard shall be had not only to the value of the land to be purchased by the acquiring authority, but also to the damage, if any, to be sustained by the owner of the land by reason of the severing of the land purchased from the other land of the owner, or otherwise injuriously affecting that other land by the exercise of the powers conferred. . . .[12]

It seems reasonably clear that severance and injurious affection are intended, primarily as a matter of valuation rather than law, to plug a gap. If land worth £10,000 is cut into two equal pieces, one of which is compulsorily acquired at a market value of £5,000, the normal assumption, prima facie, is that the owner thereafter owns land worth £5,000

---

12 Where a leasehold tenant with a yearly or lesser interest is being expropriated under s 20 of the 1965 Act (see above, ch 5, p 87), sub-s 2 of that section says: 'If a part only of such land is required, [the tenant] shall also be entitled to compensation for the damage done to him in his tenancy by severing the land held by him or otherwise injuriously affecting it'.

and £5,000 in money, total £10,000, in place of his former undivided £10,000 of land value. But it may be that whereas the undivided land was a viable unit—say a farm or a factory or a filling-station—each separated half of it may not be, and therefore is to be valued not at £5,000 but (say) £4,000. To avoid leaving the owner with only £4,000 in money and £4,000 in land, total £8,000, which would mean unjust deprivation of £2,000, rational valuation principles backed up by the statutory provisions mentioned above require the gap to be plugged by a further payment of £2,000 on account of the depreciation caused by the severance. If, however, the deficiency of £2,000 is caused by what is done by the acquiring body in carrying out their project for which the land was taken, being injurious affection akin to nuisance, and not by a disproportionate reduction in value of the land either retained or acquired it must be compensated just the same. Either way the owner retains land worth £4,000 and gets £6,000 in compensation, of which £4,000 is purchase price at market value. And frequently the loss of £2,000 cannot be attributable exclusively either to severance or to other injurious affection akin to nuisance. If so it is still payable but ascribed to both factors in combination.[13]

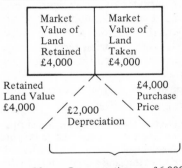

MARKET VALUE BEFORE SEVERANCE  :  £10,000

| Market Value of Land Retained £4,000 | Market Value of Land Taken £4,000 |

Retained Land Value £4,000

£2,000 Depreciation

£4,000 Purchase Price

Money Compensation  :  £6,000

| Land Value 'Before' | = £10,000 |
| Land Value 'After' | = £  4,000 |
| *Total Compensation* | = £  6,000 |

## 2  SEVERANCE

Severance on its own gives rise to little difficulty in law. In *Palmer and Harvey Ltd v Ipswich Corpn*,[14] an urban property reduced in size at-

---

**13** The leading case justifying compensation for 'severance and injurious affection' as a composite phenomenon is the *Buccleuch* case (below, p 178).

**14** (1953) 4 P & CR 5.

tracted severance compensation after another part of it had been taken for slum clearance purposes. In *Holt v Gas Light and Coke Co*,[15] a small piece of land was compulsorily purchased from a larger area used for a rifle-range. It was merely a section of ground behind the butts, but its loss reduced the safety area so that the range could no longer be used. Therefore in addition to the insignificant amount representing the purchase price of the land taken, there had to be paid a large sum for the depreciation of the remainder because it was no longer viable.

In the Australian case of *Melwood Units Pty Ltd v Commissioner of Main Roads*,[16] a 37-acre urban site was severed into unequal parts of some 25 acres ('north site') and 7 acres ('south site') respectively by the compulsory purchase of about 5 acres for a new road. To simplify a complex state of affairs, it can be taken as established that all 37 acres enjoyed in a general way 'development potential' such that their market value for housing development was about $9,000 an acre and for 'drive-in shopping centre' development (the 'highest and best use') was some $24,000 to $40,000 an acre. The necessary demand was there, and planning permission would have been forthcoming for the 37 acres but for the new road scheme. After the compulsory purchase of the 5 acres the owners sold the 25 acre site for $40,000 an acre with permission for shopping centre development. Nevertheless the Australian compensation tribunal held that the entire site was to be regarded as having a value of about $9,000 an acre; and it assessed the purchase price of the 5 acres, and severance compensation in respect of the remaining 7 acres, on this footing. The Privy Council held that the figure of $40,000 an acre should not have been disregarded: indeed it 'was the only figure available at the date of assessment. . . .' as relevant valuation evidence.

But in *Pepys v London Transport Executive*[17] the claim was for depreciation caused by vibrations from tube trains under the claimant's house in London. Now, we know from the decision of the House of Lords in *Metropolitan Rly Co v Fowler*[18] that taking a stratum of land compulsorily for an underground railway[19] is a compulsory acquisition of part of an owner's land, as distinct from an acquisition of a mere servitude (such as an easement) over it. It follows that in the *Pepys* case there was a severance; and therefore in principle a purchase price should have been paid (even if only a nominal sum) in respect of the taking of the stratum. And in addition compensation (again, in principle) should have been paid for any loss to the owner, over and above the purchase price, attributable to the severance consequent upon the taking of part of the land in the form of that stratum. Thus the claimant will in such a case be

15  (1872) LR 7 QB 728.
16  [1979] AC 426, [1979] 1 All ER 161. (See above, ch 7, p 134 and ch 8, p 155.)
17  [1975] 1 All ER 748, [1975] 1 WLR 234.
18  See above, ch 5, p 96.
19  And presumably also for mining, drainage, pipe-lines or any other purpose.

entitled in principle to 'treat' for compensation (and indeed to receive a *notice* to treat), even if in the upshot the amount should turn out to be minimal. Yet the Court of Appeal held that the claim was altogether unjustified and (reversing the Lands Tribunal on this point) that, on the analogy of an unsuccessful civil action for damages, costs must be awarded in full against the unsuccessful claimant. The justice of this is questionable, to say the least. [20]

### 3 INJURIOUS AFFECTION AKIN TO NUISANCE FROM SEVERED LAND

On compensation for depreciation by injurious affection akin to nuisance so long as it arises on land taken by the acquiring body from the claimant—ie severed from the land which he retains—the classic leading case is *Duke of Buccleuch v Metropolitan Board of Works*. [1] The defendant authority compulsorily purchased land in order to construct the Victoria Embankment alongside the Thames at Westminster. A belt of the plaintiff's leasehold land along the shore of the river was included in the purchase. He was held, by the House of Lords, to be entitled not merely to a market value purchase price for the strip of land but to the full depreciation caused to the property—the house and grounds not taken— by the loss of that strip, which exceeded any purchase price figure. It is pretty clear that the value of such a strip on its own, in the open market, would be derisory, compared with its value to the land which lay behind. This was partly a question of severance, in as much as the house lost its access to the river (there being a jetty on the foreshore), and was less desirable on that account. But it was also akin to nuisance in that the placing of a public road on the land taken produced dust, noise and loss of privacy. The *total depreciation* (£5,000), payable in full on expropriation of the riverside strip, therefore covered these factors as well as the severance and the insignificant market value of the strip.

These calculations are thus to be made on a 'before and after' basis—ie the true depreciation is quantified by deducting the value of the re- mainder of the property, after severance and injurious affection, from its value before. [2]

Although such injurious affection greatly resembles private nuisance, it should be noted from this case that it extends to loss of privacy, which is not a matter for which damages may be awarded in tort. This in turn points to the fact that the governing consideration here is not an identi- fication with the law of tort, but the making up in full of the claimant's

---

**20** For costs in the Lands Tribunal, see above, ch 6, p 123.

**1** (1872) LR 5 HL 418.

**2** But this is not always done in practice. See for example *Bolton Metropolitan Borough Council v Waterworth* [1981] 2 Lloyd's Rep 625, where loss compensated as severance and injurious affection seems in fact to have been lost development value.

loss in land value. It is fundamentally a valuation approach, not a legal approach. This kind of injurious affection is, so to speak, 'tort plus'.

For land to be the subject of severance or injurious affection compensation, it need not be absolutely contiguous. 'I am prepared to hold that, where several pieces of land, owned by the same person, are so near to each other, and so situated that the possession and control of each gives an enhanced value to all of them, they are lands held together within the meaning of the (Lands Clauses Consolidation) Act.' This statement was made by Lord Watson in his speech to the House of Lords in *Cowper Essex v Acton Local Board*.[3] In this dispute part of the claimant's land was compulsorily purchased for a sewage-works. In addition to purchase price compensation, he successfully claimed injurious affection compensation in respect of his remaining land, which he had intended to develop for housing before the local authority's project rendered it less desirable. His claim succeeded not only for land directly severed from the land taken but also for other land nearby which he intended to include in his proposed housing development even though it was separated from the rest by a railway line.

It should be noted that the claimant here was not making any far-fetched assertions. The detached portion of land nearby was, as a plain matter of valuation, to be included in the depreciation suffered. Had the facts been otherwise there would not have been anything to claim in respect of it. The acquiring body were in effect saying that, although such depreciation genuinely extended to the detached portion of land, nevertheless that land must be excluded from the claim for no other reason than the fact that it was detached. It follows from this case that, where an owner holds land in separate but closely situated parcels, the first question to ask is whether the depreciation suffered, if any, extends to more than one parcel. If it genuinely does, then prima facie there can be no justification for excluding any such parcel from the scope of the claim. In short, the acquiring body must accept that there is a genuine loss suffered in respect of such parcels and it is genuinely attributable to the taking of the claimant's land which is part of another such parcel.

A similar situation arose in a Canadian case, *Sisters of Charity of Rockingham v R*,[4] where a school owned land nearby, comprising two promontories on the shore of a lake, separated from the school by a road and railway. Moreover Lord Parmoor, in the Judicial Committee of the Privy Council, pointed out that depreciation (like purchase price) compensation is not confined merely to what has already happened but extends also to what is expected to happen—thus underlining the point

3 (1889) 14 App Cas 153. On the difficult question of valuing separate but adjacent parcels of land in the same ownership, see also *Rothera and Goddard v Nottingham City Council*, above, ch 5, p 82.
4 [1922] 2 AC 315. See p 186, below.

that valuation of land must inevitably in the normal case take account of the future, as far as the market is reasonably prepared to foresee it, and not only of the past and present. He said, '. . . the appellants are entitled to claim compensation, which must be claimed once for all, . . . in so far as depreciation is due to the *anticipated* legal use of authorised works which may be constructed upon the two promontories'. Unlike the *Cowper Essex* case, however, it was only existing use value and not development value which was at stake.

INJURIOUS AFFECTION WITH AND WITHOUT SEVERANCE

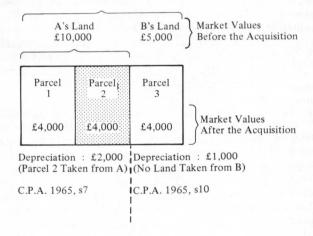

## C. Depreciation not resulting from taking the claimant's land

1  WHETHER OR NOT ANY LAND HAS BEEN TAKEN FROM THE CLAIMANT

Much more difficulty has arisen over cases where either *no* land has been taken from the claimant, or the depreciation of which he complains is caused by what is done on land not taken from *him*. Until 1973 legal significance was attributed to the second category which is wider than the former; even though in several leading cases, and in many situations arising in normal practice, the facts came into the former category.[5]

In *Edwards v Minister of Transport*,[6] land was compulsorily purchased

5  *McCarthy's* case (see p 181, below) comes within the former category; *Edwards v Minister of Transport* does not. A case which presumably ought not to be regarded as one relating to injurious affection where no land was taken, yet seems in fact to have been so regarded, is *Pepys v London Transport Executive* (above, p 177).
6  [1964] 2 QB 134, [1964] 1 All ER 483.

for a new trunk road, including a small quantity from the grounds of the claimant's house. It was held, in the Court of Appeal, that the taking of land from the claimant was not relevant to a claim for injurious affection in so far as the latter arose from what was done on land *not* taken from him. The established (but perverse) interpretation of s 68 of the 1845 Act, referred to above,[7] was held to be applicable to any injurious affection arising on land not taken from the claimant whether or not other land had in fact been taken from him for the authority's project, and was not restricted to cases where no land was taken from him for that project.

Section 44 of the Land Compensation Act 1973, which has now disposed of the *Edwards* case, is a particularly beneficial reform. It provides as follows:

(1) Where land is acquired or taken from any person for the purpose of works which are to be situated partly on that land and partly elsewhere, compensation for injurious affection of land retained by that person shall be assessed by reference to the whole of the works and not only the part situated on the land acquired or taken from him.[8]

The consequence of this is that the special rules just about to be described now apply only to claimants whose land is depreciated but from whom no land is taken. If some land is taken, however little, 'injurious affection' compensation under s 7 of the 1965 Act is payable for depreciation of land retained, regardless of the proportion of it that arises on land other than the land taken from the claimant.

It is usually said that injurious affection not arising from land taken is defined by 'the four rules in *McCarthy's* case'. This is the House of Lords' decision in *Metropolitan Board of Works v McCarthy*.[9] Again the construction of the Victoria Embankment gave rise to the actual claim; but, unlike the *Buccleuch* case, the compulsory purchase of land for the embankment did not involve the taking of any land from the claimant. What took place, however, was the blocking up and destruction of Whitefriars dock, a public dock very close to the claimant's business premises where the builders' materials in which he traded were stored and sold. A public highway over the water of the dock, connecting the road highway leading to the dock with the river highway outside it, was thus totally obstructed. The claimant argued that, not only was he affected as an ordinary member of the public using the highway (which in itself would not entitle him to compensation), but that the value of his

---

7 See p 184 (now s 10 of the Compulsory Purchase Act 1965 see below, p 183).
8 'Compensation for injurious affection' is expressly stated (s 44 (2)) to mean compensation under ss 7 and 20 of the Act of 1965 (see above, p 175) or the comparable type of compensation obtainable when what is compulsorily acquired in not 'land' as such but any 'right' over land under the Highways Act 1980 and the Gas Act 1972. (For 'rights' see above, ch 5, p 96).
9 (1874) LR 7 HL 243.

business premises was depreciated because other modes of access were very much less convenient. His right to compensation for depreciation—injurious affection—of the premises was duly upheld.

It was pointed out that this case is on all fours with the earlier decision in *Chamberlain v West End of London and Crystal Palace Rly Co*,[10] in which the railway company blocked off an existing public road and diverted it round to a new bridge that they built, all being within the proper exercise of their statutory powers. The claimant's land lay on a portion of the old road now converted into a *cul-de-sac*. He succeeded in claiming for the depreciation caused to his land thereby. This case should be contrasted with *Jolliffe v Exeter Corpn*,[11] where in advance of compulsory purchase of part of a highway it had been stopped up under highway legislation (in this case the Town and Country Planning Act 1962, s 153, not the Highways Act 1959, Part VI).

It should be noticed that here we have an analogy in tort, not strictly with private nuisance as such, but with public nuisance privately actionable, the particular species being obstruction of a highway which causes loss and damage peculiar to the claimant, over and above what he suffers as a member of the general public. It will however be seen that he can only claim injurious affection compensation in such a case if the particular loss is to land value, not a trade loss or any other kind of damage which in principle could justify an action in tort.[12]

The following extracts from the speeches in the *McCarthy* case do, among others, contain references to the famous 'four rules', but not in terms which express them as such; and it would be truer to say that the rules are derived from the cases generally. Lord Cairns LC referred to, '... whether the act done in *carrying out the works* ...' would have been actionable but for statutory authority. And Lord Chelmsford declared: 'there must be an injury and damage to the house or land itself. . . . A mere personal obstruction . . . or a damage occasioned to a man's trade or the goodwill of his business, although of such a nature that but for the Act of Parliament it might have been the subject of an action for damages, will not entitle the injured party to compensation under it.' These and many other statements are all intended as interpretations of s 68 of the Act of 1845.[13]

10  (1863) 2 B & S 617.
11  [1967] 2 All ER 1099, [1967] 1 WLR 993. Stopping up highways does not, in itself, give to frontagers any right to compensation (see the present writer's book *Concise Law of Highways*, published 1969, pp 170 to 177, 239); but there is an exception to this in relation to public path extinguishment orders (Highways Act 1980, s 121 (2)). Section 153 of the Act of 1962 has now been re-enacted as s 209 of the Town and Country Planning Act 1971. The Highways Act 1980 has replaced the 1959 Act.
12  This arises from rule (iii) of *McCarthy's* case (p 184, below). Another difference stems from rule (iv) in that case (pp 185–187, below).
13  See p 174, above.

That section has been re-enacted, without being repealed, in s 10 of the Compulsory Purchase Act 1965, which expressly says:

> This section shall be construed as affording in all cases a right to compensation for injurious affection to land which is the same as the right which section 68 of the Lands Clauses Consolidation Act, 1845, has been construed as affording in cases where the amount claimed exceeds fifty pounds. [14]

Section 10 applies only, it seems, where an authority has compulsorily acquired the land giving rise to the depreciation complained of, not acquired it by agreement. But where a *local* authority has acquired land by agreement under statutory powers before April 1974 they may by resolution (which must be confirmed by the Minister or Secretary of State concerned with the functions for which it is held) apply s 10 to it. [15] The intention is presumably to clarify the question of how the principle underlying the *Brand* case applies in such circumstances, so that some compensation may be payable yet liability in nuisance can confidently be resisted.

## 2 THE FOUR RULES IN THE McCARTHY CASE

Rule (i) of the 'four rules' is that the action giving rise to the depreciation of the claimant's land must be authorised by statute. In *Clowes v Staffordshire Potteries Waterworks Co*[16] the water company fouled a stream beside which they had compulsorily acquired land for a waterworks. It was held that their statutory authority did not extend to doing this, and so it must be remedied by an action in tort, not a claim for compensation. [17] It is essential to realise that the water company would have been liable in tort *not* because they fouled the stream but because the court inferred that the fouling was an *avoidable* consequence of their exercise of the statutory authority conferred upon them and therefore ultra vires. If convincing expert evidence had led the court to conclude that the fouling was *un*-avoidable the reasoning of the House of Lords in

---

**14** Subsection 2. The fifty pound limit is a red herring. It refers to the summary procedure in s 22 of the 1845 Act (mentioned above, on p 172) for small claims, which has been obsolete in practice since the introduction of the official arbitration procedure in 1919 (above, ch 2, p 29), like the other procedures in the 1845 Act for determining compensation disputes. Section 10 (1) of the 1965 Act says: 'If any person claims compensation in respect of any land, or any interest in land, which as been taken for or injuriously affected by the execution of the works, and for which the acquiring authority have not made satisfaction . . . any dispute arising in relation to the compensation shall be referred to and determined by the Lands Tribunal.'

**15** Local Government (Miscellaneous Provisions) Act 1976, s 14. Procedure for publicity and objections is prescribed.

**16** (1872) 8 Ch App 125. See also *Imperial Gas Light and Coke Co v Broadbent* (1859) 7 HL Cas 600.

**17** For the common law position of riparian owners see *John Young & Co Ltd v Bankier Distillery Co* [1893] AC 691 at 698.

*Brand's* case would mean that it was within that statutory authority and consequently free of liability in tort. But if the promoters had not needed any statutory authority, for example because they were not a company but a group of individuals serving a wealthy landowner who acquired the land privately and engaged them to construct a waterworks for his use, he and they would have been liable in tort *because* they fouled the stream, regardless of avoidability. [18]

Rule (ii) is that the cause of depreciation would be actionable at law but for the statutory authority. In *Re Penny and South Eastern Rly Co*[19] a claim for loss of privacy failed because this does not found a cause of action in tort. The distinction between this kind of case and the Buccleuch case discussed above, where the injurious affection arose on land taken from the claimant, is instructive.

Rule (iii) is that compensation can only be claimed for depreciation of rights in land. This was clearly the kind of loss suffered in the *McCarthy* and *Chamberlain* cases. In *Ricket v Metropolitan Rly Co*[20] the House of Lords refused to allow compensation for loss of trade, even though such loss could found an action in tort, as public nuisance privately actionable, on the authority of *Wilkes v Hungerford Market Co*.[1] In *Senior v Metropolitan Rly Co*[2] trade loss caused by temporary obstruction of a highway was included in compensation for depreciation of land; but *Ricket's* case overruled this decision.[3] Trade loss is now to be considered for compensation under the heading of 'disturbance', which means that it can only be recovered when the premises are themselves compulsorily acquired.

Of particular importance under rule (iii) is the question of rights *in alieno solo*. It has been explained earlier how the compulsory acquisition of servient land does not necessarily affect the easements or other rights

---

18  It is relevant here to notice how the principle in *Brand's* case was reformulated by Lord Blackburn in *Geddis v Bann Reservoir Proprietors* (1878) 3 App Cas 430 at 455. He said '. . . no action will lie for doing that which the legislature has authorised, if it be done without negligence . . .; but an action does lie for doing that which the legislature has authorised, if it be done negligently. And I think that if by a reasonable exercise of the powers. . . . the damage could be prevented, it is . . . negligence not to make such reasonable exercise. . . .' *And yet*: 'If a man creates a nuisance, he cannot say that he is acting reasonably. The two things are self-contradictory' (per Kekewich J in *A-G v Cole & Son* [1901] 1 Ch 205 at 207). Thus any liability in nuisance negatives reasonableness where offenders are *not* acting under statutory powers; but conversely reasonableness negatives any liability in nuisance where they are. This is hardly reasonable.

19  (1857) 7 E & B 660.

20  (1867) LR 2 HL 175.

 1  (1835) 2 Bing NC 281. See the passage discussing this matter in *Salmond on Torts* ch 5, s 31 (3).

 2  (1863) 2 H & C 258.

 3  *Ricket's* case was recently followed in *Argyle Motors (Birkenhead) Ltd v Birkenhead Corpn* [1973] 1 All ER 866, [1973] 2 WLR 487, affd. [1975] AC 99, [1974] 1 All ER 201, in which a local Act applied s 68 of the 1845 Act in terms which were held to give no wider compensation rights.

over it,[4] but that if they are interfered with this is injurious affection, which must be the subject of compensation. Clearly this is a situation where land is depreciated in accordance with rule (iii), the depreciation being that which the dominant land suffers. In the absence of any reforming legislation, it can be said that these cases provide the strongest justification for the courts' cavalier interpretation of s 68 of the Act of 1845. Thus in *Eagle v Charing Cross Rly Co*,[5] compensation was held to be payable when the claimant's premises were injuriously affected by infringement of his easement of light. And in *Long Eaton Recreation Grounds Co v Midland Rly Co*[6] compensation was similarly held to be payable for the infringement of a restrictive covenant. In the *Eagle* case the court held also that any appreciation in value, or 'betterment', of the claimant's land resulting from the acquiring body's project was not to be set off against the injurious affection compensation, in the absence of any statutory requirement to that effect.

Rule (iv) is the most controversial of all. It is that the loss must be caused by the 'execution of the works' and not by the use of the land after the acquiring authority have carried out those works. In other words, compensation may be payable if the depreciation is caused by actually building a road or railway, but not if it is caused by the use of that road or railway for traffic afterwards. This rule was in effect, laid down by the majority of the House of Lords in *Brand's* case as a straight question of interpreting the words 'injuriously affected by the execution of the works' in s 68. Lord Cairns, in the minority, urged a liberal interpretation of those words to cover subsequent use as well as construction; but Lords Chelmsford and Colonsay held to a restrictive interpretation. Thus, building a road or railway so as to block (say) an easement of way, will give rise to compensation. But building a road or railway so that the privacy, peace and quiet, or other amenities of property are reduced, will not.

In *Edwards v Ministry of Transport*, referred to above,[7] the claimant's loss of amenity by reason of the noise, lights and other injurious affection caused by traffic using the new trunk road was in consequence of rule (iv) not compensatable, regardless of the depreciation in value caused to his house, in so far as the trouble arose on land *not* taken from him. Yet in so far as it arose on land *taken* from him it was compensatable, as in the *Buccleuch* case. The part of the new road constructed over land taken from him comprised a small fraction of land not easily indentifiable, and not in the least meaningful after the road was built. Donovan LJ said, 'regard must be had only to things done on the land taken from (the claimant). Where a highway is concerned this restriction is of course

4 Above, ch 5.
5 (1867) LR 2 CP 638.
6 [1902] 2 KB 574.
7 See p 180, above. It is of course now overruled.

artificial. The noise of traffic will begin well before it reaches the plot of land which was formerly part of (his) frontage and it may continue long after traffic has passed it.' But the calculation, however artificial, had to be made, and was agreed by both sides at £1,600 out of a total depreciation of £4,000. The £1,600, therefore, represented *Buccleuch* compensation, in respect of the only land where injurious affection could give rise to it. The rest of the land of the trunk road was subject to the four rules, and rule (iv) ruled out injurious affection compensation in respect of it.

Again, in *Sisters of Charity of Rockingham v R*,[8] the Canadian case referred to earlier, compensation was only payable for the depreciation attributable to what was done on the land actually taken from the claimants. Lord Parmoor said that their claim could not be 'extended beyond mischief which arises from (the use) of the two promontories as part of a railway shunting yard'.

However, a slight liberalisation of rule (iv)—though not one which is likely to be capable of general extension—occurred in *Re Simeon and Isle of Wight RDC*.[9] The acquiring body was a local authority statutorily empowered to act as a water-authority, and they built a reservoir on land none of which was acquired from the claimant. But when they filled the reservoir, water percolating through undefined channels to wells and springs on his land nearby was diverted. This would of itself not have been actionable at common law, and so rule (ii) would not have been satisfied, but for the fact that the authority were taking this water from land in respect of which a previous owner had bound himself by a restrictive covenant, for the claimant's benefit, not to interfere with the percolating water. The interference, therefore, would have been an actionable breach of covenant, but for the statutory authority enjoyed by the acquiring body, and moreover an interference with a right in land.[10] This satisfied the first three rules. Luxmoore J held that rule (iv) was also satisfied because, in his view, filling a reservoir was 'execution of the works' just as much as the actual construction of the reservoir before it was filled.

It is of course important to realise that the *Edwards* case and the *Rockingham* case would now be decided differently under s 44 of the Land Compensation Act 1973,[11] by virtue of the fact that some land,

---

8  See p 179, above.
9  [1937] Ch 525, [1937] 3 All ER 149.
10  A contrasting case is *R v Directors of Bristol Dock Co* (1810) 12 East 429. Brewers had used river water, but the dock company's works made it 'brackish and noxious' (the effect on the beer is not stated). The Court of King's Bench refused a mandamus on the ground that: 'These persons have no more claim to compensation under the (authorising) Act than every inhabitant of Bristol would have who had been used to dip a pail into the river for water for the use of his house.' (Contrast *Pride of Derby and Derbyshire Angling Association Ltd v British Celanese Ltd* [1953] Ch 149, [1953] 1 All ER 179.
11  See above, p 181.

however small, was taken from the claimants. Indeed, it may be now of considerable benefit to a landowner to have even the tiniest fragment of his land taken, so as to ensure that he gets full compensation without having to bother with either the *McCarthy* rules or those about to be described which are enacted in Part I of the Land Compensation Act 1973. He should move heaven and earth to convey a square metre (or less, if necessary) to an acquiring body rather than have them acquire adjoining land yet none from him.

## 3 DEPRECIATION CAUSED BY THE USE OF PUBLIC WORKS

In the century after *Brand's* case it became very apparent that claimants whose land was in injuriously affected by reason of what was done by acquiring authorities on land not taken from them stood very little chance of obtaining compensation unless the mischief depreciating their land comprised an interference with some other right existing over the land taken. The essence of a nuisance situation is always present; and it must be remembered that privately actionable nuisances comprise interference with rights *in alieno solo* as well as direct interference with the plaintiff's property. The one essential factor is the damage to the condition or the enjoyment of that property, and interference with an easement which benefits it is actionable for the very same reason as interference which affects it directly. But this does not alter the fact that differences in detail may well underline the distinction between the two varieties of privately actionable nuisance. Interference that affects the plaintiff's land directly is likely to arise from use of the defendant's land rather than works of construction upon it, as in *Halsey v Esso Ltd*,[12] when fumes from the defendants' premises damaged the plaintiff's property. Conversely, interference that affects the plaintiff's land by damaging an easement which benefits it is likely to arise from works of construction rather than use, as in *Ough v King*,[13] when the plaintiff's right of light was infringed by an extension which the defendant built on to his house. There are of course contrary examples, such as *Sedleigh-Denfield v O'Callaghan*,[14] when the faulty construction of a culvert on the defendants' land caused flooding upon the plaintiff's property, and *Pride of Derby Angling Association Ltd v British Celanese Ltd*,[15] when faulty use of the defendants' works caused pollution of a river in which the plaintiffs had fishing rights. But in a general way it tends to be construction works which disrupt servitudes and misuse of property which causes the more direct types of private nuisance.

In tort this matters little because the artificial distinction between

12 [1961] 2 All ER 145, [1961] 1 WLR 683.
13 [1967] 3 All ER 859, [1967] 1 WLR 1549.
14 [1940] AC 880, [1940] 3 All ER 349.
15 [1953] Ch 149, [1953] 1 All ER 179.

construction and use of works on offending land is not relevant to privately actionable nuisance. Only because of *Brand's* case is it relevant to injurious affection. Rule (iv) of the four rules in *McCarthy's* case is the one that gives most trouble, and has effectively defeated claimants not only in *Edwards v Minister of Transport* or the *Rockingham* case but in countless other situations in which property has been depreciated as a result of the use to which land nearby is being put after a statutory body has acquired it and developed it for some public purpose. In Victorian times this would commonly be railway development; nowadays roads and airports are the most prominent examples. The problem is not the less acute for being based on an unreal distinction. It is unreal not only because the contrast of 'construction' with 'use' is immaterial in tort but also because to dissect depreciation in this way is meaningless financially. A valuer can assess a value for property in its depreciated state; and he can assess another value which would apply to that property if it had not been thus depreciated. But a distinction between the different elements of that depreciation has only needed to be drawn because public authorities have (understandably) insisted, on the ultimate authority of *Brand's* case, that they are entitled to have it drawn in order to exempt them from paying compensation which the artificial *McCarthy* rules say they are not liable to pay, regardless of their having caused it.

And so we have the situation wherein urban fly-overs, airfields, sewage works, power-stations and innumerable other kinds of public works can depreciate adjoining properties by virtue of their construction or of their subsequent use. Yet only in respect of the former factor are they compensatable; whereas the latter is normally the effective factor, though for reasons which may be more easily assumed than proved.

For a long time people put up with this situation, until absurdity was highlighted, for lawyers by the *Edwards* case, and for the public at large by the agitation caused when the building of Westway in London and other 'fly-overs' intruded urban motorways into the middle of residential areas. Eventually the Land Compensation Act 1973, Part I (ss 1–19) reformed this part of the law. It did not remove the source of the trouble by getting rid of the doctrine in *Brand's* case and the four *McCarthy* rules, but proceeded instead on a more limited footing. A new type of compensation is recognised within this area, referred to as 'Compensation for Depreciation by Public Works'. The loss to be compensated is not described as 'injurious affection'—possibly because 'injurious affection' and 'depreciation' are merely the old and new ways of referring to the same phenomenon—even though it falls squarely within the scope of 'injurious affection not arising on land taken' to which the *McCarthy* rules themselves apply. Since those rules are still law, they and Part I of the 1973 Act overlap; indeed the rules cover the same general area of depreciation as Part I and more besides. But Part I gives compensation expressly in cases of depreciation caused by *use* of works, which rule (iv) excludes; whereas depreciation from interference with servitudes, though not within the categories listed in Part I, is as shown above commonly caused by *construction* of works and not their use—the building of the Victoria Embankment in *McCarthy's* case, the building and filling of the reservoir in *Re Simeon*—and therefore rule (iv) does not exclude it. But this convenient distribution of remedies is rough and ready, not carefully devised, and so there will *still* be many cases of genuine loss inflicted on owners without any right of redress.

Section 1 of the 1973 Act openly concedes the fact that this kind of loss lies in the same area as the tort of nuisance, because it restricts liability to cases where there is express or implied immunity (the latter being the normal case, though only by virtue of the reasoning of the House of Lords in *Brand's* case). Section 17 says that if such immunity is denied, so that a compensation claim fails, that immunity cannot thereafter be asserted so as to defeat a claim in nuisance.

Statutory bodies with this immunity that are in control of works or land the *use* of which gives rise to any of certain specified 'physical factors' are by virtue of that control termed 'responsible authorities'; and if that use depreciates[16] an 'interest' in land which 'qualifies for compensation' section 1 makes them liable to pay compensation for that depreciation provided the date when that *use* began, referred to as the 'relevant date', was not earlier than 17 October 1969. Section 84 provides that the Crown is subject to this obligation along with other 'responsible authorities', except that it does not apply to 'any aerodrome in the occupation of a government department'. The 'physical factors' are specified as 'noise, vibration, smell, fumes, smoke and artificial lighting and the discharge on to the land in respect of which the claim is made of any solid or liquid substance'.

The claimant must (s 2) have held the 'interest' at the 'relevant date' unless it has been transferred to him subsequently in consequence of the death of whoever did hold it at that date. It must be an 'owner's interest'—freehold or a leasehold with three years or more to run—(i) in a dwelling, occupied as the claimant's residence if the interest entitled him to occupy it or else held in reversion, or (ii) in some or all of an agricultural unit (which includes farm dwellings) of which he occupies the whole, or (iii) in all or a 'substantial part' of any other property, which he occupies by virtue of that interest, with a rateable value not exceeding £2,250 under the valuation current from April 1973. In other

16 Proof that the use of the relevant works has in fact depreciated a claimant's interest is a hard task. Claimants failed in this attempt in *Hickmott v Dorset County Council* (1976) 35 P & CR 195 (road widening in a village), *Streak and Streak v Royal County of Berkshire* (1976) 32 P & CR 435 (new motorway), and *Shepherd and Shepherd v Lancashire County Council* (1976) 33 P & CR 296 (refuse dump). However, in *Davies v Mid-Glamorgan County Council* (1979) 38 P & CR 727, the claimant succeeded (successive extensions to an airfield).

words, claimants must be owner-occupiers for all property which is not residential. But *any* leaseholder validly claiming enfranchisement of a dwelling under the Leasehold Reform Act 1967 is treated as having an 'owner's interest' if the 'relevant date' (above) has occurred between the date of his notice claiming the freehold or an extended lease and the date of that acquisition.[17]

Section 3, as amended by the Local Government, Planning and Land Act 1980, ss. 112–113, prescribes the procedure for claiming compensation. The claimant must serve on the 'responsible authority' (above) a notice, giving the relevant particulars of the claim, not earlier than 12 months after the 'relevant date'. A claim can, however, be made (though not the payment of compensation) during the first 12 months if at the 'relevant date' the owner has already contracted to dispose of his interest outright or, if it is not a dwelling, to lease it. Provided that the 'relevant date' was 13 November 1977 or later, the claim period will be the six years allowed under the Limitation Act 1980[18] for sums recoverable by virtue of any statute. If the 'relevant date' was earlier, the claim period is only two years,[19] unless delay thereafter can be shown to have been caused by insufficient publicity. The claim period of either two or six years begins on what is termed the 'first claim date'.[20]

The assessment of the compensation is made according to prices current on the first day of the 'claim period', in relation to the actual use of works on the offending land of the authority at that date and any reasonably expected intensification thereafter. The interest in land for which the claim is made is taken as at the date of service of the notice of claim (s 4). The benefit of any works or grants already available in respect of soundproofing must be treated as enjoyed by the claimant; but any mortgages and other dealings with the claimant's land occurring after the 'relevant date' must be disregarded, likewise any use of that land beginning after that date. But development value must be ignored in so far as it depends upon planning assumptions (other than those within the scope of the Eighth Schedule to the Town and Country Planning Act 1971 for which compensation has not become payable) or upon planning permissions not yet acted on (s 5).

If it happens that the land subject to the claim, or any nearby land held on the 'relevant date' by the claimant in the same capacity—for his own benefit, or as trustee, or as personal representative—enjoys for any reason an *increase* in value attributable to the same works, s 6 requires this to be set off against the compensation (but the special rules of

17 If any depreciated property interest is jointly owned, all the joint tenants must claim: *Williams v British Gas Corpn*, (1980) 41 P & CR 106.
18 Section 9 (repeating earlier Limitation Acts).
19 Under the 1973 Act, s 3 as originally enacted.
20 The 'first claim date' is the day after the period of 'twelve months from the relevant date' expires.

assessment laid down in ss 4 and 5 do not apply). As this is a set-off it will not be suffered by any benefited owner who is not at the same time suffering a loss compensatable under Part I of the 1973 Act, nor to the extent (if any) it exceeds such compensation when payable in any particular case.

Section 7 states that a claim will not be payable unless the amount exceeds £50. Section 8 provides that there can only be one payment for any given piece of land except where there is an entitlement to compensation for more than one interest in a dwelling by virtue of s 2. It also provides that compensation must not duplicate any payable under s 7 of the Compulsory Purchase Act 1965 (as discussed earlier in this chapter). Such duplication ought not to arise, in as much as the latter compensation will be payable in respect of severance or other injurious affection of land retained by an owner in consequence of the taking of other land from him, whereas Part I of the 1973 Act applies where no land has been taken from the claimant; but presumably there may be uncertainty where acquisitions and projects occur in successive stages. Section 8 also enacts that where part only of land *is* taken (including acquisitions by agreement) within the meaning of s 7 of the 1965 Act, the acquiring authority must enter details, in the local land charges registry, of: (i) the works for which the land taken is required, and (ii) that part of the land which is not taken. If land not acquired is subject to a compensation payment under the 1973 Act, and is compulsorily acquired at a later date, that payment must then be taken into account.

It may happen, however, that depreciation within the meaning of Part I is caused by a change in use after the carrying out of public works as a separate circumstance and not as an intensification reasonably foreseeable when the works themselves first came into use. Section 9 of the 1973 Act therefore gives a right to compensation, in accordance with the foregoing rules, for such depreciation in its own right, provided that it is attributable to: (i) the alteration of a highway carriageway or of any other public works, or (ii) a change of use (other than mere intensification) of 'any public works other than a highway or aerodrome'. However, compensation is expressly ruled out in respect of depreciation from 'physical factors' caused by *aircraft* unless they occur in relation to new runways, or major realignment or extension or strengthening of existing runways, or substantial additions to or alterations of 'taxiways' or 'aprons' chiefly for the purpose of accommodating additional aircraft.

Part I of the 1973 Act came into effect on 23 June 1973. Section 14 provides that no 'claim period' must end before 22 June 1975, two years after that date, even if it related to a 'relevant date' earlier than the Act, since it will be remembered that such a date can have occurred as early as 17 October 1969. Special provisions governed cases where owners had already disposed of land (including grants of tenancies of premises other than dwellings) between the date of publication of the Bill (17 October

1972) and the commencement of Part I, provided that they had done so after the 'relevant date'.

Disputes over claims are referable to the Lands Tribunal from the beginning of the 'claim period' (s 16). Interest on the compensation is payable from the same date, or from the date of service of notice of claim if later, which should encourage expedition by both sides in the settling of claims (s 18). Mortgagees who receive compensation must apply it as if it were the proceeds of sale of the mortgaged property; and trustees for sale, and tenants for life under strict settlements, must apply it as capital money (s 10).

To faciliate the proper handling of claims under Part I, s 15 provides that 'responsible authorities' must officially record the dates when highways and other public works are first used as such, and furnish a written statement on demand. The Secretary of State's certificate of aerodrome works is conclusive.[1]

## D.  Depreciation compensation today

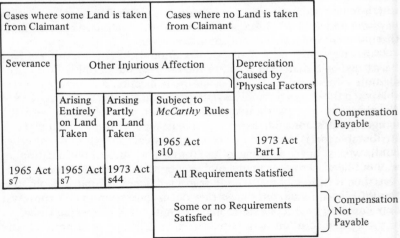

ACTUAL LOSS SUFFERED BY DEPRECIATION

It has been shown how the Compulsory Purchase Act 1965, while not repealing ss 63 and 68 of the Act of 1845, re-enacted them, taking good care not to reform the law by mistake in the process. Section 7 of the Act

---

1  For acquisition of land 'affected by public works', or intervening land, and 'works of mitigation', together with related matters such as sound-proofing grants, see below, ch 11, pp 238–240.

of 1965 virtually repeats s 63; while s 10 repeats s 68, to the extent of preserving its original form as a procedural section, worded in terms which became obsolete more than half a century ago, the substance of which is, however, qualified by a statement that it must be construed exactly as s 68 was construed—ie with bold disregard for the plain meaning of its words. Thus the original provision, and its subsequent perversion in a good cause, are reverently preserved together.

The Land Compensation Act 1973 does not repeal s 10, but reduces the scope of its practical application by assimilating injurious affection of the *Edwards* type to that of the *Buccleuch* type,[2] so that all that is left is injurious affection exclusively of the *McCarthy* type. Its scope is reduced still further by the introduction of the new compensation for depreciation caused by 'physical factors',[3] which will reach many of the cases that fail to qualify for compensation, despite the genuine nature of the loss suffered, even under the *McCarthy* rules because they are caused by the use and not the execution of the works. What chiefly remains to section 10 in practice is the type of case in which the depreciation is not caused by 'physical factors'. But fortunately the most important examples of such depreciation are those which will in fact be likely to satisfy the *McCarthy* rules—particularly the all-important rule (iv) in as much as the loss will be attributable to the execution and not the use of the works—namely interferences with easements, restrictive covenants and other such rights *in alieno solo* benefiting the depreciated land.[4] Section 63 of the Land Compensation Act 1973 now provides that interest is payable in accordance with s 32 of the 1961 Act,[5] on compensation for injurious affection where no land is taken from the claimant, calculated from the date of the claim.

Apart from the 'physical factors' compensation under Part I of the 1973 Act there are no express rules legally prescribed for assessing depreciation compensation. Rule (vi) of s 5 of the Act of 1961, referring to 'disturbance or any other matter not directly based on the value of land' continues to bear the implication that 'market value' under rule (ii) of that section is in fact applicable in these cases, since they are clearly 'based on the value of land'.[6] The planning assumptions in ss 14 to 16 of the 1961 Act, although they are expressed to apply only to land taken, may probably be pressed into service by analogy on the ground of

2 Section 44 (see above, p 181).
3 Part I (see above, p 189).
4 *Re Simeon* (see above, p 186) is a leading example of such a case. Note that any depreciation claim which satisfies some but not all of the rules contained in Part I of the 1973 Act, and so does not qualify under them, may yet succeed under s 10 if (a very big 'if') it complies with the *McCarthy* rules including rule (iv).
5 See above, ch 4, p 65.
6 See above, ch 7, p 144.

reasonableness, in so far as it makes sense to do so in valuation terms, and on an impartial basis.[7]

But this is principally a valuation matter. On the law side, the analogy with actions for damages in tort must always be remembered, even though in one kind of injurious affection loss can be compensated beyond what is allowed in tort, while in the other kind there are many situations which do not give a right to compensation even though an action in tort would lie. But it is generally considered, on the authority of the decision of the Court of Appeal in *Re London, Tilbury and Southend Rly Co and Gower's Walk School Trustees*,[8] that the *measure* of compensation is the same as for damages in tort.[9]

It has been held, in particular circumstances, that if land is compulsorily purchased and the purchase price compensation is assessed to include development value for building, injurious affection to adjoining agricultural land retained by the owner cannot be claimed if the depreciation asserted would in any case have followed from the development of the land acquired. That is to say injurious affection compensation on such a footing is incompatible with the inclusion of prospective development value in the compensation for the price of the land acquired.[10]

This rule, if correct, is analogous to the decision in *Horn v Sunderland Corpn*, concerning disturbance, discussed in the next chapter.[11] Statements in that case by Sir Wilfred Greene MR, and in *Chamberlain v West End of London and Crystal Palace Rly Co* by Erle CJ, it will be remembered,[12] show that, apart from any items of loss not reasonably foreseeable at the time, all heads of compensation should be brought together into one single claim made 'once and for all'. Indeed, any amount representing severance and injurious affection is not truly calculable in isolation but needs to be arrived at in relation to the purchase price of land taken, as part of the same valuation exercise. But whether this happens in reality is by no means certain.

7 See above, ch 8, p 156.
8 (1889) 24 QBD 326.
9 Light to a set of windows enjoying an easement of light was obstructed. Compensation was held to be recoverable not only for this but also for loss of light to another set of windows not enjoying an easement of light, the cause of the obstruction of light to both sets of windows being the same. Had the second set of windows been affected alone, or had the cause not been the same, the loss of light to them would not have been compensatable (see Megarry and Wade *The Law of Real Property* ch 13, Part IV, s 6B3.) For the Defence Acts and injurious affection see *University College Oxford v Secretary of State for Air* [1938] 1 KB 648, [1938] 1 All ER 69.
10 *VG John v Gelligaer UDC and Rhymney Valley Water Board* (1964) 192 EG 309 and 423.
11 See p 200, below.
12 See above, ch 6, p 113.

# Chapter 10

# Disturbance and other loss

## A. Disturbance as an element in expropriation

### 1 PURCHASE MONEY TO INCLUDE DISTURBANCE

In an ordinary free sale on the open market, it is unlikely that the purchaser will pay the vendor's removal expenses, or incur any other incidental costs for the vendor's benefit. It is not of course impossible. There may be special factors affecting the bargain between the parties so that it becomes worth the purchaser's while to pay such sums (though if the purchaser believes the land to contain oil or buried treasure, unknown to the vendor, he might well arouse the latter's suspicions by making extravagant offers of extra payments to tempt him to sell it). It is true that all land is unique. This is said to be a justification in the eyes of equity for making the remedy of specific performance available for the enforcement of contracts for the sale of land, as distinct from contracts for the sale of most kinds of goods. But the concept of 'the market' is generalised: it could scarcely be a concept if it were not. Physically, land may be unique; but what really matters most of all in law is the economic benefits of land. These are not unique, in as much as they are expressible in money and therefore capable of evoking comparisons between the financial value of one piece of property and that of another.

On the whole, therefore, market conditions will apply to sales of land. The purchaser either agrees to pay a price acceptable to the vendor, or he does not, and the vendor has no way of jockeying him into the payment of extras without giving corresponding benefits in return. It happens sometimes, of course, that special rules of law prohibit high prices when land, like other commodities, is in short supply; and then there arises an incentive to get round the prohibition by demanding extra payments. These in turn may be prohibited. Thus in the law of landlord and tenant the Rent Act 1977, Part IX, imposes restrictions on the payment by tenants of 'premiums' and special charges for furniture to landlords of residential accommodation; and the Costs of Leases Act 1958 prohibits any requirement that one party's costs be paid by the other (unless there is express agreement in writing to that effect). But these are special cases. If vendors have the whip-hand over purchasers, in normal circumstances this results simply in a higher purchase price rather than in the imposition of complicated requirements for extra payments.

But in compulsory purchase both practice and law diverge here from free market transactions. The acquiring body is required to pay to the expropriated owner compensation for 'disturbance' over and above purchase price compensation. There are circumstances, expressly provided for by statute, in which authorities are given a *discretion* to pay compensation for disturbance. But these do not apply to expropriated owners, who are entitled to such compensation as of right. The right is regarded as statutory, yet it is not expressly laid down in any statutory provision. It would be more accurate to say that 'disturbance' is compensatable in so far as it can be shown to be a part of an expropriated owner's 'true loss', the latter being greater in such a case than the mere market value purchase price of the land. In fact the 'true loss' may well extend even beyond disturbance: there is no logical reason why it should be so confined, and there are particular reasons why it should not. Rule (vi) of s 5 of the Land Compensation Act 1961 expresses this well enough when it states that, 'The provisions of rule (ii) shall not affect the assessment of compensation for disturbance *or any other matter* not directly based on the value of land.'[1]

Severance and injurious affection, which are 'directly based on the value of land', are expressly provided for by statute, as already discussed. They are also separate from market value of land compulsorily acquired. Only in this last respect do they resemble disturbance. Disturbance, like the 'extra 10 per cent' rule for purchase price payments condemned by rule (i) of s 5 (though unlike that rule it has been approved instead of being condemned) seems to have originated in a general feeling that the statutory provisions for compensation must be interpreted as favourably to owners as possible.

The court's approval of disturbance compensation was obtained in *Jubb v Hull Dock Co.*[2] A brewer was awarded £400 compensation by way of purchase price for his brewery premises, plus £300 for loss of business in the period before settling into alternative suitable premises for his brewing operations. Lord Denman CJ upheld the payment of the £300, which the dock company had challenged, on the ground that it was sufficiently covered by the relevant statute, a private Act conferring powers on the company. Unfortunately an examination of the section which the judge relied on shows that it was in fact concerned with injurious affection: '. . . compensation for the damage occasioned to any such lands by the execution of the works'. This misinterpretation of a statutory provision is worthy to set beside that accorded to s 68 of the Land Clauses Consolidation Act 1845, which has already been discussed.

Nevertheless there have not been any comparable complications in respect of disturbance, so the result has been beneficial, at least in expropriation cases.

The courts seem to have taken a cautious line over the proposition so precariously founded upon *Jubb's* case. In *Horn v Sunderland Corpn*,[3] Scott LJ stated the rule to be simply that personal loss is compensatable, if at all, only as an element in the purchase price of the land taken. It follows from this that, in the absence of special statutory provisions, disturbance compensation cannot be claimed in respect of land *retained* by the claimant. It is true that in *Senior v Metropolitan Rly Co*[4] a tailor had obtained compensation for loss of trade caused to his retail shop by a temporary obstruction of the highway, a type of loss which is clearly disturbance in modern law when it is compensatable at all. But in *Ricket v Metropolitan Rly Co*[5] the House of Lords overruled that decision. The House held, in effect, that loss in respect of property *retained* can only be compensated for on the footing of severance or injurious affection, and that injurious affection arising (as in *Senior's* case and *Ricket's* case) on land *not* taken from the claimant is not compensatable where it occurs in the form of trade loss but only where it occurs in the form of depreciation of land values.[6]

It is clearly established that disturbance compensation is regarded as an integral part, though separately assessed, of purchase price compensation. In *Horn v Sunderland Corpn*, Greene MR, said that 'the sum to be ascertained is in essence one sum, namely the proper price or compensation payable in all the circumstances of the case'. The leading authority for this in the House of Lords is the decision in *IRC v Glasgow and South Western Rly Co*[7] where the sum of £52,658 for a compulsory acquisition included £9,499 for loss of business, a clear example of disturbance. The fact that the decision was arrived at on a basis favourable to the Revenue may provoke cynical reflections; but the authority, such as it is, of *Jubb's* case does seem to require that disturbance be regarded merely as an element in the purchase price of land. The point at issue in 1887, was whether stamp duty should be computed on the sum inclusive of the £9,499, and it was held that this must be so. Lord Halsbury LC said:

...the value under the circumstances to the person who is compelled to sell... may be naturally and properly and justly taken into account; and when such phrases as 'damages for loss of business' or 'compensation for the goodwill' taken from the person are used in a loose and general sense, they are not

3 [1941] 2 KB 26, [1941] 1 All ER 480.
4 (1863) 2 H & C 258.
5 (1867) LR 2 HL 175.
6 Compensation for trade loss may be authorised by statute in special cases, for example, by s 231 of the Highways Act 1980 (private street works). See *Lingke v Christchurch Corpn* [1912] 3 KB 595.
7 (1887) 12 App Cas 315.

inaccurate for the purpose of giving verbal expression to what everybody under-
stands as a matter of business; but in strictness the thing which is to be ascertained is the price to be paid for the land. . . .

This view of the law has been endorsed recently by the House of Lords
in *Woolfson v Strathclyde Regional Council*.[8] It means that a claimant can
only obtain disturbance compensation if he is both expropriated and
displaced. The displacement, as will be seen, is the essence of disturbance—ie the fact of being turned out of the premises. But compensation
for this is not obtainable on its own account. It is deemed to be part of
'the price to be paid for the land', to use Lord Halsbury words. Therefore a successful claimant must be expropriated of a legal or equitable
freehold or leasehold, and be paid a purchase price for it, however small,
in which the amount of the disturbance, however large, can be included.

## 2 LIMITS OF COMPENSATABLE LOSS

In recent years the courts have occasionally made helpful general statements about disturbance . In *Lee v Minister of Transport*[9] Davies LJ said:
'Disturbance must, in my judgment, refer to the fact of having to vacate
the premises.' In *Harvey v Crawley Development Corpn*,[10] Romer LJ
remarked that loss may be properly compensatable as disturbance,
'provided, first, that it is not too remote and, secondly, that it is the
natural and reasonable consequence of the dispossession of the owner'. It
is clear from these statements that loss must result from actual interruption of beneficial occupation of land. A landlord or mortgagee will have
primarily an investment interest in the property, and so will not be
'disturbed', except perhaps in some cases in respect of 'goodwill'—a
matter which will be discussed below. Moreover a landlord of furnished
premises, which are compulsorily purchased, is presumably disturbed in
respect of his furniture and other belongings on those premises even
though it is of course the tenant who is being displaced. And in *Roberts v
Coventry Corpn*,[11] the claimant failed in her claim for disturbance on
account of the depreciation in value of shares she held in the company
which was the yearly tenant of the land compulsorily purchased. It made
no difference that she was also the landlord (and so compensatable in
respect of her freehold reversion to the tenancy) or that it was in fact a
family company, F. Roberts & Sons Ltd, in which she held a majority of
the shares and her sons the remainder. Lord Goddard CJ said brusquely
that the loss in question was 'far too remote'.

Where related companies are landlord and tenant respectively, the
normal rules governing disturbance compensation mean that only the

8 (1978) 38 P & CR 521 (see below, p 199).
9 [1966] 1 QB 111, [1965] 2 All ER 986.
10 [1957] 1 QB 485, [1957] 1 All ER 504.
11 [1947] 1 All ER 308.

occupying tenant company can claim it, and even then not unless that company is being expropriated as distinct from merely being dispossessed.[12] In *Melias Ltd v Manchester Corpn*[13] the premises acquired were occupied by the parent company on a periodic tenancy, and a subsidiary company were the freehold landlords. The Lands Tribunal held after considering all the facts (including each company's memorandum of association) that they could not reasonably be regarded as all part of the 'same' concern. Therefore disturbance compensation could only be paid by reference to the tenant company, and even then only because it had been 'required to give up possession . . . before the expiration of (its) term' within the meaning of s 20 of the 1965 Act.[14]

The Lands Tribunal took a somewhat similar view of the facts of *DHN Food Distributors Ltd v London Borough of Tower Hamlets*.[15] Three related companies ran a 'cash and carry' grocery business from a warehouse in Bow, in the East End of London. The parent company owned and ran the business itself and the two subsidiaries owned respectively the premises and the vehicles used. The directors were the same persons for all three. On compulsory purchase the acquiring authority argued that only the parent company could be regarded as disturbed (by the interruption of the business); but because it suffered no expropriation (the freehold in the land being taken from the subsidiary company in which the legal estate was vested) it could not claim disturbance compensation. The Lands Tribunal's acceptance of this was reversed on appeal. The Court of Appeal held that all three companies should be regarded, in the words of Shaw LJ 'as a single entity'. Goff LJ said that 'this is a case in which one is entitled . . . to pierce the corporate veil', and that the three companies 'had no separate business operations whatsoever . . .'. Disturbance compensation was therefore payable.

But the House of Lords has made it clear that this decision must be applied very narrowly. In *Woolfson v Strathclyde Regional Council*[16] the facts were similar, except that the company holding the legal estate in the business premises being acquired did not have identical membership

---

12 But a firm which is merely dispossessed and not expropriated may now be entitled to a statutory 'disturbance payment' (see below, p 213).

13 (1972) 23 P & CR 380.

14 See ch 5, p 87.

15 [1976] 3 All ER 462, [1976] 1 WLR 852. A similar case is *Smith, Stone and Knight Ltd v Birmingham Corpn* [1939] 4 All ER 116 in which a parent company and its subsidiary respectively held the freehold reversion and a periodic tenancy of premises being compulsorily purchased. The former was expropriated, the latter merely received notice to quit in the usual way. It was held that the distinction between the companies was formal only, the one being the agent of the other, and therefore disturbance compensation was payable. If this case had been decided in the same way as the *Melias* case, no disturbance compensation at all would have been payable, because the company in occupation was merely dispossessed and not expropriated.

16 (1978) 38 P & CR 521.

with the company which occupied and used them, even though the bulk of the shares were in the same ownership. The two companies were not a 'single entity'. Therefore the 'corporate veil' must not be 'pierced'. Businessmen who create two companies must take the disadvantages of having two corporate persons in law, along with the advantages.

This problem will arise less often in future, because of the existence, for disturbance cases occurring on or after 17 October 1972, of the new right to 'disturbance payments' under s 37 of the Land Compensation Act 1973. These, however, are not available to licensees (as distinct from short-term tenants whose terms end without renewal) except on a purely discretionary basis.[17]

There are circumstances in which loss by disturbance, even though genuinely incurred, cannot be met by compensation. In an unreported case, *Mizen Bros v Mitcham UDC* (1929):

the land was used as a market garden and was in a high state of cultivation. It had erected on it greenhouses and other trade fixtures. The value of the land (including greenhouses and fixtures) as market-garden land did not exceed £12,000, but the land was ripe for immediate development for building and on that basis was valued by the arbitrator at £17,280, a sum which could only be realised if vacant possession were given, the seller being at liberty to remove the greenhouses, etc., and plants and crops. The arbitrator assessed the value of tenant right, fixtures and disturbances (assuming that the owners were entitled to claim it) at £4,640, a sum which, when added to the valuation of £12,000 on a market-garden basis, fell short of the value assessed on a building basis.

This account of *Mizen's* case appears in the judgment of Greene MR in *Horn v Sunderland Corpn*. The question was this: was it lawful to award £4,640 disturbance compensation in addition to £17,280 calculated as the purchase price on the footing that the land enjoyed a market demand for building development? The Queen's Bench Divisional Court[18] in *Mizen's* case held that it was not lawful, and the Court of Appeal in *Horn's* case, by a majority, agreed.

In *Horn's* case itself, the facts were similar. Horn claimed £22,700 purchase price compensation on the footing that his farm, compulsorily acquired by Sunderland Corporation for housing, enjoyed a market demand for building development. He also claimed disturbance compensation for having to vacate the farm. Greene MR said that if 'circumstances are such as to make it impossible for the owner to claim that he has suffered damage through disturbance for which he ought to be compensated, then he is not entitled to have the price or compensation increased by an addition for disturbance *even if he has in fact been disturbed*'. Such circumstances as this exist, as in *Horn's* case and *Mizen's* case, where there is an inconsistency in the claim. The inconsistency

17 See below, p 214.
18 Deciding a special case stated by the arbitrator.

arises out of asking for disturbance, which presupposes unwillingness to leave the property, at the same time as full development value of the land, which presupposes willingness to give up the present use of the property in order to free it for development. The proper rule, avoiding the inconsistency, is this: The claimant may choose either full development value without disturbance, or existing use value with disturbance. Whichever of these sums is the higher is his 'true loss', and so properly compensatable.[19]

It may be asked why the law should strain at allowing disturbance on top of development value if it allows disturbance at all, since in any case disturbance will not be paid in a free market transaction. Probably the true answer is that it is merely a question of drawing a line somewhere, and also that disturbance compensation is in itself a concession justified partly by the element of compulsion and partly by a general belief that 'market value' in a compulsory acquisition may well be less than the price which the land might be expected to fetch in a free transaction, at any rate so long as inflation prevails. But it may also be part of the explanation to say that disturbance on top of existing use value, though no doubt artifical, does not at any rate involve an inherent contradiction, whereas disturbance on top of development value clearly does.

The court in *Horn's* case[20] also commented on the general statutory basis, or lack of it, underlying the payment of compensation for disturbance. Greene MR pointed out that rule (vi) of s 2 of the Act of 1919, re-enacted in s 5 of the Act of 1961, although it contains apparently the only express statutory reference to the matter,[1] 'does not confer a right to claim compensation for disturbance. It merely leaves unaffected the right which the owner would before the Act of 1919 have had in a proper case to claim that the compensation to be paid for the land should be increased on the ground that he had been disturbed.' As to what is a 'proper case', Scott LJ commented austerely that, 'rule (vi) does not purport to give statutory validity to every pre-1919 judicial determination on the subject of "disturbance", still less to perpetuate exaggerations in the practice of juries or arbitrators'.

## 3 TIME OF LOSS

If, as Romer LJ said, compensatable disturbance must be 'the natural and reasonable consequence of the dispossession of the owner', can items of expenditure be claimed which have been incurred not only before the authority acquired the property but before service of notice to treat? In fact they can. The phrase 'consequence of the dispossession' must be understood causally, not chronologically. In two Scots decisions, *Smith v*

---

19 Compare the situation in regard to injurious affection (see ch 9, p 194).
20 [1941] 2 KB 26.
 1 See the comment by Lord Sorn in *McEwing's* case, p 205 below.

*Strathclyde Regional Council*[2] and *Aberdeen City Council v Sim*,[3] claims for costs incurred in removal were upheld even though they antedated the compulsory purchase, because it could firmly be said that they reasonably anticipated it. The Court of Appeal adopted this approach and applied it in *Prasad v Wolverhampton Borough Council*;[4] though the claim in this case was in the event remitted to the Lands Tribunal for a finding of fact on whether the expenditure really had been reasonably incurred in anticipation of the compulsory purchase.

But this principle should not be pushed to the point where claimants who remove from premises substantially as free agents are allowed to claim as if they have been 'dispossessed'. That would be an abuse of the system.

## B. Varieties of disturbance compensatable as of right

Bearing in mind the highly generalised criteria which judges have put forward as a basis for interpreting what is to be understood by 'disturbance', it is highly likely that its categories are never closed. All the same, several well-known varieties have long since been established by the cases. Some are themselves quite general to occupation of land, whether residential or commercial. Others are chiefly commercial (using this word in the widest sense to include farms, factories, offices, and workplaces generally). The point about them all is that they have a strongly practical significance and represent a definite financial setback to the owner who claims for them.

### 1 LOSSES IN GOODWILL, PROFITS AND STOCK

The examples of chiefly commercial disturbance which appear from the cases (subject to the general requirement of being the natural and reasonable consequences of dispossession and not too remote) are loss of goodwill, loss of profits and depreciation of stock. The difference between goodwill and profits is essentially the difference between capital and interest, between a lump sum and a rent. Goodwill, therefore, is the capital value of a business as a going concern—the sum it would fetch on the open market—and a competent valuer experienced in this field

2  (1980) 42 P & CR 397.
3  (1982) 264 Estates Gazette 621. This is a particularly strong decision, because the claimant moved to other premises on failing to reach agreement with the acquiring authority when attempting to sell his house to them of his own accord (but admittedly their urban renewal policies were the cause of his move). The house was in fact compulsorily purchased, but not until a year or so later.
4  [1983] 2 All ER 140 [1983] 2 WLR 946, overruling the earlier Lands Tribunal decision to the contrary effect in *Bloom (Kosher) & Sons Ltd v Tower Hamlets London Borough Council* (1978) 35 P & CR 423.

would be called upon to value it as a capital asset just as a freehold or leasehold would be valued. If a shop is to be sold, the owner will be anxious to get a proper market price for the goodwill of his business as well as for the freehold or leasehold of the shop premises. What its market value is, will be an open question of expert fact, to be decided on the basis of a valuation in the light of all the relevant circumstances; and it may be relatively significant or insignificant. What the business profits are, however, is perhaps more a question for an accountant.

As with land, the value of goodwill is usually a continuing thing and depends greatly on future prospects as well as past performance, assessed objectively on the basis of the beliefs of people in general as reflected in 'the market'. Thus there has to be a great deal of estimation of the future—a task which judges, perhaps unnecessarily overawed, sometimes regard as 'difficult indeed',[5] but a lapse of time occasionally makes it necessary to consider a value retrospectively, which in turn makes it possible to do so in the light of what has actually taken place. In *LCC v Tobin*,[6] an optician in the East End of London moved to new premises when his former shop was compulsorily purchased. A claim for disturbance was made in respect of the difference between the goodwill attached to the former shop, and now extinguished, and the goodwill in prospect at the new shop. When the Lands Tribunal heard the case, the trade at the new shop had already been developing for a couple of years. Wynn-Parry J said in the Court of Appeal:

Now the duty of the tribunal was to estimate the capital value of the business in the new premises as at the point of time immediately after the move into those premises. Had they been hearing the case at that time, any figure at which they arrived would necessarily have been wholly an estimated figure. In fact, they were sitting nearly two years after the move. In those circumstances they were bound to have regard to what had actually happened during the interval.[7]

A judicial comment on goodwill may be quoted from an earlier Court of Appeal decision, *Cooper v Metropolitan Board of Works*,[8] when Cotton LJ said: 'The goodwill which attaches to a particular house increases the value of that house. . . . But there may be other kinds of goodwill attaching to personal reputation . . . a thing personal to the man whose skill and whose name have acquired that goodwill.' The point here is that any kind of goodwill which a compulsory purchase of commercial premises reduces or destroys will normally be the subject of disturbance compensation; yet if it pertains to the property rather than to the person, the loss may be attributable not to the dispossessed occupier but to a mortgagee

---

5 In *Tobin's* case, below.
6 [1959] 1 All ER 649, [1959] 1 WLR 354.
7 Compare *Bwllfa and Merthyr Dare Steam Collieries* (1891) *Ltd v Pontypridd Waterworks Co* ch 7, p 141, above.
8 (1883) 25 Ch D 472.

or landlord or some other party entitled to a capital interest in the property. But in most cases the goodwill is probably the occupier's alone and does not 'attach to' the property.

The question may then arise, as it did in *Tobin's* case, whether the dispossessed owner can take his goodwill in whole or in part to new premises. If not, it will become extinguished. The more localised in nature the business happens to be, such as the typical suburban 'corner shop', the less transportable the goodwill is likely to be. A mail-order business, on the other hand, may well be transportable anywhere. This is a question of expert fact. So is the reason for loss of goodwill: it must not be taken for granted that if goodwill is reduced or extinguished at the time of compulsory purchase the purchase will be the cause of this. In *Bailey v Derby Corpn*,[9] a master builder's yard and workshops were compulsorily purchased. The builder acquired alternative premises nearby; yet by reason of ill-health he decided not to re-establish his business in them but to let them to a firm of decorators. The Court of Appeal upheld the decision of the Lands Tribunal that disturbance compensation for the full value of his business on its consequent extinction was not payable. The Tribunal, in the words of Lord Denning MR, awarded instead 'compensation on the basis that he might have removed his business. It gave him £1,200 for the loss of profits he would have made; £420 for the cost of removal; £25 for stationery; £50 for travelling; £152 for costs incurred. The total compensation altogether, with the value of the land (£1,750), was nearly £3,600.' The Master of the Rolls later summed up the legal position as follows:

It seems to me that counsel is starting from the wrong point when he says that compensation is to be given for the loss[10] of his business. It is not. All that is acquired is the land. The compensation is given for the value of the land, not for the value of the business.[11] The business still remained the claimant's. The only other thing to which he is entitled is compensation for his loss by reason of the acquisition of the land. It seems to me that, while costs of removal and loss of profits are recoverable, the losses which flow from his subsequent ill-health or accident are not the proper subject of compensation.

And Russell LJ stated succinctly, in regard to the disturbance caused by the compulsory acquisition, 'the ill-health was not produced by that disturbance'.

9 [1965] 1 All ER 443, [1965] 1 WLR 213.
10 Perhaps 'loss' is ambiguous in this context; 'expropriation' is better.
11 The distinction between marketing a business—goodwill—and marketing premises where that business is carried on is all too easily overlooked. In *Wilkinson v Middlesbrough Borough Council* (1981) 45 P & CR 142, (see above, ch 7, p 143) there was an unsustainable claim to 'equivalent reinstatement' compensation for premises acquired from a veterinary practice. Even if it were proved that the practice could not survive the displacement it is hard to see that 'equivalent reinstatement' would be appropriate rather than disturbance compensation for extinguishment of goodwill.

Reasonable though this is, the decision in *Bailey's* case upset the landed profession. Section 46 of the Land Compensation Act 1973 was therefore enacted, under which an occupant of business premises who is over 60 years of age may, if the entire premises are compulsorily purchased but he retains the goodwill, give an undertaking neither to dispose of that goodwill nor to carry on (directly or indirectly) what is substantially the same business within an area and period specified by the acquiring authority, in return for an increase in his compulsory purchase compensation to include disturbance[12] in the form of extinguishment of the goodwill. Thus business proprietors of advancing years may spare themselves the trouble of selling a marketable asset (because if it is not marketable they would be entitled to compensation anyway) but still collect its value out of public money.

Repayment of the extra compensation may be demanded if the above undertaking is broken. Premises consisting of all or part of a hereditament with a rateable value exceeding £2,250[13] are excluded from s 46, and so are all cases where compensation is being assessed for disturbance losses earlier than 17 October 1972. In the case of partnerships, *all* the partners must be over 60 and join in the undertaking. In the case of companies, *all* the shareholders and the company as well must join in the undertaking and all the shareholders (or, if they hold less than 50% of the shares, their spouses) must be over 60.[14]

As in *Bailey's* case, loss of profits is a proper item of compensation; but it must consist of profits which would have been made in the existing course of business.[15] Future profits from a business operation not yet started are a different matter, so that if for example compulsory acquisition of land prevents it from being used for a prospective purpose the loss of profits expected to have accrued from the carrying out of that purpose is not a proper item of compensation for disturbance. In *McEwing & Sons Ltd v Renfrew County Council*,[16] builders were prevented from completing housing development on land compulsorily purchased from them for building a school. They obtained purchase price compensation, plus disturbance compensation for such matters as abortive expenditure, but nothing for loss of prospective profits arising from their intended development of the land. Lord Sorn, in the Court of Session (who incidentally observed that 'the word "disturbance"

---

12 'Disturbance' here includes 'disturbance payments' (see below, p 213).
13 £750 where the compensation fell to be assessed by reference to a date earlier than 1 April 1973. These figures are the same as those applicable to blight notices (see below, ch 13, p 257).
14 These requirements effectively restrict the benefit to small family companies.
15 In *Watson v Secretary of State for Air* [1954] 3 All ER 582, [1954] 1 WLR 1477, a farm tenant was held entitled to compensation for the year's profits he would have obtained had he continued to farm the land being acquired from him.
16 (1960) 11 P & CR 306.

appears for the first time in the Acquisition of Land Act 1919'), noted the builder's assertion that the land taken was the 'only sizeable remaining site in Greenock suitable for private housing . . .' He went on: 'but the claimants are builders and their business as builders has not been brought to a stop'. Had their business been wholly or partly dislocated, in other words, this would have been compensatable; but there was no evidence of lack of other work for them to undertake, or that their ability to undertake it had been at all impaired.[17] As for the development value of the land taken, that was properly accounted for in its purchase price.

The relationship between future profits from the use of land and the prospective development value of that land was put in a nutshell by Lord Moulton in a Privy Council case: *Pastoral Finance Association Ltd v Minister (New South Wales)*.[18] 'Now it is evident that no man would pay for land, in addition to its market value, the capitalised value of the savings and additional profits which he would hope to make by the use of it.'

Depreciation of the stock of a business, like loss of goodwill, varies greatly according to the nature of the stock and other circumstances. Perishable goods will obviously suffer more than durable goods. The loss in each case is a question of fact. Equipment and other goods must be regarded similarly. Thus in another Scottish case, *Venables v Department of Agriculture for Scotland*,[19] the sporting tenant of a deer forest on a 99-year lease was held to be entitled on dispossession, to compensation for loss in value of sporting equipment, including a car and a launch. This means that, broadly speaking, there is no difference between business and domestic disturbance in regard to chattels.

## 2 REMOVAL COSTS; ADAPTATION OF PREMISES AND CHATTELS; PROFESSIONAL FEES

Other examples of disturbance are normally appropriate to residential as well as commercial premises (if the natural and reasonable consequence of dispossession and not too remote): removal expenses, additional travelling costs,[20] adaptation of premises and of chattels, professional expenses and fees payable in the course of obtaining new premises.[1] The latter may be claimed, provided that they are reasonably incurred, even in respect of abortive attempts at purchase, as the Court of Appeal held in *Harvey v Crawley Development Corpn*.[2] In that case, Denning LJ (as he

---

17 See also *Collins v Feltham UDC* [1937] 4 All ER 189, and *Wimpey & Co v Middlesex County Council* [1938] 3 All ER 781.
18 [1914] AC 1083.
19 1932 SC 573.
20 For these, see *Rutter v Manchester Corpn* (1974) 28 P & CR 443.
 1 See Lord Denning MR's account of the list of items of compensation in *Bailey's* case, p 204, above. For loss in respect of chattels, see footnote 19 above.
 2 [1957] 1 QB 485, [1957] 1 All ER 504.

then was), speaking of a dispossessed house owner, said: 'If he pays a higher price for the new house, he would not get compensation on that account, because he would be presumed to have got value for his money: but he does get the costs which he has to pay a surveyor and lawyer to get it. It seems to me that the costs are then the subject of compensation under the heading of "disturbance" as specified in rule (vi).' Whether higher loan charges bona fide incurred for a necessary purchase of dearer premises could be recovered under the heading of 'disturbance' is an open question: in principle they ought. As for the adaptation of chattels: 'Mrs. Harvey gets compensation for having to move out her furniture and put it into the new house: she gets compensation for having to alter the curtains and carpets and remake them to fit the new windows and floors.'

Counsel had suggested in argument that this sort of compensation for disturbance is inappropriate because it really amounts to 'reinstatement', which is only permissible when the Lands Tribunal expressly sanctions the assessment of compensation on the basis of 'equivalent reinstatement' under rule (v) of s 5 of the Act of 1961, as discussed in a previous chapter. Romer LJ said: 'The fact that in some sense reinstatement or replacement may be involved does not appear to me to disqualify the claim.' In fact 'equivalent reinstatement' is primarily intended as an alternative mode of assessing the purchase price of land, and whatever additional amount by way of disturbance is required to make up the 'true loss' in such a case can normally be justifiably included in the compensation[3]

In line with the 'value for money' approach to 'Crawley costs' (as disturbance items are sometimes called) is the decision of the Court of Appeal in *Service Welding Ltd v Tyne and Wear County Council*.[4] The claimants attempted to get disturbance compensation to cover bank charges and loan interest (not a 'bridging loan') which they had incurred when building themselves a new factory. This claim was rejected, on the ground that such expenses are frequently incurred as part of the normal capital cost of obtaining a new asset: it is value for money.

One form of disturbance that is perhaps incompatible with 'equivalent reinstatement', always depending of course on the facts of a particular case, is the adaptation of new premises. The Lands Tribunal accepted this as a proper head of disturbance compensation in *Powner and Powner v Leeds Corpn*.[5] The cost of transferring to suitable new premises is

---

3 'Equivalent reinstatement' compensation and its relationship with both the principle in *Horn v Sunderland Corpn* (p 200, above) and prospective development value (see ch 7, p 143, footnote 12) do not seem to have been satisfactorily analysed so far, in decided cases or otherwise.

4 (1979) 38 P & CR 352. Contrast the *Tamplin* case (below); and see also *Simpson v Stoke-on-Trent City Council*, (above, ch 6, p 126) for a case involving a 'bridging loan'.

5 (1953) 4 P & CR 167.

precisely what 'equivalent reinstatement' is about. But the latter is almost always appropriate when the value of the land taken is practically restricted to a non-marketable, and thus usually a non-commercial, existing use; whereas adaptation is normally appropriate where the land taken has at the very least an appreciable market value in respect of an existing use which is commercial in nature.

It must be remembered, when talking of 'premises', that fixtures 'adhere to the realty' and are normally to be treated as part of the premises and not as chattels; though there is no reason why a freehold vendor should not stipulate in the contract of sale for the removal of anything he wishes from the premises. 'Tenant's fixtures', of course, may in certain circumstances be removed by the tenant, depending variously on whether they are trade, domestic or agricultural fixtures.

A recent case involving fixtures is *Tamplins Brewery Ltd v County Borough of Brighton*.[6] The authority compulsorily purchased the premises comprising the claimants' bottling department, and put forward a disturbance claim assessment in which an estimated saving in operating costs in consequence of having the benefit of new bottling equipment in new premises more than outweighed the loss of the old equipment. The claimants, however, put forward a substantial figure, arrived at by claiming the cost of buying the new equipment less an estimated saving in operating costs which was much smaller than the authority's estimate. The Lands Tribunal (surprisingly) accepted the claimant's approach in principle, but with detailed modifications which produced a lower total. It is regrettable that the opportunity was not taken to examine and apply legal principles relevant to the question of fixtures; and the outcome will give little guidance in future cases.[7]

Yet there is legal authority on the main issue. The effect on compulsory purchase compensation of rights over fixtures was considered by the Court of Chancery in *Gibson v Hammersmith and City Rly Co*.[8] The court emphasised that the right of removal, such as it is, confers a choice upon an owner, whether he be a tenant, as stated, or a freeholder who decides that he will only enter into a contract to sell subject to a prior removal of such fixtures as he chooses. It follows that in a compulsory purchase, the acquiring body can compel neither the removal of fixtures, nor their retention, so as to reduce compensation, in the absence of any

---

6  (1970) 22 P & CR 746; also (1971) 222 Estates Gazette 1587, CA.

7  The Court of Appeal later remitted the case to the Lands Tribunal for further consideration, having said little beyond commenting that all three assessments seemed unsatisfactory. The statement by Denning LJ in *Harvey's* case (above) that the purchase of a new and more expensive house was 'value for money', and thus not an item calling for compensation, seems prima facie to be relevant also to the purchase of new and more expensive bottling equipment, at any rate in regard to the capital cost as distinct from any loan charges incurred.

8  (1863) 2 Drew & Sm 603.

statutory provisions to that effect. But the owner can make the choice, and so avoid a reduction of compensation, or at all events any reduction below his 'true loss'. In *Gibson's* case the owner was entitled to choose to sell the land to the acquiring body without removing fixed machinery from his ironworks, the market value of the premises equipped with the machinery being in the circumstances greater than the combined values of the premises stripped of machinery and of the detached machines. Had the values been different, the owner would have been free to choose to sever the fixed machinery and claim disturbance compensation for consequent loss reasonably incurred in selling the machines or adapting them for use in new premises.

Increased operating costs, which were among the factors in the *Tamplin* case, were put forward in their own right as a disturbance item in *J Bibby & Sons Ltd v Merseyside County Council*.[9] The Court of Appeal expressed the view that they may well be compensatable—but only if (i) they are incurred unavoidably, and (ii) no benefit is derived from them. The disturbance claim in regard to them failed in this case.

### 3 DISTURBANCE AND THE INCIDENCE OF TAX

One pitfall in regard to disturbance is the fact that, although the compensation will be included in a capital sum, it may (partially at least) represent income. The problem is then whether a given quantity of compensation if viewed alternatively as capital or as income is equally liable to tax. If the tax element is not properly taken into account the claimant might obtain *and keep* as compensation an amount which, if undisturbed, he would have had to surrender in tax. There is an analogy here with common law awards of damages which compensate for lost income that would have been taxable if received. The House of Lords, having previously held, in *British Transport Commission v Gourley*,[10] that in a successful action for damages an amount equivalent to any tax that would have been incurred must be deducted from the equivalent quantity of damages awarded, went on therefore to adopt a similar approach in cases of compulsory purchase compensation. In *West Suffolk County Council v W Rought Ltd*,[11] business premises were compulsorily purchased for the purpose of widening a bridge at Brandon in Suffolk. Included in the compensation was a disturbance payment in respect of a temporary loss of profits, which would have been subject to tax if actually earned. It was held that the estimated amount that would have been payable in tax ought to have been deducted from the compensation.

Fifteen years later the Lands Tribunal took this principle further

9 (1980) 39 P & CR 53.
10 [1956] AC 185, [1955] 3 All ER 796.
11 [1957] AC 403, [1956] 3 All ER 216.

when in *Rosenberg & Son (Tinware) Ltd v Manchester Corpn*[12] it held that removal costs included in the disturbance claim then being assessed should be calculated with a deduction in respect of tax. The justification for this is that the Inland Revenue was believed—no longer correctly as it turned out—to allow compulsory purchase removal expenses as an income tax deduction. This concession would mean, if the underlying assumption had been right, that the claimants were somewhat better off than if they had moved of their own accord, so that the amount of that financial benefit represented an element in their incidental expenditure which did not call for compensation.

The peculiarity of this situation in regard to compulsory purchase has perhaps been somewhat obscured by the analogy with the common law. As has been said, disturbance compensation, though treated as part of 'the proper price' for the land taken and therefore as part of a capital sum, in fact covers losses in the nature of income as well as losses in the nature of capital. When income was taxed but capital was not, that compensation which, though capital, was received in lieu of lost income would naturally not be taxable even though that income, had it actually been received, *would* have been taxable. So long as Parliament failed to enact a rule that such elements in compensation for disturbance would be subject to equivalent taxation, the only choice that remained lay between (i) allowing a claimant to *obtain* an undeserved benefit, and (ii) allowing the acquiring authority to *retain* an undeserved benefit. Following the example of the *Gourley* case, the House of Lords in the *Rought* case not surprisingly came down in favour of choice (ii). Either way, the Inland Revenue were the losers, as far as compensation received by the vendor was concerned; though stamp duty, payable by the purchasing authority,[13] is another matter.

But in the interval between the *Rought* decision and the *Rosenberg & Son (Tinware) Ltd* decision, taxation of capital gains had been introduced.[14] Contrary to the principle applied in the *Rosenberg* case, therefore, the Inland Revenue were empowered to tax any 'readily identifiable amount in respect of temporary loss of profits',[15] assessed to capital gains tax (or, in regard to a company, to corporation tax on capital gains). No deduction, therefore, was any longer to be made from compulsory purchase compensation for such items. The amounts in question would be taxable as accruing in lieu of equivalent sums which, had those

12 (1971) 23 P & CR 68.
13 See Compulsory Purchase Act 1965, s 23 (above, ch 4, p 64), and the *Glasgow and South Western Rly Co* case (above, p 197).
14 In the Finance Acts 1969 and 1971.
15 See Board of Inland Revenue Statement dated 22 March 1973. The Board condescended to waive the capital gains tax payable on such items where an equivalent amount had already been deducted from a claimant's compensation for compulsory purchase.

actually been realised, might have been income and therefore liable to *income* tax; but being themselves capital sums, were instead liable, if taxable, to *capital* taxation.

The question is now governed by the Capital Gains Tax Act 1979, ss 20 (1) (a), 43 (4) and 110. Disturbance compensation is taxable in so far as any of its components represent taxable capital or taxable income items.[16] No longer may acquiring authorities make deductions from disturbance compensation in respect of alleged tax savings. An authority which attempted to do this was restrained by the Court of Appeal, and it is to be hoped that the attempt will not be repeated.[17]

## C. Statutory disturbance and 'other matters'

### 1 EXPROPRIATION DISTINGUISHED FROM DISPOSSESSION

Disturbance compensation so far discussed is statutory in little more than name. It has been elaborated in case law on the basis that compulsory purchase statutes authorise it to be paid, but by implication rather than express wording. The reasoning requires that, since it is 'part' of the purchase price of land taken, there must in every case be a compulsory purchase price figure for it to be part of: in short, it is parasitic and cannot stand on its own two feet. Therefore, although it must result, as Romer LJ said, from 'the dispossession of the owner',[18] dispossession is not sufficient; there must also be expropriation, that is to say the acquisition compulsorily from the claimant or by agreement under the shadow of compulsory powers, of a freehold or a leasehold by virtue of which he physically occupies the property. Reversioners may not as a rule claim disturbance; neither may occupiers whose occupancy the acquiring body can terminate validly at common law by withdrawal of a licence, notice to quit, notice to terminate, forfeiture, or refusal to renew a tenancy, on the strength of the authority's acquisition of the landlord's or licensor's interest.

It has been shown already how statutory protection of tenants does not prevail against compulsory purchase. It is true that many business or farm tenants have a statutory entitlement to compensation in lieu of security of tenure when deprived of the latter for reasons not arising from their own default. These compensation payments are obtainable from the landlord, and an acquiring body which must pay them will do so as landlord and not as acquiring body. This kind of payment, whether made under the Landlord and Tenant Acts or the Agricultural Holdings Acts,

16 Compensation may also be liable, as regards *purchase price*, to capital gains tax (except in so far as *development value* is liable to development land tax—see below, ch 14).
17 *Stoke-on-Trent City Council v Wood Mitchell & Co Ltd*, [1979] 2 All ER 65.
18 See above, p 201.

is often called 'disturbance' in practice; but it is not 'disturbance' in the compulsory purchase sense. Yet because it is given in lieu of security of tenure it bears a strong resemblance in practice to compulsory purchase compensation with disturbance included, being a payment in return for what is to all intents and purposes expropriation rather than a mere dispossession such as any leasehold tenant undergoes at the end of his term whether it is long or short.

Residential tenants, and for that matter some business and farm tenants, get no compensation on losing their security of tenure. What they have paid for they have used up in the form of the period of time bought by each instalment of rent. But this makes sense in terms of purchase price compensation, not disturbance. As far as the latter is concerned these distinctions of tenure make no sense. If the house in which Smith lives is held by him freehold, on a lease for 21 years, or on a lease with a year left to run, the distinction between those periods of time will be reflected, reasonably enough, in the market value figures of the compulsory purchase price compensation in each case. If Smith's reasonable removal costs are £500, he will have that £500 *added* to the purchase price figure awarded to him; the authority must meet that expense not he. And if the shop in which Jones has carried on his business as a grocer is held by him on the same tenure as Smith's house, and his reasonable removal costs are £500, the same will apply.

Yet if Jones's security of tenure exists only by grace of the Landlord and Tenant Act 1954 and he loses it for no default on his part, his compensation, even when the landlord responsible is a public authority, will not be an expropriation purchase price, nor will it include his reasonable removal costs of £500; it will be a pre-ordained figure under the 1954 Act, calculated by reference to the rateable value of the shop premises. And if Smith's security of tenure exists only by grace of the Rent Act 1977 and he loses it on whatever ground, he will get no compensation for any of his loss, certainly not for his £500 of removal costs, though he may well be re-housed. These are the rules that apply apart from the incidence of the Land Compensation Act 1973.

Anomalies in compensation for loss of property through compulsory purchase are not in issue here (they are discussed elsewhere) merely anomalies in disturbance compensation, which are plainly due to the peculiarities in the legal basis of such compensation and its consequent parasitic nature. Attempts have been made by Parliament to mitigate the evil; but until 1973 they took the form of providing only discretionary powers to pay disturbance compensation to sufferers who were not entitled to disturbance of right because they were merely dispossessed and not expropriated.

These provisions were mostly repealed by the Land Compensation Act 1973, except for the reasonable discretionary disturbance compensation which is payable under the Agriculture (Miscellaneous

Provisions) Act 1963[19] in respect of removal expenses and trade disturbance incurred by displaced occupiers of agricultural land. Part III of the 1973 Act substituted for them a set of provisions which for the first time give a clear statutory entitlement to money for disturbance as of right. It will be seen, however, that not all of these provisions benefit dispossessed as against expropriated occupiers, even though that was the real pretext for reform.

## 2 DISTURBANCE PAYMENTS

Section 37 of the 1973 Act entitles dispossessed occupiers in appropriate circumstances to claim, from the public authority responsible for the dispossession in each case, 'disturbance payments', which must on no account be confused with 'disturbance compensation' available to *expropriated* occupiers. The claimant must have been displaced on or after 17 October 1972 from property, other than agricultural land, in consequence of (i) its purchase by a body with compulsory powers, or (ii) the making of a demolition, closing or clearance order, or the acceptance of an owner's undertaking to do works, under the Housing Acts in respect of it, or (iii) redevelopment (including change of use) by a public authority holding it for any purpose for which it was acquired under compulsory powers or subsequently appropriated. Alternatively he may claim if permanently displaced from his dwelling, on or after 31 July 1974, by reason of an 'improvement notice' served under the Housing Act 1974, Part VIII,[20] or of improvement or redevelopment by a registered housing association or one treated as a local authority for grant purposes.[1]

The claimant will nevertheless be entitled to the payment only if he is 'in lawful possession' of the property, apparently both (i) at the time of dispossession and (ii) earlier at the time of first publication of the draft Bill or compulsory purchase order, or the making of the agreement for purchase or the housing order, or the acceptance of the housing undertaking, as the case may be. If the displacement occurs because of redevelopment after a local authority *appropriation* this may well be a serious matter because the original acquisition of the land may have occurred long ago.

'Lawful possession' is not defined, but presumably it is to be distinguished from unlawful possession giving rise to liability for an action at law for recovery of the land. The meaning of 'possession' in English land law, though not precisely defined, is by strong implication to be regarded as an attribute of freehold or leasehold ownership in law or equity, thus excluding mere lawful *presence* on land by permission as a

---

**19** Section 22.
**20** Housing Act 1974, s 130 and Sch 13.
 **1** Housing Rents and Subsidies Act 1975, s 17 and Sch 5.

licensee. If this applies, a lodger could not claim under s 37. Moreover even a claimant in 'lawful possession' is precluded from obtaining a 'disturbance payment' if he holds an interest for the extinguishment or acquisition of which he is in any case entitled to be compensated—that is to say a freehold or leasehold which is being expropriated—unless it is an 'unfit house' within the meaning of the Housing Acts and the compensation is accordingly restricted to 'site value' under those Acts as if the house did not exist; but even in that case he will still be ineligible if he is entitled to the 'owner-occupier's supplement' prescribed by those Acts, which covers the difference in value (where it exists) between 'site value' and a greater sum representing the value of site plus house. If the claimant is also a business tenant denied the grant of a new tenancy for reasons not based on his default, and consequently entitled to compensation under s 37 of the Landlord and Tenant Act 1954, he may choose either but not both.

A person displaced in consequence of the events giving rise to a 'disturbance payment' claim, but not 'entitled' to one, may still receive one at the discretion of the authority concerned so long as he is not entitled to 'compensation for disturbance under any other enactment'. Authorities may lawfully therefore make disturbance payments to deserving licensees if they so wish.

The amount of a disturbance payment[2] must equal the claimant's reasonable expenses incurred in moving plus, in the case of business claimants, loss suffered by reason of the disturbance to the trade or business as a result of the displacement (taking into account the reasonable likelihood of continued occupation but for the displacement and the availability of other premises). If a dwelling has been structurally modified for a disabled person and a local authority grant was available for that work, the disturbance payment must include a reasonable sum to cover the making of comparable modifications to the new dwelling.

Disputes over the amount of any disturbance payment are to be settled by the Lands Tribunal. All payments carry interest at the rate currently prescribed under s 32 of the Land Compensation Act 1961, from the date of displacement.

The major question inevitably raised by the wording of these provisions is whether the scope of 'disturbance payments' matches the scope of 'disturbance compensation'. The Lands Tribunal in *Nolan v Sheffield Metropolitan District Council*[3] has gone far to establish that this is in fact the case, by upholding the claimant's contention to that effect and rejecting the authority's attempt only to pay removal costs.

2  Land Compensation Act 1973, s 38.
3  (1979) 39 P & CR 741. In *R v Islington London Borough Council, ex p Knight* [1984] 1 All ER 154, a 'secure tenant' rehoused by agreement was denied a disturbance payment.

## 3 COMPENSATION FOR FARMERS AND FARM LOSS PAYMENTS

As already stated, 'disturbance payments' do not apply to agricultural land. To understand the current position over disturbance in relation to farms it is necessary to unravel some complex legal provisions.

If the farmer is a periodic tenant—usually in practice a yearly tenant—or a fixed-term leaseholder whose term has come to an end or will shortly do so, his security of tenure under the Agricultural Holdings Act 1948 will not prevail against compulsory purchase, though (as stated in an earlier chapter[4]) s 48 of the 1973 Act requires it to be recognised as subsisting *for compensation purposes* when assessing the value of expropriated interests.

If he occupies his farm under a periodic tenancy and this is not merely terminated by notice to quit but is *expropriated*, the payment required in this circumstance by virtue of s 20 of the Compulsory Purchase Act 1965[5] must be assessed accordingly. Since there is unlikely to be any 'profit rent', that is to say any appreciable property benefit exceeding the value of the outgoing rent payable to the landlord, this will probably not make much difference; but in any case the substance of any compulsory purchase compensation paid to a short-term tenant will in practice chiefly comprise disturbance of the orthodox type which can always, if validly incurred, be included in expropriation compensation, for reasons examined earlier in this chapter.

In addition to this, s 12 of the Agriculture (Miscellaneous Provisions) Act 1968 requires an acquiring authority which takes possession of any or all of an agricultural holding, or expropriates any or all of a tenancy in it, to pay to the tenant of the holding the sum which *would have been due to him* under s 9 of that Act from his *landlord* if his departure had been otherwise than in consequence of compulsory purchase, to 'assist in the reorganisation of the tenant's affairs'. The prescribed amount is four times the yearly rent. That sum under s 9 (as distinct from s 12) is payable in circumstances when 'compensation for disturbance' is also payable under s 34 of the Agricultural Holdings Act 1948 by the landlord to the tenant, namely when a valid notice to quit is served upon the tenant in circumstances involving no default by him (nor his death); and the amount payable under s 34 is between one and two times the yearly rent, depending on the size of the loss incurred by reason of having to move.

Thus when under the Agricultural Holdings (Notices to Quit) Act 1977, a farm tenancy is terminated by *notice to quit* (from the original landlord, or the acquiring authority replacing him) the tenant, if entitled to the normal 'compensation for disturbance' from the landlord under s 34 of the 1948 Act, is also entitled to a 'reorganisation of affairs'

---

4 See above, ch 5, p 94.
5 See above, ch 5, p 87. A notice of entry should have been served.

payment under s 9, not s 12, of the 1968 Act. If, though entitled to these, he is *expropriated*, he claims under s 12, not s 9.

If, however, the farmer is a tenant for an interest greater than a yearly tenancy there are further complications. He can only be turned out by his landlord as such—whether the original one or an authority expropriating the reversion—by *notice to quit* under the 1977 Act (as above) taking effect when (and not before) his interest comes to an end at common law by effluxion of time and is thereupon transformed into a yearly tenancy by that Act, in which case s 34 of the 1948 Act and s 9 of the 1968 Act again apply.

But if the acquiring body *expropriate* him (by notice to treat, with or without notice of entry depending on whether or not they take possession of the farm before his lease or tenancy is compulsorily assigned to them) he is compensated in the normal way, with the benefit of s 48 of the 1973 Act as mentioned above. If so, ordinary disturbance compensation is included—which, as with an expropriated periodic tenancy, is likely in practice to comprise the bulk of the amount claimable. In addition, he will be entitled to the payment due from the authority under s 12 of the 1968 Act for 'reorganisation of affairs' as referred to above. Yet this time it is specially provided by s 12 that if the tenancy is for a term of two years or more no such payment is due unless the amount of expropriation compensation (which, it must be re-emphasised, *includes* disturbance) should happen to fall short of the aggregate of compulsory purchase compensation (including disturbance) plus compensation under s 12 payable in the ordinary case of a yearly tenancy. Even so the amount in such a case must be equal to that shortfall but no greater.

Thus if compensation under the 1948 Act paid by a landlord to a yearly farm tenant on whom he has served notice to quit under the 1977 Act were *twice* an annual rent of £1,000, it follows that the 'reorganisation of affairs' payment by that landlord under s 9, being *four* times that rent, would be £4,000, bringing the aggregate amount payable up to £6,000. If instead the yearly tenant were expropriated, and his compensation were assessed at £100 for the nominal market value of his tenancy as a capital asset plus £2,400 disturbance, totalling £2,500, the addition of the same 'reorganisation of affairs' payment of £4,000 under s 12 would bring the aggregate total to £6,500. Expropriation compensation for a tenancy of two years or more would have to fall short of £6,500 for any amount to be payable under s 12 of the 1968 Act; and it would have to be no greater than £2,500 if the s 12 figure were to be assessed at the full £4,000.

If the farmer is a freeholder, the ordinary rules of expropriation compensation once again apply, including disturbance, and there are of course no complex problems of the kind raised by the landlord-tenant relationship. But whatever his interest in the land, in a normal case a farmer dispossessed through compulsory purchase, whether by expropriation or by notice to quit, will receive an appreciable sum in respect of disturbance. Where the rules fail to give disturbance as of right in particular cases s 22 of the Agriculture (Miscellaneous Provisions) Act 1963 gives acquiring authorities discretion to pay reasonable sums for removals and trade loss to occupiers of farms; which may be particularly relevant in the case of licensees and also periodic tenants who for some reason fail to get 'compensation for disturbance' under the 1948 Act. But the 1973 Act prescribes a new compensation procedure for dispossessed farmers in certain cases, called the 'farm loss payment'.

A 'farm loss payment' may be claimed, as of right, under s 34 of the 1973 Act, from an acquiring authority by whose action the farmer is displaced on or after 17 October 1972 from the *whole* of an 'agricultural unit' which he occupies. But he must be a freeholder or a leaseholder with three years unexpired, so that this provision is not intended to benefit yearly or other short-term tenants. Also, he must start to farm another 'agricultural unit' in Great Britain within three years after the displacement; and he must occupy the whole of the new unit 'in right of a freehold interest therein or a tenancy thereof' which he has acquired during the period extending from the date on which the authority was authorised to acquire his original farm to the date on which he starts to farm the new one. But if he is entitled to a payment under s 12 of the 1968 Act (above) for 'reorganisation of affairs' he cannot obtain a 'farm loss payment', even (apparently) if the s 12 payment is very small. Nor can he obtain it if he has himself instigated the acquisition by a 'blight notice'.

Section 35 of the 1973 Act prescribes the amount of the 'farm loss payment' on the basis of a normal year's net profits from farming. More precisely, it is the average annual profit from the original holding over the period of three years ending in the displacement, or the actual period of occupation if less. A sequence of accounting years ending not earlier than one year before the displacement may be used, or any three years' consecutive accounts of profits; and there must be a deduction of an amount representing 'the rent that might reasonably be expected to be payable' for the land taken (not the actual rent as such—if any) if it were let for agricultural purposes to a tenant responsible for rates, repairs and other outgoings,' whether in fact it is let or not. Profits already compensatable as 'disturbance' are not to be included, otherwise the claimant would be paid twice over for their loss.

If the new unit is less valuable than the original one there must be a proportionate reduction in the amount of the payment, calculated in relation to the *existing use value of the freehold* as agricultural land, at prices prevailing at the date of displacement for the land taken and at the date of the start of farming for the new unit, ignoring the main dwelling (if any) but applying rules (ii)–(iv) of s 5 of the Land Compensation Act 1961, which have been discussed in an earlier chapter.[6] But the benefit of

6 See above, ch 7, pp 136–142.

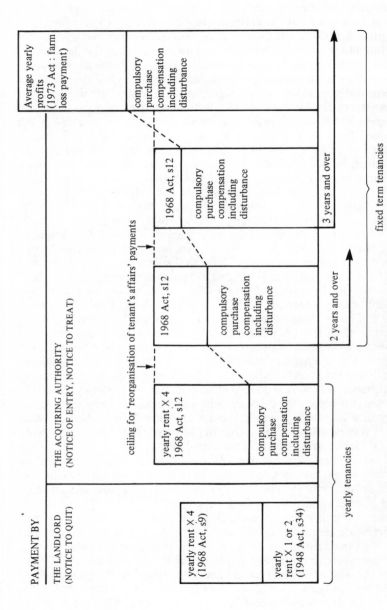

PAYMENT BY

THE LANDLORD (NOTICE TO QUIT)

THE ACQUIRING AUTHORITY (NOTICE OF ENTRY, NOTICE TO TREAT)

Average yearly profits (1973 Act : farm loss payment)

compulsory purchase compensation including disturbance

ceiling for 'reorganisation of tenant's affairs' payments

1968 Act, s12 — compulsory purchase compensation including disturbance

1968 Act, s12 — compulsory purchase compensation including disturbance

yearly rent × 4 1968 Act, s12 — compulsory purchase compensation including disturbance

yearly rent × 4 (1968 Act, s9)

yearly rent × 1 or 2 (1948 Act, s34)

yearly tenancies

fixed term tenancies

2 years and over

3 years and over

NOTE. 'Reorganisation' payments preclude 'farm loss' payments. Disturbance compensation must not duplicate items included in 'reorganisation' payments, nor be duplicated by items included in 'farm loss' payments.

any development value in the purchase price compensation for the land taken is to be offset by a reduction in the amount of the payment. Disputed assessments go to the Lands Tribunal.

Section 36 of the 1973 Act requires that a 'farm loss payment' must be claimed not later than one year after the start of farming of the new unit. Interest is payable, as currently prescribed under s 32 of the Land Compensation Act 1961, from the date of the claim, which may also include reasonable valuation and legal expenses. An authority acquiring by agreement may include the equivalent of a 'farm loss payment' in the compensation.

## 4 HOME LOSS PAYMENTS

Section 29 of the 1973 Act makes provision for 'home loss payments'; but in spite of the similarity of name the basis of these is very different from that of 'farm loss payments'. They are payable, by the public body responsible for the dispossession in each case, to any person displaced from a dwelling on or after 17 October 1972 in consequence of (a) its purchase by a body with compulsory powers, or (b) the making of a demolition, closing or clearance order, or the acceptance of an owner's undertaking to do works, under the Housing Acts in respect of it, or (c) the carrying out of redevelopment (including change of use) by a public authority holding it for any purpose for which it was acquired under compulsory powers or subsequently appropriated. They have also been made payable to any person permanently displaced from a dwelling, on or after 31 July 1974, in the circumstances specified by the provisions of the Housing Act 1974 and the Housing Rents and Subsidies Act 1975 already referred to in connection with 'disturbance payments' earlier in this chapter (see above, p 213).

In *R v Corby District Council, ex p McLean*,[7] the applicant sought an order of mandamus to compel the respondent council to make a home loss payment to him. He had been displaced from a post-war 'pre-fab.' bungalow situated on the council's land (being land acquired for housing purposes). The 'pre-fab.' was corroded, and the council proposed to remove several such bungalows and build more durable houses in their place. This was done and the applicant was rehoused. He justified his claim for a home loss payment on ground (c) above, namely redevelopment. The council argued that this was not the cause of displacement. They claimed that the only cause was the bungalow's unfitness for habitation. The Queen's Bench Divisional Court granted the application for mandamus, holding that the carrying out of redevelopment (in the words of Lord Widgery CJ) 'should be given its ordinary common sense meaning and can go back to and include the act of demolition which precedes the substitution of new buildings. . . .' It is submitted that this

7 [1975] 2 All ER 568, [1975] 1 WLR 735.

is a welcome decision. The council's attempt to avoid making the payment rested in effect on the notion that prefabricated houses are so different from ordinary houses that displaced residents ipso facto fall outside the benefit of s 29; but Lord Widgery CJ said: 'I do not see why in principle . . . a distinction should be made in these cases . . .'.

Thus far 'home loss payments' go on a similar footing to 'disturbance payments'. But they are not confined to cases of displacement without expropriation, as 'disturbance payments' are. On the other hand, they are available only in respect of residential property. A claimant must have occupied a substantial part of the dwelling as his main residence for the last five years under 'any interest', which presumably means a freehold or leasehold in law or equity, or a statutory tenancy or protected furnished letting under the Rents Acts, or a contract of employment. If the occupant leaves of his own accord he cannot claim[8]; yet any other occupant—presumably a sub-tenant—who has to leave in consequence may still do so. An occupant who has himself initiated the acquisition under a 'blight notice' is also debarred from claiming. Caravan dwellers are entitled to claim (s 33) if no alternative site is available to them on reasonable terms; the five years' continuity of residence they have to show relates to the same site but not necessarily the same individual caravan standing.

The amount of a 'home loss payment' is the rateable value of the property from which the claimant is dispossessed multiplied by three, but not less than £150 nor more than £1,500 at present (s 30).

Originally the claim had to be made not later than six months after the displacement (s 32); but this time limit was abolished and replaced by the normal six years' limitation period applicable under the Limitation Act 1980, s 9, running from the accrual of the right to claim on the date of displacement.[9] A claimant may if necessary take advantage of any predecessors' periods of occupancy under the kind of interest, letting or contract prescribed above, so long as there has been continuity of residence by the claimant himself for the requisite five years; this includes transfers of rights in the dwelling during the five-year period as well as cases where a person entitled to make a claim dies during the *claim* period before doing so. Continuity is not lost by reason of changes of rooms within a dwelling, so long as the dwelling itself is unchanged. If the requisite interest, letting or contract is shared by co-owners, they share the benefit of the payment. If the authority concerned acquires by agreement, the compensation may include an item equivalent to a 'home loss payment'.

Similar in some respects to a home loss payment, but (among other things) discretionary instead of claimable as of right, is a sum which an acquiring authority may pay, under s 43 of the 1973 Act, to cover

8  But see *R v Islington London Borough Council, ex p Knight* [1984] 1 All ER 154.
9  Local Government, Planning and Land Act 1980, s 114.

reasonably incurred expenses of a displaced residential occupant in obtaining a comparable dwelling. The displacement must have occurred in consequence of one of the events giving rise to the duty to rehouse displaced residents imposed by s 39 of the Act, as extended by the Housing Act 1974 (see below). The price of acquiring the new dwelling is *not* covered by this provision (which is hardly surprising because, whereas it will probably be bought outright, the dwelling from which the occupant is displaced must have been held under an interest no greater than yearly tenancy). The contract to acquire the new dwelling must be made within a year of the displacement.

### 5 REHOUSING

Section 39 of the 1973 Act also imposes on certain bodies a new rehousing obligation, which replaces that formerly enacted by s 144 of and Sch 9 to the Housing Act 1957.

Local authorities empowered to provide council housing under Part V of the Housing Act 1957, and new town authorities, have a duty to ensure that, if no other suitable accommodation is available, they will rehouse residential occupiers (including caravan dwellers[10]) displaced from any dwelling in consequence of: (i) its purchase by a body with compulsory powers, or (ii) the making of a demolition, closing or clearance order, or the acceptance of an owner's undertaking to do works, under the Housing Acts in respect of it, or (iii) redevelopment (including change of use) by a public authority holding it for any purpose for which it was acquired under compulsory powers or subsequently appropriated. The duty has been extended to apply to residential occupiers displaced from any dwelling, on or after 31 July 1974, by reason of an 'improvement notice' served under the Housing Act 1974, Part VIII.[11] Displaced occupants must have been in residence when the compulsory purchase order or Bill was published in draft, or when the relevant housing order or undertaking or acquisition agreement was made or notice served. The Greater London Council may by agreement undertake to carry out the rehousing duty of a London Borough in any particular case.

The duty to rehouse does not, however, arise where the occupant has become displaced in consequnce of serving a 'blight notice', or is a trespasser, or is being permitted to occupy the premises temporarily pending their demolition, or is in receipt of any loan for housing obtained under s 41 of the 1973 Act or under new town or housing legislation. Nor does it arise where the displacement is in consequence of a compulsory purchase in relation to which the Secretary of State decided at some date before 23 May 1973 that rehousing is necessary.

---

10 Land Compensation Act 1973, s 40.
11 Housing Act 1974, s 130 and Sch 13.

Where the authority causing the displacement is not the same as the authority on which the duty falls, s 42 requires the former to indemnify the latter against the net loss which will be incurred in discharging the duty, in any of the ten years starting with the year in which the rehousing takes place. This consists of rehousing in a council dwelling, or any other dwelling covered by the authority's housing revenue account replaced by a similar council dwelling in any of the four years beginning with the year before he is rehoused. The indemnity may be met by periodic payments or a lump sum, and must be the latter if the 'net loss' consists not of providing a dwelling, but of making a loan for housing (referred to above) on which the borrower defaults if the consequence of the default is that the amount unpaid exceeds the net proceeds of resale or the dwelling for which the money was lent.

## 6  COST OF PREPARING THE CLAIM FOR COMPENSATION

One final item of compensation which must be considered here has explicitly been declared to be, in the words of rule (vi),[12] not 'disturbance' but an example of 'any other matter not directly based on the value of land'. This is the cost of preparing the compensation claim itself. Lord Denning MR in *Minister of Transport v Lee*,[13] speaking of the phrase 'any other matter', said: 'This includes, I think, the fees which the owner has to pay to his surveyor, valuer, or agent to prepare his claim.' Russell LJ, agreeing, said: 'No one could suggest any meaning that could be given to the words ... unless it were a reference to the established practice of including in the value of the land an allowance for the expense to which the owner was put in establishing the value of the land, as something which was not already embraced in the word "disturbance".'

The right to claim for the cost of preparing the claim had already been established by the Court of Appeal in *Tobin's* case.[14] Morris LJ (as he then was), said: 'Whether in a particular case it is necessary to have legal assistance in preparing a claim, or the services of an accountant, will be a matter for decision having regard to the circumstances of the particular case. But if such assistance and such services have properly and reasonably been obtained, then I see no reason why the expense incurred should not be included as part of the compensation claimed.'

Professional fees incurred in preparing the claim must not, of course, be confused with professional fees incurred in obtaining alternative premises. The latter are indisputably 'disturbance' items, and have been discussed on that footing earlier in this chapter (page 206).

12  Of the 1961 Act, s 5.
13  See p 198, above.
14  See p 203, above.

Part three

# Compulsory purchase in planning

Chapter 11

# Land required for planning purposes[1]

## A. Positive planning

### 1 NEED FOR GENERAL REDEVELOPMENT

When a public body of any kind compulsorily purchases land, the purpose of the acquisition will normally be, to devote that land to a definite use in the public interest. In addition, the intended use will usually involve development of that land, in the sense in which the term 'development' is interpreted by statute for the purposes of planning control. So if a local authority should compulsorily purchase land for council housing, that land will of course be used to build houses or flats. If on the other hand it contains houses already, and the authority intend to use those existing houses as council houses[2] without reconstruction, then the acquisition will not involve a project of development, but this is uncommon.

The carrying out of the development will require actual or deemed planning permission under the Town and Country Planning Acts;[3] though this is not so where the Crown is the developer, since the Crown is not subjected to planning control.[4] It is necessary to keep in mind the distinction between, on the one hand, obtaining lawful authority to purchase land compulsorily for a specific purpose and, on the other hand, obtaining permission to carry out any development necessary to give effect to that purpose. The distinction, which is quite clear-cut, at least in the abstract, is that between the law relating to compulsory purchase and the law relating to planning.

But it is possible to have compulsory purchase of land actually for the purposes of planning; and because this is so, it is important not to confuse the planning question with the compulsory purchase question. Moreover, a 'planning purpose', unlike most if not all other purposes for which land is compulsorily acquired, does not of itself involve a

---

1 See *Compulsory Purchase under Planning Legislation*: V. W. E. Moore, 34 Conv (NS) 311.
2 As in *Moore v Minister of Housing and Local Government* [1966] 2 QB 602, [1965] 2 All ER 367.
3 Town and Country Planning Act 1971, ss 22, 23, 24, 40, 64.
4 See *Ministry of Agriculture v Jenkins* [1963] 2 QB 317, [1963] 2 All ER 147.

reasonably definite and obvious use of the land acquired. Compulsory purchase of land for a hospital, a power station, an aerodrome, a motorway or a sea-wall, is for a reasonably definite and obvious purpose. But compulsory purchase for a 'planning purpose' is not. The legal significance of 'planning purposes' is discussed below.[5]

The origin of this kind of compulsory purchase seems to lie in the Town and Country Planning Act 1944. This Act, passed towards the end of the war with a view to preparing for peace-time reconstruction and replanning, made the innovation of empowering local authorities to carry out 'positive' in addition to 'negative' planning. That is to say they would not merely approve or disapprove the proposals of private developers—'negative planning', as it is sometimes disparagingly called—but would also be able to take positive action themselves to *promote* development in accordance with an acceptable plan. This need not mean that they would actually do the development in all cases. 'Development' of itself in each particular instance is usually too specific to count as 'planning'. But they would provide the plan for a given area, to which all development must be related, and as far as possible take the necessary initiative to get the plan carried out. They would do this either by ensuring that land was held by, or transferred to, owners who would be ready to develop it in accordance with the plan, or by obtaining and developing the land themselves if they considered this course of action to be necessary or desirable. At the national level and in the national interest the central government would exercise the required co-ordination and control.

The key to 'positive planning', as distinct from 'negative planning', has to be compulsory purchase. The authority in question must be able, even if only as a last resort, to acquire land the use or development of which is to be controlled in order that the positive plan for the area may be fulfilled. Although these positive plans will be included in the local planning authority's development plan for the area which is administered by that authority, they will none the less be separate entities in their own right. This is because the local authority concerned will enjoy, within the precise area that each positive plan covers, an initiative in replanning which the authority cannot lawfully exercise outside such areas. Compulsory purchase powers have been essential to their positive plans from the beginning.

The beginning took the form of the provision, enacted in s 1 of the Act of 1944, that: 'Where the Minister . . . is satisfied that it is requisite, for the purpose of dealing satisfactorily with extensive war damage, in the area of a local planning authority, that a part or parts of their area . . . should be laid out afresh and redeveloped as a whole, an order . . . may be made by the Minister (of Town and Country Planning)'

5 See p 230, below.

declaring that the land designated by the order should be subject to compulsory purchase. Such orders were called 'declaratory orders' and the land designated in them became known as 'declaratory areas'. The words 'Minister . . . is satisfied' were alleged, in *Re City of Plymouth (City Centre) Declaratory Order* 1946, *Robinson v Minister of Town and Country Planning*,[6] to mean '*reasonably* satisfied', so as to imply an objective test which could be challenged in the courts. This was meant to profit by Lord Atkin's famous minority interpretation of the words 'Secretary of State has *reasonable* cause to believe' in Regulation 18B, concerning internment in wartime, of the Defence (General) Regulations 1939, which he put forward in *Liversidge v Anderson*.[7] But the Court of Appeal held that the word 'reasonably' should not be implied into the 1944 Act. Its absence pointed clearly to the conclusion that Parliament intended to confer an administrative discretion, not a judicial duty, upon the Minister.

Because of the diffuse and complex nature of this new power of compulsory purchase, it was thought that the 1944 Act could not serve as the authorising Act, pure and simple, for such acquisitions. The choice of specific land could not be left directly to a compulsory purchase order, as in an ordinary case. Instead, there had to be a new, intermediate stage in the procedure. The local area in which positive planning was to be exercised in each case—the 'declaratory area'—had first to be settled by the 'declaratory order', made by the Minister on the application of the local planning authority concerned. The standard procedure was applied, of preparation in draft, prior publicity, and a hearing for objectors, before the Minister confirmed his draft order.[8] After the declaratory order took effect the next step was for the local authority concerned to select each quantity of particular land within the 'declaratory area', required from time to time in accordance with the programme for redevelopment, by means of a compulsory purchase order in the usual way. After the compulsory purchase order had been made the way was open for the actual acquisition of individual estates and interests in land by the customary notice to treat procedure or, in urgent cases, by the newly devised 'expedited completion' procedure[9] which was the fore-runner of the general vesting declaration. Thus the elaborate procedure for compulsory purchase was made even more elaborate by the insertion of the extra stage, in between the general statute itself (the Act of 1944) and the compulsory purchase order in each case.

It may be that the term 'authorising Act', in this context, needs to be applied not to the general statute alone, but to that statute plus the

---

6 [1947] KB 702, [1947] 1 All ER 851.
7 [1942] AC 206, [1941] 3 All ER 338.
8 Town and Country Planning Act 1944, s 1.
9 Town and Country Planning Act 1944, Sixth Schedule; Town and Country Planning Act 1947, s 39. See ch 4, p 73, above.

relevant declaratory order. However that may be, the position now is no longer quite the same as it was under the 1944 Act.

## 2 COMPREHENSIVE DEVELOPMENT AND ACTION AREAS

The Town and Country Planning Act 1947 absorbed the 'declaratory order' stage of proceedings into the development plan system which it set up. The 'declaratory area' now became an 'area of comprehensive development'; and land in or near any such area could be 'designated' for compulsory purchase.[10] These new areas could be defined for dealing not only with war-damage ('blitzed' land), but also with bad or obsolete development ('blighted' land), with 'overspill' population or industry to be moved away from 'blitzed' or 'blighted' land, and with any other purpose specified in the development plan itself.[11] The introduction of 'blighted' land took the new procedure into the field already partly occupied by slum-clearance procedure under the Housing Acts. But it should be noted that a resolution of a *housing* authority declaring an area to be a 'clearance area' does not require approval or confirmation by a Minister, though the Secretary of State for the Environment (the 'Minister' at the time of writing) does have to be notified.[12] It should also be borne in mind, on the other hand, that slum clearance concentrates primarily upon houses, other types of property being included only incidentally; whereas comprehensive development is general in its scope.

The new procedure was normally in practice, though not in theory, confined to the town rather than the countryside. 'Comprehensive development' is therefore virtually synonymous with the American term, 'urban renewal'.[13] Even more narrowly than this it has so far tended to mean, in the normal case, 'town centre redevelopment'. The old, congested town centres have in fact been the commonest location of 'blitzed' as well as 'blighted' land, though not of course 'overspill'. On the other hand, it has been found more commonly convenient in practice to deal with 'overspill', at least in bulk, by means of 'new towns' and 'town development', both of which involve independent projects governed by separate legislative provisions.[14]

Comprehensive development areas, like declaratory areas, required ministerial confirmation quite separately from the confirmation which would be needed for any compulsory purchase order made in relation to them. But the confirmation was obtained for the development plan as a

---

10 Section 4 (3).
11 'Blitzed' and 'blighted' were terms at one time in vogue for the kinds of land referred to: see Heap *An Outline of Planning Law* (4th edn) pp 27–28.
12 Housing Act 1957, s 42. But 'clearance' and 'declaratory' areas are comparable.
13 Comprehensive development in a rural area is possible.
14 New Towns Act 1981; Town Development Act 1952.

whole, or any subsequent amendment of it as a whole, not separately for the area as such.[15] It is important to note that compulsory purchase of land for planning was not lawful without prior designation of the area containing that land for comprehensive development.[16] It was often administratively convenient, in the sense of furnishing planning authorities with a coherent, comprehensive picture of future public development of every kind, to 'designate' generally, despite the fact that this was not necessary in cases of compulsory purchase for purposes other than planning: in other words for council houses, schools, roads, reservoirs and so on. But this administrative convenience was offset by the unfortunate fact that prior publicity by 'designation' for compulsory purchase in the development plan frequently made land difficult or impossible to sell at a proper market price.[17] Here was 'blight' in its newer sense.[18] The additional procedural stage required by the 1944 Act for 'declaratory areas', and extended by 'designation' for compulsory purchase in general, had become hard to justify. It is true that the 1947 Act system of designation was re-enacted in the Town and Country Planning Act 1962. But in the end it was quickly dispatched by s 27 of the Town and Country Planning Act 1968.

There is at present a gap in the story—or perhaps a breathing space. Areas of comprehensive development already created are being dealt with in accordance with the plans made for them; but new ones are not being made since the Act of 1968 brought to a halt the previous system of making development plans. The new system, involving 'structure plans' which continue to require the approval of the Secretary of State, as the previous plans did, and detailed 'local plans' which will not in normal cases need such approval, is now governed by the Town and Country Planning Act 1971.[19]

Section 7 (5) of the 1971 Act provides as follows:

A local planning authority's general proposals under this section with respect to land in their area shall indicate any part of that area (in this Act referred to as an 'action area') which they have selected for the commencement during a prescribed period of comprehensive treatment, in accordance with a local plan prepared for the selected area as a whole, by development, redevelopment or improvement of the whole or part of the area selected or partly by one and partly by another method, and the nature of the treatment selected.

15 Town and Country Planning Act 1962, s 10.
16 Ibid, ss 4, 67–68.
17 See the remarks of the Permanent Secretary to the Ministry of Housing and Local Government, published in Vol 34 of the *Journal of the Royal Institution of Chartered Surveyors* in December, 1954.
18 See ch 13, below.
19 Part II and Schs 4 to 7, 25. These provisions are being brought into effect gradually in different parts of the country by separate statutory instruments (s 21), which will take some time.

This will be part of the 'structure plan'.

Section 11 (6) of the same Act provides as follows:

Where an area is indicated as an action area in a structure plan which has been approved by the (Secretary of State), the local planning authority shall (if they have not already done so), as soon as practicably after the approval of the plan, prepare a local plan for that area.

Thus an 'action area plan' is to be a 'local plan' which enjoys priority, that is to say when the new development plans are sufficiently far advanced in any local planning authority's area to have reached this stage.

The 'action area' of 1971, having descended from the 'declaratory area' of 1944 by way of the 'comprehensive development area' of 1947, resembles it in as much as ministerial approval is necessary for the relevant structure plan, and in as much as the same kind of practical action will ensue. This action will comprise the acquisition of land, where necessary, under compulsory powers by an appropriate local authority and the co-ordinated redevelopment of the area by that authority and other landowners. But the 'action area' differs from its predecessors, first in that it will not have the effect of 'designating' land for compulsory purchase, and second (which may be more important) in that the compulsory purchase of land 'for planning purposes' does not seem to depend as a necessary condition upon being included in it.[20] Nevertheless, putting the matter on the practical level, town centre redevelopment will largely be organised in 'action areas' from now on.

The scope of this 'positive planning' was enlarged for a while by the Community Land Act 1975; but the scheme of that Act was rejected in the wake of the change of government in 1979. The Act was repealed by the Local Government, Planning and Land Act 1980,[1] and is therefore now of historical interest only.

# B. Planning purposes

### 1 DEVELOPMENT, REDEVELOPMENT, IMPROVEMENT AND PROPER PLANNING

The phrase 'for planning purposes' has been used in the Planning Acts without being defined. But s 133 of the 1971 Act states that 'any reference to the acquisition of land for planning purposes' in that Part (VI) of the Act refers to ss 112 or 119, or to ss 68 or 71 of the 1962 Act. Those sections authorise the acquisition, by compulsion and by agreement respectively, of land intended for official acquisition, either as being in

20 See s 112 of the 1971 Act (below, p 231).
1 Section 101. For the Community Land Act, see the third edition of this book.

an area of comprehensive development, or as being otherwise required to secure its use in conformity with the development plan. Section 68 of the 1962 Act and s 112 of the 1971 Act deal with compulsory acquisition. Section 71 of the 1962 Act and s 119 of the 1971 Act deal with acquisition by agreement.

Section 119 of the Act of 1971 empowers any county, London borough or district council, and in some instances the GLC, to acquire land by agreement 'for any purpose for which a local authority may be authorised to acquire land under s 112 of this Act', and also buildings of special historic or architectural interest with (if necessary) land adjoining them. Generally, what has been said in an earlier chapter about procedure for acquisitions by agreement applies here.

Section 112 of the Act of 1971, therefore, as amended by the Local Government, Planning and Land Act 1980,[2] gives us the key to the phrase 'for planning purposes'. It is a comprehensive authorising enactment for compulsory purchase of land for these purposes, and empowers the Secretary of State to authorise any local authority, that is to say any county council or district council, the Greater London Council or any London borough council, to compulsorily purchase:

(a) any land which is in their area, and which is suitable for and is required in order to secure the carrying out of one or more of the following activities, namely development, redevelopment and improvement;

(b) any land which is in their area and which is required for a purpose which it is necessary to achieve in the interests of the proper planning of an area in which the land is situated.

In considering the suitability of land for development, redevelopment or improvement, regard must be had to the development plan 'so far as material', to existing planning permissions, and to 'other considerations which . . . would be material for the purpose of determining' any applications for planning permission. Adjoining land can be included in the acquisition for 'executing works for facilitating [the] development or use' of the land acquired, or for giving in exchange if it 'forms part of a common or open space or fuel or field garden allotment'. The Secretary of State may substitute some other such local authority as acquiring authority, but only after consulting those local authorities in whose areas the land is situated. 'It is immaterial by whom the local authority propose that any activity or purpose . . . should be undertaken or achieved'; they need not do it themselves.

Acquisitions take place using the standard procedure under the Acquisition of Land Act 1981. Section 132 (1) of the Act of 1971 empowers the Secretary of State to disregard objections to the compulsory purchase

2 Section 91.

order which are, in substance, really objections to the development plan.[3]

'Development' is a term to be used in accordance with the definition in s 22 of the Act of 1971, meaning an operation on land or a material change of use of land. 'Redevelopment' and 'improvement' are not defined nor is 'proper planning'. Presumably 'proper planning' must relate to 'development, redevelopment or improvement'—particularly the first—in accordance with the current development plan and especially the relevant 'action area' plan if there is one. 'Proper planning' will then be 'positive planning'.

It may be added that s 214 of the 1971 Act makes provision for extinguishing highways over land held 'for planning purposes', and that, if any alternative highway is to be provided, s 218 empowers the local highway authority or the Secretary of State to compulsorily purchase the necessary land, using the standard 1981 Act procedure.

## 2  OTHER PLANNING PURPOSES

There are other provisions which can be regarded as authorising enactments for compulsory purchase within the field of planning. In the 1971 Act itself, s 114 empowers the Secretary of State to compulsorily purchase, or to authorise the county council or district council for the area (the Greater London Council or the appropriate London borough council if it is in London) to compulsorily purchase, a 'listed' building of special architectural or historic interest, not being an officially protected ancient monument or a building in use for 'ecclesiastical purposes', if he considers it is not being properly looked after. Adjoining land may if necessary be included in the purchase. Procedure is to be in standard form under the Acquisition of Land Act 1946. But s 115 prohibits the acquiring authority from acting until at least two months after serving on the owner a 'repairs notice'[4] specifying works to be done and telling him of the statutory procedure. Within 28 days after service on him of the usual statutory notice that the draft compulsory purchase is made, the owner may appeal to the magistrates to stay the proceedings if he can satisfy them that the building is in fact being properly looked after. Either side can appeal from the magistrates to the Crown Court.

On compulsory purchase of a listed building, compensation must be assessed on the assumption that any 'listed building consent' would be available to the owner for works of alteration or enlargement, except for any work which has already been refused consent and has attracted compensation accordingly, and except for demolition other than for the

---

3 Sections 9 and 13 (as amended) of the 1971 Act govern the procedure for hearing objections to structure and local plans respectively.
4 Not to be confused with a repair notice under the Housing Act 1957, s 9.

purposes of carrying out Schedule 8 development.[5] But if he has deliberately allowed the building to fall into ruin, a direction can be included in the compulsory purchase order that the purchase price shall consist of no amount beyond 'minimum compensation', that is to say on the footing that no planning permission or listed building consent would be forthcoming for any works other than restoring the building to its previous state.[6] Appeals lie to the magistrates, and to the Crown Court, in a similar way to appeals under s 114.

The Act of 1971 also[7] authorises the Secretary of State, as distinct from local authorities, to 'acquire compulsorily any land necessary for the public service', and includes a power 'to acquire an easement or other right over land by the grant of a new right.[8] Procedure is to be in standard form under the Acquisition of Land Act 1981. As in the case of s 112, the Secretary of State can ignore objections to the compulsory purchase order which are in substance objections to the development plan (s 132 (1)).

The Local Government, Planning and Land Act 1980[9] extends this by empowering the Secretary of State to acquire compulsorily other land needed with such 'public service' land, (a) for 'proper planning' of the area, or (b) so that all the land can be used in 'the best, or most economic, way', or (c) to give in exchange for any land to be acquired which 'forms part of a common or open space or fuel or field garden allotment'. It also allows land to be acquired for these various purposes and 'other purposes' in addition; and it extends 'public service' to include the service in the United Kingdom of 'any international organisation or institution' or any office or agency thereof, 'whether or not the United Kingdom or Her Majesty's Government in the United Kingdom is or is to become a member', or 'of a foreign sovereign Power or the Government of such a Power'. If land acquired for any of these purposes is to be disposed of, any other land needed 'to facilitate' this can be acquired under a parallel provision in the Commissioners of Works Act 1852,[10] and any land so acquired by agreement can be acquired in advance of need and put to such other use in the meantime 'as the Secretary of State shall determine'.

Acquisitions of land for new towns under the New Towns Act 1981, or for 'town development' under the Town Development Act 1952, or for

---

5 Town and Country Planning Act 1971, s 116 (as amended by the Town and Country Amenities Act 1974, s 6).
6 Ibid, s 117.
7 Ibid, s 113.
8 See above, ch 5, pp 96–99. No such right can be acquired under this provision over land forming 'part of a common, open space or fuel or field garden allotment' within the meaning of the Acquisition of Land Act 1981, s 19 (4).
9 Section 122, substantially re-enacting the Community Land Act 1975, s 37.
10 Section 2.

'country parks' under the Countryside Act 1968, are also, in a sense, acquisitions for planning, both urban and rural. But a detailed account of these provisions lies outside the scope of this work.

## 3 APPROPRIATION FOR PLANNING

In addition to acquisition it should be borne in mind that there is also the question of appropriation. Appropriation takes place when land, which has already been acquired, and is being held, by virtue of statutory authority for a prescribed purpose, is to be used instead for a different purpose. This will be an infringement of the statute in question unless the appropriation is itself in terms authorised by statute. Lawful appropriation—which in practice seldom arises except in regard to local authorities, because they are multi-purpose administrative bodies whereas statutory undertakers are, on the whole, single-purpose bodies—therefore amounts in effect to compulsory purchase at one remove or more, since the land in question will originally have been acquired under proper statutory powers for purpose A before it is 'appropriated' under proper statutory powers to purpose B or C. For example, land bought for council housing may ultimately be used instead for a highway.[11]

The Local Government Act 1972, s 122, confers a general power of appropriation upon local authorities. The Town and Country Planning Act 1959, s 23, provides that ministerial approval is, in principle, no longer necessary for appropriations by local authorities (and certain analogous bodies); but the exceptions to this relaxation are manifold. For instance, land compulsorily acquired by a local authority for purpose A still requires ministerial approval before being appropriated to purpose B, the minister in question (in most cases the Secretary of State for the Environment) being the one 'concerned with the function for the purposes of which the land was acquired by the authority', meaning purpose A.[12] Commons and other open spaces, cottage holdings and allotments also need various kinds of ministerial consent before appropriation, by virtue either of s 23 of the 1959 Act or of s 121 of the 1971 Act. The latter section, concerning commons and other open spaces, and fuel or field garden allotments, but not London Green Belt land, requires an order for appropriation made by the local authority and confirmed by the Secretary of State. But the order will be subject to special parliamentary procedure, unless the Secretary of State gives a certificate in the same

11 See also *Capital Investments Ltd v Wednesfield UDC* [1965] Ch 774, [1964] 1 All ER 655, in which the defendant council was held to be entitled to sell to the county council, as a site for a school, land acquired under the Housing Act 1957, Part V. But this was because building a school was a valid purpose in connection with the provision of housing in the area, in accordance with s 105 (1) (a) of that Act. For appropriation generally, see ch 4, pp 78–79, above.
12 1959 Act, s 23 (2) (b).

manner as for a compulsory purchase order of such land, as described in an earlier chapter.[13] Where this involves making land available in exchange, such land may be obtained by compulsory purchase. Commons, open spaces and fuel or field garden allotments held for planning purposes can be so used regardless of any restrictions contained in other Acts, whether general or special in scope.

## C. Dealing with land acquired

### 1 DISPOSAL TO DEVELOPERS

When land has been acquired or appropriated 'for planning purposes' under ss 112 or 119 of the 1971 Act (or under the 1962 Act) the question arises of what may be done with it. With ordinary compulsory purchases there is no great problem: the published purpose is usually obvious and definite enough. Compulsory purchase of a 'listed building' under s 114 of the 1971 Act has as its purpose 'the preservation of the building' (sub-s 4), and this too is apparently regarded as sufficient. But if land is 'held for planning purposes' after being acquired either by compulsion or by agreement, a special group of provisions in the 1971 Act come into play. They do not apply to acquisitions by the Secretary of State 'for the public service' under s 113,[14] presumably because that formula is regarded as sufficient in itself.

Section 123 of the 1971 Act, as amended by the Local Government, Planning and Land Act 1980,[15] allows the local authority holding the land to

dispose of the land to such person, in such manner and subject to such conditions as may appear to them to be expedient in order to secure the best use of that or other land and any buildings or works which have been, or are to be, erected, constructed or carried out thereon, whether by themselves or by any other person, or to secure the erection, construction or carrying out thereon of any buildings or works appearing to them to be needed for the proper planning of the area of the authority.

'Positive planning' is considered on the whole to be best achieved by making land available, by sale or lease, to a variety of developers, so long as they are prepared to develop in conformity with the development plan in general and with any old-style 'comprehensive development area' plan or new-style 'action area' plan that may be in force, for 'town-centre redevelopment' or otherwise.[16]

13 See ch 3, pp 55–56.
14 See p 233, above.
15 Schedule 23 (para 11); Sch 34 (Part XIII).
16 Before open space land is disposed of there must be local press publicity and any objections must be duly considered (1971 Act s 123 (2A)).

The Secretary of State's consent is needed for disposal of land which is or was a common 'and is held or managed by a local authority in accordance with a local Act', and for any disposal (except for a term not exceeding seven years) at less than market value.[17]

Preferential treatment is to be given to 'persons who were living or carrying on business or other activities' on land acquired if they 'desire to obtain accommodation on such land, and . . . are willing to comply with any requirements of the authority as to the development and use of such land' (sub-s 7). But to a large extent this provision embodies a pious hope. This is partly because the areas in question are often being redeveloped in such a way as to ensure that many of the previous occupants will be 'relocated'; but more especially because the rents of the redeveloped premises are likely to be well above the levels at which previous business tenants (at least) can afford to pay them, even if they are fixed on a concessionary basis.

In *A Crabtree & Co Ltd v Minister of Housing and Local Government*, the plaintiffs tried to invalidate the compulsory purchase of their premises in Keighley for town centre redevelopment, by claiming that sub-s(7) had been infringed.[18] They alleged that the local authority had disregarded the plaintiffs' own proposals for redevelopment and unjustifiably taken their land in order to dispose of it to a development company.

Their claim failed. In the first place, sub-s(7) is clearly intended to encourage the offering of premises to previous occupants *after* redevelopment, not to enable them to do the redeveloping themselves (even though they may in fact be in the running as commercial developers). In the second place, it clearly imposes no *duty* on the authorities such that any individual can enforce it, but merely expresses the desirability of certain action in purely general terms. In the third place, the process of planning, positive as well as negative, is in essence an administrative and not a judicial one; it is a policy question for each authority concerned to decide on what scale land shall be made available for redevelopment, and what types of development are desirable there. It is true that the subsection speaks of 'any requirements of the authority as to the development and use of such land'; but the authority are plainly not *bound* by these words to impose any requirements of this kind. Even if they do, different kinds of 'development' can occur simultaneously on a small scale for individuals as well as on a larger scale appropriate to the main projects which an authority may have in view; and the 'requirements' can apply to the smaller without affecting the larger development.[19] Finally, the subsection speaks of 'due regard to the price at which any such land has

17  Section 123 (2).
18  (1965) 17 P & CR 232. The provision then was 1962 Act, s 78 (7).
19  For example, alterations to individual buildings by occupiers acquiring from large-scale developers.

been acquired' from an owner who is eligible to be considered for preferential treatment. But it was accepted by the court that this form of words is a survival from the original provision in the 1944 Act, passed at a time when '1939 values' were being applied to land transactions, and is not in fact relevant now that owners are being expropriated at market value.[20]

## 2 DEVELOPMENT OR APPROPRIATION BY THE LOCAL AUTHORITY

It is possible that the local authority concerned may wish to redevelop the land themselves rather than dispose of it to developers; indeed some necessary projects, such as providing roads as part of the schemes of redevelopment, are of a kind that may be of no interest to private developers, or of a kind that clearly come within the authority's own functions. Section 124 of the 1971 Act accordingly provides that a local authority's functions 'shall include power for the authority, notwithstanding any limitation imposed by law on the capacity of the authority by virtue of its constitution, to erect, construct or carry out any building or work on any land . . . which has been acquired or appropriated by [the] local authority for planning purposes'. They may repair, maintain and insure buildings or works so provided, and 'deal therewith in a proper course of management'. They may delegate the carrying out of the work to an 'authorised association'. This means

any society, company or body of persons whose objects include the promotion, formation or management of garden cities, garden suburbs or garden villages, and the erection, improvement or management of buildings for the working classes and others, and which does not trade for profit or whose constitution forbids the issue of any share or loan capital with interest or dividend exceeding the rate for the time being fixed by the Treasury.

It is, of course, also possible that land held for planning purposes may not in fact be needed for those purposes after all. If so, s 122 of the 1971 Act, as amended by the Local Government, Planning and Land Act 1980,[1] states: 'where land has been acquired or appropriated by a local authority for planning purposes and is for the time being held by the authority for [those] purposes . . . the authority . . . may appropriate the land for any purpose for which they are or may be authorised in any capacity to acquire land by virtue of or under any enactment not contained in this part of this Act'.[2] The consent of the Secretary of State is needed for appropriation of land which is or was a common 'and is held or managed by a local authority in accordance with a local Act.[3]

---

20 See ch 7. Part II of the Town and Country Planning Act 1944 applied '1939 values'.
1 Schedule 23 (para 10); Sch 34 (Part XIII).
2 Before open space land is appropriated there must be local press publicity, and any objections must be duly considered (s 122 (2B)).
3 Consent may be general or particular, conditional or unconditional (s 122 (2), (2A)).

3 LESSER RIGHTS; SPECIAL TYPES OF PROPERTY; JOINT BODIES

Certain ancillary provisions should briefly be noted. Private rights of way and of having and maintaining any apparatus on land will be extinguished, and any such apparatus will vest in the authority, subject to compensation, if land is acquired or appropriated for planning purposes.[4] The erection of buildings or carrying out of works on land held for such purposes may proceed notwithstanding any infringement of a 'restriction as to the user of land arising by virtue of a contract', or of an 'easement, liberty, privilege, right or advantage annexed to land and adversely affecting other land, including any natural right to support'. Compensation for these infringements is to be assessed as for 'injurious affection', of whichever kind may happen to be appropriate in any particular case. There is a more elaborate procedure, however, if the apparatus or works of statutory undertakers are affected, involving notices, counter-notices by the undertakers, and ministerial orders to settle the matter.[5]

Local authorities developing, appropriating or disposing of land held for 'planning purposes' must 'have regard to the desirability of preserving features of special architectural or historic interest, and in particular, listed buildings'.[6] Where land held for 'planning purposes' is subject to restrictions because it is a burial ground on consecrated land, or is a common or open space or a fuel or field garden allotment, these restrictions are overridden.[7] The certificate of the Secretary of State will override any protection conferred by the Rent Act 1977 upon tenants of residential premises, if local authorities need to go into physical possession of those premises.[8]

Lastly, it may be noted that, after consulting the authorities concerned, the Secretary of State may if he wishes set up a joint body to whom land acquired for 'planning purposes' may be transferred. The joint body will consist of representatives of the local authority already holding the land and of some other local authority as appropriate.[9]

4 LAND AFFECTED BY PUBLIC WORKS

One form of public activity on land which may involve compulsory purchase in a planning context is the mitigation of adverse effects of public works. This is of course connected with injurious affection or depreciation of land, and derives from the Land Compensation Act 1973, Part II, just as compensation for depreciation caused by 'physical

4 1971 Act, s 127.
5 Ibid., s 230.
6 Ibid, s 125.
7 Ibid., ss 128, 129.
8 Ibid, s 130 (3).
9 Ibid, s 131.

factors' derives from the same Act, Part I, as discussed in an earlier chapter.[10] The purpose of Part II[11] is to deal with the harmful effect on use and enjoyment of nearby land from public works, caused by noise, vibrations, fumes and similar 'physical factors' which may give rise alternatively to compensation under Part I. Acquisition and compensation are the two sides of the same coin.

Much of Part II originally related to highways, but those provisions— ss 22 to 25—have since been repealed and re-enacted in the Highways Act 1980. The substance of the relevant law, therefore, is now contained in that Act, ss 246, 253, 272, and 282, as regards land affected by highways, but is still contained in the 1973 Act, s 26, as regards land affected by other public works.

Highway authorities are empowered to acquire land, compulsorily or by agreement, 'for the purpose of mitigating any adverse effect which the existence or use of a highway constructed or improved by them, or proposed to be constructed or improved by them, has or will have on the surroundings of the highway'.[12] The term 'surroundings' presumably means any nearby land which, as a straight question of fact, can be proved to suffer some 'adverse effect' to the extent of being depreciated in value ('injuriously affected'). Three tracts of land are thus involved: land A, which comprises the 'surroundings' and suffers the 'adverse effect'; land B, which is to be acquired as a result; and land C, which is the highway. Land B is, therefore, so to speak, a 'buffer zone' between A and C. Land A may well comprise many separate properties lying on either side or both sides of the highway. The 'mitigation' will consist of the provision of embankments, fences, trees or other practical screening and sound-deadening devices, as appropriate.

Alternatively land A itself may be acquired, as 'land the enjoyment of which is seriously affected' by highway use or highway works (construction or improvement); but this can only be done by agreement, and the property interest acquired in this way must be one 'qualifying for protection' for the purpose of serving a blight notice.[13]

Compulsory acquisition under these provisions must have been begun before the date on which the highway, as constructed or improved, is opened to the public, and so must acquisitions by agreement of land which is itself 'seriously affected' by construction or improvement works; in other acquisitions by agreement the contract must be made

10 Sections 1–19 (as amended): see ch 9, pp 187–192, above.
11 Sections 20–28 (subsequently repealed in part).
12 Highways Act 1980, s 246 (1). (The standard procedure for compulsory purchase orders, now under the Acquisition of Land Act 1981, is to be followed, and such orders are to be confirmed by the Minister of Transport, or the Secretary of State for Wales. The land acquired is deemed to be needed for the construction or the improvement, as the case may be).
13 Ibid, s 246 (2). (For blight notices, see below, ch 13).

within one year after that opening date.[14] Land may be included in an acquisition in order to be exchanged for other such land 'forming part of a common, open space, or fuel or field garden allotment'.[15]

The carrying out of works of 'mitigation' is itself authorised in general terms for highway authorities;[16] and they are empowered in addition to enter into agreements with other landowners as to the carrying out of such works on 'land adjoining, or in the vicinity of, a highway', or the restriction or regulation of the use of such land including 'restricting the lopping or removal of trees, shrubs or other plants on the land'.[17]

The acquisition of land to mitigate 'adverse effects' of public works, *other than* highways, on 'the surroundings of the works' is governed by s 26 of the 1973 Act. The authorisation of such acquisitions is essentially the same as it is in regard to highways, but with the exclusion of the provisions relating to compulsory purchase: ie acquisitions can only be by agreement. The acquiring body is the 'responsible authority' in charge of the particular public works.[18]

Highway authorities and other 'responsible authorities' may meet the cost of obtaining temporary alternative accommodation for residential occupiers and their households where the nature of works being carried out makes this reasonably necessary.[19]

It may also be noted that the Secretary of State for the Environment is authorised to make regulations empowering or requiring highway authorities and other 'responsible authorities' to sound-proof buildings against noise from the construction or use of public works, or to pay grants towards the cost of doing so.[20]

14 Ibid, s 246 (3). Compulsory acquisitions are 'begun' when the *draft* compulsory purchase order is published (see above, ch 3, p 41): ibid, s 246 (4).
15 Ibid, s 246 (5).
16 Ibid, s 282. (It includes 'the planting of trees, shrubs or plants of any other description and the laying out of any area as grassland').
17 Ibid, s 253. (The burden of such agreements 'runs' to bind successors in title).
18 These are 'any works on land (not being a highway or aerodrome) provided or used in the exercise of statutory powers': Land Compensation Act 1973, s 1 (3). The carrying out of mitigation works is authorised, much as it is for highways, with the addition of a power to 'develop or redevelop any land acquired . . . under section 26' (ibid, s 27).
19 Ibid, s 28.
20 Ibid, s 20. See the Noise Insulation Regulations 1975, SI 1975/1763, which relate to sound-proofing residential buildings within 300 metres of highways. For aerodromes, see the Civil Aviation Act 1982, s 79.

# Chapter 12

# Purchase notices

## A. Land incapable of beneficial use

### 1 INVERSE COMPULSORY PURCHASE FOR ADVERSE DECISIONS

All compulsory purchase in planning is to some extent out of the ordinary. Particularly is this true of what may be termed 'inverse compulsory purchase', where the compulsion is applied by the vendor against the acquiring body instead of the other way about. It is not the less a compulsory purchase on this account. The statutory requirements must be strictly adhered to; and compensation is assessed on the same basis as in the more orthodox kinds of expropriation. Procedure is simplified, however, to this extent, that there is no need for a compulsory purchase order. The lawful application of compulsion to particular land is achieved without it, when an owner of a specific property brings himself within the legal requirements. For the same reason, a notice to treat or vesting declaration is not needed either. Once the vendor's notice has been accepted without challenge, or upheld on challenge, all that remains is the question of compensation; and it will be remembered that certain of the leading cases discussed earlier in this book in relation to the principles of assessment of compensation arose out of 'inverse compulsory purchase'.[1]

There are two kinds of inverse compulsory purchase. The earlier form to be introduced was procedure by 'purchase notice', which is discussed in this chapter; the later was procedure by 'blight notice', which will be discussed in the next. When modern planning control came in under the Act of 1947, it was enacted that where restrictions on development would leave land virtually useless—in other words, where its existing use is practically non-existent—the owner could, if he wished, serve a purchase notice in order to have it taken off his hands. The difficulty here is that, because the existing use was virtually nil, and because the owner was not entitled to prospective development value (the underlying principle of the 1947 Act), his compensation could only relate to the existing use and must therefore in strictness be purely nominal. In other words,

---

1 See the two *Jelson* cases (pp 131 and 164, above), the *Devotwill* case (p 164, above), the *Provincial Properties (London) Ltd* case (p 159, note 20, above), the *Morris and Jacombs* case (p 132, above) and the *Trocette Property Co* case (p 133, above).

the procedure must be nothing more than the unloading of a useless possession.

Yet it is unlikely that this ever really happened. The land so transferred often had a very real value to the authority that acquired it: for example all or part of a derelict residential site might be required for road widening or for inclusion in some project of public development, and this might be the very reason why the owner was prohibited from redeveloping it. In such a case the entire effective value of that land would be development value. The theory of the 1947 Act that owners should be restricted to existing use value might be bearable so long as that value amounted to something, such as a house or a farm. But when that value was nothing, and a reasonable possibility of some development value existed, restriction to existing use value could not be bearable.

On the other hand, the worst case of this kind would occur when a site had previously contained a building which had been destroyed by bombing or fire or otherwise. The replacement of a destroyed former building comes within 'existing use' or 'Eighth Schedule' development (to be considered later);[2] and the value of it was in fact allowed to its owner by the 1947 Act (and still is) *in the event of compulsory purchase* but not otherwise, provided that it existed before 1948.

## 2   WHAT THE OWNER MUST PROVE

The first half of Part IX of the 1971 Act now contains the main statutory provisions for serving purchase notices. Section 180 empowers the 'owner' to serve such a notice, requiring that his interest in stated land be purchased, after an application for planning permission to develop that land has been refused, or granted subject to conditions, provided that the land 'has become incapable of reasonably beneficial use in its existing state'.[3] 'New development' (meaning development involving appreciable change in the property such as replacing a large old house by a block of flats), must be disregarded; but one would have thought that this was self-evident in view of the words 'existing state', which in fact suggest that *any* kind of development must be disregarded.

Much of the trouble experienced with this part of the law arises from failure to take proper account of the distinction between actual use or development potential of land, and their value. Since owners are not now deprived of prospective development value (except by adverse planning decisions) but merely taxed in respect of it, the rationale of purchase

2  See ch 16, p 316 (formerly 'Third Schedule').

3  In *Smart & Courtenay Dale Ltd v Dover RDC* (1971) 23 P & CR 408, the Lands Tribunal held, on a preliminary point of law, that 'the land' in s 180 means all the land covered by the adverse planning decision; so that if the claimant does not own all that land he cannot serve a purchase notice. This seems unnecessarily strict; 'the land' refers back to 'any land' which is surely a sufficiently flexible expression to cover such cases.

notice procedure can be both clear and acceptable: namely that it only applies in cases where *existing use* of land is negligible and development is prohibited; that the negligible value of the existing use justifies 'inverse compulsory purchase', and that development value can be realised in the compensation for the acquisition to the extent that the 'assumptions as to planning permission' discussed in an earlier chapter,[4] can be applied.

If the application for planning permission could not itself be made because the proposed development also requires an industrial development certificate, and this has been refused, the local planning authority can be required to state if they *would* have given an adverse decision; and if they would, purchase notice procedure is applicable.[5]

'Incapable of reasonably beneficial use' does not mean merely 'less valuable'. As Lord Parker CJ said in *R v Minister of Housing and Local Government, ex p Chichester RDC*,[6] 'I suppose that in every case where land is worth developing and permission to develop is refused . . . it will be less useful to the owner, than if it were developed.' In that case the landowner enjoyed some agricultural and some residential use (but not much) from the land in dispute. He was refused permission to redevelop the land residentially, and served a purchase notice. The Minister upheld the purchase notice and expressly gave the reason that, 'the land in its existing state and with its existing permissions is substantially less useful . . . than it would be with permission for the permanent redevelopment for residential purposes'. This reason was wrong on the face of it, as has been demonstrated. The local authority therefore succeeded in having the Minister's decision quashed in the Queen's Bench Divisional Court by an order of *certiorari*. And in *General Estates Co Ltd v Minister of Housing and Local Government*[7] the Court of Appeal upheld a Ministerial decision that land used as a sports field, and denied planning permission for redevelopment, was not 'incapable of reasonably beneficial use in its existing state'.

In *Wain v Secretary of State for the Environment*,[8] the Court of Appeal held that, if only part of a property is 'incapable of reasonably beneficial use' the whole cannot be made the subject of a purchase notice. The facts were that in respect of a tract of open land, for which planning permission had been refused, a clearly-defined part was virtually useless in its existing state, but the rest might conceivably be used at certain times for grazing. The court said that the latter part must therefore be excluded from the purchase notice served by the owner on the local authority.

4 See ch 8, p 156, above.
5 1971 Act, s 191 (2).
6 [1960] 2 All ER 407.
7 (1965) 195 *Estates Gazette* 201.
8 (1981) 44 P & CR 289.

In *Purbeck District Council v Secretary of State for the Environment*,[9] Woolf J upheld a purchase notice relating to a tract of useless marsh-land, for which planning permission had been refused. The fact that it had been marsh-land since time out of mind was not a valid objection. But adjacent land which had become unusable because of a breach of a condition in an earlier planning permission could not be the subject of a purchase notice.

An ironical commentary on the law of purchase notices is the case of *Adams and Wade Ltd v Minister of Housing and Local Government*.[10] Planning permission was given for housing development on a field, subject to a condition that a screen of trees was to be planted and maintained along the boundary of the adjoining public road for reasons of amenity. The permission was accepted in these terms; the houses were built and sold off to purchasers. When no land remained unsold except for the site of the intended trees, the local planning authority received a disagreeable surprise in the shape of a planning aplication for development of that very site, instead of planting it with trees. Naturally this was rejected with indignation, being obviously contrary to the condition in the earlier permission; whereupon the applicants played their next card by serving a purchase notice. The rejection of this was duly contested in the High Court, on the point of law whether the words 'incapable of reasonably beneficial use' should or should not apply to a situation wherein the actual use of land, however negligible in economic benefit, had been accepted as a quid pro quo for permitting lucrative development of other land. The court gave judgment for the owners, holding that the wording of what is now s 180 clearly applied to the situation. No special exceptions were prescribed to cover such a case, and there was nothing in the statute which required any amenity benefit to other land to be taken into consideration.

Parliament overruled this decision by enacting s 184 of the Act of 1971, which describes such land as having 'restricted use' and empowers the Secretary of State to refuse to confirm a purchase notice in these cases,[11] 'if it appears to him that the land ought, in accordance with the previous planning permission, to remain undeveloped or, as the case may be, remain or be preserved or laid out as amenity land in relation to the remainder of the larger area for which that planning permission was

9 (1982) 80 LGR 545.

10 (1965) 18 P & CR 60. Compare this case with the *Morris and Jacombs* case (above, ch 7, p 132), in which the condition subject to which planning permission was granted was to retain a small portion of the site not for amenity but for additional access. It may be that this will lead in due course to an amendment of s 184 so as to extend its scope to include access as well as amenity.

11 He can only refuse to confirm where the whole of the land to which the notice relates was the subject of the previous planning permission: *Plymouth City Corpn v Secretary of State for the Environment* [1972] 3 All ER 225, [1972] 1 WLR 1347 (compare this with the case mentioned in footnote 3 on p 242, above).

granted'. He may do this 'although satisfied that the land has become incapable of reasonably beneficial use in its existing state'. It is immaterial whether the requirement concerning that land was imposed as a condition of the planning permission or whether it was 'contemplated (expressly or by necessary implication)' in the application for that permission.

It should be noticed that only an 'owner' may serve a purchase notice. 'Owner' is defined in s 290 (1) of the Act of 1971 to mean 'a person, other than a mortgagee not in possession, who, whether in his own right or as trustee for any other person, is entitled to receive the rack rent of the land, or, where the land is not let at a rack rent, would be so entitled if it were so let'. That excludes reversioners entitled to a nominal or ground rent. In *London Corpn v Cusack-Smith*,[12] freeholders in reversion upon a long lease at a ground rent were for this reason held, by the House of Lords, not to have the right to serve a purchase notice, despite the fact that the leaseholders had been statutorily exempted from paying rent because the premises had been bombed. Planning permission for rebuilding had been refused because the site was included in a road-widening scheme. The leaseholders thereupon served a purchase notice and succeeded; but the City Corporation were not willing to take the freehold at that stage.[13]

Where the adverse planning decision is not a refusal but a conditional consent, s 180 is only satisfied where compliance with the conditions will leave the land still incapable of reasonably beneficial use; and in any case the availability of some other planning permission will preclude a purchase notice unless that permission also does not render the land capable of reasonably beneficial use. It will be seen presently that the Secretary of State can dispose of a purchase notice by directing that planning permission be given for the land to which it relates.

# B. Serving a purchase notice

## 1 THE LOCAL AUTHORITY AND THE SECRETARY OF STATE

The procedure for a purchase notice is for the owner to serve it upon the district (not the county) council for the area within 12 months after the date of the adverse planning decision. In London it will be the London borough council or the Common Council of the City.[14] There need not be a decision of the Secretary of State; though it is likely that most owners would appeal to him first from an adverse planning decision of the local planning authority before serving the notice. It will be seen that the local

12 [1955] AC 337, [1955] 1 All ER 302.
13 That is, to buy out their own landlords.
14 1971 Act, ss 180 (1), 290 (1).

planning authority as such are not the recipient of the notice; but in many cases they will be the same body as the local authority who do receive it, depending on whether they are the county planning authority or the district planning authority.[15] If they think the notice is justified they should, under s 181 of the 1971 Act, accept it, or state if some other authority or body of statutory undertakers have agreed to accept it. Otherwise—which is the equivalent of a rejection—they should transmit a copy of it to the Secretary of State, and notify the owner that they have done so, with a statement of reasons. They must do this within three months of receiving the notice.[16]

Acceptance of the purchase notice means that the body concerned 'shall be deemed to be authorised to acquire the interest of the owner compulsorily' under Part VI of the Act of 1971.[17] This means deemed to acquire it 'for planning purposes' in accordance with the provisions already discussed in ch 11, or for the purposes for which statutory powers of compulsory purchase exist by virtue of the authorising Acts applying to any statutory undertakers who may accept the notice.[18] A notice to treat, which cannot be withdrawn, is deemed to have been served on the date of service of the purchase notice.[19]

If the notice is referred to the Secretary of State he must, under s 182, inform the owner who served it, the council which received it, and also the local planning authority, of his intended course of action in dealing with it; and if he intends to substitute any other body for the council which received it he must also inform that body. He must give all these parties at least 28 days to apply for a hearing before an inspector, after which he may carry out either his original decision or a different decision. If he decides that the notice is not justified under the requirements of s 180, then he is empowered to state that he will not confirm it.[20] But if he decides that it is justified, s 183 (1) states that 'he shall confirm the notice',[1] unless he decides instead to take any of certain alternative courses open to him. These are: that he may grant the planning permission for which the owner had applied, or relax conditions 'to enable the land to be rendered capable of reasonably beneficial use . . .'; or that

---

15 See the Town and Country Planning General Regulations 1976 SI 1976/1419, reg 14. A case in point is that involving Chichester RDC (see p 243, above).

16 See 1971 Act, s 181 (1), (3). The 12-month period for serving a purchase notice is prescribed by the Town and Country Planning General Regulations 1976, reg 14 (see previous note).

17 1971 Act, s 181 (2), (4). See *Hyatt v Dover Corpn* (1951) 2 P & CR 32.

18 In other words they are to use it for their own proper functions.

19 1971 Act, ss 181 (2), 208.

20 Ibid, s 183 (5). But s 185 empowers the Secretary of State to refuse to confirm even if the purchase notice appears to be justified, in certain special cases under office development control; nor need he take any of the alternative courses described below, under s 183 (2), (3) and (4).

 1 Subject, however, to s 184 (see above, p 244).

he may direct an alternative planning permission to be granted, if applied for, in relation to all or any of the land if it 'could be rendered capable of reasonably beneficial use within a reasonable time by the carrying out of any other development'. In the latter case he is empowered, if he thinks fit, to confirm the notice as to part only of the land and direct one or more substitute planning permissions to be available for the rest. Or he may confirm the notice but substitute another local authority, or statutory undertakers, in relation to all or any part of the land, 'having regard to the probable ultimate use of the land'.[2]

Section 186 provides that within nine months of the service of the purchase notice, or six months of the transmission to him by the local authority of a copy of it, whichever period is the shorter, the Secretary of State must either have confirmed it, or taken one of the decisions alternative to confirming it, or stated that he declines to confirm it. If he does none of these things it is deemed to be confirmed in respect of the local authority which received it. The consequences of actual or deemed confirmation are the same as the consequences of acceptance by the local authority; except that the deemed service of notice to treat is 'on such date as the (Secretary of State) may direct', or on the expiry of the six or nine months' time limit, in the case of actual, and of deemed, confirmation respectively.[3]

Sections 242 and 245 of the 1971 Act provide that the Secretary of State's decision cannot be challenged in any court,[4] except within six weeks in the High Court which, 'if satisfied that the order or action in question is not within the powers of this Act, or that the interests of the applicant have been substantially prejudiced by a failure to comply with any of the relevant requirements in relation thereto, may quash that order or action...'. Either the owner or 'the authority directly concerned' may apply to the High Court under this procedure.[5] If the Secretary of State's decision is quashed, 'the purchase notice shall be treated as cancelled, but the owner may serve a further purchase notice in its place'; and for the purpose of time limits which will apply to a further purchase notice the adverse planning decision is then treated as having been made on the date of the quashing.[6]

It must be emphasised that, in so far as any purchase notice succeeds in being accepted or confirmed, it results in a normal compulsory purchase. Compensation must then be assessed in the ordinary way. It is provided—but this is unlikely to occur often in practice—that if the Secretary of State directs the granting of an alternative planning permission in lieu of confirming a purchase notice in whole or in part, and

2 1971 Act, s 183 (2), (3) and (4).
3 Ibid, s 186 (1) to (3). For acceptance by the local authority, see p 246, above.
4 Ibid, s 242 (1), (3).
5 Ibid, s 245 (1) to (4).
6 1971 Act s 186 (4), (5).

the amount of prospective development value which results is less than the value of 'existing use' development within the categories of the Eighth Schedule to the 1971 Act, then the local authority must pay the difference to the owner as a form of planning compensation. It will be assessed as for compulsory purchase compensation.[7]

It should also be stressed that local authorities and the Secretary of State must deal with purchase notices as a matter of law rather than as a matter of policy—except in so far as it is possible either to substitute another public body for the local authority receiving a particular notice or to direct the granting of an alternative planning permission in place of the one refused. This is quite different from the width of general policy discretion allowed in dealing with planning applications.

## 2 PURCHASE NOTICES IN SPECIAL CASES

Rejections of planning applications, or granting them subject to conditions, are not the only categories of adverse planning decision, even though they are the main ones. Other varieties of adverse decision also carry the right to serve a purchase notice. This applies to revocation, modification and discontinuance orders under s 45 and 51 of the 1971 Act, to which the procedure already described in this chapter applies subject to necessary modifications. Thus, instead of confirming a purchase notice in these cases, the Secretary of State may revoke or amend the order which gave rise to it, or any conditions in that order, as the case may be. Any compensation paid under these procedures must not duplicate compensation payable in respect of such an order.[8]

It is also provided that purchase notices may be used in relation to tree and advertisement control. But there the requirement is that a tree preservation order, or regulations for control of advertisements must make the necessary provision.[9] The regulations for control of advertisements[10] do not make any such provision, and apparently never have. Any tree preservation order may do so; but the model form of order, upon which individual orders are presumably based in practice, makes no mention of purchase notices.[11]

However, s 190 of the 1971 Act does specifically provide for purchase notices in regard to 'listed buildings'. These are buildings of special architectural or historic interest entered on a list compiled by the Secretary of State.[12] Where a 'listed building consent', to demolish, alter or

7  Ibid, s 187 (2) to (5). And see ch 16, p 325, below.
8  Ibid, s 187 (1), 188, 189.
9  Ibid, s 191 (1).
10  Town and Country Planning (Control of Advertisements) Regulations 1969, SI 1969/1532.
11  Town and Country Planning (Tree Preservation Order) Regulations 1969, SI 1969/17, the Schedule to which contains the 'model' or standard form of tree preservation order.
12  1971 Act, s 54.

extend a listed building 'in any manner which would affect its character' as such, is refused or granted subject to conditions, or is revoked or modified, then the purchase notice procedure described in this chapter applies to the case, with necessary modifications.[13] Thus the land affected by such a purchase notice includes the 'listed building' to which it relates, together with any land comprising the building, or contiguous and adjacent to it, and owned with it, being land as to which the owner claims its use is substantially inseparable from that of the building and that it ought to be treated, together with the building, as a single holding.[14]

Purchase notices can also be served under housing legislation in regard to 'obstructive buildings', which a local authority may wish to demolish because their closeness to other buildings makes them dangerous or injurious to health, though they are not (if they are houses) unfit for habitation.[15] Section 74 of the Housing Act 1957 provides that, if the local authority exercise their power to make a demolition order for an obstructive building, the owner may offer it for sale to them, so that they have the task of demolition themselves, at any time within the two months' period for vacating the building under the order. Compensation is to be assessed as for a compulsory purchase in the normal course of slum clearance in regard to property to be acquired other than at 'site value'.[16]

13 1971 Act, s 56 and Eleventh Schedule. Further details of procedure for listed building purchase notices are contained in the Nineteenth Schedule. Listed building purchase notices (like other purchase notices) must be served within 12 months of the adverse decision: Town and Country Planning (Listed Buildings and Buildings in Conservation Areas) Regulations 1977, SI 1977/228, reg 7.
14 Ibid, s 190 (3).
15 Housing Act 1957, s 72.
16 See ch 8, p 166, above.

# Chapter 13

# Blight notices

## A. Blight situations

The second type of 'inverse compulsory purchase' occurs in cases of adverse planning proposals. Purchase notices are appropriate to adverse planning *decisions*, if these leave land virtually useless. 'Blight notices', however, are designed to deal with a threat, not to the usefulness of land but to its marketability, which is what results from adverse *proposals*. It may also be observed, as far as the practical question of compensation is concerned, that attention in regard to *purchase* notices is focused upon development value as distinct from existing use value, since the whole question arises from the fact that existing use value in such a case is virtually nil. But, in regard to *blight* notices, a property's development value, although it may be important in particular cases, is incidental and attention is focused instead upon the existing use value, which ought to be appreciable but is in fact impaired by the 'blight' which has occurred.[1]

The word 'blight' has been made respectable, and indeed a term of art, by statute. But it is obviously slang and is still used as such in popular speech. It is most important to remember that its official meaning is carefully defined by statute; and any word which gets this treatment cannot possibly mean exactly the same in ordinary speech as it does officially. The statutory meaning will be examined shortly; but the ordinary meaning is much wider, and in effect is synonymous with 'depreciation', except perhaps that it has a stronger flavour of undeserved catastrophe, like greenfly or the Black Death. If land is put up for sale and a substantially lower price is obtained than the vendor was led (or led himself) to believe would be forthcoming—at any rate if calculated on a basis of comparison with similar transactions—he is sure to regard it as 'blight'. This will almost certainly be so if the cause can be traced to some actual or proposed public project of development nearby, such as a new main road, or school, or sewage pumping station. A private development may also be regarded in the same light, since it depends on a public decision in the shape of a planning permission which in turn comes into being in the context of the development plan. Again an

---

1 For development value as distinguished from existing use value, see ch 8, above.

adverse planning decision concerning the owner's own land may well be described as 'blighting' it because some or all of the prospective development value of the land is extinguished thereby.

In so far as these different varieties of depreciation can be reliably established by expert valuation, they could all be covered by compensation from public funds; though it must be admitted that this is not likely to happen in the foreseeable future. Where 'blight' is officially recognised, it would be possible to calculate the depreciation in each case and to pay compensation accordingly; but this is probably simpler in theory than in practice. The solution adopted, however, is to turn the owner's entire asset into money by an outright purchase, so that all that has to be calculated is a 'proper', undepreciated market value figure for the property in accordance with the normal rules for assessing compulsory purchase compensation. The amount of depreciation, if it needed to be ascertained, would presumably be the difference between this figure and the actual market figure being offered for the 'blighted' property.

Thus there is in fact an 'inverse compulsory purchase' here, just as there is with purchase notices, though in a different context. In fact, until the term 'blight notice' was officially adopted considerable confusion prevailed, because many people chose to call this type of acquisition procedure a 'purchase notice'. The statutory provisions never gave any warrant for this. They merely evaded the issue by not giving the procedure a name at all; and until 1968 the only term which could reasonably be used was 'notice to purchase'.

## 2 WHAT THE OWNER-OCCUPIER MUST PROVE

The blight notice, in its orginal anonymous form, was first introduced by the provisions of the Town and Country Planning Act 1959, Part IV. These provisions were repealed and are re-enacted in the second half of Part IX of the Act of 1971. The Town and County Planning Act 1968 introduced the term 'planning blight' and amended the existing law; and the kinds of situation in which blight notices can be served have been considerably extended by Part V of the Land Compensation Act 1973, notably by making such service possible at an earlier and less definite stage in the procedures which give rise to the 'blight' suffered. Apart from these alterations in detail the law on this matter is essentially the same as when it was first introduced. The intention behind the enactment of this part of the law in 1959 was not to confer a benefit on landowners generally but only upon owner-occupiers, whether residential, agricultural or commercial, and in the case of commercial owner-occupiers only the 'small men'. Larger firms, and investment owners of whatever kind, were not to be assisted in this way no matter how much their interest might be 'blighted'. One type of investment owner was brought within the scope of the provisions, namely a mortgagee of an owner-occupier who is himself within them, provided that the mortgagee has a power of sale which has become exercisable.[2]

There are three main elements which must exist in any situation before a blight notice can be enforced. First, all or part of the land must come within 'the specified descriptions'; second, the interest to be sold must be one 'qualifying for protection'; and third, a genuine attempt must have been made, but without success, to sell the interest at a reasonable figure on the open market.[3] In *Lade and Lade v Brighton Corpn* the Lands Tribunal upheld a claim that in the circumstances there had been 'reasonable endeavour to sell' a second-hand and antiques shop merely by putting a notice in the window although normally such a course would be inadequate.[4]

If all requirements are satisfied and the blight notice takes effect, then the procedure goes forward as a normal compulsory purchase. No compulsory purchase order, of course, is needed; and notice to treat is deemed to have been served, by virtue of s 196 of the Act of 1971, either two months after the blight notice was itself served, if it has not been challenged or it has been restricted to part only of the land by agreement, or else on a date to be specified by the Lands Tribunal if it *has* been challenged but upheld in regard to all or part of the land. The deemed notice to treat cannot be withdrawn; but unless the acquiring authority have entered into possession of the land the blight notice itself can be withdrawn by the owner before the compensation has been determined by the Lands tribunal, or within six weeks thereafter; and this in turn counts as a deemed withdrawal of the deemed notice to treat.[5] It may be noted that, originally, severance and disturbance compensation could not be claimed in blight notice acquisition; but this restriction was repealed in 1968.[6]

It may also be noted that, whereas a purchase notice if challenged is referred to the Secretary of State, a blight notice if challenged is referred to the Lands Tribunal—not on the question of compensation, since that

2  1971 Act, s 201. He is an investment owner on the point of disposing of his investment.
3  1971 Act, s 193 (1), as amended by the 1973 Act, s. 77, which repealed the additional requirement previously in force that the failure to sell must have occurred *since* the land came within the 'specified descriptions'.
4  (1970) 22 P & CR 737. The shop was in a 'very second-rate street', and only visiting dealers were likely to be interested in buying it. See also *Mancini v Coventry City Council* (1982) 44 P & CR 114, in which the claimant's property (dwelling, plus workshop for making ice-cream) was placed in an estate agent's hands, but there were no takers; the Lands Tribunal regarded this as a reasonable endeavour to sell.
5  Town and Country Planning Act 1971, ss 198, 208.
6  Town and Country Planning Act 1962, s 143, repealed by the Town and Country Planning Act 1968, s 37 (1) and Eleventh Schedule. For a case involving s 143, see *Minister of Transport v Lee*, ch 10, pp 198 and 222, above. See also *Elmer-Smith v Stevenage Development Corpn* (1972) 23 P & CR 371.

cannot arise unless the notice succeeds, but on the general question of whether the notice ought to succeed.[7] Also, the proper recipient of a purchase notice is the local authority, but the proper recipient of a blight notice is the 'appropriate authority'. This term is defined by s 205 (1) of the 1971 Act to mean 'the government department, local authority or other body by whom, in accordance with the circumstances by virtue of which the land falls within any of the specified descriptions, the land is liable to be acquired or is indicated as being proposed to be acquired'. Disputes between two or more authorities over which of them is the 'appropriate authority' go to the Secretary of State, 'whose decision shall be final'.[8]

### 3 THE SPECIFIED DESCRIPTIONS

The question of what are these 'specified descriptions' is more than a little complicated; but the underlying factor is that they all involve adverse planning proposals for the land in question of such a kind that compulsory purchase is either foreshadowed or has actually begun. It may be asked why there is a need for 'inverse compulsory purchase' when actual compulsory purchase is on the way. The answer lies in the delay involved, so that the owner cannot properly market his land in the meantime as he is entitled to do, and also in the possibility that until the threatened purchase has actually been completed no-one can be sure that it will be. On the other hand, a prospective acquiring authority may even be anxious to help owners and avoid blight, if circumstances permit. If so, they can take advantage of ss 46, 48 and 49 of the Town and Country Planning Act 1959, which authorise the acquisition of land in advance of requirements, in regard to 'town development' and highways.[9]

Section 192 of the 1971 Act sets out, as follows, ten categories of 'specified description', which have since been extended in scope by Part V of the Act of 1973.

1  The land is shown in a valid structure plan as being required for the functions of some public body, or for an 'action area'; unless there is also a local plan for the district which specifies any land in that district as being so required.[10] This category is now extended to include

7  1971 Act, s 195.
8  Ibid, s 205 (2).
9  For new towns, see the New Towns Act 1981, s 10.
10  1971 Act, s 192 (1) (a). In the absence of any such local plan for the district in question, Sch 24 (para 58) of the 1971 Act continues in force the Town and Country Planning Act 1962, s 138 (1), which includes as a 'specified description' any land which is shown in an *old-style* development plan as being required for the functions of some public body. The 1973 Act (s 68) extends this to cover alterations submitted to, or modifications publicised by, the Secretary of State in respect of such plans (see next footnote). For action areas, local plans and structure plans see ch 11, p 229, above, and the 1971 Act, Part II.

structure plans, or alterations to such plans, which are still at their earlier stage of submission to the Secretary of State, and also modifications to such plans when publicised by him.[11]

2   The land is shown in a valid local plan as being so required.[12] This category is now extended to include proposed local plans, or alterations or modifications thereto, when publicised.[13]

3   The land is shown in a development plan, otherwise than in either of the above categories, as the site or part of the site of a highway as it will be constructed or altered.[14]

4   The land is liable to be compulsorily purchased by virtue of a valid order or scheme under the Highways Act 1980, or the previous Acts of 1959 and 1971, as the site or part of the site of a trunk or special road, or a road joining a classified road, as it will be constructed or altered.[15] This category is now extended to include an order or scheme which has been publicised but is still before the Minister of Transport or the Secretary of State and as yet has neither come into force nor been rejected.[16]

5   The land is shown on plans approved by a resolution of a local highway authority as the site or part of the site of a highway as it will be constructed or altered.[17]

6   The land is the site or part of the site of a trunk or special road which the Secretary of State, by written notice to the local planning authority 'together with maps or plans sufficient to identify the proposed route of the road', states that he 'proposes to provide'.[18]

7   The land is subject to a compulsory purchase order empowering any authority to acquire rights over it[19] but notice to treat has not been served.[20]

---

11  1973 Act, s 68. When any prospective plans referred to in this section come into force, or fail to do so, a blight notice can no longer be served under it; but if a counter-notice has been served and is not yet disposed of (see below, p 259) the 'appropriate authority' may serve a substituted counter-notice 'specifying different grounds of objection' within 2 months after any such prospective plans have in fact come into force.

12  1971 Act, s 192 (1) (b).

13  1973 Act, s 68. (See footnote 11.)

14  1971 Act, s 192 (1) (c).

15  1971 Act, s 192 (1) (d).

16  1973 Act, s 69. Substituted counter-notices can be served as described in footnote 11 if a scheme or other comes into force. Land required under the Highways Act 1980, s 246, is also included (1973 Act, s 74): see below, p 256, footnote 11.

17  1971 Act, s 192 (1) (e).

18  1971 Act, s 192 (1) (f).

19  See for example the Local Government (Miscellaneous Provisions) Act 1976, s 13, and the Highways Act 1980, s 250.

20  1971 Act, s 192 (1) (g), as extended by 1973 Act s 75. A compulsory purchase order which has been publicised, but is still before the appropriate minister or Secretary of State and not yet made or rejected, now comes within this category (1973 Act, s 70).

8 The land is subject to a local authority's published intention to acquire it as part of a 'general improvement area' under Part II of the Housing Act 1969.[1]

9 The land is liable to be compulsorily purchased under a 'special enactment',[2] which means private legislation or subordinate legislation specifically referring to the land.

10 The land is covered by an effective compulsory purchase order,[3] but is not yet subject to a notice to treat.[4]

In addition to the above 'specified descriptions', Part V of the 1973 Act provides some more, as follows:

11 The land is included in a plan approved by resolution of the local planning authority[5] as shown to be required for the functions of some government department, local authority or statutory undertaker; or the local planning authority decide to safeguard it for development for any of those functions (whether or not the Secretary of State so directs).[6]

12 The land is included in a New Town designation order[7] which has been publicised in draft, or in such an order which has been approved.[8]

13 The land is included in a clearance area,[9] or is surrounded by or adjoining such an area and the local authority decide to acquire it. A counter-notice cannot then deny the intention to acquire.[10]

14 The land is included in a plan approved by resolution of the local highway authority of acquisition under s 246 of the Highways Act 1980; or the Secretary of State informs the local planning authority in

1 1971 Act, s 192 (1) (h).

2 Within the 'limits of deviation', if any, specified in it: 1971 Act, s 192 (1) (i).

3 Including one publicised but not yet made or rejected, under the provision mentioned in footnote 20 on p 254, above.

4 1971 Act, s 192 (1) (j). Notices to treat must be served within three years of the compulsory purchase order (see ch 4, p 60, above), as authorities know well.

5 When exercising any of their powers under Part III of the 1971 Act.

6 1973 Act, s 71.

7 Under the New Towns Act 1981, s 1.

8 1973 Act, s 72. A blight notice cannot be served in respect of a *draft* order after it has come into operation (since it may have been modified) or is rejected. The Secretary of State is the 'appropriate authority' (see above, p 252) for acquisition until a development corporation is established for the new town, but the Land Compensation Act 1961 applies in such a case as if a development corporation were in fact acquiring the land (see above, ch 7, in particular s 6 of the 1961 Act). He must transfer any land so acquired to the appropriate development corporation if a designation order is made which includes that land, or in other cases as he thinks fit.

9 Under the Housing Act 1957, Part III. 'Site value', plus 'well-maintained' and owner-occupiers' payments, apply accordingly.

10 1973 Act, s 73. For counter-notices see below, p 259, below.

writing that he means to acquire it under that section for a trunk or special road.[11]

15  The land is within the minimum width prescribed for new streets,[12] or fronts on to a new street and is within the minimum width prescribed for it,[13] and comprises all or part of a dwelling already built (or being built) when that width is prescribed or of the curtilage of such a dwelling. A counter-notice cannot then deny the intention to acquire.[14]

It is essential to note that no-one can serve a blight notice merely because purchasers fight shy of buying his land. It has to be clearly within one of the above 'specified descriptions'. If the line of a new road points straight to X's land, but stops short of it, that fact will no doubt be very ominous for X but will not of itself justify a blight notice. Nor will the 'zoning' of land in the development plan. In *Bolton Corpn v Owen*,[15] the owner-occupier of a house in an old part of a town centre served a blight notice on the local authority because the development plan included the property within 'an area scheduled for residential development'. That is to say it was 'zoned' for housing. He claimed that it was 'allocated for the purpose of (the) functions of a local authority', in that because of its position it was sure to be taken for clearance and new council housing. The Court of Appeal held that this contention was ill-founded, because 'the development plan is silent as to how the proposed development is to be carried out'. The Lands Tribunal had drawn the inference, from the facts of the case, that the area in which the house lay 'could as a matter of practical politics only be redeveloped by the local authority exercising its functions as such . . .'[16] But Willmer LJ pointed out that this sort of inference was not warranted in the light of the careful wording of the specified description, and said, 'I do not think it was permissible for the member of the Lands Tribunal to speculate upon the probability or otherwise of the area in question being cleared and re-developed by the appellants in the exercise of their functions as housing authority, rather than by private enterprise.' The specified descriptions, in other words, are plainly drafted in such a way as to rule out all cases of possible private development of land. The only apparent exception to this is private development at one remove, after acquisition of the land by a local authority 'for planning purposes' within the action area: in other words private development in a public context.

11  1973 Act, s 74. Such acquisitions are for dealing with adverse effects of highway works (see above, ch 11, pp 238–240).
12  By an order under the Highways Act 1980, s 188.
13  By an order under the Public Health Act 1925, s 30, applying bye-laws or local Acts.
14  1973 Act, s 76. But if the appropriate authority have already acquired an interest in the same land under a blight notice, or by agreement in lieu of one, no such notice can be served. For counter-notices, see below, p 259.
15  [1962] 1 QB 470, [1962] 1 All ER 101.
16  Contrast the 'practical possibility' argument in *Davy v Leeds Corpn* (ch 7, p 146, above).

4 INTERESTS QUALIFYING FOR PROTECTION

Interests 'qualifying for protection' must, in accordance with s 203 of the 1971 Act, be freeholds, or leaseholds with at least three years to run, held by an 'owner-occupier'. Owner-occupation requires physical occupation for at least six months, up to the date of service of the blight notice, or up to any date not more than 12 months before service of the notice provided that in the intervening period before service of the notice the land (except in the case of a farm) was unoccupied. The 12 months' period may be extended by any length of time required for deciding any dispute over which body is the 'appropriate authority'. Residential property must be occupied 'as a private dwelling'.[17] In *Minister of Transport v Holland*,[18] the Court of Appeal held that the owner of a house who had moved and left it empty but continued to store various belongings could not be regarded (contrary to the finding of the Lands Tribunal) as its 'owner-occupier'.

The unit of property must be either an 'agricultural unit'—a farm—or a 'hereditament'. The latter term is defined as 'the aggregate of the land which forms the subject of a single entry in the valuation list for the time being in force for a rating area'. Occupation of a hereditament, as distinct from a farm, need not be of the whole so long as it is of 'substantial part'. Occupation 'for the purposes of a partnership firm' counts as occupation by the firm—the 'partners for the time being'—and not any individual partner.[19] Business and other occupation, as distinct from residential or agricultural occupation, is subject to a value limit above which a hereditament is not subject to blight notice procedure. This is currently fixed at a net annual value for rating of £2,250.[20] In *Essex County Council v Essex Incorporated Congregational Church Union*,[1] a church and church hall were made the subject of a blight notice. They were entered in the rating list as 'exempt'. The House of Lords, reversing the Lands Tribunal and Court of Appeal, held that this meant the premises were not within the limit, 'Exempt' is not the same as 'nil'.

Section 79 of the Land Compensation Act 1973 provides that if a blight notice is served in respect of an interest 'qualifying for protection' in a farm and part of that farm is land not within any of the 'specified descriptions'—in other words, not officially 'blighted'—the 'unaffected (ie officially blighted) area' can be included in the notice on the ground that it cannot be reasonably farmed, even in combination with other

17  1971 Act, s 203 (3).
18  (1962) 14 P & CR 259.
19  1971 Act, ss 203, 204.
20  Town and Country Planning (Limit of Annual Value) Order 1973, SI 1974/425. This is, of course, intended to restrict the availability of blight notices in respect of business premises to 'the small man'. £2,250 was substituted for £750 in consequence of the rating revaluation which took effect on 1 April 1973.
1  [1963] AC 808, [1963] 1 All ER 326.

available land (if any) in the farm or in another 'agricultural unit' currently owner-occupied by the claimant either freehold or leasehold with three or more years to run. The possibility of challenging this inclusion will be considered below.[2]

## B. Serving a blight notice

### 1 NOTICES AND COUNTER-NOTICES

If all the foregoing requirements are satisfied an owner-occupier with an interest 'qualifying for protection' can be advised to serve a blight notice, under s 193 of the 1971 Act,[3] on the 'appropriate authority' by whom 'the land is liable to be acquired'.[4] He may do so whether his freehold or leasehold ownership extends to the whole or only to part of the 'hereditament', but not in respect of part only of the land over which his interest extends.[5] The same applies to a farm; but as stated above the *occupation*, as distinct from ownership, of a farm must be of the whole of the unit.[6]

Section 201 of the 1971 Act empowers a mortgagee, with a power of sale currently exercisable over his mortgagor's interest in all or part of a hereditament or farm (though not in respect of any mortgagor's interest subsisting in less than the area of the mortgagee's own interest),[7] to serve a blight notice in respect of the interest he is empowered to sell. He must have tried, and failed, to sell the interest on the open market at a reasonable price. He cannot serve the blight notice unless the mortgagor could have done so; but he is given an extra period of six months in which to serve it, plus any further period necessary to settle any outstanding dispute over which is the 'appropriate authority'.[8] But a mortgagee cannot serve a blight notice if the mortgagor has already served one which is still outstanding, and vice versa.[9]

If an owner-occupier with an interest 'qualifying for protection' dies

2 See p 262, below (1973 Act, ss 80–81); and compare with ch 5, p 105–108, above.
3 As amended by the 1973 Act, s 77.
4 Explained above, on p 253.
5 Thus if X, the freeholder of Blackacre, leased West Blackacre to Y for (say) 21 years, of which three or more remain unexpired, Y can serve a blight notice. But if X leased all Blackacre to Y, Y cannot serve a blight notice for West Blackacre.
6 1971 Act, s 203 (2). Sections 192, 193 and 203, when read together, suggest that an owner-occupier whose *interest* comprises only West Blackacre may serve a blight notice in respect of it even if only East Blackacre is blighted (by being within the specified descriptions) provided that he has made reasonable endeavours to sell his interest but failed because of that blight, and provided also that he *occupies* at least a 'substantial part' of Blackacre as a whole, or all of it if it is a farm. But the authority can say that they want only East Blackacre (see pp 259–262, below).
7 Ibid, s 201 (2).
8 1971 Act, ss 201 (1), (3), 205 (3) (b).
9 Ibid, s 201 (4).

before he has served a blight notice, his personal representative can do so instead, provided that he has made reasonable attempts to sell the land but, because of its actual or impending inclusion within any of the 'specified descriptions', he has failed to obtain a reasonable price, and provided also that no corporate body enjoys the beneficial interest. The land can be part of a hereditament or farm but not less than whatever part comprises the interest.[10]

The authority which receives the blight notice may accept it, in which case a normal compulsory purchase goes forward as described earlier in the chapter. Or they may challenge the blight notice, under s 194 of the 1971 Act, by serving a counter-notice within two months of the date of serving the blight notice (or of the date when any dispute over which body is the 'appropriate authority' is settled, if later). This counter-notice, which must be in a form currently prescribed in the Town and Country Planning General Regulations 1976,[11] must state one or more grounds for objection specified in ss 194 or 201 (6) of the 1971 Act. There are seven main grounds, but they come down in effect to four, as follows:

(1) No part of the land comes within 'the specified descriptions'.
(2) The claimant, when serving the blight notice, was not entitled to an interest 'qualifying for protection' in any part of the land.
(3) He has not genuinely tried and failed to sell the land for a reasonable price on the open market since it came within 'the specified descriptions'.
(4) They do not currently intend to acquire any of the land; or they intend to acquire only a specified part of the land. Alternatively in the case of two of the specified descriptions, they do not intend to acquire within the next *15 years*.[12] These two specified descriptions[13] are listed above as no. 1 and no. 3.[14]

Section 201 (6) of the 1971 Act empowers them to object, where appropriate, that any of the necessary requirements empowering a mortgagee to serve a blight notice is not fulfilled.

Where a personal representative serves a blight notice under s 78 of the

10 1973 Act, s 78 (1), (2). Special rules relating to counter-notices in these cases will be mentioned below. Nothing in the section empowers the serving of concurrent blight notices by a mortgagor and a mortgagee (s 78 (4), and see previous footnote).
11 SI 1976/1419 (reg 18 and First Sch).
12 This objection, if upheld, will tend to reduce the claimant's effective marketable interest to a term of 15 years. But see below, p 261, as to 'hardship'.
13 Town and Country Planning Act 1971, s 192 (1) (a) and (c). 'Development plan' includes structure and local plans in so far as they are currently in force: ibid, s 20 (1).
14 See p 254, above. They relate respectively to being shown: (i) in a structure plan as being needed for the functions of some public body or for an 'action area', or (ii) in a development plan as being the site, or part of the site, of a highway when constructed or altered.

1973 Act (referred to above[15]), the grounds upon which any counter-notice may be served are as follows:

(1) No part of the land comes within the 'specified descriptions'.
(2) The authority do not currently intend to acquire any of the land; or they intend to acquire only a specified part of the land.[16]
(3) The claimant is not the deceased's personal representative.
(4) The deceased was not entitled to an interest 'qualifying for protection' in the land.
(5) The claimant has not made any genuine attempt to sell at a reasonable price which was rendered unsuccessful because of the land's actual or impending inclusion within any of the 'specified descriptions'.
(6) A corporate body enjoys some or all of the beneficial interest.[17]

Section 256 of the 1971 Act empowers local authorities (including the GLC) to advance money to assist other persons to purchase the property in cases where the land is not required for 15 years, subject to any conditions which they may wish to impose. The land, if subject to rates, must be within the rateable value limit specified above.[18]

## 2 REFERENCE TO THE LANDS TRIBUNAL

The claimant who receives a counter-notice can only proceed if within two months he requires the objection raised by the authority that served it to be referred to the Lands Tribunal under s 195 of the 1971 Act. The burden of proof lies on the claimant in most cases; that is to say it is for him to satisfy the Lands Tribunal that the authority's objection is 'not well-founded'. But where the authority are objecting on the ground that they do not intend to acquire any of the land, or that they intend to acquire only part of it, or that they do not intend to acquire for ten years or some longer period, the burden of proof lies on them; so that in such cases the authority must satisfy the Lands Tribunal that their objection is 'well-founded'.

In *Bolton Corpn v Owen*, the Lands Tribunal wrongly found for the claimant on the basis that the burden of proof lay upon the authority to show that the claimant's land was not within 'the specified descriptions' and had not been discharged. The Court of Appeal pointed out that the decision would have to be reversed on this ground alone, apart from the substantive ground mentioned earlier.[19]

The words 'well-founded' are not very precise. In *Duke of Wellington Social Club and Institute Ltd v Blyth Borough Council*[20] the Lands

15 See above, p 259.
16 Section 194 of the 1971 Act applies here (see above, p 259).
17 1973 Act, s 78 (3).
18 Currently £2,250: see p 257, above.
19 See p 256, above.
20 (1964) 15 P & CR 212.

Tribunal held that where an authority object that they do not intend to acquire, such an objection can be judged to be 'not well-founded' if the consequence of it will be to inflict hardship on the claimant. This can perhaps be summed up in two propositions. The first is that a (genuine) lack of intention to acquire is a policy matter on which *the authority alone* are competent to pronounce; and as a general rule such lack of intention must be accepted for fear of imposing unreasonable burdens of acquisition on authorities. But the second proposition is that hardship to claimants is as serious in principle as hardship to authorities; and therefore authorities ought to bow to claimants in individual cases where hardship to the latter is sufficiently established. It is hoped that this view will prevail.[1]

In *Mancini v Coventry City Council*,[2] the claimant's property had been shown in the development plan as part of a site to be redeveloped for educational purposes (Lanchester College). The authority's counternotice to his blight notice was upheld on the ground that the plan had been altered to include the premises in a residential zone. This was said to have 'alleviated' hardship for the claimant, though not to have eliminated it.

If the Lands Tribunal upholds the objection, the blight notice fails, unless the objection is that only part of the land is required, in which case the notice succeeds but only in respect of that part.[3] If a compulsory purchase order is in force, a successful blight notice merely hastens the acquisition under that order, so that all that remains is to assess compensation. In such cases s 197 of the 1971 Act makes it clear that any special rules of assessment, either in relation to slum clearance under Part III of the Housing Act 1957,[4] or to 'minimum compensation' under s 117 of the 1971 Act,[5] still apply. But s 199 of the 1971 Act provides that if a compulsory purchase order or a special enactment is in force, and the 'appropriate authority' successfully object to a blight notice on the ground that they do not intend to take any of the land, or that they only intend to take a specified part of it, then the order or enactment 'shall cease to have effect', either completely, if the authority do not intend to take any of the land, or partly, if they do not intend to take part of it.[6]

Where a blight notice served in respect of a farm includes an 'unaffected area' as provided in s 79 of the 1973 Act (referred to above[7]), any

1 It is particularly important if the appropriate authority resist a blight notice on the ground that the land is not needed for the next 15 years (see above, p 259).
2 (1982) 44 P & CR 114.
3 See *Lake v Cheshire County Council* (below, p 262, note 12).
4 For 'cleared site' value see ch 8, pp 166–167, above.
5 See ch 11, p 233, above.
6 Otherwise the authority could cynically deny an intention to acquire, and then acquire later when it suited them to do so. Yet they can procure a fresh authorisation.
7 See above, p 257.

counter-notice may, under s 80, allege that the assertion that the 'unaffected area' cannot reasonably be farmed is not justified; what is more, it *must* do so if it alleges also that the authority only wish to take a specified part of the 'affected (ie officially blighted) area'.[8] If the Lands Tribunal upholds the counter-notice on the first ground and no other, it must declare the blight notice to be valid in respect of all the 'affected area' but not more. If it upholds the counter-notice on *both* grounds, but no other ground, it must declare the blight notice valid only in respect of the part of the 'affected area' the authority require and no more. In either case it must specify a date for the deemed notice to treat.

If the Lands Tribunal upholds, or the claimant concedes, an allegation in a counter-notice that an assertion under s 79 of the 1973 Act that the 'unaffected area' of a farm cannot be reasonably farmed is not justified, with the consequence that a blight notice is restricted to the 'affected area', or to the part of that area which the authority require and no more, s 81 deems the 'appropriate authority' to be authorised to acquire that land and to have served notice to treat on the date specified under s 80 (above) or the date on which the claimant conceded, as the case may be.[9] But if any 'unaffected area', or any part of an 'affected area' which the authority say they do not require, is in fact included in a blight notice after all, the compensation for it must not include prospective development value.[10]

In cases where an authority object that they only acquire part of the land specified in a blight notice, the claimant may always assert his right under s 8 of the Compulsory Purchase Act 1965, as discussed in an earlier chapter,[11] to demand that they take all or nothing. If this happens, then the Lands Tribunal, in deciding whether or not the objection should be upheld, must also apply the 'material detriment' and 'amenity or convenience' rules, in accordance with that section, if the property is 'a house, building or manufactory' or 'a park or garden belonging to a house'.[12]

---

8　In such a case the Lands Tribunal must regard the remainder of the 'affected area' as other available land which may, if combined with the '*un*affected area', cause the latter to be capable of being reasonably farmed after all.

9　Section 81 applies where a personal representative acts in place of a deceased claimant just as it does in other cases.

10　As specified in the 1973 Act, s 5 (see above, ch 9, p 190).

11　See ch 5, pp 101–104, above.

12　1971 Act, s 202. See *Lake v Cheshire County Council* (1976) 32 P & CR 143, in which the Lands Tribunal found that the land in question did not fall within s 8 of the 1965 Act. On the general question whether the authority were entitled to resist a blight notice for an entire property when they wished to take only part, their counter-notice to this effect was upheld because it was found on the facts that there would be no 'detriment' to the land not taken if they succeeded in taking only part.

Part four

# Betterment taxation and planning compensation

Chapter 14

# Betterment and development value taxation

## A. Betterment as an overall rise in value

### 1 DIRECT LEVY, SET-OFF AND RECOUPMENT

In 1427, a statute of Henry VI gave authority to commissioners to impose upon landowners a levy in respect of improvements in value accruing to their lands in consequence of the building of sea walls which protected those lands from flooding.[1] A power to distrain was given in order to deal with landowners who refused to pay. These 'commissioners of sewers' as they were called—'sewers' being until recent times a term referring to land drainage rather than household drainage—have had a continuous history down to the present day; though they are now constituted as river authorities. Their mode of finance has been transformed into a system of levying rates, but distress is still used for enforcement.[2]

In the seventeenth century, Acts were passed for redevelopment in London, both before and after the Great Fire, and they provided for the levying of charges on owners of property of which the value was increased—'melioration' was the term used—by public works such as street widening. In default of agreement juries would be empanelled, as under the Lands Clauses Acts later, to assess disputed values.[3]

In the nineteenth century further Acts were passed, again notably in respect of London, providing for the levying of charges on the improvement of property values in consequence of public works. It was assumed, on the other hand, that losses would normally be compensated for in the form of compulsory purchase compensation, either by way of purchase price or of injurious affection; and courts settling compensation disputes in such cases, whenever the law was in issue, took the line that increases in values could not be dealt with, even by way of 'set-off' against compensation, unless statute clearly so provided. In other words, although compensation for losses in land values, and levies on gains in land values, were each to some extent provided for by law, they were so provided quite separately and piecemeal, despite the fact that on a general viewing they could be regarded as the two sides of the same coin.

1 Uthwatt Report 1942, ch IX.
2 General Rate Act 1967, Part VI.
3 Uthwatt Report, ch IX.

The account in earlier chapters of this book of compensation provisions has already shown how even compensation was legislated for in a haphazard manner. The law giving authority for charges to be imposed on increases in land values was more haphazard still.

By this time the word 'betterment' had come into use, together with a variation in methods of levy. The London County Council obtained statutory powers for various public works in a series of Acts, beginning shortly after the Council came into existence in 1889, and tried three different methods. The first was the direct levy or 'improvement charge', as under the legislation of earlier times. This was soon dropped, largely as a result of its unpopularity. The second and third were called 'set-off' and 'recoupment'. 'Set-off' was limited in its effect for this reason, that it could only occur when compensation was being paid and could only, even when established, be deducted to the extent of any compensation being paid to the same owner. Perhaps because it was of limited scope (though erratic in consequence of its limitations, and even unfair, in that owners would only be caught by it in as much as they had a coincidental claim to compensation) it was used in other private local Acts and also in some public general Acts. Eventually it found its way into the Land Compensation Act 1961, as discussed in an earlier chapter,[4] and is generally applicable in cases of compulsory purchase compensation today.

'Recoupment' was less restricted in scope. At first sight it does not seem to have found much favour except in private local Acts. Nevertheless the general system of compulsory purchase of land 'for planning purposes' seems wide enough to make the practice of 'recoupment' possible today in all but name; and the practice of co-operation between local authorities and private developers in a 'consortium points to the mode of its effective operation.[5] 'Recoupment', whether called by that name or not, depends on the acquisition by a public authority, of sufficient land for a project of development to make it possible to resell (or lease) some of that land, after using the rest for the project, at values enhanced by that project. This kind of enterprise, however, may only be appropriate to projects of general urban redevelopment, rather than to particular projects involving compulsory acquisition, such as for building schools or hospitals. To put it another way, the enhancement of value of land by projects of public authorities is perhaps unlikely except where urban redevelopment, and maybe road development, is being undertaken.[6] Also, the value that is enhanced is perhaps likely to be prospective development value as much as existing use value; and this in turn raises questions of planning control.

4 See ch 7, p 146, above.
5 On this, see O. Marriott *The Property Boom.*
6 See the observations of Lord Denning, MR in *Wilson v Liverpool City Council* (ch 7, p 130, above).

A prominent example of a project in which 'recoupment' played a part was the construction by the London County Council of Kingsway and Aldwych, completed in 1905. In an account of the whole enterprise published for the official opening, the Clerk of the Council wrote:

The total estimate of the gross cost of the complete scheme of improvements, without deducting recoupment, was . . . put at £6,120,380. The recoupment from the disposal of building land was estimated at £4,363,200, thus leaving the cost which would ultimately fall upon the rate-payers at £1,757,180.

He went on to comment:

This result is most encouraging, and shows that the policy advocated by Mr Shaw-Lefevre of allowing the Council to acquire sufficient property to enable it to benefit from the improved values caused by the improvement, instead of leaving the improved values to adjoining owners, is the best practical means for carrying out what is needed in London. [7]

The upshot of these developments, however, was to show that 'set-off' and 'recoupment', though relatively effective for securing 'betterment' for the public benefit, are limited in scope. When public general legislation appeared in the field of town and country planning, the general question of taxing betterment reverted to the direct method, betterment charges. Thus the Town and Country Planning Act 1932 provided that, where a planning scheme could be shown to have produced 'betterment', a levy of 75% should be imposed on the owners of the land enjoying that 'betterment'. This was intended to be the counterpart of paying compensation to owners whose land was depreciated—'injuriously affected'—by the scheme. But little or nothing was in fact obtained by way of betterment charges under the Act of 1932.

## 2 THE UTHWATT REPORT

The Second World War produced a new attitude to the question of land use, including the control of land values; and the need to prepare for reconstruction after the war led, among other things, to the setting up of an expert committee on Compensation and Betterment under the chairmanship of Lord Justice Uthwatt. The Final Report of that Committee, [8] known generally as the *Uthwatt Report* and published in 1942, produced an elaborate scheme of proposals.

The underlying principle of the Uthwatt Report was that 'betterment' should be appropriated to a large extent by the community or the state. It

---

7 *Opening of Kingsway and Aldwych by His Majesty the King, Accompanied by Her Majesty the Queen* (King Edward VII and Queen Alexandra), 18 October 1905; published by the London County Council (pp 12 to 13). The Rt Hon G. J. Shaw-Lefevre (Lord Eversley) was Chairman of the Improvements Committee of the LCC, 1898 to 1900. He was also First Commissioner of Works in Gladstone's fourth cabinet (1892–94) and President of the Local Government Board in Lord Rosebery's cabinet (1894–95).

8 Cmnd 6386 (published September 1942).

set down a definition of 'betterment' as it was then generally understood, namely, 'any increase in the value of land (including the buildings thereon) *arising from central or local government action*, whether positive, eg by the execution of public works or improvements, or negative, eg by the imposition of restrictions on other land'. It drew what it regarded as a fundamental distinction between 'developed land' and 'undeveloped land'; and it defined 'development', by and large, in terms of *half* the modern statutory definition of that word in the Act of 1971,[9] namely building and other operations or works of construction, but not changes of use. The prospect of development, and the value of that prospect, were not related directly to the definition of 'betterment'. And unfortunately for precision of thought, it was not realised that 'central or local government action' must be clearly given the meaning of *'particular* projects or restrictions causing *particular* increases in the value of nearby land', as against 'projects and restrictions in general'.

One main set of proposals concerned the bulk of *undeveloped* land, being land in the country as distinct from the towns. Developed land in the country and undeveloped land in the towns were excluded from these proposals. They were that owners should be deprived of all value of prospective development of undeveloped land in the country, on being paid compensation once-for-all for the loss, and should retain only the existing use value. The prospective development value should go to the state. When a project of development for any such land was sanctioned, the land (at its existing use value) would be bought by the state, which would then *lease* it to the developer on the same sort of terms as a private lessor would lease land for development. The owner from whom the land was taken should be given preference if he himself wished to do the development. This can be summed up as the system for expropriating development rights.[10]

The other main set of proposals concerned *all land when developed*. There should be a general valuation, every five years, in conjuction with rating valuations, wherein each 'hereditament' for rating was to have the annual value of its site assessed at its existing use. The first such valuation would provide a 'datum'. Every quinquennial valuation after the first should, if producing a figure higher than the 'datum', have the 'datum' value deducted from it; and improvements to the land—actual development, in other words—should have their value deducted likewise. The remainder, if any, was 'betterment'. A charge of 75% (as under the 1932 Act) was then to be levied upon this 'betterment'. It would be an annual value in each case; but the levy would be retrospective because it was based on 'betterment' which had occurred during the previous quinquennium. All calculations would be made in relation to the original

9 Section 22.
10 Uthwatt Report, ch IV.

'datum'; and if a revaluation produced an annual value figure which, with the allowed cost of improvements, fell below the original 'datum', then no annual betterment levy would be charged in the ensuing quinquennium. This can be summed up as the system for betterment levy on annual values of developed sites.

In effect, three types of landed property (excluding special categories such as land owned by the Crown, charities, and so forth) need to be distinguished in regard to the proposed working of these two related sets of proposals. The first is developed land, whether in towns or in the country; the second is undeveloped land in towns; the third is undeveloped land in the country.

Developed land in towns and in the country would be subject to the system of betterment levy on annual values straight away. Further development would require permission only if the land came within a planning scheme under the Act of 1932. Whether this was the case or not, the cost of development works would be set off against any increase in value, arising from market demand and availability for development,[11] at the next quinquennial revaluation.

Undeveloped land in towns would come under planning control under the 1932 Act in the same way as developed land. Demand and availability might increase its value; but valuation for betterment would not occur until the land was actually developed in accordance with any necessary permission. Presumably the 'datum' for that land would be fixed at that valuation but not before.

Undeveloped land in the country would come under planning control just the same as land in the other two categories. But development value would have been transferred to the state in return for payment. Again, valuation for betterment would not occur until the land was actually developed, and would then fix the 'datum' for it.

It should be noted that betterment levy would, like rates, fall on the occupier of land, whether he was paying a rent or had acquired it for a lump sum purchase price, or a combination of the two. This is because, in the words of the Report, the levy ought to be 'borne by the person who is for the time being in enjoyment of the increase'. Like a lump sum purchase price, a rent fixed at the beginning of a tenancy would not be affected by the increase, which would therefore accrue to the tenant and not the landlord. But if the tenancy included a rent revision clause, as many modern leases and tenancies do, that might well mean that the levy should fall on the landlord to the extent of the revision increase.

A subtle question now arises as a result of the Uthwatt Report proposals; did they in fact alter the meaning of 'betterment'? There seems to be nothing in the Report to say that they were intended to do so. Liability to betterment charges depended, of course, on there being increases in

11 See *Viscount Camrose v Basingstoke Corpn* (ch 8, p 150, above).

value of land. Now, if the accepted definition of betterment was unchanged, the Report will have been attributing such increases in the value of land, after deducting the actual cost of works ('improvements'), to 'central or local government action, whether positive . . . or negative'.[12] It is clear that this means public works and restrictions but *not* private development or any other factor, such as inflation. Yet the mode of identifying and taxing 'betterment' was deliberately chosen so as to avoid having to identify the cause of that 'betterment' (other than the actual cost of work). Hence it begins to look as if 'betterment' for the purposes of the Uthwatt scheme of charges was intended to mean, in principle, *increase in value from any cause whatever* (other than the actual cost of works). There might of course be no practical difference between this and 'central or local government action', but only so long as no factor other than 'central or local government action' came into play. This would be a foolish assumption to make on any long view, as the course of post-war inflation has shown; and doubtful even on the short view. In any case the theoretical difference is clear enough.

## B. Betterment as prospective development value

### 1 EXPROPRIATION OF PROSPECTIVE DEVELOPMENT VALUE

Thus the tacit definition of 'betterment' underlying the Uthwatt Report's proposals seems to have been wider than the stated definition in the Report. But a possible third definition was also implied in the Report, by virtue of the scheme for expropriating development rights in undeveloped land in the country. This, it will be remembered,[13] consisted of the expropriation of prospective development value by the state, in return for a once-for-all payment for compensation, leaving the owner in each case with the land and its existing use value. The Report did not treat this as the taking of betterment. Indeed the scheme for betterment charges, based on quinquennial valuations of the annual value of developed sites, would have applied to such land as much as to any other land, after the state had leased it out to developers and they had developed it. Moreover there was apparently no suggestion of imposing any levy on compensation, either the once-for-all compensation on expropriation of these prospective development values, or any compensation payable under the 1932 Act system for planning restrictions, despite the

---

12 See p 268, above.
13 See pp 268–269, above. As a result of the difference in meanings of the term 'betterment', the term 'worsenment' ('worsement' in the Uthwatt Report) is no less ambiguous. In America the late Professor Donald Hagman (of Los Angeles University) and colleagues have favoured 'windfalls' (see below, p 277) and 'wipeouts' as synonymous for 'betterment' and 'worsenment' (or 'depreciation') respectively. See their book *Windfalls for Wipeouts* (West Publishing Corp, 1978).

fact that such compensation would represent land values. (All that the Report did here was to recommend a reduction in scope of planning compensation). Nevertheless the distinction between existing use value and prospective development value, and the proposal that the state should take over the latter, led in fact to the post-war system for both identifying and taxing 'betterment'. It was unconsciously implied, in other words, that 'betterment' could be identical with 'prospective development value'.

The Town and Country Planning Act 1947 enacted a thorough-going two-part reform of the system for the public control of land use in this country. The first part, planning control of development, is with us today and maybe for a long time to come, having survived various major changes in political direction. The second part, control of land values, did not long survive the first of those major political changes. But it seems to be inescapable that, rightly or wrongly, the two parts went together, and the survival of one without the other has produced a highly anomalous situation. The situation immediately after 1947 need not have been regarded as sacrosanct, certainly; but even if unacceptable, it did require a more intelligent adjustment than it in fact received.

The Act of 1947 did not adopt the Uthwatt proposals, except partially in matters of detail; though the underlying spirit was no doubt very similar. The system of planning control, then *and now*, rests on the assumption that the existing use of land—and the value of that use—is the owner's; but the prospect of developing the land—and the value of that prospect—is the community's. If the value, on the other hand, is *not* regarded in this way, the financial result of planning control is peculiar, as is the case today. Thus, X wishes to develop his land in 1984. There is a market demand for its development. If for good planning reasons the local planning authority give permission, X would get existing value plus prospective development value. If for equally good planning reasons they do not, X would be left with existing use value only. Merit is irrelevant. The good of the community rules the decision. The world of property owners is thus divided in true Gilbertian style into the happy ones who get high values in the wake of planning permissions and the unhappy ones who do not.[14]

The 1947 Act provided an answer for this; and if that answer was too drastic to be acceptable it ought to have been displaced in favour of something no less internally consistent. The 1947 answer was this: planning control plus development at the disposal of the community, therefore prospective development value should by the same token be put at the disposal of the community also. After all (the assumption goes)

14 Compare the song from 'The Mikado' beginning: 'See how the fates their gifts allot. A is happy, B is not . . .' (etc). This song might be thought to have an affinity with the *Pointe Gourde* doctrine (see above, ch 7, p 129).

those owners who effectively realise development value, have paid for their land in its existing use, and they pay to develop it; but they do not pay for prospective development value. That is a windfall, created by all the infinitely various actions, individual and collective, of members of the community which affect land; therefore, if it goes to anyone, by right it should go to the community. This may be repugnant, but it is logical.

What this means is that 'prospective development value' was treated in 1947, and is treated now, as the equivalent of 'betterment'. It seems pretty certain that the Uthwatt Report's proposals for expropriation of development rights led to this result. Betterment levy under the Land Commission Act 1967 certainly went on the assumption that 'betterment' has this meaning[15] and all that has happened since then is that the taxation of betterment has been transferred from the levy to capital gains tax (though subsequently it was decided to tax development gains as income[16]) and then to development land tax. Thus in effect we continue to have betterment levy; and no new meaning of 'betterment' has emerged.

On the 'appointed day', 1 July 1948, when the Act of 1947 came into effect, the prospective development value of all land was transferred to the state,[17] and planning control over the development of all land came into effect. All freeholders and leaseholders of land already enjoying prospective development value at that date were invited to submit claims for compensation to a central government body set up to handle the matter, the Central Land Board.[18] From the same date, all persons who obtained planning permission for development of land were to be liable to pay a 'development charge' in respect of the whole of the prospective development value of the land accruing in consequence of the permission—a 'betterment levy' of 100%.[19] Whether the value did accrue, and what its amount would be, would naturally depend on market demand as well as planning permission; and its calculation was just as much a normal question of valuation expertise after the 'appointed day' as before it.

But it should not be supposed that compensation for loss of development value on the one hand, and the development charge on the other, simply cancelled each other out. The compensation was to be once-for-all, as in the Uthwatt scheme. But schemes of development are not once-for-all. Land can be subjected to a series of developments. Therefore each would have attracted a development charge, if permitted, tailored to the development value it would create. Indeed, a series of develop-

15 Land Commission Act 1967, s 27 (1).
16 See below, p 276.
17 See the diagram set out in ch 16, on p 317, below.
18 1947 Act, Part VI.
19 Ibid, Part VII.

ments one after the other, may continue indefinitely into the future. Nor on the other hand was there any reason why a particular project, and its value, would embrace the entire development value in existence in respect of land on the 'appointed day'. There might be a series of minor development projects before the full development potential, as it existed in 1948, was realised.

## 2 ONCE-FOR-ALL COMPENSATION

Part VI of the 1947 Act provided for the system of submitting claims for compensation. A 'global fund' of £300 million was set up; and established claims were scheduled to met in 1953, against this fund, in the form of an allotment of government stock. Claims had to be submitted to the Central Land Board, which after negotiation either rejected them or accepted them with or without modification. Very small claims were not to be accpeted at all, under what came to be called the 'de minimis' rule. The actual basis of calculation of loss was to be the difference between the 'unrestricted' and the 'restricted' value of the claimant's interest; and the 'restricted' value rested on an assumption that planning permission would only be granted for the limited categories of development within the Third Schedule to the Act, which will be discussed in a later chapter.[20] These categories represent very little departure from the existing (or recent) use of the land, and are therefore often known by the paradoxical name of 'existing use development'. In practice, valuers normally treat 'existing use development' value as an integral (and marginal) part of existing use value—except perhaps in so far as the value of the right to rebuild a destroyed building or structure is substantially different from the value of the derelict site per se.

In the event of the 'global fund' being insufficient, certain types of claim were given a prior right to settlement in full—depending on the amount of near readiness in practice, or 'ripeness', for the land for actual development—and the rest were to be settled as fully as possible in proportion. It was calculated in due course that in fact the accepted claims would exceed the fund, and that claims without priority could only be met up to 80%. Then in 1951, the first of the major political changes referred to on p 271, above took place. After a delay, the system of development charges was abolished. As a result it was decided that there was no need to pay any compensation. The 'global fund', the established claims upon it, and the Central Land Board, all became redundant. Nevertheless the established claims were not forgotten but presently applied, after further delay, in a strangely modified manner, which will be considered in the next chapter.

20 See ch 16, p 316, below.

3 BETTERMENT LEVY AND CAPITAL GAINS TAX

In 1965, 'betterment', in its post-war sense of prospective development value, was once more subjected to tax. This came at the end of a decade and a half of freedom during which it was never really clear whether the notion that the community should have any share in betterment was totally rejected de jure or merely suspended de facto. In 1964 there had occurred the second of the above-mentioned major political changes, which resulted in a swing back in favour of that notion. This time the government decided not to act on the view that planning control logically entailed the total transfer of prospective development value to the community, but instead to treat the question more or less as a taxing operation. In other words, 100% development charges were not re-introduced nor was there a once-for-all compensation scheme. But it was made clear that 'betterment' was still to be identified with prospective development value; and a system was devised whereby a share of it should be appropriated for the community's benefit. No move was made back to the pre-Uthwatt concept of betterment, as an overall rise in value of particular land—without differentiation betwen its existing use and the prospect of development—occuring as a result of 'central or local government action'.

The Finance Act 1965 introduced capital gains tax; and for two years 'betterment' was included under the general heading of capital gains, and taxed accordingly. But this was meant to be a temporary arrangement; and in 1967 the taxation of this asset, as had been intended, was given separate attention by the introduction of 'betterment levy'.

Part III of the Land Commission Act 1967 enacted the provisions governing the levy. Section 27 (1) stated: 'A levy, to be called "betterment levy" . . . shall . . . be charged where the development value, or part of the development value, of land is realised on or after (6 April 1967).' Six 'Cases', lettered from A to F, covered the various situations. All except Case C comprised the realisation of 'development value' in money terms on outright sale, grant of a tenancy, receipt of compensation, or receipt of money for granting or relaxation of rights in alieno solo. The rate of levy was fixed at 40%,[1] though some increase of this was foreshadowed.

The two principal categories were Case A and Case C, the other four cases being largely variations on the basic theme of Case A. Under Case C an owner would obtain permission for 'material development' of land and begin to carry it out himself. 'Material development meant development which was not merely marginal in scope.[2] Under Case A the owner would dispose of land to a purchaser with the benefit of planning

---

1 Betterment Levy (Prescribed Rate) Order 1967, SI 1967/544.
2 Land Commission Act 1967, s 99 (2); Material Development Regulations 1967, SI 1967/494.

permission. Each of these occurrences was a 'chargeable act or event' by virtue of which 'the development value . . . is taken to be realised', thus giving rise to liability to pay levy. The levy was always payable in money; and under all Cases except C the development value was realised in money as well: so that the money was there out of which to pay the levy (and pocket the remainder). But under Case C the development value was only realised in terms of land value, so that the money would need to be obtained from elsewhere to pay the levy: no hardship in theory, yet likely to be so in practice.

The calculation was made by taking 'market value'—the purchase price received in money under a normal Case A disposition, but enjoyed as land value and not money under Case C—and deducting from it the 'base value', plus any relevant ancillary expenditure. 'Base value' could be, at the levy payer's option, either the price paid on a previous transfer of the land (subject to certain exceptions),[3] which was appropriate where a *previous* owner had obtained planning permission, or else the 'current use value', plus 10%[4] (in special cases 20%),[5] plus any compensation for severance, which was appropriate where the *present* owner had obtained planning permission. 'Market value' under Case C required, however, a notional calculation involving notional or actual rent capitalised, since there would be no actual sum realised in any transaction.[6]

Public bodies did not pay levy, nor did statutory undertakers or charities for land used for their functional purposes.[7] Vendors to public bodies, however, paid levy just as if the purchaser was a private person, unless selling to the Land Commission itself, which deducted the levy at source.[8] (The Land Commission also had important functions involving the acquisition and disposal of land, but these were separate from its collection of levy.[9]) Disputes over assessment of levy were to be referred to the Lands Tribunal.[10]

On the third major political change, in 1970, there appeared once more to be a swing away from the notion that the community should have a share in betterment. The Land Commission (Dissolution) Act 1971 abolished the Commission and declared that levy was not payable on acts or events after 22 July 1970. But development value of land did not go free. Capital gains tax once again took the place of betterment levy for the purpose of taxing betterment, as it had done from 1965 to 1967.[11]

3 Land Commission Act 1967, Fifth Schedule.
4 Ibid, Fourth Schedule.
5 This and other modifications of levy were enacted in the Finance Act 1969, ss 43–49.
6 Land Commission Act 1967, Fourth Schedule, Part III.
7 Ibid, ss 56–59, 63, 84.
8 Ibid, s 73.
9 Ibid, Part II.
10 Ibid, ss 47–49.
11 Finance Act 1971, s 55. The rate of capital gains tax was basically 30% (Finance Act 1965, s 20 (3)). From 1967 to 1971 it was charged on the existing use value only, not the

Subsequently Parliament decided to tax development gains as income.[12] But by this time, in 1974, a fourth major political change opened the way to yet another attempt to tax betterment on a separate basis by the introduction of development land tax.

## C. Development land tax

### 1 'WINDFALLS' AND WHITE PAPER

On 12 September 1974 the White Paper *Land*[13] was published, an event already referred to in chapter 12. For the foundation of future policy it raised what may be regarded as a moral issue, namely that development value in land should be 'restored to the community'. No evidence has ever been adduced to show that development value in land is, or ever was, in any way the property of 'the community', that is to say the nation or people; though this does not of course mean that a case cannot be made for transferring it to them. On the other hand it is hard to see that anyone else is 'entitled' to it either, in any moral sense, though owners of property have since time immemorial been able to realise and enjoy it. Development is paid for, in hard cash or by hard work; but development value is not. Since the latter is the value merely of the *prospect* of development, this distinction is plain enough.

Prospective development value, *alias* betterment in the modern connotation of that term, is a market phenomenon. So long as there is a market in land there will always be a likelihood of some prospective development value being enjoyed by persons with land to sell, if circumstances are right in particular cases. Since all modern legislation on land, on compulsory purchase, on taxation, and on related subjects, presupposes the continuance of a land market, it must presuppose also the continuance of prospective development value in land essentially unchanged. Indeed no basis for land valuation other than market value which is not purely arbitrary has ever been seriously envisaged. It is true that the White Paper *Land* looked to the evolution of a 'new land market', but the nature of this marvel is not revealed: perhaps it was a misprint for a 'nil land market' and pardonably left to the imagination.

So there is very little morality on either side of the question of whether prospective development value should be in private or public ownership. Americans have developed the habit of calling it a 'windfall', and so it is.

development value of land, since the latter was subject to levy. For a case illustrating the incidence of tax on 'betterment' during the period 1971–76, see *Watkins v Kidson* (above, ch 8, p 154).

12 Finance Act 1974, s 38, enacting for a temporary period proposals put forward by the government in office in December 1973.

13 Cmnd 5730.

What remains to be considered therefore is expediency. It might be thought expedient to transfer some of this 'windfall' from private to public pockets. The White Paper *Land* duly proposed this, but took the view that in principle the whole of it should be transferred, with the concession that some small fraction should probably be left for private persons to enjoy. The obvious way to transfer the 'windfall' was to tax it, at 100 per cent or some lesser rate according to taste.[14]

The eventual outcome of all this in terms of taxation is the Development Land Tax Act 1976, which was brought into effect on 1 August 1976.[15] Subject to considerable later modification, it remains law today.

## 2 REALISED DEVELOPMENT VALUE

Development land tax is levied not on development value but on '*realised* development value'. There are two kinds of occurrence when development value is to be treated as 'realised': (i) when an owner actually disposes of an interest in land; (ii) when he is deemed to do so.[16] 'Interest in land' is widely defined to include any estate or interest in or any right in or over land or affecting its use or disposition, but *not* interests of mortgagees or chargees (other than owners of rentcharges) or beneficiaries under settlements.[17] Thus most legal and many equitable rights are covered. 'Disposals' include assignments of part of the property, and grants of lesser rights in it, and also cases of depreciation for which compensation is received.[18]

Any transaction within reason is, in principle, a disposal (except as regards land in an 'enterprise zone').[19] Compulsory purchases are included as well as free market transactions. Essentially, a disposition of land otherwise than by way of gift occurs in two stages: contract, followed by conveyance, the former transferring title to the recipient in equity and the latter doing so at common law. The 1976 Act provides that the date of a disposal in furtherance of a contract is the date when the contract becomes unconditionally binding.[20]

The effect of this in regard to compulsory purchase was in issue in *IRC v Metrolands (Property Finance) Ltd*.[1] Notice to treat was deemed to be served in respect of the taxpayers' land, by virtue of a purchase notice,

---

14 The Community Land Act 1975, ss 7 and 25, envisaged an alternative method in certain cases, which was to exclude it from compulsory purchase compensation assessments as from a 'second appointed day'. That day never arrived, because the Act was repealed (see above, ch 11, p 230).
15 Development Land Tax (Appointed Day) Order 1976, SI 1976/1148.
16 Development Land Tax Act 1976, ss 1, 2.
17 Ibid, s 46.
18 Ibid, s 3.
19 Finance Act 1980, s 110, which exempts all such land from the tax.
20 Development Land Tax Act, s 45.
 1 [1982] 2 All ER 557.

before 1 August 1976 when the tax was brought into effect; but compensation was not settled until 11 August 1976. Notice to treat, as stated in an earlier chapter,[2] does not constitute a contract until compensation is settled in accordance with it, therefore the House of Lords held that there was no disposal until the later date.

An owner is *deemed* to dispose of his interest in land (and immediately to reacquire it) at market value, provided that it is a 'major interest', immediately before the start of a project of 'material development' on that land.[3] Any interest is a 'major interest' unless (a) it is currently valued at less than £5,000 and gives no right to possession or (b) it exists totally in reversion to a leasehold term exceeding 35 years[4] and does not benefit from any development value in the land. 'Material development' is development *outside*: (i) the classes of any general development order which is then in force,[5] (ii) comparable categories prescribed in the Act itself.[6] These categories are: (1) altering buildings, including enlargement by up to *one-third* in cubic content above their original size (this was raised from *one-tenth* by the Finance Act 1981, s 133); (2) rebuilding buildings currently in existence or destroyed within the previous ten years, including similar enlargement by up to *one-tenth*; (3) increasing any use (dating back to 12 September 1974) within any building or other land by up to *one-tenth*, in cubic content or area respectively; (4) resuming a previous use of land after a period of disuse or some temporary use; (5) carrying out building or other operations relating to use of land for agriculture or forestry, or for advertisements, or for car-parking (up to six years only); and (6) making certain changes of use (with or without intervening periods of disuse). These changes of use are changes strictly *within* one of the following: (i) residential and non-residential non-profit-making uses; (ii) shop and office uses; (iii) hotel and related uses; (iv) industrial and storage uses; (v) other general commercial uses. Increases in cubic content referred to above are, however, to be disregarded in so far as they relate to fire-escapes, to garages and parking, to lifts or stairs, or to heating or air-conditioning or similar installations. (Groups of buildings within one curtilage are treated as single buildings.) Increases in cubic content are calculated in relation to the *original* building—ie as it existed on 12 September 1974, or as it was first built if later than that date. 'Material development' is thus development which is not on an insignificant scale.

Any actual or prospective owner intending to develop land may give

2  Chapter 2, p 24, above. For deemed service of a notice to treat in the case of a purchase notice, see above, ch 12, p 246.
3  Development Land Tax Act 1976, s 2 and Sch 1.
4  It is assumed that tenants will exercise options to extend or renew their tenancies (ibid, s 44).
5  Ibid, s 7 (7).
6  Ibid, Sch 4, Part II.

advance notice of this to the Inland Revenue; and then, provided that the development is started within two years of that notification, liability to the tax will be assessed as at the time of the notification regardless of changes (notably increases) in market values in the meantime. The notice can be withdrawn; and it becomes void at the end of the two-year period if development has not started. No other party, for example a tenant or a reversioner, is affected.[7]

In short, therefore, an owner is in essence liable to the tax if he either develops his land himself or sells it to a developer. The tax he will actually have to pay, if any, is found by taking the price at which the land is sold (or *deemed* to be sold) on a particular occasion later than 1 August 1976, and deducting any incidental costs of sale; this gives a figure representing the 'net proceeds' of disposal on that occasion. From this figure is deducted in turn a sum termed 'base value'; and the remainder (if any) is the 'realised development value' of the owner's interest.[8]

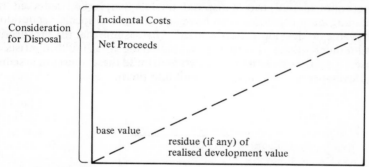

In principle 60% of the amount of this remainder is payable in tax to the Inland Revenue; though the first £50,000 of 'realised development value' accruing to any one person in the current financial year (with certain exceptions, to prevent tax evasion) is exempt.[9] There are various specialised provisions for tax exemption or tax deferment which are discussed below.

## 3 BASE VALUE (INCLUDING SPECIAL ADDITIONS)

The central factor in understanding whether a person ultimately incurs liability to pay this tax is the concept of 'base value'. There are three 'bases' to choose from in establishing what sum represents 'base value', and a prospective taxpayer is entitled to choose the highest of them.[10]

7 Finance Act 1980, s 114.
8 Development Land Tax Act 1976, s 4 and Sch 2. Partnership firms are treated as individuals: ibid, s 31.
9 Finance Act (No. 2) 1979, s 24. Until 12 June 1979, only the first £10,000 was exempt, and the next £150,000 was taxable at 66⅔%, subject to which the rate was 80%.
10 Development Land Tax Act 1976, s 5 and Sch 3.

Base A is the one which most closely reflects the general principle of the tax; Base B and Base C are variations on this main theme. They are applied to the 'net proceeds'.

The underlying idea is that the amount of the 'net proceeds' of disposal is analysed in order to distinguish three components, namely (i) the value of the current (existing) use of the land, (ii) the value of its development prospects, and (iii) money spent on improving it. Assume, for example, that the owner's interest in a piece of agricultural land is now sold for a market value figure of £20,000. The sum of £1,000 is incurred as incidental costs of disposal (fees, etc). Its current use market value today as agricultural land is (say) £8,000 and an amount of £2,000 (say) has been spent on improvements such as better drainage or access. If the current use value of £8,000 is deducted from £20,000, the remainder, £12,000, can be regarded as *gross* development value or 'development potential'. If the £2,000 spent on improvements, plus £1,000 incurred in respect of incidental costs of disposal, total £3,000, is then deducted, the remaining amount, £9,000, can be regarded as, so to speak, *net* development value or 'development potential'. Also assume that the prospective development giving rise to the market value of £20,000 consists of houses; if so, the owner is either starting to build these houses or is selling to a developer for the purpose of building them.

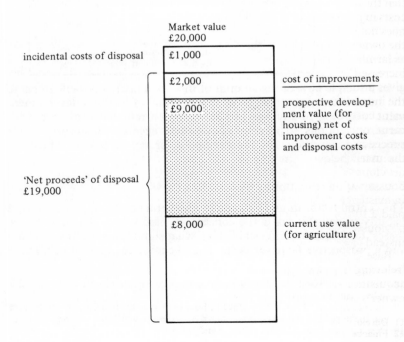

That figure of £9,000, however, is to be further analysed *retrospectively*, in order to discover whether, given that prospective development value exists now, its present appearance is or is not its first. If it, or any part of it, can be traced back and shown to have been present in an earlier net disposal figure, then that amount was 'realised' at an earlier time and is not being 'realised' now. It is most important to grasp that the essence of this tax assessment process comprises (i) ascertaining the up-to-date value of land and (ii) relating this figure to one or more figures representing value in the past.

Thus in our example, if £6,000 was 'realised' in an earlier transaction, in principle only £3,000 is 'realised' development value now, whereas if no amount was 'realised' in an earlier transaction, in principle, the whole £9,000 is 'realised' development value now. Bases A, B and C exist to give landowners a choice in the manner of dealing with this question.

Base A is applied by taking the cost of the property when the owner acquired it (including incidental costs such as professional fees incurred), then adding to that figure any amount by which the value of the current use has gone up in the meantime (ignoring any period before 6 April 1965), and adding also the cost of any improvements but only in so far as they are 'relevant'—ie they have increased the prospective development value as distinct from the current use value. (It may be noted here that the term 'improvements' includes expenditure on such items as legal costs in protecting or enhancing the title—eg paying off a mortgage—but does not include expenditure on upkeep.[11]) Thus if in the above example the owner had purchased the property a few years ago for £6,000 purely as farmland, and *half* of the expenditure of £2,000 on improvements has increased its existing or 'current' use value as farmland, Base A then gives a total of £9,000, made up of the acquisition figure of £6,000 plus the increase in the current use value £2,000, plus the 'relevant' improvement costs which are those which related to development value enhancement only (£1,000). Deduct this from £19,000 (which is the 'net proceeds' after deducting £1,000, for incidental costs of disposal, from the market value figure of £20,000) and £10,000 remains as 'realised development value', attributable in principle to the prospect of the housing development referred to. But if a planning permission had been in existence at the time when the owner acquired the land, and he had paid £10,000 (ie £4,000 over and above its value as farmland), then obviously the base value in accordance with Base A will be £13,000 instead of £9,000 and the 'realised development value' will fall to £6,000.

Base B comprises the current use value, increased by 15%,[12] plus 'relevant' improvement costs; but it disregards the cost of the property's acquisition. It will therefore produce a higher figure than Base A if the owner's cost of acquisition had included little or no development value,

11 Development Land Tax Act 1976, s 5 (3) and Sch 3, Part I.
12 Finance Act 1980, s 116 (1). The increase was previously 10%.

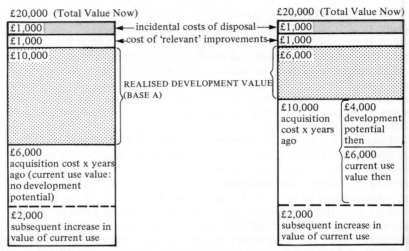

NOTE: The unshaded portions constitute 'base value'. Any 'special additions' to Base A will increase them, with the result that Realised Development value will shrink or disappear altogether.

amounting at any rate to less than the current use value today with the additional fifteen per cent.

Base C comprises the owner's cost of acquisition, increased by 15%, plus the cost of improvements generally (ie not merely the 'relevant' improvements), also increased by 15%.[13] It will produce a higher figure than Base A if the amount of improvement expenditure additionally allowable exceeds any addition to the current use value of the property since acquisition, but not otherwise. It will produce a higher figure than Base B if the amount of the improvements additionally allowable, plus any element of development value in the owner's acquisition cost, outweighs any addition to the current use value of the property since acquisition (allowing for the fifteen per cent increase in each case), but not otherwise.

It is probably true to say that the most important factor influencing the choice between Bases A, B and C will, in the long run, be the question whether the planning permission which gives rise to the prospective development value of the land at the time of assessment was obtained by the present vendor or by a predecessor. If a predecessor obtained it, the prospective development value will have been 'realised' partly or wholly on a former occasion and be now free of tax to that extent. But if the

13 Finance Act 1980, s 116 (1). It was previously 10%. As from 9 March 1981, the Finance Act 1981, s 129, raises this Base C percentage from 15 to 50 for *deemed* disposals (ie starting 'material' development: see above, p 278) in cases where the land is owned as stock-in-trade and the development is residential.

present vendor obtained it this will not be the case, so that Base A and Base C will be of little help to the owner; and it will be left to Base B to offset the development value in so far as it is possible to do so by enhancing the figure representing the current use value.

In the short run, however, this consideration is offset by the existence of a 'special addition' to Base A[14] which in many cases may well increase by a considerable amount the figure so calculated. It applies where the property interest in question was acquired before May 1977. The additional sum is a percentage of the owner's *acquisition cost*. The percentage is to be the number of years or parts of years (not exceeding four) that have elapsed since the acquisition, multiplied by 10 (or 15 if the acquisition dates back to White Paper Day or earlier). But this special addition to Base A is *not* to be made where the interest currently disposed of has to be treated as having been 'acquired' in a previous transaction which was in fact merely a 'deemed' disposal and reacquisition by virtue of the start of a project of 'material development' (as described above), if the 'net proceeds' on the occasion of the 'deemed' disposal contained any 'realised' development value. If however they did not, there will be a 'special addition' to Base A after all; but it is not a percentage of the 'deemed' acquisition cost. Instead it is a percentage of a *fraction of the earlier value of the property* at the time when it was actually acquired. The fraction in question is the proportion (if any) of the Base A figure relating to the 'deemed' disposal which *exceeds* the amount of the 'net proceeds' on the same occasion. Moreover in these cases the number of years (up to four) taken for the purpose of ascertaining the percentage of that fraction is the number which have elapsed since the time of the 'deemed' acquisition on starting the development; but whether the multiplier is to be 10 or 15 depends on the *earlier* date when the property was actually acquired.

Nor is this all. Where the 'special addition' to Base A applies (whichever percentage is to be used for it), and there is also an amount in respect of 'relevant' improvements as described above, a *further* addition applies. This is calculated as a proportion of the cost of those improvements, namely the amount of the special addition just described divided by the acquisition cost of the land.[15]

These intricate rules can be considered in relation to the example discussed above, where there is a sale (or 'deemed' sale) of agricultural land with development potential of which the 'net proceeds' are £19,000. Assume that the owner acquired it, actually and not notionally, on or before White Paper Day. Because he did so before May 1977 he qualifies for the special addition to Base A. If the sale was after 1978 these facts justify a percentage of four (years) multiplied by fifteen. Thus the percentage of the acquisition cost for the special addition is 60. So in

14 Development Land Tax Act 1976, s 6. This was to encourage sales.
15 Development Land Tax Act 1976, s 5 (5) and Sch 3, Part II.

regard to the alternative acquisition costs suggested above, the special addition to Base A at 60% will therefore be £3,600 if the owner's acquisition cost was £6,000, and £6,000 if it was £10,000, bringing the respective amounts of 'base value' under Base A up to £12,600 (from £9,000) and £19,000 (from £13,000). In consequence the 'realised development value' would fall to £6,400 (from £10,000) and to nil (from £6,000) respectively.

But each of those calculations also included £1,000 for 'relevant' improvements. That justifies the inclusion of the further addition as well; and this will (on the above facts) be 60% of that £1,000, namely £600, giving complete totals of £13,400 and £19,600 respectively. Deducted from the 'net proceeds' of £19,000, this ultimately reduces the figures for 'realised' development value under Base A to £5,800 in one case; in the other it has already fallen to nil. The figure of £19,000 obviously includes a sizeable element of development value, but much or all of this disappears on these calculations.

Applying the calculation for Base B to the exactly same facts, we get the following result. The 'relevant' improvements amount to £1,000. The current use value on disposal today as farmland is £8,000 which, increased by 15%, gives £9,200: total, £10,200. This amount when deducted from the 'net proceeds' of £19,000 still leaves £8,800 of realised development value.

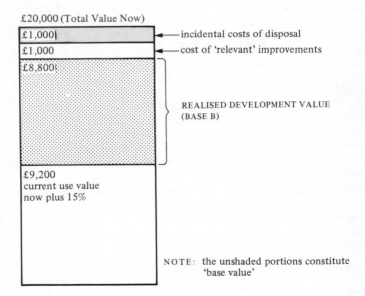

£20,000 (Total Value Now)

£1,000 ◄——— incidental costs of disposal

£1,000 ◄——— cost of 'relevant' improvements

£8,800

REALISED DEVELOPMENT VALUE (BASE B)

£9,200
current use value
now plus 15%

NOTE: the unshaded portions constitute 'base value'

Applying the calculation for Base C to those facts, we get the following results. The owner's acquisition cost increased by 15% is either £6,900 or £11,500. The figure for *all* improvements increased by 15% (only payable under Base C) is £2,300, giving a final amount of either £9,200 or £13,800. This amount when deducted from the 'net proceeds' of £19,000 still leaves either £9,800 or £5,200 (respectively) of realised development value.

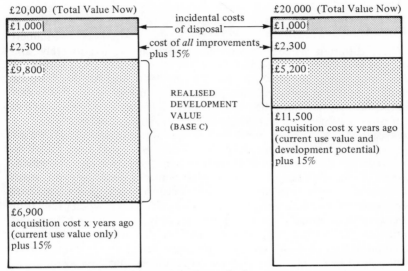

NOTE : the unshaded portions constitute 'base value.'

In those cases where the percentage increase is 50 instead of 15, the figure for the cost of all improvements goes up to £3,000, while the acquisition cost figures go up to £9,000 and £15,000 respectively, which brings down the realised development value to £7,000 and £1,000.

Here certain qualifications need to be made to what has been said about 'base value'. First, 'market value' calculations must disregard (i) mortgages and other forms of security,[16] and (ii) any depression of price in respect of an excessive quantity of land being put (or deemed to be put) on the market at once.[17] Second, 'current use value' assumes *no* planning permission except for development within the Eighth Schedule to the Town and Country Planning Act 1971 and development already started;[18] and again mortgages and other forms of security must be

16 Development Land Tax Act 1976, s 7 (5).
17 Ibid, s 7 (1).
18 Ibid, s 7 (2), (3) and Sch 4, Part I. (For the Eighth Schedule see below, ch 16. Any reduction of the 'unexpended balance' (see ch 15) on compulsory purchase must be disregarded (s 7 (6)).

disregarded.[19] Third, the cost of an acquisition must exclude any contribution to it made from public funds.[20] Fourth, where a disposition occurs between certain related companies or other 'connected' persons within the meaning of the Finance Act 1965 Part III (for the purpose of preventing tax evasions), then for 'base value' calculations on a subsequent disposal (or 'deemed' disposal) no 15% increase is to be made to the cost of improvements in Case C and no special additions are to be made in Case A.[1]

### 4 ANCILLARY RULES

Where different parcels of land have been assembled together and disposals from this assembled land are then made, a special set of complex rules is laid down in Sch 2 to the 1976 Act. All that need be noted here is that for calculation purposes the time of acquisition is that of the latest acquisition; the cost of acquisition is the aggregate cost; and current use value is calculated separately for each piece of land before it is aggregated. These rules, however, do not apply to any disposal subsequent to a previous disposal of part of the aggregated land.

Other detailed matters dealt with in Sch 2 are: pro rata apportionments of charge to tax on part disposals; grants of leases (separate rules additional to rules already applicable because such grants are 'part disposals'); apportionments for base value calculations when projects of 'material development' are begun on part only of an owner's land; and adjustments to sums representing consideration for disposals to take account of the following factors—mortgages, rentcharges, obligations to pay rent to reversioners, foreign tax, compulsory purchase disturbance compensation, insurance, contributions from public funds, payments of purchase price by instalments, contingent risks and liabilities, and the cost of acquiring mortgagees' and beneficiaries' interests.

Gifts of land are ignored, so that for later disposals it is the donor's acquisition and not the donee's which is taken into account. Disposals at an under-value, however, are not ignored, unless they are in fact acquisitions by charities, in which case they are ignored just as if they were gifts.[2] Disposals within groups of related companies are likewise ignored as if they were gifts;[3] but there is a 'deemed' disposal when a company leaves the group.[4] (Amalgamations are treated as inter-group disposals.[5])

Options are disposals of land; consideration given for them when they are granted is combined with the consideration for the disposals which occur when they are subsequently exercised.[6]

**19** Development Land Tax Act 1976, s 7 (5). If compensation is received for depreciation of land (s 3 (2)—see above, p 277, note 18) the current use value is to be that of the land *before* it is depreciated (s 7 (4)).      **20** Ibid, s 5 (4).
**1** Development Land Tax Act 1976, s 5 (6).      **2** Ibid, s 10.
**3** Ibid, s 20.      **4** Ibid, s 21.      **5** Ibid, s 22.      **6** Ibid, s 8.

Where there are 'bare' trusts (eg property vested in nominees) the beneficiaries are treated as the legal owners;[7] but for settled property the beneficial interests are ignored.[8] A mortgagee who realises his security is treated as a bare trustee for the mortgagor; foreclosure is treated as a disposal by the mortgagor to the mortgagee;[9] similar rules are applied in liquidation and bankruptcy.[10] The purely technical transfer of a deceased owner's land to his personal representatives does not count as a disposal.[11]

## 5 DEFERMENTS AND EXEMPTIONS

Where there is a 'deemed' disposal by an owner carrying on a business such that 'material development' for industrial purposes connected with that business gives rise to 'realised' development value, liability for tax is (subject to certain exceptions) deferred until the next actual disposal or until the property in question ceases to be used in that way.[12] 'Material development' by statutory undertakers for their operational purposes raises a comparable right of deferment.[13] Liability is also deferred in respect of 'deemed' disposals by the Housing Corporation, and by registered housing co-operatives, until the next actual disposal is made for payment.[14] In these various cases of deferment of liability to tax, that liability when it eventually accrues is back-dated to the time of the 'deemed' disposal.[15]

There is a general deferment of liability to the tax where a person has developed for his own use, starting between 9 March 1981 and 1 April 1984, in accordance with a valid planning permission. There is a charge to the tax in the event of an actual disposal afterwards, but not in the event of a *deemed* disposal (ie further development) nor of an inter-group disposal or an amalgamation or reconstruction disposal as between companies, nor of a lease-back disposal. It makes no difference if the developer ceases to use the premises himself, nor if there are short-term lettings of up to a year each which succeed each other at intervals of not less than a year, nor if there is a letting for the purpose of the property becoming tied premises.[16]

---

7 Development Land Tax Act 1976, s 28. Co-ownership is treated like a bare trust, proceeds on disposal being apportioned (s 29). Partners are treated as individuals (s 31).
8 Ibid, s 30.
9 Ibid, s 32.
10 Ibid, s 33.
11 Ibid, s 9.
12 Ibid, s 19.
13 Ibid, s 23.
14 Ibid, s 26 (2). But actual disposals *between* housing associations since 1 August 1976 are treated as gifts (this includes the Housing Corporation but not unregistered self-build societies—ie those which the Housing Corporation has declined to register in accordance with its powers under the Housing Act 1974, Parts I–III).
15 Ibid, s 27.
16 Ibid, s 19A (inserted by the Finance Act 1981, s 132).

'Deemed' disposals by housing asociations which are self-build societies or approved housing co-operatives are *exempt* from liability to tax[17] as are charities.[18]

Where an owner has held land as stock-in-trade (ie the proceeds of sale of such land would be included in the owner's accounts as trade profits) continuously since White Paper Day, he and his personal representatives are exempt from tax.[19] There is full exemption from tax on 'deemed' disposals and fifty per cent exemption on actual disposals, for mineral development.[20] There is exemption from tax also on a sale by an individual owner of a private residence on land not exceeding one acre, provided that his ownership is of six months' standing and he has resided in the property for at least half of the last two years (this also applies to personal representatives of such owners, if they dispose of the property within two years, and to settlement trustees of beneficiaries in residence for the stated period).[1] There is exemption from tax also where anyone who has owned land since White Paper Day builds on it a single dwelling house for occupation by the owner or by certain specified relatives, and a similar exemption in respect of a second such house provided that it is built in the grounds of an existing house belonging to that owner.[2]

There is, finally, a general rule of exemption from tax which applies to any case of 'deemed' development where the project of 'material development' in question is begun *within three years* of the acquisition of the land, provided that no appreciable *realised* development value would have accrued to the owner if the project had been started immediately after acquisition. In other words any development value must have been 'realised' by a previous owner, and the development must be put in hand reasonably promptly.[3]

As for local authorities, government departments and other similar public bodies, they are altogether exempt from tax, because they represent the public ownership into which the proceeds of development land tax are intended to be transferred.[4]

---

17 Development Land Tax Act 1976, s 26 (1).
18 Finance Act 1980, s 111; Finance Act 1982, s 155. Before 25 March 1980 charities were liable to the tax in certain circumstances, sometimes on a deferred basis.
19 Development Land Tax Act 1976, s 16 and Sch 5.
20 Ibid, s 17.
1 Ibid, s 14.
2 Ibid, s 15.
3 Ibid, s 18. The Finance Act 1981, s 131, provides that the law must be assumed to have been the same at the time of the acquisition as it is at the time of the disposal—in other words the law currently in force is notionally back-dated. Among other things, this gave to taxpayers the right to back-date the 50% addition to acquisition cost under Base C (see above, p 282, footnote 13).
4 Development Land Tax Act 1976, s 11 (the Finance Act 1981, s 130, adds urban development corporations).

## 6 COLLECTION OF TAX

Section 41 of and Sch 8 to the 1976 Act enact details of the system of collection which is the function of the Inland Revenue[5] but administered in a strictly centralised procedure and not by offices of local tax-collectors. In cases where 'realised' development value accrues on an actual (not a 'deemed') disposal and the price for the disposal is payable in one sum, or in instalments not extending beyond a period of seven years, and exceeds £10,000, the person chargeable to tax must give notice of the transaction to the Board of Inland Revenue within one year, unless the instrument of transfer is produced to the Board within that time under the existing procedure for land transactions in accordance with s 28 of the Finance Act 1931. Such notice is, however, dispensed with in respect of outright (not part) disposals of dwelling houses on land not exceeding one acre if the price is £25,000 or less.

Schedule 8 as first enacted also provided that in the case of *deemed* disposals, and of actual part disposals in the form of grants of leases at rents not exceeding commercial rents, taxpayers might elect to pay in eight yearly or 16 half-yearly instalments over a period of eight years beginning 12 months after the date of disposal. In regard to *deemed* disposals after 25 March 1980 that has been extended to a period of nine years beginning 24 months after the date of disposal.[6]

Local authorities, government departments and similar bodies, which as stated above are exempt from tax, were at first empowered to deduct it themselves when they were the purchasers in actual (but not, of course, deemed) disposals of land—in other words where they compulsorily purchased land or bought it by agreement under statutory powers; but this ceased to apply after 5 August 1980.[7]

Ad hoc tax collection was also imposed on persons buying land from foreign residents. They must deduct half the price payable for 'development land' (ie land enjoying planning permission for a project of 'material development' which has not yet began) on behalf of the Inland Revenue; but there are various exceptions to this duty.[8]

## 7 OTHER CAPITAL TAXATION

Complex provisions are enacted in s 34 and Sch 6 to avoid any overlap with other direct taxes. In effect, this means capital gains tax and capital transfer tax. The details fortunately lie outside the scope of this book;

---

5 In bankruptcy and winding-up development land tax has priority in the same way as income tax (ibid, s 42). Capital money held under a strict settlement or trust for sale may be used to pay the tax (ibid, s 43).
6 Finance Act 1980, s 113. Taxpayers' liability under s 27 of the 1976 Act (see above, p 287, footnote 15) is subject to the same concession.
7 Development Land Tax Act 1976, s 39 and Sch 7; Finance Act 1980, s 112.
8 Development Land Tax Act 1976, s 40.

but the essence of the matter is that the same financial benefit accruing to a taxpayer often attracts, in principle, more than one tax. Thus the exemptions from development land tax, referred to earlier in this chapter, may well merely subject that financial benefit to some other tax, most probably capital gains tax. Subject to this, it can be said in a rough and ready way that increases in existing (current) use value are liable to capital gains tax whereas increases in development value are liable to development land tax. Liability to capital gains tax on compulsory purchase compensation is dealt with in the Capital Gains Tax Act 1979, ss 110 to 111B.[9]

In addition the predecessor of the development land tax has to be considered, namely development *gains* tax (being capital gains tax formerly charged on development values in land), which in principle came to an end on 1 August 1976, including the special variety of it taking the form of taxation of first lettings. Such tax nevertheless remained payable instead of development land tax in certain transitional cases. These are: (i) first disposals of land after 1 August 1976 where a project of 'material development' was begun before that date, or where a disposal before that date was treated as involving neither a gain nor a loss; (ii) first lettings after 1 August 1976 where the premises in question were created by the carrying out of development begun before 18 May 1976.[10]

9 Sections 111A and 111B were added by the Finance Act 1982, s 83. For the relation of capital gains tax to disturbance compensation, see ch 10, pp 209–211, above.
10 Development Land Tax Act 1976, ss 35–38.

Chapter 15

# Planning compensation and the unexpended balance

## A. Restriction of development value

### 1 RELATION OF COMPENSATION TO BETTERMENT

Betterment and planning compensation now go hand in hand. Before the Act of 1947 each was regarded as applying to particular situations, rather than generally. As shown in the previous chapter, betterment was then taken to mean particular cases of increases in land values caused by particular projects of public works nearby.[1] Planning compensation consisted of payment for particular cases of depreciation of land values caused by particular planning schemes. But the strategy of the Act of 1947 transformed them both. It borrowed from the Uthwatt report the concept of distinguishing existing use of land, and its value, from the prospect of development of land, and its value. But unlike the Uthwatt Report it did not apply the distinction solely to undeveloped land in the country. It applied it generally; and in consequence that distinction has been, ever since 1947, of fundamental importance to the law of planning and compulsory purchase alike.

The interrelation of betterment and planning compensation expresses itself in two questions. Should any or all of prospective development value, when it accrues, being currently termed 'betterment', be appropriated by the community? How that question has been answered appeared in the previous chapter. And on the other hand, if it does not accrue, because the interests of the community, expressed in the form of planning restrictions, prevent it from doing so, should the community pay any or all of its value to the deprived landowner by way of compensation?

The first point which may be made in answering the latter question is this, that if all of the prospective development value of land, when it accrues, were to be taken in betterment tax, it would be obviously absurd to pay compensation for the loss of any of that value in planning restrictions. The once-for-all compensation scheme intended by the Act of 1947[2] does not conflict with this argument, because it was intended solely to benefit owners who enjoyed prospective development value on

---

1 See ch 14, p 268, above.
2 See ch 14, p 273, above.

30 June 1948, and not later. It follows from this point, in strict logic, that if *all* prospective development value when it accrues were to be taken away in betterment tax, then *no* compensation should be paid for loss of prospective development value in consequence of planning restrictions. Conversely, if there is *no* betterment tax there ought to be *full* compensation for planning restrictions. The former of these two conclusions was adopted by the 1947 Act, and largely put into effect, but subsequently discarded. The latter has not been adopted, not apparently has its adoption even been proposed.

Both of these extreme propositions rest on the logical view that development value in the form of land values and development value in the form of money are the strict equivalent of one another, differing only in form. That is why 'land values in money' must include 'compensation'. Granted that this is so, it should next follow that, if both of the above propositions are unacceptable because they are extreme, then there ought to be a logical compromise. For example, if an owner were to *retain* 60% of accrued betterment (and pay 40% in tax) where development is permitted, he should *receive* 60% compensation from public funds (and leave the remaining 40% in those funds) where it is restricted. If the best solution is an equal division—'equality is equity'—then an owner ought to pay in tax 50% of accrued betterment, meaning actual development value, keeping the other 50%, and be entitled to receive 50% of any 'lost betterment', meaning lost development value by way of planning compensation for development restrictions. But betterment tax should only be payable when the betterment has been realised in money or money's worth on a disposal of the land; and allowance should be made for incidental expenses.

The position since 1952 has been that the owner keeps all or (since 1965) some of actual betterment in accrued land values; yet only in special cases does he receive the equivalent of lost betterment in planning compensation—a 'state lottery' indeed. As Sir David Cairns said in the Court of Appeal in *Peaktop Properties (Hampstead) Ltd v Camden London Borough Council*:[3] 'There is no general right to compensation for the refusal of planning permission.'

The bulk of the law relating to planning compensation is to be found in Parts VII and VIII of the Act of 1971, re-enacting the 1954 and 1962 Acts. Differences of treatment depend on the following distinctions. First, there is a distinction between restrictions on development imposed *at the outset*, that is to say in response to the planning application submitted for permission to carry out that development, and restrictions imposed *subsequently*, that is to say by revocation, modification or discontinuance orders. No such distinction in respect of development value was made by the Act of 1947; it was introduced by the Town and Country

3  (1983) 46 P & CR 177.

Planning Act 1954.[4] Second, there is a distinction *within* the category of restrictions upon development imposed at the outset, drawn between 'new development' and 'existing use development' or 'Third Schedule' development—so called because the categories of which it is composed were set out in a series of classes specified in Sch 3 to the Acts of 1947 and 1962.[5]

The relevant provisions are now the Eighth Schedule to the 1971 Act. 'New development' is defined in s 22 (5) of the Act of 1971 as development outside the classes specified in Sch 8. This distinction was in fact made by the Act of 1947, which treated the value attaching to the prospect of such development as being purely marginal to the value of the existing use on 1 July 1948, and conceded it to owners accordingly.

The result of drawing these two distinctions has led, in the present law of planning compensation, to a more far-reaching one. This is that *all* restrictions on development imposed after the original planning permission, as by revocation, modification and discontinuance orders, together with restrictions imposed *at the outset on existing use development*, give a corresponding right to full compensation (subject to certain qualifications); but restrictions at the outset on *new* development do not. Part VIII of the Act of 1971 deals with planning compensation as of right, and will be discussed in the next chapter. Part VII comprises a special body of provisions whereby planning compensation of a limited kind is available for restrictions, at the outset, on new development.

It will be apparent that these restrictions which are compensated for, if at all, under Part VII of the 1971 Act, comprise the main body of development restrictions of the normal type. Restrictions to be compensated for as of right are uncommon in their occurrence—largely because planning authorities know full well that equivalent compensation as of right will have to be paid if they are imposed—or marginal in their scope. In fact even the prospect of paying marginal compensation was found to be so alarming in certain kinds of case that Parliament passed the Town and Country Planning Act 1963 to restrict the categories of 'existing use development' still further than was originally the case under the Third Schedule.[6] Unfortunately, planning authorities are aware that 'the community' makes development value available the easy way, through the medium of higher market prices, when planning permission is given, whereas 'the community' will have to pay in hard cash if the equivalent of development value is to be paid in compensation when planning permission is withheld or restricted. It is the old problem: justice is not to be had on the cheap.

4 Part IV.
5 See below ch 16, p 316.
6 See below, ch 16, p 325.

## 2 THE STRANGE COMPROMISE

The Town and Country Planning Act 1954 had to take account of the fact that Parliament, which had restored full development value to owners who obtain planning permissions, was unwilling to see them totally deprived of compensation in the normal case of loss of development value by planning restrictions, and yet at the same time could not face the logical consequence of awarding full compensation in lieu of lost development value. There are only two ways of avoiding payment in this situation: either deny all right to compensation, or grant all planning permissions asked for.

To escape from the dilemma, a kind of Alice-in-Wonderland compromise was worked out. It was decided that the claims for compensation made, and accepted by the Central Land Board, under the Act of 1947, although truly redundant now that development charges were abolished, should be applied to this new situation. To have asked for one thing was now to be made the qualification for getting something different. The claims had been made on the central government, and it is true that they would still have to be met (if at all) by the central government. But they had been made in the light of development potentialities in 1948, yet would be met in respect of planning situations arising at any time in the future after 1954. They had been made in respect of the loss suffered by owners of land, yet would be met in respect of the value of land itself.

The point of most substance, however, is that compensation is not payable in accordance with facts which are relevant now, such as current market demand and consequent loss of value in consequence of the imposition of restrictions. Instead it is payable in accordance with the claim (if any) that the owner of the land saw fit to make in relation to the state of affairs which existed in 1948, to the way in which that claim was handled by him or on his behalf and by the Central Land Board, and to the market values then prevailing. In fact, 1947 prices had been chosen as the basis for assessment.[7]

Part I of the Act of 1954 provided for compensation to be paid by the Central Land Board for losses (such as the payment of development charges) other than those caused by planning restrictions, between the 'appointed day' (1 July 1948) and the end of 1954. Part V of the Act provided for compensation to be paid by the Minister of Housing and Local Government for losses caused by planning restrictions during the same period. Payments were not to be made beyond the amount of any established claim previously made under the 1947 Act. For the future, any claims not affected or exhausted by such payments were to be

---

7 Part VI of the 1947 Act applied the principle that expropriation of prospective development values should date from 7 January 1947—the date when that Act was originally introduced into Parliament as a bill—and compensation should therefore relate to prices prevailing at that time.

available for compensation to be paid by the Minister of Housing and Local Government for planning restrictions after 1954. (Part II of the Act). Compensation was also to be paid by local planning authorities for revocation and modification orders after 1954 (Part IV of the Act); but it will of course be realised that this was to be compensation as of right,[8] without regard to established claims under the 1947 Act.

As far as compulsory purchase is concerned, it should be noted that Part V of the Act of 1947 had provided that compulsory purchase compensation was to be assessed at existing use value, plus Third Schedule development value but excluding other development value. This of course was fully consistent with the expropriation of development value imposed on owners in general by virtue of the introduction of planning control and the development charge system. In other words an owner of land would be confined to the same restricted value whether he retained his land with the benefit of planning permission, or retained it subject to planning restrictions, or relinquished it in consequence of compulsory purchase. When the abolition of development charges put an end to this consistency by making owners of land who enjoyed planning permission better off financially than owners of land who were subject to planning restrictions, it became an interesting question whether owners of land subject to compulsory purchase would find themselves in the same boat as the former, or the latter, or neither. Part I of the Act of 1954 empowered owners whose land had been compulsorily acquired already at existing use value to obtain from the Central Land Board the full value of any established claim there might be, plus interest; and the Board in turn was entitled to be reimbursed by the acquiring authority. Part III of the Act of 1954 provided that for future acquisitions the compulsory purchase compensation was to include, in addition to existing use value, no more than the value of any outstanding established claim there might be, plus interest (after 1954 known as an 'unexpended balance', for reasons to be explained).

Thus, compulsorily expropriated owners were in effect placed in the same boat as owners subjected to planning restrictions, and not in the same boat as owners enjoying planning permissions. The resultant uproar when they found themselves in the wrong boat led eventually to a further change in the law, when the Town and Country Planning Act 1959, Part I, subsequently re-enacted in the land Compensation Act 1961, transferred them to the other boat in all cases where notice to treat was served after 29 October 1958. These provisions, which are of course applicable today and have therefore been discussed earlier in this book in relation to present-day acquisitions,[9] enact the procedure based on

8 See p 293, above.
9 See ch 8, above.

planning assumptions which now gives the benefit of development value to expropriated owners.

# B.  The unexpended balance of established development value

## 1 ONCE-FOR-ALL COMPENSATION TRANSFORMED

The story of planning compensation can now be resumed by referring to Part VII of the Act of 1971, which re-enacts the relevant provisions of the Act of 1954. Section 135 of the 1971 Act refers to the claims accepted by the Central Land Board under Part VI of the 1947 Act, calling them 'established claims'. They relate, of course, to estimated loss of development value under that Act by freeholders and leaseholders. Section 137 terms the benefit of such claims 'claim holdings'. Thus if, from 1947 onwards, X was freehold owner-occupier of Blackacre and his claim for (say) £7,000 loss of development value was accepted in full by the Central Land Board in 1949, the benefit of that £7,000 'established claim' was a 'claim holding'. Had X been the freehold reversioner to Y, a lessee for a term of 99 years, X's claim might have amounted to (say) £700 while Y's claim amounted to £6,300, total £7,000.

These rights were personal property and capable of being transferred, divided or combined. Any compensation paid under Parts I and V of the 1954 Act then had to be taken into account; and that and other 'adjustments' were made accordingly by virtue of provisions now contained in the Fifteenth Schedule to the 1971 Act: including where necessary a proportionate division of 'claim holdings' if the land itself had been divided. Thus if X as freehold owner-occupier had divided Blackacre into two, in a value ratio of 3:2, there would then be two claim holdings, East and West Blackacre, respectively valued at £4,200 and £2,800. And any or each of the various amounts might have been retrospectively reduced or exhausted by virtue of any relevant compensation payments or other 'adjustments'. Such calculations would of course be child's play to experienced valuers. [10]

It will be apparent that, whatever calculations had to be made in respect of past events viewed from 1 January 1955, when the 1954 Act came into effect, the continued use of established claims in connection with the payment of *future* planning compensation would, though possible, be highly artificial. What was done was to transform the rights founded upon them from personal property to a sort of property in land. Their real nature is no different from before. They amount to payments

10 For division of compensation money between life beneficiaries and remaindermen under trusts of property, so as to do retrospective justice to the former, see *Re Chance, Westminster Bank Ltd v Chance* [1962] 1 All ER 942.

by the central government, from a fund *not* directly contributed to by the recipients, nor by anyone else, but created by the central government itself out of its ordinary resources—presumably as representing the 'community' in the spirit of 1947. It is true that the system has frequently resulted in the recipients obtaining value they have lost; but it is in fact a coincidence that this is so.

Section 136 of the 1971 Act enacts that the personal property termed 'claim holdings' was transformed into rights in land termed the 'original unexpended balance of established development value' on 1 January 1955. Not only were the claim holdings retrospectively 'adjusted' in relation to all previous compensation matters outstanding, but they were, if necessary, further divided so that there would be no area of land to which an 'unexpended balance' attached by virtue of any claim holding relating to a *smaller* area. Thus if X, as freeholder of all Blackacre, had leased West Blackacre to Y, X's claim holding of Blackacre would not lead to there being an unexpended balance for all Blackacre. As expressed in s 136 (2) (b), it was necessary that 'there was not subsisting any claim holding whose area consisted of part only of that land, whether with or without other land'. Thus there would have to be a separate unexpended balance for West Blackacre and another for East Blackacre. This was considered necessary so as to arrive at manageable units for calculating and dealing with unexpended balances in and after 1955.

But since there would often be more than one claim holding, or part of a claim holding, relating to each such area of land, all had to be aggregated for the area. In the words of s 136 (3):

There shall be attributed to the land . . . (a) the value of any claim holding having an area consisting of that land, and (b) such fraction of the value of any claim holding whose area included that land as attached to that land, and the original unexpended balance of established development value of that land shall be taken to have been an amount equal to eight-sevenths of the amount or aggregate amount so attributed.

The increase of one-seventh was intended to be in lieu of interest.[11]

For example, suppose that from 1947 onwards Blackacre was held, as stated in an illustration earlier in this chapter, by Y on a long lease from the freehold reversioner, X, and that Y enjoyed a claim holding valued at £6,300 and X enjoyed a claim holding valued at £700.[12] The 'original unexpended balance' in 1955, assuming that there were no 'adjustments', would have been calculated by aggregating these sums (£7,000) and increasing that aggregate by one seventh (total £8,000). Had the land been divided into East and West Blackacre with a value ratio of 3:2, but

---

11 Covering the period 1948 to 1955. But it is nevertheless in itself capital and not interest: *Re Hasluck, Sully v Duffin* [1957] 3 All ER 371, [1957] 1 WLR 1135.
12 See p 296, above.

| WEST | EAST |
|---|---|
| £ | £ |
| X:   280 | X:   420 |
| Z: 2,520 | Y: 3,780 |
| ——— | ——— |
| 2,800 | 4,200 |
| $\times \frac{8}{7} = 3,200$ | $\times \frac{8}{7} = 4,800$ |

| Value ratio = 2 | Value ratio = 3 |

the freehold from 1947 onwards was always to be united in X while during that period Y was to be long leaseholder, as above, of East Blackacre and Z was to be long leaseholder of West Blackacre, their respective claim holdings would have been as follows: X, £700; Y, £3,780; Z, £2,520. To comply with section 136, X's freehold claim holding would have been divided into two fractions, with a value ratio of 3:2, for East and West Blackacre (ie £420 and £280). Then, if there were no 'adjustments', the original unexpended balance of East Blackacre would have been calculated as follows: X's fraction of claim holding, £420; Y's claim holding, £3,780; aggregate total, £4,200; aggregate increased by one seventh, £4,800. The corresponding figures for West Blackacre would be: X, £280; Z, £2,520; aggregate, £2,800; increased aggregate, £3,200.

## 2 HOW THE UNEXPENDED BALANCE BECOMES EXPENDED

Since the purpose of these unexpended balances is to fix limits to the amounts of compensation to be paid for restrictions imposed at the outset on new development, it is important to understand on what principles the system is run. The fundamental principle is that, since the balances represent (up to a point) development value that owners are not allowed to enjoy, they should diminish to the extent that owners do in fact succeed in enjoying development value after all. There are three main ways in which this can happen.

Section 140 deals with the first possibility: actual receipt of planning compensation. To the extent that it is in fact paid for restrictions at the outset on new development, it is deducted from the unexpended balance. This is of course a statement of the obvious, since the balance represents a strict limit on compensation. Thus if X was entitled on 1 January 1955, to an original unexpended balance of £8,000 and he receives £8,000 in compensation, that puts paid to the balance. If X received £7,000 in compensation, there will still be an unexpended balance to the extent of the remaining £1,000, but it will no longer be the 'original' unexpended balance. Owners cannot have their cake and eat it. The original unexpended balance is the cake.

Section 141, which deals with the second possibility, provides that if development value comes to be enjoyed in terms of actual land value, the owners who get the benefit are also to be treated as consuming their cake, and the unexpended balance is diminished accordingly. The start of new development on the land in question *at any time after 1 July 1948* has this effect, because the balance on 1 January 1955 was derived from a loss agreed to have been suffered already on 1 July 1948; though, of course, for most practical purposes s 141 is concerned with recent or present development. The Sixteenth Schedule to the 1971 Act governs the calculation of the 'value of the development'. Prospective development value, not the cost of the actual development, is in question, so the development itself is disregarded. The land is first valued on the footing that the development was permitted but had not occurred. Then from that figure is deducted the value of the same land on the footing that the development was *not* permitted. *Current* market values are used. The remainder is then to be deducted from the unexpended balance when calculating a normal current claim for compensation.

Section 142 deals with the third possibility, and provides that compulsory purchase of land extinguishes the entire unexpended balance, if any, attaching to the land. If, however, any freehold or leasehold interest is not included in the acquisition, the proportion of the unexpended balance relating to that interest will be saved from extinction; and the mode of calculating this proportion is set out in the Seventeenth Schedule. Acquisitions by agreement under compulsory powers are treated as compulsory acquisitions. It is of course assumed—though not expressly stated—that the unexpended balance must be included in the calculation of compensation for the acquisition in accordance with the Land Compensation Act 1961.[13] The owner is thus deemed to have swallowed his cake.

Section 143 can be regarded as ancillary to s 142. It provides that where compulsory purchase compensation includes severance or injurious affection compensation for other land retained by the expropriated owner, then if that part of the compensation itself includes an element of loss of development value, any unexpended balance attaching to that other land is to be diminished accordingly. Receipt of that

13 This is because the unexpended balance in principle represents prospective development value. See ch 8, above for means whereby prospective development value can be included in compensation for compulsory purchase by virtue of 'assumptions as to planning permission'. But this does not altogether guarantee that development value and the unexpended balance correspond *in detail*; so the wisest course is always to make known, and include in the claim, the amount of any relevant unexpended balance when assessing compulsory purchase compensation.

element of the compensation counts as consumption of some of the cake belonging to the land retained.

Any or all of these events may affect the unexpended balance relating to land. They may not necessarily affect all of the land's area; and, if so, s 144 provides for an apportionment. The unexpended balance relating to the land will then be replaced by separate balances for the parts respectively affected and not affected by the events in question. For information about the existence of any unexpended balance, whether apportioned in this way or not, it is best to apply to the Secretary of State, as the central government authority in succession to the Central Land Board. His duty, under s 145, is to furnish authorities acquiring land under compulsory purchase powers with a certificate of any relevant unexpended balance existing immediately before service of a notice to treat in respect of the land, should they apply for it. As for other persons, his duty is only to issue a certificate of the *original* unexpended balance in 1955, with details of the state of the land on 1 July 1948; but he may if he wishes give details of subsequent events affecting that balance. If an apportionment is necessary—and it will be seen later that the Secretary of State may, under s 158, apportion any compensation paid among different parts of the land—or if an acquiring authority is to be notified of a deduction from an unexpended balance because actual development has been undertaken, the Secretary of State must first notify all persons affected by the apportionment or deduction, giving them 30 days to make representations. Any resultant objection may be referred within a further 30 days, if the objector so requires, to the Lands Tribunal for decision before the certificate is issued.

## C. Payment and repayment of compensation

### 1 COMPENSATION FOR RESTRICTIONS ON NEW DEVELOPMENT AT THE OUTSET

These provisions help make it possible to ascertain, at any given time, if land enjoys an unexpended balance, original or otherwise, and what the amount of that balance is. Only if such a balance exists will it be possible to obtain compensation for depreciation caused by restrictions imposed at the outset upon new development; and s 146 so provides. Under s 152, the person entitled to any freehold or leasehold so depreciated is empowered to claim the amount of depreciation, or the amount of the unexpended balance, *whichever is the less*. It must be assumed that there are not, and will not be, restrictions on any development which is not new development (s 153).[14] If more than one owner is entitled to claim,

14 On this see ch 16, pp 316–25, below. An owner is entitled to get the value of prospective development marginal to existing use (as distinct from 'new' development) listed in Part

as a lessor and a lessee may be, each should take care to do so, because if the combined total of their losses in value exceeds the unexpended balance (if any), a dilatory claimant may make it possible for a prompt claimant to obtain full payment instead of the due proportion sanctioned in such a case. A calculation should always be made retrospectively; that is, a claim is envisaged, and then previous events are considered to see whether an unexpended balance originally existed, and if so whether all or any of it currently remains.

Section 154 prescribes the procedure for making an application for compensation. Within six months of the adverse planning decision (or longer if the Secretary of State so allows) the claimant must submit his claim to the local planning authority, which must in turn transmit it to the Secretary of State together with any further details required in accordance with the relevant regulations. These are the Town and Country Planning (Compensation and Certificates) Regulations 1974,[15] which lay down details of the procedure to be followed and the forms to be used.

The adverse decision may be either that of the Secretary of State (normally by way of appeal) or of the local planning authority. If it is the decision of the latter, no appeal having been made, the Secretary of State nevertheless has power, under ss 38 and 39 of the Act of 1971, to head off the claim for compensation by directing that a more favourable decision be substituted as he largely could have done had the applicant in fact appealed to him from the local planning authority's adverse decision in the first place.[16] If the original application could have referred to *other* development which the Secretary of State now considers could be permitted, but did not, then whether the adverse decision had been the local planning authority's or his own he may direct that permission for such development be granted.[17] But all parties affected must first be afforded a hearing before an inspector; and the Secretary of State must give due regard to the current development plan and other relevant planning factors.[18]

II of Sch 8 to the Town and Country Planning Act 1971, because if he does not get unconditional planning permission to carry out such development he will instead get compensation for loss of the value of that development in consequence of such restriction. He will alternatively be entitled to have such value (and in addition the value of prospective marginal development listed in Part I of Sch 8) included in his compensation if his land is compulsorily purchased.

15 SI 1974/1242.

16 Any claim for compensation then takes effect (if not withdrawn) in relation to the substituted decision: 1971 Act, s 155 (2).

17 Ibid, s 38 (3).

18 Ibid, s 39 (1), (2). Subsection 3 provides that the Secretary of State must give notice of any direction he ultimately makes to the local planning authority concerned and to any person with an outstanding compensation claim; and s 155 (1) then empowers any such person within 30 days to notify the Secretary of State that he is modifying his claim (unless, of course, he is in any case abandoning it).

A claimant for compensation who, in response to his claim, receives a beneficial planning decision in one of the ways just described, or whose claim is regarded as being unjustified for any other reason, will be invited by the Secretary of State to withdraw it. If it is not withdrawn, the Secretary of State is required, by s 156 and the Regulations already mentioned, to 'cause such investigations to be made and such steps to be taken as he may deem requisite for a proper determination of the claim', and to notify his findings to the claimant and any other parties affected. Any person affected may dispute the findings, or any apportionment among different parties, within 30 days by notice in writing to the Lands Tribunal, so long as he has not already given the Secretary of State an acceptance in writing. Then, unless there is a revision by agreement, the Lands Tribunal must settle the dispute and 'either confirm or vary the . . . findings, or . . . the apportionment, and shall notify the parties of their decision'. But the Lands Tribunal are forbidden to change any apportionment to the extent to which it is shown to be consistent with some previous apportionment—for instance one made in connection with the exercise of the Secretary of State's functions under s 145, discussed above.[19]

## 2  COMPENSATION NOTICES AND REPAYMENT

The Secretary of State must pay the compensation when it has been established. An amount over £20 must, under s 158, be notified to the appropriate district council in whose area the land lies, and that council must register the notice as a local land charge. The Secretary of State must also 'apportion the amount of the compensation between different parts of the land to which the claim for compensation relates', if this is practicable, and include details of the apportionment in the 'compensation notice'. The point of local registration, being an addition to the recording of the details as a matter of normal administrative routine by the Secretary of State, is that future purchasers of the land or part of the land can be made aware of the fact of payment in the course of an ordinary conveyancing search. The importance of this arises from the fact that the compensation may have to be repaid, as follows.

Section 159 provides: 'No person shall carry out any new development to which this section applies on land in respect of which . . . (a 'compensation notice') is registered . . . until such amount (if any) as is recoverable under this section . . . has been paid or secured to the satisfaction of the Secretary of State'. This refers to subsequent development 'of a residential, commercial or industrial character' consisting 'wholly or mainly of the construction of houses, flats, shop or office premises, or industrial buildings (including warehouses) or any combination thereof', and also the winning and working of minerals, and any other

19  See p 300, above.

development to which the Secretary of State considers it 'reasonable that this section should apply' in view of the probable development value. But if what happens is a compulsory acquisition, s 257 empowers the Secretary of State as a rule to recover payment from the acquiring authority.

In other words prospective development value, in so far as it has already been realised in the form of compensation, will be realised twice over if lucrative development then takes place—though in its second manifestation it will come as land value rather than money. Realisation of development value in this form has, of course, already been indicated as precluding subsequent realisation in the form of compensation, because it diminishes the unexpended balance, under s 141,[20] in cases where it occurs *before* the question of paying compensation arises. It must follow logically, therefore, that if compensation has been obtained already it ought to be repaid. Repayment will restore the amount to the unexpended balance (s 161); but the value of the development will itself diminish the balance (under s 141). At all costs the landowner must not have his cake and eat it, even though there are many circumstances when he can do neither.

Section 160 provides that in these circumstances the entire compensation must be repaid, or a proportionate part of it if the subsequent development relates to part only of the land. However, it may be that the intended new development will create *less* development value than was covered by the compensation. If so, full repayment is due just the same. But if the Secretary of State can be persuaded that to require repayment in full will make it not worth the developer's while to go ahead, he can if he chooses remit part or all of the repayment. Where part is remitted the compensation notice must be amended.

It is clear from the wording of s 159 that an owner cannot be compelled to repay compensation unless a compensation notice has been registered as a local land charge. If the Secretary of State has not issued such a notice, or if the local authority have not registered it, or if it is registered but not disclosed on an official search, then a purchaser of an interest in the land will be acting in ignorance of it. Section 17 (3) of the Land Charges Act 1925[1] said that an official certificate of search of the local land charges register 'shall be conclusive', so that a registered item which should be disclosed in it, but is not, is to that extent to be treated as if it were not registered. In *Ministry of Housing and Local Government v Sharp*,[2] a compensation notice was negligently omitted from a certificate of search of the local land registry at Hemel Hempstead. A prospective developer purchased the land in question from the previous owner, who

---

20 See p 299, above.
1 Now re-enacted in the Land Charges Act 1972, s 10 (4).
2 [1970] 2 QB 223, [1970] 1 All ER 1009.

in 1960 had obtained £1,828 compensation for refusal of permission for new development but had applied again in 1962 and been granted permission. The purchasing developer, being unaware of the compensation notice, refused to repay the compensation, and the Ministry conceded the point. The action was in fact brought against the authority and the registrar for damages in tort for negligence by reason of the official failure to disclose, and it succeeded (against the authority, though not the registrar) in the Court of Appeal.

The moral to purchasing developers is, on no account repay the money in such a case. In *Stock v Wanstead and Woodford Borough Council*,[3] the same situation had occured except that the purchaser incautiously paid up when the Minister demanded. He then sued the local authority for damages, on the ground that the failure to disclose the compensation notice on the official search made them liable to him. The alleged liability was for the loss he incurred by being obliged to make a payment which had he known he would have set off against the purchase price agreed with the vendor. But the court rejected the proposition that he had been obliged to make the payment. By virtue of the Land Charges Act 1925, s 17 (3), he need not have done. His action failed.

# D. The scope of compensation

## 1 CASES EXPRESSLY EXCLUDED

Unfortunately, it is not enough even to show that one's land enjoys an unexpended balance when claiming compensation for restrictions imposed at the outset on new development. Certain kinds of adverse planning decision are specified by the Act of 1971 as conferring no right to compensation regardless of the unexpended balance. Conversely, however, there are special situations where such compensation is payable even in the absence of what is, strictly speaking, an adverse planning decision.

Section 147 (1) excludes compensation in consequence of adverse decisions on applications for consents to display advertisements, and, which is more far-reaching, for planning permissions to carry out 'any development which consists of or includes the making of any material change in the use of any buildings or other land'. Since so many forms of building development also include clear changes of use of a 'material' kind, as when farm land or buildings are developed or redeveloped for housing, or when houses are reconstructed as commercial buildings or vice versa, this rule on the face of it would reduce the right to compensation quite drastically. But the official interpretation of the rule

3 [1962] 2 QB 479, [1961] 2 All ER 433.

(fortunately) seems to be this:[4] that restricted new development is excluded from compensation *in so far as* it involves a material change of use but *not in so far as* it consists of any building or other operation. Thus a project of development which involves building a house on a farmer's field is ineligible for compensation, if restricted, only in so far as it involves a change of use from agriculture to residence.[5] In so far as it involves a building operation, as it obviously does, it remains eligible.

Section 147 (2) excludes compensation in so far as an adverse decision consists of imposing in a planning permission any conditions relating (in effect) to density, design, layout, use, or access to a highway, or any condition whatever in a permission to win and work minerals. A service road, however, is not in itself an 'access to a highway' in this context.[6]

Section 147 (4) excludes compensation for refusal of permission to develop made on the ground that the development is premature, either because of priorities in the development plan as approved or amended by the Secretary of State, or because of the deficiency during a reasonably specified period of water supply and sewers. Any such reason for refusal can only be persisted in for seven years for it to be effective to exclude a right to compensation.

Section 147 (5) excludes compensation for refusal of permission to develop made substantially on the ground of danger of flooding or subsidence.

Section 149 excludes compensation for adverse decisions received by authorities who have acquired the land in question under compulsory powers, or adverse decisions relating to 'operational' land of statutory undertakers or the National Coal Board. But special statutory provision is made elsewhere for restrictions on 'operational' land.[7]

Section 148 excludes compensation in so far as some alternative permission already exists for 'development of a residential, commercial or industrial character, being development which consists wholly or mainly of the construction of houses, flats, shops or office premises, or industrial buildings (including warehouses), or any combination thereof'. Whether this wording includes, say, hotels is a moot and subtle point. It

---

4 Assurances to this effect were given in Parliament; but it would have been better to include appropriate wording in the statutory provision.

5 Section 33 (2) of the 1971 Act gives permission for a building, the *construction* of which is authorised by a planning permission, to be *used* for the purpose for which it has been designed.

6 Compensation is also excluded in respect of express or deemed conditions imposing time-limits on carrying out development or on applying for detailed approval under outline planning permissions, and express or deemed conditions in industrial development certificates or office development permits (s 147 (3)).

7 See ss 237–40 of the 1971 Act. 'Operational land' is land used for the operational purposes of a body of this kind, such as the railway lines of British Rail or the coal mines of the National Coal Board, as distinct from investment property, houses, offices, showrooms and the like.

is provided that the imposition of conditions, if any, of the kind specified in s 147 (2), referred to above, can in effect be disregarded. And in this connection it should be noted that, under s 153 (5), there is a general rule governing the assessment of compensation which restricts its amount to depreciation below the value which would accrue to the land in the event of a grant of planning permission subject to any of the conditions of the kind specified in s 147 (2) which 'might reasonably have been expected'. For good or ill, this further restricts (at least in theory) the amount of lost value which can be compensated for.

## 2 CASES EXPRESSLY INCLUDED

There are two provisions *allowing* compensation to be paid in converse cases where, strictly, there is no adverse planning decision to complain of. Section 150 allows a favourable decision to be treated as adverse in so far as the project of development submitted includes buildings or works which the Secretary of State certifies as having been included because the applicant knew that, otherwise, the planning permission would in any case have contained conditions requiring their inclusion. And s 151 provides that, in a case where an industrial development certificate was required before submitting the planning application, but was refused by the Department of Trade, the applicant must be told whether he would have received an adverse planning decision; if so, he will be entitled to compensation (if any) accordingly.

## 3 RELATIONSHIP WITH OTHER COMPENSATION

Diminution in land value is not necessarily attributable to restrictions imposed at the outset on planning permission for new development. In particular cases distinctions may have to be drawn, and depreciation may be attributable, wholly or in part, to restrictions of a different kind. This may give rise to compensation as of right. Such compensation is described in the next chapter, where a notable example is given of a case in which such a distinction had to be drawn between depreciation (non-compensatable) caused by a planning refusal and depreciation (compensatable) caused by a preservation order.[8]

---

8 *Hoveringham Gravels Ltd v Secretary of State for the Environment* [1975] QB 754, [1975] 2 All ER 931. See below, p 316.

# Chapter 16

# Planning compensation as of right

## A. Varieties of compensation as of right

The kinds of loss for which planning compensation is payable as of right do not bulk large in practice, but in spite of that the law relating to them is not altogether straightforward. For the very reason that it is payable as of right the authorities concerned take care, understandably, that they do not have to pay it if they can reasonably avoid doing so. Once, when a situation developed in which it began to look as if there would have to be a notable increase in payments of one variety of planning compensation as of right, the Town and Country Planning Act 1963 was hurriedly passed to reduce the liability to pay it. This was expedient, but hardly edifying.[1]

The quality which these varieties of compensation have in common, apart from being payable as of right, is a negative one, namely that they are not caused by the imposition of restrictions upon projects of new development at the outset.[2] They do not, in other words, arise in the circumstances of a normal planning refusal or conditional planning permission. Apart from this it should be noted that, unlike 'unexpended balance' compensation, which is paid by the Secretary of State, all varieties of planning compensation as of right (except where ancient monuments are concerned[3]) are payable by *local* planning authorities. But as in other cases questions of disputed compensation are referred to the Lands Tribunal.[4]

There may be said to be four main kinds of planning compensation as of right. First, there is compensation for withdrawal of development rights already in existence; second, compensation for unjustified loss in enforcement proceedings; third, compensation for restrictions imposed

---

1 See p 325, below.
2 See ch 15, p 293, above.
3 See p 315, below.
4 1971 Act, s 179. Section 178 provides that, as far as is appropriate, the 'market value' rules in the Land Compensation Act 1961, s 5, are to be applied (see ch 7). Dispute has arisen on whether an authority must pay interest on compensation awarded. In the absence of statutory provision to the contrary it has been held in relation to a revocation order (see below) that interest is payable not from the date of the order itself but only from the date when compensation is quantified: *Hobbs (Quarries) Ltd v Somerset County Council* (1974) 30 P & CR 286.

in the interests of amenity; and fourth—the most difficult kind—compensation for restrictions imposed on marginal development, otherwise known as 'existing use' or Third Schedule (now Eighth Schedule) development. The main provisions, though not all, are contained in Part VIII of the Town and Country Planning Act 1971 (ss 164 to 179).

## B. Deprivation of accrued development value

### 1 REVOCATION AND MODIFICATION CASES

Section 164 of the Act of 1971 empowers 'a person interested in the land' to obtain compensation from the local planning authority for 'loss or damage which is directly attributable' to a revocation or modification order. Abortive expenditure is also compensatable; but nothing is to be paid in respect of work or loss (apart from depreciation of land value) earlier than the planning permission revoked or modified—not even, it seems, if that permission were retrospective.[5] Abortive expenditure includes not only the cost of works on the land, but also of preparatory matters such as plans.[6] Application for compensation must normally be made within six months.[7]

In *Pennine Raceway Ltd v Kirklees Metropolitan Borough Council*[8] the Court of Appeal held that the phrase 'person interested' must not be construed narrowly to mean a 'person with an interest', in 'a strict conveyancing sense' (ie presumably as meaning 'legal estate owner') as Eveleigh LJ put it. The claimants were licensees, who spent a great deal of money on adapting the licensor's land in question for motor racing, abortively because planning permission was then revoked. The Lands Tribunal's refusal to award compensation was reversed on appeal. But it was pointed out that in any case the claimant had an equitable interest by way of proprietary estoppel.[9]

As far as depreciation of land values is concerned, this represents new development value. Section 164 (4) provides that in calculating the loss it must be assumed that permission for 'existing use' development would be granted.[10] Therefore if it is a permission to carry out such development, and *not* new development, which is revoked or modified (possible, but not very likely, in practice) the only remedy seems to be to re-apply

5  1971 Act, s 32, provides for retrospective planning permission.
6  A decision to this effect had previously been given in *Holmes v Bradfield RDC* [1949] 2 KB 1, [1949] 1 All ER 381.
7  Town and Country Planning General Regulations 1976, SI 1976/1419, reg 14.
8  [1982] 3 All ER 628.
9  For equitable interests in land by proprietary estoppel, see above, ch 5, p 83.
10  The Lands Tribunal stressed in *Burlin v Manchester City Council* (1975) 32 P & CR 115, that such development (within the Eighth Schedule to the 1971 Act) was the *only* development for which permission could be assumed as a result of the revocation order.

for such permission and then, on refusal, claim Eighth Schedule compensation in the manner to be described later in this chapter. What is not altogether clear is whether depreciation of land values is confined to freeholds and leaseholds. But reference may be made to s 166, which provides for apportionment (where practicable), and registration of 'compensation notices' as local land charges for amounts over £20, exactly as for 'unexpended balance' compensation[11] except that the local planning authority and not the Secretary of State must discharge these duties. The section states that, ' "interest" (where the reference is to an interest in land) means the fee simple or a tenancy of the land and does not include any other interest therein'. On general principles, and the authority of cases such as *Oppenheimer v Minister of Transport* (discussed in an earlier chapter[12]), freeholds and leaseholds in equity, such as options, equitable leases and other estate contracts, must be included.

Different in form from but closely similar in substance to revocation and modification orders are cases in which planning permission for development is conferred automatically by a development order but is afterwards withdrawn, either by revoking or amending the order, or by exercising a power of direction under it, and a specific permission for that same development is then refused or only granted conditionally. There is, it is true, no original specific permission in favourable terms, and no subsequent revocation or modification order; but permission is first conferred and then restricted or taken away just the same. Section 165 therefore provides that such a situation is to be treated, for compensation purposes (including the time limit for applications), as if there had been an actual revocation or modification order. But sub-s (3) denies the benefit of s 165 to the 'operational land' of statutory undertakers. As for the specific adverse decision itself, s 149 (4) of the 1971 Act provides that a claim under s 165 debars a claim in respect of the unexpended balance.

It is apparent from these provisions that loss of prospective development value is being compensated for just as it is in cases of restrictions imposed on new development at the outset. The only difference is, that the amount is not restricted to the limit imposed by any unexpended balance. Indeed there may not be one for the land in question, and this will not make any difference. But if there *is* an unexpended balance, the question arises whether the payment of revocation compensation should diminish it in the same way that payment of compensation for restrictions on new development at the outset would do by virtue of section 140.[13] Section 167 therefore gives the Secretary of State an option (provided he receives notification of a 'compensation notice' under s 166) to contribute to the compensation any amount he chooses, so long as it

11 See ch 15, p 302, above (1971 Act, s 158).
12 See ch 5, p 83, above.
13 See ch 15, p 298, above.

does not exceed either the amount of the compensation itself or that of the unexpended balance. But he can only do this if he would have been *obliged* to do so had the same restrictions as are imposed by the revocation or modification been imposed at the outset in response to a planning application; and the Town and Country Planning (Compensation and Certificates) Regulations 1974,[14] Part VI, provide that, in the event of a contribution being paid, the unexpended balance will be diminished accordingly, just as under s 140. Before contributing, the Secretary of State must notify all parties affected, and give them 30 days to submit written objections, which he must consider. If any such party, having persisted in an objection, disputes the Secretary of State's subsequent decision, that party has 30 days more in which to refer the matter, in writing, to the Lands Tribunal. By this procedure anyone interested in preserving the unexpended balance may be able to do so by showing that the revocation or modification is not, in effect, to be regarded as parallel to an adverse decision on an original planning application.

The final turn of the screw in these procedures is that the repayment of compensation may, under s 168, be demanded from the recipient or his successor in exactly the same circumstances as under ss 159 to 160, described in the last chapter. The Secretary of State will receive the repayment, but in this case he must pay the money over to the local planning authority, deducting only any contribution he may have made under s 167.

## 2 DISCONTINUANCE CASES

A somewhat similar liability of a local planning authority to pay compensation may arise in consequence of a discontinuance order. The difference between discontinuance and revocation orders is that the latter are only valid to the extent that planning permission has been granted but not acted upon, that is to say development is permitted but has not been carried out. If it has been partly carried out, a revocation order is only valid in respect of the other part still to be done (though abortive expenditure in respect of the first part will be subject to compensation— so long as it really is abortive). Crypto-revocation, covered by s 165 (above), is to be regarded similarly: as illustrated by *Cole v Somerset County Council*,[15] in which the court held that automatic permission under the General Development Order 1950[16] could not be withdrawn in circumstances in which it had already been acted upon. Presumably a discontinuance order would have been the correct procedure in that case.

Section 170 requires the local planning authority to pay compensation to anyone who, in consequence of a discontinuance order, 'has suffered

14 SI 1974/1242.
15 [1957] 1 QB 23, [1956] 3 All ER 531.
16 Now replaced by the General Development Order 1977, SI 1977/289.

damage in consequence of the order by depreciation of the value of an interest in the land to which he is entitled, or by being disturbed in his enjoyment of the land'. And anyone complying with such an order is entitled to have his reasonable expenses reimbursed, subject to a deduction for the value of materials removed. Thus not only the loss of development value but also the net cost of reversing the development itself—by demolition, or removal of anything from the site—must be covered by the compensation. Application must normally be made within six months.[17]

One of the few court decisions in this whole area of the law arose in fact from a discontinuance order: *Blow v Norfolk County Council*.[18] The appellant was required to discontinue the use of land at Runton Mill, close to the sea near Cromer, as a caravan site. As Lord Denning MR said: 'This meant that he should receive the amount which the land, if sold in the open market by a willing seller, might be expected to realise, ie if sold as a caravan site, in excess of what it would fetch if sold for agricultural purposes'. The Lands Tribunal awarded a figure lower than had been put forward on the authority's behalf before negotiations broke down. The Court of Appeal held that the Tribunal did wrong in ignoring the higher figure on the ground that it was put forward in correspondence 'without prejudice', because the reliance on 'without prejudice' had in fact been waived. The Tribunal had been right, however, to hold that the value of the land as a caravan site should be reduced because of an uncertainty as to how much of the site could lawfully be used for caravans. Lord Denning said: 'A purchaser would obviously give more for a site with established rights, ie with planning permission, than he would for a site as to which there was a question-mark'. The claimant's appeal was allowed on the 'without prejudice' point, and the case remitted to the Tribunal accordingly.

## C. Enforcement and amenity compensation

### 1 STOP NOTICE CASES

Compensation for unjustified loss in enforcement proceedings occurs in respect of 'stop notices' served under s 90 of the 1971 Act, as amended.[19] Because a local planning authority may fear that the period during which an enforcement notice is in suspense, while being challenged, is likely to be used for pressing on with unauthorised development so as to present a fait accompli, they may cover this period (which could conceivably extend into years rather than months in the event of an appeal to the

17 Town and Country Planning General Regulations 1976, SI 1976/1419, reg 14.
18 [1966] 2 All ER 579, [1967] 1 WLR 1280.
19 Town and Country Planning (Amendment) Act 1977, s 1.

courts) by serving a 'stop notice'. This will prohibit the carrying out of any specified activity constituting (or included in) the alleged breach of planning control attached in the enforcement notice, subject to certain exceptions.

Section 177 of the 1971 Act, as amended,[20] provides that compensation may be payable by the authority 'in respect of any loss or damage directly attributable to the prohibition contained in the notice', but only in certain cases. These are: if the stop notice itself is withdrawn; or if the enforcement notice which it supports is withdrawn for any reason *other* than a change of policy over the alleged breach of planning control to which it relates; or if that enforcement notice is quashed for any such reason or else is varied 'so that matters alleged to constitute a breach of planning control cease to include one or more of the activities prohibited by the stop notice' (again, on grounds other than any such change of policy). The claim must normally be submitted within six months of the withdrawal, quashing or varying.[1] Compensation may be claimed by any 'person who . . . has an interest in or occupies the land' at the time when the stop notice is first served.

## 2 TREE PRESERVATION CASES

Compensation for restrictions imposed in the interests of amenity occurs in six kinds of case. The first two concern tree preservation orders. Section 174 of the 1971 Act says that these may specify cases in which compensation is to be paid for 'loss or damage'. The Secretary of State's 'model' tree preservation order—and the Town and Country Planning (Tree Preservation Order) Regulations 1969,[2] which contain it, say that orders must be 'substantially in the form' of this model—duly provides for payment of such compensation, by the local planning authority, 'in consequence of' any refusal, conditional grant, revocation or modification of a consent, under the order, to fell or lop trees which the order preserves. Application must normally be made within 12 (not six) months of the decision. But that decision may be accompanied by a certificate that the trees specified in it are to be preserved either 'in the interests of good forestry, or (in the case of individually preserved trees only, not areas of woodland) because of their 'outstanding or special amenity value'; and any such certificate not quashed by the Secretary of State on appeal will preclude the payment of compensation for those specified trees. Compensation paid must not, of course, be paid twice over on another application. If the felling which is restricted would, had it been permitted, have 'injuriously affected' other land of the 'owner' (meaning a freeholder, or a leaseholder with three years

20 Town and Country Planning (Amendment) Act 1977, s 2.
1 Town and Country Planning General Regulations 1976, SI 1976/1419, reg 14.
2 SI 1969/17. See reg 4 and the Schedule.

to run), this must be taken into account in the assessment of compensation.[3]

A decision of the Lands Tribunal which is of interest here is *Bollans v Surrey County Council*.[4] The claimant was denied consent to interfere with trees which the authority claimed should continue to be protected for reasons of amenity. He planned to clear and replant the land for commercial reasons; the authority asserted that the land on its own was not viable for commercial forestry.[5] He accepted the refusal and claimed compensation. The Tribunal rejected his claims for compensation: for 'loss of amenity', as being irrelevant; for extra maintenance, loss to his estate and loss of profits on the sale of trees, as being totally unsupported by evidence; and for fees paid for forestry and legal advice when applying for consent, on the ground that these were not incurred 'in consequence of' the refusal of consent, but in advance of it. He was, however, awarded £26 for 'loss of growing timber'.

Tree preservation orders may also give rise to compensation under s 175 of the 1971 Act. If protected trees are 'felled in the course of forestry operations permitted by or under' a tree preservation order, subject to a direction for replanting, but the Forestry Commissioners consider the replanting not to be a commercially viable forestry operation, and refuse financial assistance—in short if the compulsory replanting is to be for amenity and not for good forestry—the person required to comply with the direction may apply, normally within 12 months of it,[6] to the local planning authority for compensation 'in respect of such loss or damage, if any, as is caused or incurred in consequence of compliance with the direction'.

### 3 BUILDING PRESERVATION CASES

For 'listed' buildings of special architectural or historic importance, ss 171 and 172 of the 1971 Act provide that compensation may be claimed from the local planning authority on a refusal, conditional grant, revocation or modification of consent to alter or extend (but, apparently, not demolish) a listed building, provided that the decision was made by the Secretary of State. In the case of a refusal or conditional grant the works restricted must not constitute development, other than that automatically permitted under a development order; and compensation will be strictly in respect of depreciation in value of the claimant's interest in the property on the assumption 'that any subsequent application for the like

---

3 See arts 1, 5 and 8 to 12 of the 'model' order. The 12 months' time-limit will be found in art 11 (2). The provision for certifying that preservation is for 'good forestry' or 'amenity value' will be found in art 5.
4 (1968) 20 P & CR 745.
5 The claimant grew Christmas trees which he sold by retail, as a 'barrow boy' carrying on business in the London Borough of Wandsworth.
6 Town and Country Planning Act 1971, s 175 (4).

consent would be determined in the same way'. The Secretary of State may, however, have undertaken to grant consent for some other works, and the effect of this on the alleged depreciation must be taken into account. In the case of revocation or modification of consent, the same considerations apply as those which govern compensation under s 164 of the 1971 Act, discussed earlier in this chapter.[7] All claims must normally be submitted to the local planning authority within six months.[8]

Section 173 of the 1971 Act applies where a building is not 'listed', but the local planning authority think it ought to be and have therefore given it a temporary protection under a 'building preservation notice' while they exercise persuasion upon the Secretary of State. If they fail, and the building is not listed, the building preservation notice will lapse. On making application to the local planning authority, normally within six months[9] of the lapse, 'any person who at the time when the notice was served had an interest in the building shall be entitled to be paid compensation by the authority in respect of any loss or damage directly attributable to the effect of the notice'. This right to compensation may perhaps be compared with that conferred by s 177 in respect of stop notices.

### 4 ADVERTISEMENT CASES

Under advertisement control, rights to compensation are almost non-existent; and it will be remembered how, in respect of the unexpended balance, s 147 (1) of the 1971 Act specifically excludes compensation for adverse decisions on applications for consent under what are now the Town and Country Planning (Control of Advertisements) Regulations 1969.[10] But s 176 of the 1971 Act does provide for compensation in respect of any advertisement displayed on 1 August 1948, or any site used for the display of advertisements on that date, in any case where a person is required under those Regulations to carry out works for the removal of such an advertisement or the discontinuance of such a use. He may within six months of completing such works[11] apply to the local planning authority for 'compensation in respect of any expenses reasonably incurred by him in that behalf'. This right, though of course far more limited in scope, bears some resemblance to the right to compensation under s 170 in respect of a discontinuance order, discussed earlier in this chapter.

---

7  See p 308, above.
8  Town and Country Planning (Listed Buildings and Buildings in Conservation Areas) Regulations 1977, SI 1977/228.
9  Ibid.
10  SI 1969/1532. (For s 147 (1), see ch 15, p 304, above.)
11  Ibid, reg 30.

## 5 PEDESTRIAN PRECINCT CASES

Another kind of right to compensation for restrictions in respect of amenity is to be found in s 212 of the Act of 1971, which empowers a local planning authority, as 'a proposal for improving the amenity of part of their area' to reduce a highway which is a carriageway to one which is only a footpath or bridleway. The authority must pass a resolution to this effect, and then apply to the Secretary of State to make an order after consultation with the highway authority to 'provide for the extinguishment of any right which persons may have to use vehicles on that highway'; but the procedure is not available for a trunk road or 'a principal road for the purposes of advances under s 235 of the Highways Act 1959'. An order may provide for the continuance of some use by vehicles, as specified, normally for access to premises along that highway.

The compensation claim may be made to the local planning authority, normally within six months,[12] by any 'person who, at the time of an order under . . . this section coming into force, has an interest in land having lawful access to a highway to which the order relates'. It must be 'in respect of any depreciation in the value of his interest which is directly attributable to the order and of any other loss or damage which is so attributable'. The meaning of 'lawful access' is access which does not contravene planning control. An order may be revoked; but there does not seem to be any requirement for repaying compensation in respect of any land value which may be re-created by the revocation.

## 6 ANCIENT MONUMENTS

Finally, mention should be made of the right to compensation where the amenity to be preserved is an ancient monument. The Historic Buildings and Ancient Monuments Act 1953, ss 10 and 11, empowered the Secretary of State for the Environment to make an interim preservation notice (in cases of urgency) or a preservation order (for permanent effect). Anyone with a property interest in the momument 'injuriously affected'—ie depreciated—in consequence of this was 'entitled to receive such compensation as may be appropriate in the circumstances . . .'. The Act gave a wide discretion as to the contents of a preservation order, compensation procedure included.

These provisions were repealed by the Ancient Monuments and Archaeological Areas Act 1979,[13] which has introduced a new system of 'scheduled monuments' and 'schedule monument consents'. Section 7 of this Act provides that compensation is payable for refusal of such

12 Town and Country Planning General Regulations 1976, SI 1976/1419, reg 14.
13 Section 64 and Sch 5, repealing Parts II and III of the 1953 Act with effect from 9 October 1981.

consents to anyone who 'incurs expenditure or otherwise sustains any loss or damage' as a result, obtainable from the Secretary of State.

In *Hoveringham Gravels Ltd v Secretary of State for the Environment*[14] a preservation order had been made in respect of an iron-age hill fort near Birmingham (Berry Mound Camp Preservation Order 1971). The claimants, who owned it, had previously applied for planning permission to extract sand and gravel for commercial use; but permission had been refused because mineral workings would have destroyed it. Yet automatic permission was available under the Town and Country Planning General Development Order 1963[15] to extract sand and gravel for *agricultural* purposes on the same property; and it was to prevent this that the preservation order was made. The owners therefore claimed compensation under the 1953 Act. They put this at £57,000, the difference between the respective market values of the land available (a) for commercial mineral extraction and (b) for use only as an ancient monument. The Secretary of State offered £100, the difference between the respective market values of the land available (a) for mineral extraction for agricultural purposes and (b) for use only as an ancient monument.

The compensation dispute was referred to the Lands Tribunal, which awarded £57,000. The Court of Appeal held this to be wrong in law, because it rested on the factual assumption that planning permission would, but for the preservation order, have been granted for commercial mineral extraction, whereas in truth the *refusal* of such permission was the very thing that had led to the threat of agricultural use and the making of the preservation order to prevent it. Thus the only use prevented by that order was the agricultural, not the commercial, and the relevant depreciation was accordingly confined to £100.

# D.  Marginal development value

### 1  DEVELOPMENT MARGINAL TO EXISTING USE

The most problematical kind of planning compensation 'as of right' relates to restrictions upon marginal or 'existing use' or Schedule 8 development. It will be remembered that s 22 (5) of the 1971 Act defines 'new development' as development which is not Schedule 8 development.[16] The distinction between development marginal to existing use and 'new' development dates back to the 1947 Act, although the term 'new development' was not in fact introduced until the 1954 Act. Existing use development in relation to the existing use of land on 1 July 1948 was in effect a concession to owners by the 1947 Act. Its value was paid,

---

14  [1975] QB 754, [1975] 2 All ER 931.
15  SI 1963/709 (see now SI 1977/289).
16  See above, ch 15, p 293.

ACTUAL COST OF
DEVELOPMENT

prospective
development
value

New development
value

Marginal development
value (Schs 8 and 18)

EXISTING USE VALUE

| | | |
|---|---|---|
| taxed at 100% | (1947) |
| „ „ nil | (1952) |
| „ „ 30% | (1965) |
| „ „ 40% | (1967) |
| „ „ 30% | (1971) |
| „ as income | (1974) |
| „ at 80% | (1976) |
| „ „ 60% | (1979) |

(The shaded area represents the section of value dependent
on planning permission—in whatever form it may be granted)

in addition to existing use value, as compensation when land was compulsorily purchased. Its value was also paid—subject to some important exceptions, as will be seen—as planning compensation when existing use development was restricted not only by a refusal or conditional grant of planning consent but also by revocation or modification. Conversely, on a grant of permission for such existing use development, no development charge was payable; and for the purposes of assessing claims to once-for-all compensation out of the £300 million funds for loss of prospective development value enjoyed on 1 July 1948, calculations were made for depreciation of land values on the basis that the owner would continue to enjoy the value of that existing use development. This meant that claims must relate purely to the difference between full development value on the one hand, and existing use value plus existing use development on the other as at that date.

Prospective development value was restored to owners in full, as of right, in the 1953 and 1954 Acts, but only in relation to the actual grant of planning permissions and to compensation for their revocation or modification. Its realisation by owners in the event of compulsory purchase has depended, since the 1959 Act, on the application of the 'planning assumptions'; and its realisation by owners in the event of restrictions imposed at the outset on new development has depended, since the 1954 Act, on the rules relating to the 'unexpended balance'.[17] But in all these

17 See ch 15, above.

cases the assumption is made that owners continue to enjoy the value of existing use development separately in its own right, so that it must always be excluded from the figure calculated in relation to prospective development value as such. The awkwardness arising from this if permission for existing use development is itself revoked or modified was touched on earlier in this chapter.[18]

It was not intended that the concept of existing use development should be significant for any purpose whatever except compensation—it is 'only money', so to speak. Except for rather doutbful motives,[19] a developer is unlikely to devise a project of development in such a way that it will be contained within the limits of existing use development. But if the question of compensation arises, either because of planning restrictions or because of compulsory purchase (including 'inverse compulsory purchase'[20]), then existing use development will have to be considered in relation to it. The value of that 'potential' must be paid automatically as part of compulsory purchase compensation (unless planning compensation has already become payable in respect of it).[1] And if a project of development which is subject to an adverse planning decision, namely a refusal of permission or a grant subject to conditions, *turns out to be* within the scope of existing use developments, then the value of that prospective development—with certain exceptions—will be payable, as of right, as compensation. The exceptions are the classes of development contained in Part I of Sch 8 to the Act of 1971. The other classes are in Part II of that Schedule.

Schedule 8 re-enacts Sch 3 to the Act of 1947,[2] with the important difference that since 1954[3] its benefit is no longer virtually confined in its application to the state of property on 1 July 1948 but is to be considered in regard to the state of property 'at a material date'. This is the date in relation to which any compensation is payable.[4]

2  COMPENSATION FOR RESTRICTIONS ON MARGINAL DEVELOPMENT

Section 169 of the Act of 1971 enacts that on a refusal, or a conditional grant, of permission for development within any of the classes in Part II of Sch 8, planning compensation shall be payable by the local planning authority in respect of the resulting depreciation in value of the land—if any—provided, in every case, that the decision was made not by that authority but by the Secretary of State, and provided also that a purchase notice has not been served.

18  See pp 308–309, above.
19  See p 325, below for consideration of these.
20  See chs 12 and 13, above.
 1  Land Compensation Act 1961, s 15 (see ch 8, above).
 2  See above, ch 15, p 293.
 3  Town and Country Planning Act 1954, s 71 and Sch 7.
 4  Town and Country Planning Act 1971, Sch 8 (para 12).

There may not have been any depreciation. In *A L Salisbury Ltd v York Corpn*,[5] planning permission to rebuild an existing shopfront was refused because the local planning authority wanted the owners to fall into line with adjoining shop-owners and consent to a covered pedestrian arcade being provided at pavement level, each shop having its ground floor premises set back accordingly but not the floors above. On a claim for planning compensation in consequence of the refusal, the Lands Tribunal held that there was in fact no depreciation; because if the arcade project were to be carried out, instead of the appellants' own project which had not been permitted, it would attract more pedestrian customers and thus be beneficial to the value of the shop.

Application must be made to the local planning authority, normally within six months of the Secretary of State's decision.[6] It must be assumed that 'any subsequent application for the like permission would be determined in the same way'; but any undertaking by the Secretary of State to grant permission for some other development must be taken into account. If the claim relates to a conditional grant of permission, conditions 'regulating the design or external appearance of buildings, or the size or height of buildings' may be partly or wholly ignored, if the Secretary of State thinks it reasonable to do so 'having regard to the local circumstances' and directs accordingly.[7]

If an application for permission for development within Part II of Sch 8 cannot be submitted because it requires an industrial development certificate and this has been refused, the local planning authority may be required to give notice in writing of whether they would themselves have refused permission. If they do, compensation will be payable under s 169 just the same.[8]

An adverse planning decision in respect of development within Part I of Sch 8 has been ineligible for planning compensation ever since the Act of 1947. The reasons for this are obscure, but may have something to do with the fact that the rebuilding of destroyed premises is included, so that extensive payments of compensation might have imposed too heavy a burden on public redevelopment schemes immediately after the Second World War. On the other hand the value of development within Part I, as well as Part II, was and is allowed automatically as part of compulsory purchase compensation; so that when public bodies themselves became ready to develop they would then pay this value. But the initiative for compulsory purchase is not solely a matter for acquiring authorities. There is always 'inverse compulsory purchase'. This affords to owners the practical possibility that, if their land is 'incapable of reasonably beneficial use' as a result of an adverse decision on an

5 (1960) 11 P & CR 421.
6 Town and Country Planning General Regulations 1976, SI 1976/1419, reg 14.
7 1971 Act, s 169 (3), (4).
8 1971 Act, s 169 (5).

application for permission to carry out development within Part I, they can compel the local authority to buy it. If the application was to rebuild a derelict building, or one built before 1 July 1948, and destroyed since 7 January 1937, a purchase notice[9] ought to succeed; but if the building is not derelict the purchase notice will probably fail.

## 3 TYPES OF MARGINAL DEVELOPMENT

There are eight paragraphs setting out this Sch 8 development. They all presuppose an existing use which does not contravene planning control. If that use is permitted only for a limited period in any case, the application to it of Sch 8 is similarly limited. Paragraphs 1 and 3 are modified, in respect of floor space, by Sch 18. The reason for this, and for the 'nil cube' rule in paras 3 and 7, will be explained below,[10] but first of all the paragraphs in the form in which they now exist must be considered. Paragraphs 1 and 2 are in Part I; paras 3 to 8 are in Part II.

Paragraph 1 comprises: the proposed rebuilding, 'as often as occasion may require', of any building in existence on 1 July 1948, or at the time of the relevant planning decision,[11] or destroyed between 7 January 1937, and 1 July 1948; or works for making good any war damage which only affect the interior of the building or do not 'materially affect' its external appearance. Any proposed rebuilding must not involve an increase beyond *either* of two limits in relation to the original building (ie *both* must be observed): namely an additional cubic content measured externally, of 10% (or, for a dwelling-house, an extra 1,750 cubic feet, if greater); and an additional gross floor space for any use, also measured externally, of 10% if the present building is 'original' to its site, but nil if the present building resulted from a rebuilding since 1 July 1948, of a previous building on the site. 'Cubic content' is measured externally.

Paragraph 2 comprises the proposed 'use as two or more separate dwelling-houses of any building . . . used as a single dwelling-house' on 1 July 1948, or at the time of the relevant planning decision.

Paragraph 3, which is the first of those in Part II of the Schedule, comprises the proposed alteration, whether involving improvement, enlargement or otherwise, 'as often as occasion may require' of any building now in existence (or an aggregate of buildings within the same curtilage if used for the same concern), so long as it does not involve an increase beyond either of two limits (ie both must be observed). These are: an additional cubic content, measured externally, of 10% (or, for a dwelling-house, an extra 1,750 cubic feet, if greater) if the building dates back to 1 July 1948, but nil if the building was built since that date, whether 'original' to its site or not; and an additional gross floor space

---

9 See ch 12, above.
10 See p 325, below.
11 The phrase used is 'at a material date' (see para 12 of the Schedule).

also measured externally, for any use of 10% if the building is 'original' to its site, but nil if it resulted from a rebuilding since 1 July 1948, of a previous building on the site.[12] 'Enlargement' of a building includes putting up within its curtilage any additional building to be used with it.

Paragraph 4 comprises proposed building or other operations, on land used for agriculture or forestry on 1 July 1948, or at the time of the relevant planning decision, 'for the purposes of that use', so long as they do not relate to dwelling-houses, market gardens, nursery grounds, timber yards or 'other purposes not connected with general farming operations or with the cultivation or felling of trees'.

Paragraph 5 comprises the proposed winning and working of minerals, on land occupied with agricultural land, which are reasonably required for the use of that land for agriculture (including fertilisation, and maintenance or alteration of agricultural buildings or works).

Paragraph 6 comprises a proposed change of use of a building or land, at the time of the relevant planning decision, from one use to another within 'any general class specified' in the Town and Country Planning (Use Classes for Third Schedule Purposes) Order 1948,[13] or any such change within a general class specified within the Order occurring after an interval lasting since 1 July 1948, during which the property was unoccupied, so long as the earlier use did not end before 7 January 1937. This Use Classes Order bears a considerable resemblance to the Town and Country Planning (Use Classes) Order 1972,[14] which lists classes of use for determining changes which are not development at all. It must follow from this that a change of use within a use class in the 1948 Order, which is at the same time a change within a use class in the 1972 Order, is not development in any case,[15] and therefore planning control and the Eighth Schedule cannot effectively apply to it. But the two Orders are not absolutely identical.

Paragraph 7 comprises a proposed extension of a use in a building or other land of which only part was so used on 1 July 1948, or at the time of the relevant planning decision. For land, the extension must not be more than 10% in area over the use as it was on 1 July 1948. A use beginning since that date seems not to be covered. For buildings the extension must not be more than 10% in cubic content, measured externally, over the use as it was on 1 July 1948, or the date when the use began if later, so long as *the building itself* dates back to 1 July 1948; but if the building was built since that date, paragraph 7 does not apply to it at all.

12  The scope of this paragraph should be compared and contrasted with that of para 1; and see p 325, below.
13  SI 1948/955. It was the 'Third Schedule' until 1971.
14  SI 1972/1385.
15  Except when prohibited in a planning condition: *Kingston-upon-Thames Royal London Borough Council v Secretary of State for the Environment* [1974] 1 All ER 193, [1973] 1 WLR 1549.

SCHEDULES 8 AND 18 : TOLERANCES ('ascertained by external measurement')

| | Building previously destroyed | | TYPE OF POTENTIAL DEVELOPMENT | Existing building | | | |
|---|---|---|---|---|---|---|---|
| | Either built after 1.7.48 OR destroyed before 7.1.37 | Built before 1.7.48 AND destroyed after 7.1.37 | | Built before 1.7.48 | Built after 1.7.48 | | |
| | | | | | ORIGINAL | REBUILT | |
| | NOT WITHIN SCHEDULES 8 and 18 | + 10% cube + 10% square | Rebuilding (compulsory purchase compensation only) | + 10% cube + 10% square | + 10% cube + 10% square | + 10% cube + NIL square | |
| | | | Alteration (planning and compulsory purchase compensation) | + 10% cube + 10% square | + NIL cube + 10% square | + NIL cube + NIL square | |
| | | | Extension of use in a building (planning and compulsory purchase compensation) | + 10% cube | + NIL cube | + NIL cube | |

Paragraph 8 comprises a proposed deposit of waste materials or refuse in connection with mineral working, on part of a site so used on 1 July 1948, or at the time of the relevant planning decision, 'so far as may be reasonably required in connection with the working of those minerals'.

There is a wealth of difficult detail in these paragraphs. For cases other than claims for compensation under s 169, a generalised figure is presumably sufficient to set a value on existing use development; but for claims under s 169 itself it is necessary to scrutinise carefully each particular project contained in a planning application to see whether it comes within Part II of Sch 8 or not. The wording of Sch 8 seems to imply that for development to come within paras 1, 3 and 4 it must consist of operations *only* (presumably building, engineering and related operations)—thus excluding projects involving material changes of use.[16] Conversely, development coming within paras 2, 6, 7 and 8 must consist of material changes of use *only*; while development in para 5 must consist of mining operations *only*.

In *National Provincial Bank v Portsmouth Corpn*[17] a planning application to reconstruct a building of which the upper floors had been wrecked by bomb damage led to a dispute over whether the project came within para 1, as rebuilding, or para 3, as alteration and improvement. It was held on the facts that this was a case of rebuilding, and so came within para 1.

In *Sorrell v Maidstone RDC*,[18] planning permission was refused for rebuilding on the site of huts in an old army camp. This being clearly within para 1, no compensation could be claimed under s 169; but a purchase notice was served and accepted. In a dispute over the value of existing use development when assessing the compensation, it was held that the rebuilding must be regarded as confined to the sites of the previous huts, but could be envisaged as involving the construction of substantial durable dwellings and not mere slavish copies of the defunct huts.

Again, in *Walton-on-Thames Charities Trustees v Walton and Weybridge UDC*,[19] there had been 50 'pre-fabs', with roads and sewers, *existing in* 1948 on land owned by the claimants. When these structures were removed the claimants applied for permission to redevelop the site by building 50 'dwelling-units', but it was refused. They then served a purchase notice, which was accepted, and claimed, as part of the compensation, existing use development value within para 1 of the Eighth Schedule. The council objected on the ground that the 50 'pre-fabs' were only temporary and so could never have been 'rebuilt'. They failed, and

16 In the *Peaktop Properties* case (see below), however, Sir David Cairns said, in the Court of Appeal, that he was 'not satisfied' as to this.
17 (1959) 11 P & CR 6.
18 (1961) 13 P & CR 57.
19 (1970) 21 P & CR 411.

the claim for existing use development value in respect of rebuilding 50 houses duly succeeded.

The most important leading case, however, is *Peaktop Properties (Hampstead) Ltd v Camden London Borough Council*,[20] in which the claimant company owned two blocks of flats, and applied for planning permission to build an additional storey on to each block. The crucial facts were agreed, in Sir David Cairns's words in the Court of Appeal, to be these: '(1) that both blocks of flats could be taken together and the relevant dimensions were the total cubic contents and total gross floor space of the two together and of the projected additions of both together; (2) that the projected additions so calculated would be under 10% of the cubic contents but 11.49% of the floor space'. Permission was refused, whereupon the company claimed compensation as of right from the local planning authority under s 169 of the 1971 Act. The authority disputed the claim on two legal grounds, on both of which they failed in the Lands Tribunal. They appealed to the Court of Appeal, where they failed again on one ground, but succeeded on the other and so won the appeal.

The first ground was self-contradictory: that the proposed development was not an 'enlargement' under Sch 8 because the extra flats would be separate entities and there would be a 'material change of use' of the property because the addition of 'further dwelling-houses' would be essentially the same as 'the division of a dwelling-house into two or more dwelling-houses'. This 'startling proposition' (in the words of O'Connor LJ) was rejected. A building cannot be both extended and not extended in the same breath; nor can a division per se be an extension.

The second ground was that, since the proposed works would enlarge the gross floor space for residential use by more than 10%, the project was outside Sch 8 because the limit specified in Sch 18 which was exceeded was an additional limit imported into Sch 8. On this point the company argued 'that the true effect of the provisions is to limit the compensation to be paid to a sum to be calculated on the basis that the addition to the building did comply with Sch 18'. Sir David Cairns said: 'The Act creates enough problems as it is, and there is no call for the court to add to them by putting an artificial construction on provisions that are clear'. A proposal to increase floor space by over 10% does 'not comply with the requirements of Sch 18'. If a project is outside the twin limitations imposed by the two Schedules by even the slenderest of margins in regard to only one of them, the project as a whole is outside the combined benefit of those two Schedules. Stephenson LJ said he could see no reason to put a strained construction upon them 'in aid of developers who have not taken the trouble to meet the plain condition laid down by Parliament of their entitlement to be paid money out of the pockets of other ratepayers'.

**20** (1983) 46 P & CR 177.

The Town and Country Planning Act 1963 was responsible for cutting down the scope for paras 1, 3 and 7 of the Eighth Schedule. It abolished the '10% tolerance' in respect of cubic content in paras 3 and 7 for all buildings which do not date back to 1948; and it imposed the limitations on extensions of gross floor space for any use in paras 1 and 3 which had not been in force before. The reason is instructive. Local planning authorities had come under pressure from developers who realised that Sch 8 in its previous form, conferring, as it does, an indefeasible right to compensation, could be exploited with devastating effect. They could obtain permission to develop sites by new building to the fullest intensity that a local planning authority would allow, and then demand either a further permission to extend by 10% cubic content, or compensation as of right in lieu. In respect of vast urban blocks of offices, flats, hotels and the like the development value involved was huge, especially as modern comparatively low ceilinged rooms meant that: 'With a 10% addition to the cube, the increase in floor space may well be of 40% in some cases'.[1] So the Act was quickly passed and the public purse preserved. The 1971 Act incorporated the volume limitation in Sch 8, and set out the floor-space limitation in Sch 18 (imported into Sch 8 by s 278).

## 4 MARGINAL DEVELOPMENT AND PURCHASE NOTICES

Finally, in this connection, s 187 of the 1971 Act should be mentioned. It concerns purchase notices, discussed in an earlier chapter,[2] from which it will be remembered that where a purchase notice is justified in principle the Secretary of State may, instead of confirming it, direct that an alternative planning permission be made available. Normally this would cause no problem. But the value of any interest in the land with the benefit of the alternative permission might conceivably happen to be less than its existing use value together with its existing use development value under the Eighth Schedule. If ever this should be so the person entitled to it may, normally within six months,[3] apply to the local planning authority for compensation in respect of the deficiency in value, in much the same way as under s 169.

1 Government White Paper: 'London, Employment, Housing: Land' (Cmnd 1952, February 1963). The cause of the trouble was the addition, by the Act of 1954, of the phrase 'at a material date' (see p 320, footnote 11, above).
2 See ch 12, in particular p 248, above.
3 Town and Country Planning General Regulation 1976, SI 1976/1419, reg 14.

# Index

327

**Land**—*contd.*
'relevant'—*contd.*
set-off, 146–148
'zoned', 158, 159
re-sale or other disposal, 78
'restricted use', 244
sale of, specific performance of. *See* SPE-
CIFIC PERFORMANCE
selection of—
'Lands Clauses Acts', 14, 15
provisional order, 39
specific purposes, 38, 39
servient, compulsory purchase, 184, 185
severance of. *See* SEVERANCE
size of, 159
soil part of, 80
'special needs', for valuation, 140
special potential, 139–142
stock-in-trade, as, exempt from development land tax, 288
'superfluous', 78
underground, compulsory purchase, 96,
97
unexpended balance relating to. *See* DE-
VELOPMENT VALUE
unlawful or injurious use, value where,
142
unsuitable for development, 159
use of—
adverse decision, condition in, compensation excluded, 304, 305
'material change' in, compensation refused, 304, 305
valuation of. *See* VALUATION
value of. *See* VALUE
'white', 160
'zoned', development for, 158, 159, 163,
164
'zoning', blight notice, 256
**Land charge**
estate contract, registration as, 84
**Land commission**
abolition of, 275
betterment levy, 275
**Landlord**
agricultural holding, of, 94, 95
business tenancy, of, 92, 93
certificate issued to, changed use of land,
92n
'disturbed', cannot be, 198
furnished premises, of, disturbance, 198
notice to treat served on, 66
rehousing of his tenants following compulsory purchase, 91, 221, 222

**Landlord**—*contd.*
related companies tenant and, disturbance compensation, 198, 199
reversion, value of, 90
**Landowner**
meaning, 80
powers of government over, 2
**Lands tribunal**
appeals from, 21n
apportionment of compensation, 302
assumption as to new town, dispute, 148,
149
assumptions, valuation, 165
betterment levy disputes, 275
blight, compensation, assessing, 252
blight notice—
dispute, 252, 256
objections to, 260
common, rights of, compensation, 77
compensation—
assessment by, 29, 30, 63, 76, 77, 114,
116n, 122–125, 252
dispute, 29, 30, 62, 192
planning application, 33
planning, disputes, 302
re-assessment by, 75
severance of farm land, for, 107
time for claim, 123
consolidation of proceedings by, 124
contribution to compensation, dispute,
310
costs of hearings, 123, 123n, 124
decision, final, 30
decision in writing, 125
disturbance compensation, assessing,
203
'equivalent reinstatement', sanctioning,
207
expert witnesses, 122, 123, 165
facts, deciding, 163
hearing dates, 123n
interest on award, 125,127
interests omitted from purchase, compensation for, 77, 78
law, question of, decision dependent on,
125n
limitation, 72
market value disputes, 142
mortgaged land, compensation, 75, 76
notice to treat, compensation where, 63
planning compensation, right, as of, disputes, 307
procedure, 30, 123–125
reference to must be made formally, 124